Autobiography of
HERBERT W. ARMSTRONG

Volume 2

Library of Congress Catalog Card Number 87-50567
ISBN 0-943093-01-5 (Vol. 2)
ISBN 0-943093-02-3 (Two vol. set)
ISBN 0-943093-04-X (Vol. 2, pbk.)
ISBN 0-943093-05-8 (Two vol. set, pbk.)

Printed in the United States of America.

First Edition

The paper used in this publication meets the minimum
requirements of American National Standard for Information Sciences—Permanence of Paper for Printed Library
Materials, ANSI Z39.48-1984.

HERBERT W. ARMSTRONG
1892–1986

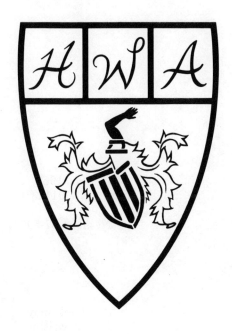

Table of Contents

40

First Vision of Worldwide Work

THE "lean years" continued through 1938 and the succeeding decade. It was a constant struggle and hardship. Growth seemed so very slow. Yet, viewed today in retrospect, expansion has been consistently rapid. Occasional setbacks were discouraging. But the forgings-ahead were far greater than the slips backward.

By June, 1938—four and a half years after *The Plain Truth* started as a mimeographed "magazine"—the first two printed editions finally had been produced. Old files, more recently examined, have shown that the May-June, 1938, number was not actually the first, but the second edition to come off a real printing press. And they were only eight-page editions. Until then all issues had been ground out on a hand-fed, hand-cranked, antiquated neostyle, ancestor of the mimeograph.

But the expense of producing those two printed issues threw us into a financial hole again. So back to the frail old neostyle we went, hand-producing a combined July-August, 1938, issue, which finally was mailed July 28 that year.

New Facilities Needed

As the work expanded, through 1938 and into 1939, a few items of new equipment became an imperative need. I do not mean convenient *wants* —but absolutely necessary *needs.*

According to usual office standards, we might have thought we needed a better office, with sunlight and ventilation. We might have thought modern steel filing cabinets were a need. I was still using cardboard cartons, obtained free at the grocery store, as receptacles for keeping correspondence files. We might have thought that office desks to work on, if only second-hand, were needed. But we were able to work, these years, on a few old tables we found in our little, stuffy, $5-per-month office room.

But when the old antiquated neostyle finally was wearing out—about to lie down and cease functioning because of old age—and we were still obliged to crank out *The Plain Truth* by hand on this piece of primitive mechanism, then a new mimeograph became an absolute *need*—or else *The Plain Truth* had to cease publication and die a natural death along with the neostyle.

So it was that on February 4, 1939—five years after the first issue of *The Plain Truth*—a letter to our few co-workers said: "I will have to tell you that we are VERY SERIOUSLY IN NEED of a new mimeograph machine. The present one is about worn out, and we are producing this issue of *The Plain Truth* under difficulties. I can get a very good used mimeograph, almost new, one capable of turning our the large amount of work that is necessary in this office, and [that] will last for several

2

years, for $65. There is not one cent available for the mimeograph, unless some of our friends can send in a special and additional offering just for this purpose."

By April 5, 1939, a letter to co-workers found in an old file says: "At last, after many unavoidable delays, we are sending you *The Plain Truth.* This issue goes to about one thousand NEW READERS. It is still mimeographed, because we have not enough funds to print it, as we did two issues last year. It is a tremendous task, and nearly all the work is done by Mrs. Armstrong, our daughter Beverly who is office secretary, and myself."

In spite of inside office, lack of light or ventilation, lack of desks, filing cabinets and office equipment, the work was GROWING! The *Plain Truth* circulation was growing. We were not able to get it out every month. There were seven issues in 1938. The June number was only the third during 1939. It was issued as often as there was enough money for paper, ink and postage. Yet already this little mimeographed "magazine" was being read by a few *thousand* people—and a hundred thousand were hearing on radio every week the very gospel Christ Himself preached—besides there were almost continuous evangelistic campaigns reaching hundreds.

The few dimes, quarters, and dollars were producing fruits that were to last for eternity!

But now our old secondhand car was about to lie down and die of old age and much use.

Near the bottom of this letter of April 5, 1939, I find this: "Another serious *need* is a new car. The present one, five years old, is in the Albany garage for lack of a $50 repair bill. We are totally dependent on our car to transport the six of us (self and singers) to Portland and back for the Sunday broadcasts. We have to drive 600 miles every week — 2,500 miles a month—

in God's work. The present car won't hold out longer. We are doing the very best we can with what we have to do with."

This referred to the 1934-model used Graham car we had purchased as a result of Mrs. Starkey's letter sent out December 21, 1937. But we were not to be able to get another car until 1941. That old Graham blew connecting rods every few thousand miles. But it was destined to suffer some *real* punishment, with weekly trips to Seattle, before we could replace it!

God has *promised* to supply all our NEED. But during these years it was surely *bare need,* not wants— and the needs were not always as great as they appeared to us.

How many of our readers, today, realize how much *more* than bare needs *you* are enjoying? Not many have had to struggle along with *real bare needs,* as we did through those lean years!

European Union and War Predicted

The February-March, 1939, issue of *The Plain Truth* contained another article on the resurrection of the Roman Empire to come. We have warned our radio listeners of this prophesied event since the first year we were on the air—1934. We have shouted this prophecy ever since 1934 in *The Plain Truth.* This issue carried a full-page map, which I sketched and traced on the mimeograph stencil, showing the territory of the original Roman Empire.

This map included four of the sea gates that control sea-access to this entire territory. The article stressed the fulfillment of the prophecy of Genesis 22:17 and 24:60, showing how the U.S.A. and Britain were to possess the sea gates of enemy nations. This was part of the national dominance promised Abraham for his descendants. But the article also pointed out that our peoples, since receiving this Birthright inheritance, have turned from our God—our national sins have increased—and God is going to have to punish our nations at the hand of this coming resurrected Roman Empire, with invasion, captivity, and slavery. These four vital sea gates, the article explained, must be taken from Britain before the "beast" power—revived Roman Empire—can rise. Britain, since, has lost Suez and exercises no real control over the other three.

This tremendous prophecy *was* fulfilled, in the form of the insignificant "sixth head of the beast," by Mussolini very shortly after this article appeared. But the all-important seventh and last "head" is being formed, today, before our very eyes! It is rising out of the Common Market in Europe—out of which ten nations or groupings of nations will ultimately combine to form a new European Union!

During March and April, 1939, about 1,000 new requests were received for annual subscriptions to *The Plain Truth!* The work was GROWING!

The August issue of *The Plain Truth,* 1939, contained an article captioned: "World War May Come Within Six Weeks." The war started September 1.

In an article in the November, 1939, *Plain Truth* on "The European War," a paragraph or two may be of interest:

"Finally, remember this war is merely *a resumption of the world war.* It is not, so far as present events are concerned, directly and specifically mentioned in the Bible prophecies at all. *But undoubtedly it is paving the way* for prophesied events.

"One of two things may happen: 1) the Allies may go on to smash Hitler, possibly with the help of either or both of the United States or Italy; 2) Italy might yet

5

come in on the side of Germany—the battle sector shifting at once to the Mediterranean, especially Egypt (the Suez canal gate), and Palestine (as described with maps in the February-March *Plain Truth*)."

The uphill struggle—climbing constantly in growth of the work in spite of inadequate facilities and financial backing—continued into the year 1940 and throughout the decade of the forties.

The March, 1940, *Plain Truth* was the first since November, 1939. It was still mimeographed. The circulation was 2,000 copies. More than 100,000 people were *listening* to the message weekly. Expenses were being held to $300 per month—including our family living of less than $85 per month.

Boys Growing Up

Meanwhile, our four children were growing up. The two girls now were twenty and twenty-two. The boys ten and eleven—Dick almost twelve. For the boys, this, I believe, is the happiest age ever enjoyed by any person. Surely nothing to compare is experienced by girls.

I remember so well when I was eleven. My only sister, Mabel, died that year in an attack of spinal meningitis, at age nine. However, a year later my brother Dwight Leslie and his twin sister Mary Lucile were born. During those years, with other boys of the same age, I took up wrestling—these were the days of our "heroes" Frank Gotch and "Farmer" Burns; we went swimming, skating in the winter, sledding. We dug caves. We had white mice and ferrets, and probably we stuck frogs in our pockets. I rode a bicycle everywhere.

At eleven and twelve a boy has few responsibilities—devotes himself primarily to "fun"—and yet, he does not altogether take a vacation from disappointments, humiliation and painful suffering. His problems

6

are far more serious to him than they are to Dad or Mom or other grown-ups.

I have recounted how our younger son had given me a big kiss—and when I asked what he was after now, he replied that was for picking out for him the best mother in the world. Only I didn't "pick her out"—we both have always known, somehow, that God chose us for each other. But if our boys had "the best Mom in the world" she was best, except for just one or two things.

For one thing, our sons had a mother who wanted them to swim—only she did not want them to go near the water until *after* they had learned how to swim. This problem was far more serious to young growing boys than Mother ever knew.

During the summer of 1940 we were returning to Eugene on the McKenzie Highway along the swift-flowing McKenzie River. The boys wanted to do some fishing. Finally, after much pleading, we stopped at a country store, bought a small roll of fishing line, a few hooks, and a bottle of salmon eggs.

Our elder daughter, Beverly, and her fiance, Jimmy Gott, were with us, and Jim cut two big "fishing poles" from a willow tree and tied the line to each of them.

From here on, I will let my younger son recount for you in his own words the humiliating experience he and his brother Dick suffered—all because of the "best Mom in the world."

"We were on the way returning to Eugene from a trip, I believe to Blemis' home, or else up to Belknap Springs—but at any rate, up the McKenzie Highway.

"Dick and I (I mostly, I believe) pleaded and pleaded, and finally, we stopped at a country store, and bought a small roll of fishing line, a few hooks, and a bottle of salmon eggs.

("Bev and Jim were along, I remember definitely—because Jim cut us two big club-like 'fishing poles' and tied the line to each of them.)

"So—we were carefully herded over the rocks, with deep pools swirling around through undercut areas, to the brink of the mighty rushing McKenzie at one of its fastest, deepest points.

"Having known only a little about fishing—I *did* know you had to get the bait *down* to where the fish were. We had no split shot or weights, no leaders on our lines, no reels, so casting was impossible.

"Mom picked out the spot where it was SAFEST—instead of letting us go where we thought we might find a *fish*. There we sat, with sour expressions on our faces, with the short line, a tiny gold single-egg hook and a bright red salmon egg—skipping frantically along the top of the gigantic rush of tons of blue-white water, on the edge of one of the fastest and deepest rapids along the McKenzie!

"There wasn't the *faintest, remotest* chance of ever catching a trout under those conditions—and we both knew it—but at least, we were SAFE!"

No Hallucinations

On April 2, 1940, I had to write co-workers: "The only way I have managed to keep the work going has been by personal sacrifice—taking money intended for our family living, letting my family suffer. One of my daughters has had to stop school. We are about to lose our home. We have gone without badly needed clothing. I could tell you more, but do not want to talk about ourselves—our heavenly Father knows. We are willing and glad to make any sacrifice. BUT THE POINT IS, WE HAVE NOW COME TO THE *END,* UNLESS SUBSTANTIAL HELP COMES AT ONCE. The work cannot be held up by this method of personal sacrifice any longer. As long as it was only us who suffered, I said nothing. But now the Lord's WORK will stop unless substantial help comes quickly. For the work's sake I must appeal to our helpers. I would starve before I would ask one cent as charity for myself. But I'm willing to humiliate myself in any way for the gospel's sake."

During the early years of this ministry, as I have noted before, no illusions of grandeur flooded my mind. I had no grandiose visions of conducting a great earth-girding work reaching many millions on all continents. If anyone had then suggested that this work would grow to even a tenth its present scope and power, I would have regarded it as an empty pipe-dream.

This work has not grown to its present proportions because *I* planned it that way—but because GOD planned it, expanded it, empowered it.

I was not without vision. When the broadcast first started, in January, 1934, I did envision a work reaching the entire Willamette Valley and probably Portland. After we reached Portland, I did envision going on to cover Seattle, and the entire Pacific Northwest. As the work grew, the vision for the future expanded with it. But this ministry was not started with any hallucinations, spawned in self-pride, vanity and egotism, as did a few ne'er-do-wells who have come to me, announcing: "Mr. Armstrong, I have come to announce to you that I am Elijah that was prophesied to come;" or "Mr. Armstrong, God has shown me in a dream that I am to be your right-hand man and soon to take your place."

All self-important vanity had been knocked out of me by the successive business reverses, being knocked down repeatedly, and made for years to bite the dust of poverty and humiliation. But I had come to receive a *new* confidence. It was based on faith in CHRIST—not

9

in self. It was *the* faith *of* Christ, which God had given as one of the gifts of His Spirit.

First Vision of Worldwide Scope

But in May, 1940, God had begun to bring into my mind a glimpse of the future worldwide destiny of this work, for the first time. We could not know, then, whether World War II, already under way in Europe, would continue on into Armageddon and the END of the world. We could not know, then, that God would grant *another recess* in the world war—*and for the very purpose* of allowing this WORK OF GOD to fulfill Matthew 24:14 in preaching and publishing Christ's gospel of God's KINGDOM to all the world as a witness, just before the END of this world and the coming of Christ!

But the sense of *imminence* of the END—combined with the knowledge that this very message *must* first be proclaimed—inspired a letter to co-workers dated May 23, 1940, which asked, in part:

"Dear CO-WORKERS: We enter, now, the most CRU-CIAL period of our co-labors together in the powerful proclaiming of the gospel. The ZERO HOUR has struck! Whatever is to be done, we must do quickly. Soon we shall not be permitted to carry on this great work.... But now, as never before, people WILL HEAR! People are STUNNED by the war events in Europe! Everywhere, people . . . are now beginning to realize the Bible prophecies are being fulfilled—that we are in the VERY LAST DAYS! . . . NOW is the time when Jesus said 'this gospel of the kingdom'—the good news of the coming government BY JESUS CHRIST, the kingdom OF GOD— 'shall be preached in all the world for a witness unto all nations; and then shall the END come'! "

For the first time, I saw the real meaning of that prophecy. I knew of no other preaching of this very gospel. Nowhere else was this prophecy being fulfilled. I saw, now, that THIS MESSAGE was to go worldwide—to ALL NATIONS. I did not yet envision that this very work would be used of God in its accomplishment. But I *did* now see clearly that we should *step up* our energies and, as far as it was GOD'S will to use us in this fulfillment, expand the work.

I began, much more intensely than before, to focus attention on expanding the broadcast into Seattle. Almost a year before I had taken a trip to Seattle to explore the possibilities of obtaining a good time on a radio station. But no door opened then. And, in 1939 it was financially impossible.

A Heart-touching Sacrifice

The Seattle broadcasting was started by an unusual sacrifice made by a man and wife in Clarke County, Washington, listeners over KWJJ. This family had lost all they had in the great drought of 1934 and 1935. They then migrated from South Dakota and had made a down payment on a small farm a few miles outside Vancouver, Washington. The man and a son had managed to build the outside shell of a house. The siding was not yet on. A second floor had been partially laid—just the subflooring. There was no stairway as yet—and no partitions either upstairs or down—just one large room on each floor. The children slept upstairs, gaining access by climbing up a ladder.

This man had, over two or three years' time, saved up $40 over and above bare family expenses and getting this much of a home built. The $40 was saved to buy lumber for the partitions for separate rooms in their house.

When these people heard we were trying to get started on the air in Seattle, they sent me that $40, explaining how they had saved it, and for what purpose. Since we were driving to Portland every week for the broadcast, I drove out to their little farm to return the money.

"I just couldn't take this money," I said, "when you have struggled so long to save it so you could have a home to live in."

Tears filled the woman's eyes. She shook her head, refused to accept the money back. "Mr. Armstrong," she said, "of course it would be nice for us to get up partitions and have separate rooms—but that is not an absolute NEED. We just *could not* use this money for a *temporary material home,* when it will help get Christ's message of a home for all eternity in God's kingdom to *many thousands* of people!"

I realized, then, that it was really GOD'S WILL that this money be used for His gospel—and that these people were actually receiving a spiritual blessing in giving it that far outweighed the material benefit of using it for themselves. Incidentally, these people *were* blessed materially after that, and it was not too long until their house was completed, after all. Jesus Christ said, seek *first* the kingdom of God—the spiritual values—and the material THINGS shall be ADDED. God always does add them!

On the Air in SEATTLE!

When I sent out a letter to co-workers telling of this sacrifice, and the NEED to get on the air in Seattle, there was a surprising response. We received one day in the mail the largest sum we had ever received—$100, for broadcasting in Seattle. It took our breath!

But, a few days later, two more $100 sums came, three contributed $50 each, and several sent in single dollars.

And so, finally, three long years after the broadcast expanded from Eugene into Portland, it now *leaped into Seattle!*

From Seattle, I mimeographed a new co-workers' Bulletin, the second such Bulletin in new form and dress, dated September 17, 1940. The leading caption stated the news: "NOW ON THE AIR IN SEATTLE!"

The program started there Sunday, September 15th, over 1,000-watt station KRSC—twice the power of our Portland station, KWJJ—and serving a larger population.

The exciting story of how we finally were enabled to add the Seattle area to those of Portland and Eugene in the broadcasting work was told in this Bulletin, and can best be told here in a condensation of that Bulletin:

There was a subhead, "How God Has Answered PRAYER."

Then: "I want to tell our family of co-workers some of the inside story of our finally getting on the air here in Seattle. I want you to know something of the problem we had to solve, the difficulties in our path, and how God went before us, answered prayer, and worked out everything so perfectly.

Answered Prayer

"Radio stations, especially in Seattle, do not want religious programs on their stations. I learned that a year ago when I was up here. I knew nothing but prayer could open the way for us, but I had faith God wanted us to speak His Word faithfully in this Seattle district, and I know He would not fail us.

"Mrs. Armstrong and I arrived in Seattle late Wednesday afternoon. I did not feel we could afford the high cost of one of the five larger 5,000-watt stations here. This reduced our possibilities to two stations.

13

One, KRSC, has never taken religious programs, and its owner gave me no encouragement when I saw him a year ago. The other station, same power, was throwing all religious programs off their station, didn't want any more, and the price was just double what we pay in Portland.

"It looked discouraging. But I decided to see the owner of KRSC again. He auditioned one of our programs. He became interested, said we had a splendid program that would attract a large listening audience. However, he would not take any outside religious program unless approved by the Seattle Council of Churches. He then called their secretary by telephone to his office to hear one of our programs auditioned. This man was well impressed with our program and also with *The Plain Truth,* which he carefully examined. It happened that he was familiar with the truth of our national identity in the House of Israel, and he was glad to see this truth published in the *Plain Truth* magazine.

"So the owner sidetracked a 4 o'clock Sunday afternoon news broadcast so we could have the same time we have over KWJJ in Portland, and then made me a rate just $1.40 more per broadcast than we pay KWJJ! Since this station has double the power of KWJJ, and is the highest class independent station in Seattle, I'm sure you'll realize how fortunate we were.

"There is but one explanation. God Himself worked it all out. It is surely an answer to prayer. Mrs. Armstrong and I will remain here until after next Sunday's broadcast, which I want to conduct in person; then we shall return home. While here, we are broadcasting by transcription from KWJJ. When we return home we will send transcribed broadcasts to Seattle."

The next subhead in this Bulletin was captioned: "LOS ANGELES NEXT!"

14

The *vision* of the mission to which God had called us, and in which the living Christ was using us, now expanded. World events made it clear.

The Bulletin continued:

"The Lord willing, we hope now to add a radio station in LOS ANGELES next. Such a station would add a QUARTER OF A MILLION people to those now hearing the true gospel of the kingdom.

"As I wrote in the last Bulletin, GOD'S TIME HAS COME for this last warning message to go—and to go to the millions, with great POWER! The whole world is IN ARMS! God now calls *us*, His children, TO ARMS! THE WARNING MUST GO!"

41

Impact on Pacific Northwest

N OW THAT the broadcast had started in
Seattle, the work began rapidly to
take on new life.

Up until this time, it certainly bore no resemblance
to what would be expected by most people to be the
very WORK OF GOD. How could anything have had such
humble and crude beginnings? Did anything ever start
smaller? Looking back on those years now, I am, myself, astonished! It surely couldn't have happened. Yet,
it did!

With Man—Impossible!

What man could start out, without money, without
support or backing, without any car and having to walk
or hitchhike, on his own, with an unpopular message to
which people were hostile, and expect to get that message preached and published to the millions on all
continents around the world?

16

With man, it certainly is IMPOSSIBLE!

But I was not looking to *people* for support—I was relying on GOD! There is a Scripture that says, "With man it *is* impossible, but with GOD all things are possible!"

And *that* is the answer!

Through the years I have encountered a few individuals who thought they had a vision to "preach Christ" and started out on their own, without backing, to do it. Some have gotten out some kind of mimeographed literature, or even managed to have a "tract" or two printed. But none I knew of ever grew. All soon gave up. Their work lacked the inspiration, the "spark," the vital "something" to make it tick—and GROW! The answer, of course, is that the POWER OF GOD was lacking. They *were,* in true fact, *on their own!* Christ had never called or sent them. They were *not* speaking HIS Word faithfully! Without His guidance and the dynamic power of His Spirit, their work soon came to naught.

The only reason this work survived—and grew—is that I was not, after all, "on my own."

Pitifully small as this effort was during those first few years—still it was, though assuredly not then apparent, the very WORK OF THE LIVING GOD. The divinely imparted dynamic spark was in it. People have asked, in recent years, what makes this now great work "tick." The vital energy and life that the living CHRIST has imparted is what makes it tick!

The Difference

The things God does *through man* must always start small—usually the very smallest—but they grow big, until they become the biggest. Jesus compared this to the proverbial mustard seed.

Today, for example [as this second volume goes to press], there are [nearly five] billion people populating the earth. God started this—with *one man,* out of whom he made one woman. The nations of Israel, Judah, the numerous Arabs, all started with *one man*—Abraham. The only true religion started with *one man*—Jesus Christ! Ultimately those born of God through Him will fill the earth.

This work certainly had no professional appearance in those days, although there must have been power in the broadcasts—they had the ring of sincerity and the truth the listeners had not heard before. And *The Plain Truth,* though crude in *appearance,* nevertheless reflected the years of professional writing experience. Mistakes were made. This was due to the *human* element. It was the guidance and power of God injected into it that gave it its real impetus—but God was using a mighty imperfect human instrument, and so human limitations entered into the picture too. These caused some of the setbacks, and God allowed others to test and refine and help perfect the instrument He was using.

I know of evangelists who have been skyrocketed suddenly to fame before vast audiences. They started out big and quickly became celebrities acclaimed by millions. But they were started out by organizations of MEN. It was organized religion which pumped into their great stadiums, coliseums, supertents or vast auditoriums the multithousand crowds. And all such world-famous evangelists must preach *only* what is allowed by the denominations or churches who back them, and must refrain from preaching anything contrary to their doctrines.

Suppose, for example, such an evangelist backed by the conservative fundamentalist-evangelical denomina-

18

tions should tell his audience the Bible commands them to keep the seventh-day Sabbath. Suppose a "big-time" evangelist with so-called "pentecostal" backing in his giant circus tent should shout to his thousands that "speaking in tongues" is *not* the "Bible evidence" of "the baptism of the Holy Spirit." Immediately they would be branded HERETICS. Immediately they would lose their organized backing; they would be plunged into "disgrace."

But such men come and they go. Their work is foredoomed to die. If they are backed by men, supported by organized men, they must become the willing TOOL of such organizations. But when one is truly called and chosen of God, he must become wholly yielded to God as God's servant, and he must speak God's Word faithfully, else GOD'S support is withdrawn. *What a difference!*

Redoubling Growth

Jesus Christ said, "Every plant, which my heavenly Father hath not planted, shall be rooted up" (Matt. 15:13). Again, "Except the Lord build the house, they labor in vain that build it" (Psalm 127:1). But, David was inspired to say (Moffatt translation): "Though I must pass through the thick of trouble, thou wilt preserve me: ... The Eternal intervenes on my behalf; ... *thou wilt not drop the work thou hast begun"* (Psalm 138:7-8). That PROMISE of God has sustained me through the years of opposition, persecution and trouble. God is still keeping that promise, and He will perpetually!

Looking back, now, over the actual physical circumstances, conditions, and happenings of those years, it seems utterly incredible that a work started in such a humble, crude manner without any visible backing could have survived, let alone continued to grow at the pace of 30 percent a year.

Of course this work did not double in size every day, every week, or even every year. But doubling in number of people reached, in number of precious lives converted, in radio power, and in scope of operation every two years and seven and a half months is, after all, a very rapid and almost unheard-of rate of growth. And that rate of redoubling continued nearly thirty years!

Plain Truth *Printed at Last*

If this work had the appearance, those first seven struggling years, of the pitifully insignificant and hopeless effort of an individual striving desperately "on his own," it began now rapidly to take on the appearance of a more substantial operation. Those with spiritual discernment began to recognize it for what it was—the true WORK OF GOD.

A limited fund had been raised to start the broadcast on KRSC, in Seattle.

In preparation for this, a part of this special fund had been used to have the *Plain Truth* issue for August-September, 1940, printed! This was the first printed number since the May-June, 1938, number.

But at last, with this August-September, 1940, number, *The Plain Truth* graduated permanently from the handmade mimeographed class! Along with the other phases of the work, *The Plain Truth* was growing up!

It "grew up" only to a most humble *start* as a *printed magazine,* however. This issue, and the few to follow, were printed on a very low-cost yellow paper we had used for years for the mimeographed editions. It was only eight pages. And it was issued only bimonthly. On page 4, under the masthead box, appeared this notice: "This is the first issue of *The Plain Truth* since May. There was no June or July number this year. For the immediate future we hope to be able, the Lord willing, to publish one number each two months. Later we hope to be able to send you an issue every month, and to enlarge *The Plain Truth* to sixteen pages, just double the present size. Constant improvement is our goal."

That improvement came slowly through the years—but the effort was never relinquished, and gradually the improvement did come.

Many months later, it did double to 16 pages. Circulation doubled and redoubled. After years as a 16-page magazine, it went to twenty-four and then to thirty-two pages. In publishing that first regular printed issue of *The Plain Truth,* an additional 500 copies were printed in anticipation of the first two months' response from the new Seattle broadcast.

Amazing Seattle Response

The broadcast had started on KRSC, in Seattle, September 15, 1940. By November 1 the receipt of mail from listeners was mounting rapidly. More than 500 requests for copies came from the first four or five broadcasts. The co-workers' Bulletin dated November 1 reported the subscription list of *The Plain Truth* had reached 3,000. We still had to keep the mailing list by handwriting, or typing, and in this manner personally address every copy. This required volunteer labor and several days' time. Mail response now indicated a listening audience of 150,000 with the three radio stations.

Although requests for *The Plain Truth* exceeded 500 the first five weeks from the Seattle station, there were, of course, *very* few contributions—especially when none were in any way solicited. Nevertheless, for the encouragement of older co-workers, this November 1 Bulletin stated: "Offerings are just *beginning,* now, to come from listeners to KRSC, our Seattle station. First, $1. Then, later, another dollar; then $6 the next week— $8 so far." It was now costing nearly $100 per issue to publish and mail out *The Plain Truth.*

In this issue of the co-workers' Bulletin (sent only to those who had become voluntary regular contributors), excerpts from several letters from listeners were reproduced—seventeen of those from the Seattle station, and nine from the Portland station.

Portions of some of those letters are illuminating. Here are just a few:

"FROM SEATTLE: 'Am enclosing $1 to help a little in your God-given work. How I wish it could be more, but when I can possibly, will send more. Received the copy of *The Plain Truth* a few days ago. . . . I have wondered many times when these Scriptures would be revealed, and by whom; but God knew, and He has given the wisdom to one He can trust. You have my prayers.' " This letter accompanied the second dollar received from the program on the Seattle station. Jesus Christ said His sheep hear His voice. They recognize His message. They catch the difference instantly. Some of these letters came from people who discerned that this, indeed, was Christ's own gospel—very different from that the world had heard.

"FROM BINGEN, WASHINGTON: 'Will you please send a copy of *The Plain Truth.* I thank God for men who tell the truth about His plan of salvation. There are only too few in this time of great need.' "

"FROM DEEP RIVER, WASH.: 'We listen to your broadcast every Sunday, and would like to receive the magazine. . . . I realize you do not ask for money, but I am enclosing $1 to help in God's work.' "

22

"FROM INDIANOLA, WASH.: 'The portion of your sermon, delivered over the radio yesterday, that I heard was most enlightening and constructive, and I should appreciate having you send me *The Plain Truth*. These certainly are the kind of biblical explanations that the world needs today.' "

Yes, some who hear the *World Tomorrow* program do recognize it as God's very own message, and it has been the generally unpreached truth of God's Word, and the power of His Spirit that has given this work *life,* and *vitality,* and caused it to grow from smallest beginnings!

Now just two or three portions of letters from listeners over KWJJ, Portland. These, too, are significant:

"FROM OREGON CITY: 'I received your message today and with tears streaming from my eyes, thanked our heavenly Father that the way had been opened for your Seattle broadcast.' "

"FROM LA CENTER, WASH.: 'I enjoy your broadcast so much, and regret when I have to miss one. I feel lifted, and see more light after listening. God is certainly with you in every word that you say—one can just feel His presence. I would appreciate a copy of *The Plain Truth*, please.' "

"FROM PORTLAND: 'In your last broadcast you mentioned that the public might not approve your words. From your own teachings, your *concern* is to preach the TRUTH, just as you have been doing. . . . The LORD approves. That is enough. *The Plain Truth* is most excellent. . . . This old world is now in the critical time when we need a pilot to show us whither we are headed. You are doing a great job. I know you are giving the truth to those who never heard it, and probably never would, who will not go to the present-day church and

23

42

On the Air in Los Angeles!

By MID-MAY, 1941, the weekly listening audience, over the three stations in Eugene and Portland and in Seattle, had grown to a quarter of a million people.

That seemed a huge audience. Indeed, it *was* a huge audience. The work of God, having been started so very small was, as stated before, growing up.

The circulation of *The Plain Truth* had gone up to 5,000 copies.

We had started on the air in Seattle, on 1,000-watt KRSC, on September 15, 1940. By February, 1941, the mail response indicated a listening audience of more than 150,000. Beginning with the issue of August-September, 1940, *The Plain Truth* had "grown up" from a mimeographed paper to a sixteen-page printed magazine, bimonthly. By mid-May we were receiving between 200 and 300 letters from radio listeners every week, and mailing out 5,000 copies of *The Plain Truth*.

Office Outgrown

Now we experienced "growing pains" in real earnest. Now we really did have a tremendous problem on our hands.

It was becoming an utter impossibility to continue handling this volume of mail, and a 5,000-name mailing list, and mailing out the 5,000 copies, without equipment in that unventilated inside office room.

For seven years we had struggled to build this work from nothing to its 1941 size, without equipment. We had paid $5-per-month rent for this small inside room. It was without windows, without ventilation, except for two transoms. One transom opened into the hallway. The other opened into a large adjoining room where labor union meetings were held. The only ventilation we received through this transom was stale tobacco smoke from the preceding night's union meetings. We were able to work in this office room only about two hours at a time without going outdoors for air. It was not a healthful place to work.

We had no modern office equipment, not even a desk. There were a few shelves along one wall. We had no mailing equipment. The 5,000 names on the mailing list had to be kept by handwriting or typing. Each issue, the 5,000 copies of *The Plain Truth* had to be hand-rolled into thin paper wrappers, stamped, addressed either by hand, or by myself on the one and only secondhand typewriter.

After going on KRSC in Seattle, this became an impossible task for Mrs. Armstrong and me, without help. Twice we had one girl or woman helping in the office, but now we had to ask several church brethren for volunteer help to come to the office to address wrappers, and help us roll them and stamp for mailing.

33

Then on May 14, 1941, a wonderful thing happened. A larger, sun-lit office became available to us. It was in the old I.O.O.F. Building in Eugene, on the third floor, rear northeast corner. There was an inner corner room, and a double-size outer room opening off the hallway. I could not afford to rent both rooms, but the building manager offered to let me have the inner corner office for $10 per month. He also said we could use the larger outer office part time, if necessary, until we could afford to rent the whole thing. A much larger adjoining room was available for future rental, when need and finance arrived.

This office had nice large windows—sunlight—fresh air.

Let me tell you right here, I never was so grateful for sunlight and fresh air in all my life. I had never before realized how thankful we should be for sunlight and fresh air. That is one blessing most people have, but usually take for granted without any thanksgiving! *How about you?*

I now managed to buy an office desk—after seven years. That same desk was used in the television program in 1955, seen by hundreds of thousands, coast to coast. I continued to use it as my desk, after moving the headquarters of the work to Pasadena, until 1955 or 1956. It is still doing service for one of God's ministers.

Our First Equipment

This desk was the very beginning of necessary equipment to administer the work of God. We had been forced to wait seven years for it.

About the time of moving to this larger office, I managed to buy an antiquated, secondhand, foot-operated addressing machine. With it we installed the first beginning of the Elliott system of stencils for the mailing list. These stencils are cut on a typewriter, or machine very similar to a typewriter.

That old foot-operated addressing machine made so much noise that the tenants on the floor below complained vigorously. Perhaps our many employees today working in the large, modern, air-conditioned mailing room may utter a momentary prayer of gratitude to the Great God who has provided them with the very finest and most efficient equipment the world affords.

I do not remember, now, what I paid for that ancient addressing machine. I believe we still have it stored somewhere around the Ambassador College campus. Perhaps we should get out some of this ancient crude equipment and form a museum of our own! It probably cost all of $10 or $15—we could not have afforded more, then. I'm sure many of our employees would laugh at it, today. But it was no laughing matter, then. We struggled along seven years to have it. And I very sincerely THANKED GOD for it!

Think of just the two of us—with at times the help of a girl who knew no shorthand and could not use a typewriter—handling and answering an average of 250 letters a week, besides all the other things Mrs. Armstrong and I had to do! Then having to call in a half dozen church brethren for volunteer help in addressing 5,000 copies of *The Plain Truth* BY HAND. And in those days we had to paste 1-cent stamps on every copy. Mrs. Armstrong had to cook paste of flour and water at home and bring it to the office to paste those wrappers.

About the time we moved to this new office, I managed to employ a secretary. I believe she started at $10 per week. Also, I now purchased my first filing cabinet. It was a heavy cardboard cabinet, reinforced at corners and edges with very thin metal.

If anyone doubts that this work started the very *smallest*, let him realize we had to wait *seven years* for this cardboard file cabinet—and then we could afford ONLY THE ONE. How many modern steel filing cabinets do we have TODAY? I simply don't know—but it must be hundreds—not only at Pasadena headquarters, in many different buildings on the campus, and in dozens and scores of offices around the world.

This great work of God not only *started* small. It grew very gradually. There was no mushroom growth.

Writing these things makes me realize HOW GRATEFUL we should be—HOW MUCH we have to THANK GOD for! And all this God has done without requests for money on the air, or in any of our literature—all of which is given FREE, upon request.

New Consciousness of Mission

About this time God impressed on my mind His real meaning of the prophecies in Ezekiel 33:1-19, and 3:17-21. The true significance of the entire book of Ezekiel had been revealed for some time. But now, suddenly, it took on *immediate* and *specific* and *personal* significance.

I had seen that Ezekiel was a *prophet* with a message for the FUTURE. He himself was in the captivity of the House of JUDAH—the Jews. But he was *not* set a prophet with a message to these people. The original nation Israel had been divided after the death of Solomon into *two* nations. The northern kingdom of TEN TRIBES had its capital, not at Jerusalem, but at Samaria. It was called THE HOUSE OF ISRAEL—not Judah. The kingdom of Israel had been invaded and conquered by King Shalmaneser of Assyria about 120 to 135 years *before* the Jewish captivity by Babylon.

The people of the House of Israel had been uprooted from their homes, their farms and cities, and taken to the southern shores of the Caspian Sea. But by the time of the Babylonish captivity of Judah, in Ezekiel's day, some of the House of Israel had migrated northwest to northwestern Europe and the British Isles.

Ezekiel was made a prophet to *this* nation—not the nation of Judah among whose captives he lived. His message was a warning of INVASION and TOTAL DESTRUCTION OF THE NATION'S *CITIES*. That invasion was for the far future. The prophecy came more than 120 years *after* Israel already *had* been invaded and conquered.

God did not say, "Warn the people *where you are.*" He said: "Son of man, I SEND THEE TO" the House of Israel. God said: "GO" from where Ezekiel was, with JUDAH—"GO, get thee UNTO THE HOUSE OF ISRAEL."

But Ezekiel *did not go*. HE COULDN'T! He was a CAPTIVE of the Chaldeans. And no such gigantic military invasion has ever befallen the kingdom of ISRAEL since Ezekiel's prophecy was written! The prophecies of the Bible are nearly all DUAL. They have a two-fold fulfillment—the one, often in Old Testament times, a type of the second, in these end-time days. The Assyrian captivity, more than a century before the prophecy, was the type. The warning is for *our day!*

Again, there is a story-flow—a time-sequence running through the book of Ezekiel. Other portions of the book show the prophecies pertain to the time shortly prior to the Second Coming of Christ. The 40th chapter to the end of the book deals with millennial events, yet future.

So now I saw Ezekiel was set a WATCHMAN—to *watch* international conditions as well as God's prophecies—and *when* this invasion is preparing, and near, shortly prior to Christ's coming to RULE THE WORLD, the watchman is to WARN the people who had migrated, in

Ezekiel's day, to northwestern Europe and the British Isles! But Ezekiel *never carried that warning!* It was not for HIS TIME! He was used *merely to write it!* It now became plain to me that God was to use a modern 20th-century "Ezekiel" to shout this WARNING.

The realization flashed to my mind with terrific impact that in WORLD WAR II—already then under way—America being then drawn closer to participation—that *I could see this "sword" of WAR coming!* I looked around. NO ONE had ever sounded this warning! No one was then sounding it! I saw numerous prophecies showing how terribly God is going to *punish* North America and the British Commonwealth people for our apostasy from Him. I saw our sins, individually and nationally, fast increasing!

The conviction came. *IF* God opened doors for the MASS-PROCLAMATION of His gospel, and of this warning, nationwide, I would walk through those doors and proclaim God's message faithfully, as long as He gave me guidance, power, and the means.

I had no illusions that I was chosen to be the "modern Ezekiel" to proclaim this message. But I did know that no one was sounding this alarm. I did plainly see this sword of destruction and punishment coming. I knew the time was near. Perhaps, with World War II well under way, it was even then *upon us.* We could not, then, foresee that God would grant another recess period in the series of world wars before the final round to end at "Armageddon."

And I did see, plainly, that God said: "IF the watchman see the sword come, and blow not the trumpet, and the people be not warned" that God would require the blood of the people—and now *whole peoples*—at the watchman's hand!

That was a stern warning to *me.* At least I was *one*

of the watchmen who *did* see it coming! God had already placed the broadcasting facilities of three radio stations at my disposal. A quarter of a million people now heard my voice weekly. Possibly ten or fifteen thousand people read the 5,000 copies of *The Plain Truth*.

Of course I had been sounding this warning all along—but only in the Pacific Northwest. Now I began to see that God intended to send it to ALL ISRAEL. And He had revealed to me that that meant, today, the United States, the British Commonwealth, and the nations of northwestern Europe. The idea of *my* being used, personally, in reaching Britain and these other countries did not yet take sharp focus in my mind. But I *did,* now, for the first time, begin to *think actively and definitely* about this work expanding to the entire United States!

Door Opens to Reach NATION

God works out His purposes on His definite time-schedule. This vision of urgency to warn the whole nation and renewed sense of mission came just when God was ready to OPEN DOORS NATIONALLY!

In June that year—1941—Mrs. Armstrong's sister and a friend were planning a trip to Detroit to take delivery on a new car. Somehow the suggestion came for Mrs. Armstrong and me—with them—to drive our new car as far as Chicago.

Immediately it flashed to my mind that in Des Moines, Iowa, where I had been born and reared, was an exclusive-channel 50,000-watt radio station, WHO. In those days I could tune it in any night out on the Pacific Coast. Only eight stations had exclusive channels—no other station on the continent on their channels. For our purpose, I knew that WHO was then the most valuable and desirable station in all the United States for our purpose—located not far from the geographical center of the nation.

Normally, I knew our chances of obtaining time on such a high prestige station were exactly nil. But then I remembered my uncle, Frank Armstrong, youngest brother of my father. For years he had been the leading advertising man in the state of Iowa. Perhaps his influence might help swing open the mighty door of WHO. Of course, we could not afford to buy time on so powerful a station—but I would see about it, anyway.

Let me say, here, for the benefit of those not familiar with the radio-television field, there is a vast difference in 50,000-watt stations. Some 50,000-watt stations have far less coverage than others. The quality of equipment, the location of the transmitter, and other factors make all the difference. But WHO was—and is—one of the very top prestige stations. Its signal was phenomenal. Today, there are many more stations on the air as then. Today, none of these big stations reaches out like they did then.

So we drove our new DeSoto car to Chicago, where the girls took a bus to Detroit. Then we stopped at Des Moines on the return trip.

I had not seen my uncle for fifteen years. We had arranged by telephone to have a family get-together at the home of my cousin—his daughter—and her husband, in Indianola, a county seat town thirty miles south of Des Moines.

I suppose we were all a little surprised to observe the change that had taken place in the appearance of each of us—after fifteen years.

We visited old friends of both my wife and myself around Indianola and Des Moines for a few days.

While there, my uncle called the general manager

of WHO on the telephone, told him about me, and asked him to see me. After I explained about our program, he said he could clear a late Sunday night time, at 11 p.m., except for one Sunday night, each month. The owner of WHO was Col. B. J. Palmer, owner of the Palmer Chiropractic Institute at Davenport, Iowa. Col. Palmer reserved the time of 11 to 11:30 p.m. on one Sunday night of each month for a personal talk by himself. Mr. Mailand, the station's manager, offered me the other three or four Sunday nights at this same hour, at the very low cost, for so powerful a station, of a little over $60 per half hour.

This was a tremendous opportunity—but it was still beyond our reach. I told Mr. Mailand we were not yet ready for it, but hoped to be by the following year. I had felt we ought to go on a Los Angeles station first, anyway. But now, definitely, our vision expanded to broadcasting nationally, as soon as we could grow to it.

Los Angeles Door Opens

We had planned to swing by Los Angeles on our way home to investigate possibilities on radio stations there.

If Portland and Seattle radio stations had been hostile to programming religious broadcasts, I found Los Angeles even more so—although there were a large number of religious programs on the air in Los Angeles.

Station KNX, the powerful 50,000-watt CBS outlet, carried Dr. Maclennan of the Hollywood Presbyterian Church, John Mathews, who billed himself as "the Shepherd of the air" and Charles E. Fuller of "The Old Fashioned Revival Hour." I had listened quite regularly to all three, since KNX came in like a local station at night in Eugene.

But I did not even contact KNX. I knew it was completely beyond our financial ability. To me, in those days, these three radio broadcasters on KNX were *real* "Big Time." On the human level they seemed to me as giants, and I as a dwarf, so low beside them I would not have presumed to encroach on their valuable time by attempting to meet and shake hands with them. Yet, on the spiritual plane. I realized that God had given me a message that was *not being preached*, anywhere, except on our program. But I felt very unimportant in my own eyes.

I found stations in Los Angeles closing their doors on religious broadcasts. Yet, when I went over to KMTR (it is now KLAC), I found the manager, Mr. Ken Tinkham friendly. He told me the station was cutting down on religious programs, though the station still carried several. It was only a 1,000-watt station, but Mr. Tinkham explained how the transmitter was directly over an underground river, which had the rather freak effect of giving their signal a power equal to about 40,000 watts. Underground river or not, I found it true that the station then had a better signal than any station in Los Angeles, except the 50,000-watt stations. It was heard like a local station in San Diego, 120 miles away, and even in Bakersfield, which is over the mountains.

As we talked, I could sense Mr. Tinkham warming up to Mrs. Armstrong and me. Finally, he said he would try, later, to open up a Sunday morning time for me. I had told him we were not yet ready to go on the air in Los Angeles.

An Eighteen-Day Fast

The long strain of building the work through seven and a half years, without facilities or financial resources, had been taking its toll physically. I had been losing sleep. The constant *driving* on high tension to keep up with the growing work had told on my nerves. The weekly trips of 650 miles to Seattle and back added to the grind.

So, on returning to Eugene, Mrs. Armstrong and I, with our boys, went over on the Oregon coast to one of the little-frequented beaches, and rented a small cabin. There I went on an eighteen-day fast for both physical and spiritual recharging. An unfit man cannot accomplish much. I returned to the new office in Eugene, August 12, 1941, refreshed and renewed, with new vigor. With the KMTR and the WHO doors standing ajar, just waiting to open to us, there was now redoubled incentive to push forward.

First Airplane Flight

By December of that year, I decided to ease the strain of those long drives to Seattle—at least part of the time. Consequently on Saturday night, December 6, I left my car in Portland, and took the train to Seattle. I had found that the overnight train arrived in Seattle in time for the 8:30 broadcast at KRSC, if it was on time.

But on that particular Sunday morning, the train was late. But by getting off at Tacoma, and hiring a taxicab, I was able to arrive on time.

I had found that I could take a plane leaving Seattle somewhere around noon, getting me back to Portland in time for the 4 p.m. broadcast on KWJJ. This was the first time in my life I had ever been up in an airplane.

I shall never forget that flight. About fifteen minutes after takeoff, I noticed the captain near the passenger cabin. He knelt beside the passengers in the front seats, and in low tones spoke to them. Then he repeated this to those in the second row. My curiosity was aroused.

43

When he came to me, he said he had just received word over the plane's radio that the Japanese had bombed Pearl Harbor that morning, December 7—that the United States Navy fleet stationed there had been knocked out. The captain had spoken so quietly to prevent any excitement of hysteria on the plane.

THAT MEANT WAR!

The United States, it flashed to my mind, was now drawn into World War II!

Arriving in Portland, I jumped into a cab and got to the radio studio as quickly as possible. I purchased the *extra* newspapers being sold on the streets. I carefully scanned the teletapes of latest news at the radio station. Out came my portable typewriter. A new broadcast was dashed off.

At 4 p.m. I went on the air with one of the red-hottest broadcasts of my life. I knew that all of my listeners probably knew, already, of the Pearl Harbor "day of infamy." I merely reported the very *latest* few items of news, then went into an explanation of the MEANING of it IN BIBLICAL PROPHECY. This was one of the exciting incidents of my life.

From that point on, my broadcasts took on more and more the nature of news analysis of the war. Listener interest increased now that the United States was in the war.

Music Dropped from Program

It was now, more than ever, that my twenty years' experience in the newspaper and magazine field profited the work. Not only did I have long experience in recognizing significant news, and in processes of analysis (of news as well as of business and merchandising conditions), but now, with a fourteen-year accumulation of biblical knowledge and understanding of prophecies,

44

resulting from these years of intense and concentrated (as well as consecrated) study, I was able to produce radio programs that carried even greater public interest than those of the network news analysts.

At this time news reporting and news analysis constituted by far the number one listener interest on radio. A number of nationally famous news commentators and analysts gained the public spotlight—such men as Elmer Davis, H.V. Kaltenborn, Raymond Gram Swing, Edward R. Murrow, Eric Sevareid and others— just to name a few.

But these men knew nothing of biblical prophecy. Not knowing the real purpose being worked out here below, they did not grasp the true significance on the world of the future, of the news they were analyzing. They did not know where it was leading.

On the other hand, none of the ministers broadcasting religious programs had the newspaper and analytic background, nor, I may add, the true understanding of the prophecies, to connect that entire third of the Bible with the war events.

Putting the two together—factual knowledge and analysis of war events, with biblical prophecies—put at my disposal a powerful interest-compelling message.

Radio station managers recognized this. At the time, they welcomed and encouraged it. They began to suggest dropping off the music. I have mentioned before that when the program started, the first Sunday in 1934, it was not called *The World Tomorrow*, but *Radio Church of God*. It was, actually, the format of a typical church service condensed into a half hour. Only, instead of taking up most of the time with music, announcements, and special events with a fifteen-minute sermon, out of a service an hour and fifteen to thirty minutes long, I did get in a twenty-three- to twenty-six-minute

45

sermon on a twenty-nine-and-a-half-minute program.

We started with our opening theme, then a lively two-verse hymn—never more than two verses on the air—then a short prayer with hummed music background, announcements, a short anthemette, then the sermon, then reminder of announcements about *The Plain Truth*, and sign-off over closing theme music.

But we noticed that not more than one in a couple thousand letters ever mentioned the music. What evoked interest, and brought response, was the MESSAGE.

At first I was both reluctant and afraid to drop the music. So I experimented by reducing it. No harm resulted. There was no lessening in the response or expressed interest. I reduced it still more. Finally, it was eliminated altogether. We found, as radio station managers had recommended, that our program attracted and held a much larger interest when it started off with analysis of world events and the MEANING, as revealed in biblical prophecy.

I Meet Future Son-in-Law

Shortly prior to our summer trip to Chicago and Los Angeles in 1941, our younger daughter had become engaged to Vern R. Mattson, a University of Oregon student. He had joined the Marines and at the time we reached Los Angeles was in boot camp in San Diego. Dorothy was then working in the office with the one secretary we had then employed. She insisted on coming to Los Angeles while we were there, to visit Vern.

When she arrived, it was necessary for Mrs. Armstrong to take the train back to Eugene, to help keep up the work in the office.

I drove Dorothy down to San Diego. It was the first time I had ever met Vern Mattson. I was not sure I

46

approved of the engagement. When he came to the car, he virtually ignored me. I made some embarrassed comment in an effort to be friendly.

"Look, I'm not marrying *you,* I'm going to marry your daughter!" he snapped.

Mr. Mattson may be surprised when he reads this. He probably doesn't remember it now. He didn't really mean to be rude—he was in Marine boot camp—and it has the reputation of being REAL TOUGH. He was being put through the paces without being spared, and his nerves were taut. Actually, as I learned later, he is one of the most friendly men I ever knew.

I found him to be tall—six feet three—blond, and, as Dorothy insisted, the handsomest man in the world. But with his boot camp haircut and baggy garb, he did not appear quite that handsome—to *me.* The war was to enforce a delay in their marriage for a few years— and when, after having been in the 1st Division U.S. Marines at Guadalcanal, then in an Australian hospital, back to America and Officers' School because of his outstanding war record, and commissioned a second lieutenant, with grades at the top of his class, the war finally was behind him. I do not want to get ahead of the story at this juncture, but later on—for some twelve to thirteen years—Mr. Mattson served as Controller of Ambassador College, and Business Manager of the *Radio Church of God,* in charge of business and financial affairs.

At Last—LOS ANGELES!

After boot camp, Vern was sent back to Quantico, Virginia, for final training for overseas fighting. In April, 1942, Dorothy received word the Marines were shipping out. Vern didn't know where, but thought likely they would sail through the Panama Canal, with

47

some possibility of a very brief stopover at San Diego, Los Angeles or San Francisco.

Immediately Dorothy demanded I take her to Los Angeles to be on hand if there was a brief landing at one of these three ports. Vern would not be able to get word to her until they landed. There might not be over twenty-four hours—or even less. It would be impossible for her to reach any one of these ports in time from Eugene.

Of course, I could not leave the work for any such trip, which might last for several weeks. But, on checking over the state of the work, I felt we could now, at last, dare to take the step of starting on the air in Los Angeles. To do this I needed to be there in person, and put on the broadcasts live, until we were well established in Southern California.

So with Dorothy I drove to Hollywood, since KMTR was located in Hollywood. We rented a small apartment within walking distance of the station. Mr. Tinkham managed to clear good time for us—9:30 Sunday mornings. The time had come to drop the church-service type program altogether. Since the original broadcast name, *Radio Church of God,* did not invite a listening from nonchurchgoers whom we wished primarily to reach, and since in the world's language the message of the true gospel—the kingdom of God—is about tomorrow's world, I adopted the broadcast name *The World Tomorrow!*

And so, mid-April, 1942, *The World Tomorrow* went on the air in Hollywood. In Hollywood I was able to do several things to make the program more professional. I was able to obtain the services of a big-time network announcer to put us on and take us off the air.

Although I used four or five different announcers in the next few years, I think the very first one was perhaps the best known of all—Art Gilmore. He was coast-to-coast announcer on such CBS shows as Sam Spade, Stars over Hollywood, and, I believe by that time, Amos and Andy, besides several others. Since 1947, Art Gilmore has been on *The World Tomorrow* as our announcer, and millions worldwide will hear his voice at the beginning and the sign-off of the program— except some of the foreign overseas stations. We still believe his is the best radio voice in America to precede our program. He also does the announcing on our TV programs. Our readers may be glad to know that Mr. Gilmore is a fine, upstanding, sincere and high-principled man.

Another reason for going to Hollywood was that Hollywood was radio headquarters for the nation. Most of the top-rated network shows originated there. As a result, I could get a quality of recording for our electrical transcription discs there I had never been able to obtain in Eugene. We had now reached the stage where the amateurish, home-made type of transcriptions I was able to have recorded in Eugene would no longer be acceptable on stations like KMTR or WHO. In Hollywood I could obtain the very finest professional recordings.

While in Hollywood, I recorded the Sunday programs for the Pacific Northwest stations either Thursday nights or Friday mornings, drove to the airport (then at Burbank) and got them off by air-express. These top-level professional recordings, with a nationally known network announcer, and the program name, *The World Tomorrow,* elevated our radio program, at last, to top quality professional level.

43

Impact of Daily Radio!

WE WERE now *ON THE AIR—IN HOLLYWOOD!*

The radio station KMTR (now KLAC) had the *very desirable* wavelength of 570 kilocycles on the radio dial. This, combined with exceptional and unusual mechanical and transmitter advantages gave it a daytime signal almost equal to the average 50,000-watt station.

The mail response from listeners was at least double that of any of the three stations already used in the Pacific Northwest.

And Now—DAILY Broadcasting!

Within about two weeks a new opportunity came. When Mr. Tinkham called me to his office and offered it I didn't know whether to regard it as an opportunity or a temptation to disaster.

One of the leading Los Angeles radio ministers,

50

Dr. Clem Davies, had been using two half-hour periods on KMTR daily, at 5:30 in the evening, and a morning half-hour. He was now changing to one program daily at the more expensive time of around 7:30 in the evening.

Mr. Tinkham offered me the 5:30 p.m. time Mondays through Saturdays, in addition to the 9:30 Sunday morning half-hour. The cost would be nearly six times the amount per week I was already paying KMTR. It had been a big leap ahead, in expenditures, as well as in numbers reached, to take on the Sunday broadcasting in the Los Angeles area.

The thought of meeting this tremendous additional increase in expenses was staggering. Where would the money come from? There was no time to send letters to co-workers to see whether they would—or even *could*—pledge enough to guarantee this mountainous increase in expenses. I had to grab that open time within twenty-four hours or lose it.

Our readers will remember that I had learned the costly lesson back in the period from November, 1934, to late in 1936. The door of KXL, Portland, had opened. We then were on only one station, our original KORE, Eugene. But instead of recognizing that the living Christ, who *heads* God's work, had opened this door and expected me to walk through in FAITH, I wanted to rely on pledges from PEOPLE. When our brethren and co-workers pledged only half enough, I was afraid to incur the obligation. Christ did not open that door before me again for two whole years!

Now He had opened another door. To me, at that time, this was a *stupendous* door. It probably meant at least *doubling* the entire expenses of the whole work— in one sudden jump! And I had to pay each week in advance, too!

51

I telephoned Mrs. Armstrong at the office in Eugene. The total balance we had in the bank at the moment was exactly the amount of one week's daily broadcasting.

Well, even if it was our last dollar, God had supplied TODAY'S need for this colossal opportunity He had opened to us! Jesus' sample prayer teaches us to ask, "Give us *this day* our daily bread." God does not often give us today our need for next year —though He tells us elsewhere it is right for us to lay up in the summer for the winter's need, and even to lay up ahead for our children and grandchildren.

But I had learned the lesson at great price. This decision took courage. It took faith. God had opened now the biggest door so far. He had supplied the immediate need of that particular day.

I walked promptly through that door IN FAITH! *Blind faith!* I could not see where the money for a second week's daily broadcasting could come from. How could our income for the whole work suddenly double?

I decided that was GOD'S problem and responsibility. I committed it to Him, and wrote out a check for every dollar we had in the bank. Now we were on the air, in southern California, seven days a week! That was by far the most tremendous leap ahead!

Tremendous Response

But, miracle of miracles!—for once in our experience, the impact of this early evening DAILY broadcasting was as tremendous as the test of faith had been! Not once did I ask for contributions on the air, just as I had refused to do from the first broadcast in 1934. And the mailing address for free literature and *The Plain Truth*, offered on each program, was then Box 111, Eugene, Oregon.

Not only was there an immediate tremendous increase in mail from listeners—there was a corresponding increase in tithes and offerings arriving in Eugene.

The first week rolled by quickly. On the day the second week's advance-payment for radio time was due, I telephoned our office in Eugene. The money for the second week's broadcasting was in the bank! And, a week later, there was enough for the third—and then the fourth, and on and on! God continued, week by week, to supply the NEED!

This daily broadcasting was a new experience. At that time I had always spoken on the air from written script. During those war years it was required. To write the script for a half-hour broadcast, including the study and research for material, occupied my entire time.

It now became daily routine. Early in the morning, each day, I started getting the broadcast material assembled and outlined—then putting it on the typewriter. Around 4:30 in the afternoon I pulled the last sheet of paper from the typewriter. Then the walk of a mile or so to the radio station, and on the air at 5:30.

Once a week—it was Thursday evenings—after the daily program, I went to a restaurant for dinner, checking the evening newspapers and the weekly news magazines for war news I could use—then, whipping together an outline of the material, I went on to the recording studio to record the Sunday program for the three Pacific Northwest stations. Then a drive to the Burbank airport to put the large transcription discs into the air-express office.

It was a grind. But it was *doubling* the size, scope and power of God's work, and *that* was a rewarding thrill!

Week after week this routine continued. As the weeks passed, no word came from Vern Mattson. We learned later that the 1st Division Marines had sailed through the Panama Canal and straight through the Pacific to Guadalcanal, where they made their spectacular landing in the very *first* offensive, driving the Japanese back from the vast Pacific empire they had captured.

Training a Son

As soon as school was out in early June, Mrs. Armstrong called me on the telephone from Eugene.

"I'm sending Dick down to you on the next train," she said. "He's grown too big for me to punish, and I simply can't manage him any more."

Dick was then thirteen, and only about four months from reaching fourteen. He was sprouting up.

Two problems had presented themselves with our two sons. Ted (Garner Ted, but we always called him Ted) had always been a "little fellow"—short for his age. Dick had been of normal height for his age. But our readers will remember that Mrs. Armstrong, over my protest, had insisted on starting the two boys in the first grade in school *together*. I had finally acquiesced to this. Ted had always been, as a small boy, a favorite with his women teachers.

Because Ted, sixteen months younger, had always basked in the limelight—"stolen the show" so to speak—Dick had developed an oversized inferiority complex. Here he was, sprouting up to a full man's height, almost fourteen, but seriously lacking in confidence.

From the moment Mrs. Armstrong said she was shipping Dick down to me, I knew I had to find a way to help him overcome his inferiority complex.

I decided on a definite plan. About the second day he was with us in Hollywood—after showing him

54

around Hollywood to some extent—I asked him if he would not like to go over and see a boyhood friend, John Haeber, who lived in Hawthorne, south of Los Angeles. The Haebers had spent a lot of time in Oregon, and our boys had become acquainted with John, about their age.

Next morning early I gave Dick enough money for car fare to Hawthorne and back.

"Well, Dad, I don't know the way. How shall I go?" Dick asked.

"Dick," I said, "you have to begin right now learning to be self-reliant and finding your own way around. You already have the Haebers' street address. Learn to 'carry a message to Garcia' on your own. I'm too busy getting the broadcast ready to tell you. Here's car fare. You're on your own. Find your own way. And be back here in time for dinner. Good-bye, son."

What went on in Dick's mind at that moment I never knew. But I opened the door, he went out, and he was on his own. Somehow, he worked out his problem. He arrived at the Haebers', and was back in time for dinner. That was the beginning of my program for him.

A few days later I asked him if he would like to spend the day out at the beach—at Santa Monica and Oceanside. I gave him carfare. Again, I gave him no directions whatever, but told him to find his own way.

He was a little late returning. Somehow, he had lost his return carfare in the sand. I do not remember now how he managed getting back to Hollywood—but he worked his own way out of his predicament without telephoning me for help. He lacked even the price of a telephone call, anyway.

A little later he mentioned going to the zoo. I didn't know where the zoo was, but gave him permission to go—again on his own.

Dick was learning self-reliance. He was developing initiative. He was finding his own way around. I planned to have Mrs. Armstrong and Ted come down before we ended our summer and returned to Oregon. One last thing remained in my plan before they came. I took Dick two or three times boating on the lagoons in MacArthur and Echo parks, taught him how to use the motorboats rented out there.

Now I was ready for Dick's *final exam* in his course in self-reliance, and overcoming a feeling of inferiority to Ted.

Filling the Biltmore

Dr. Clem Davies, whose time I had taken over on KMTR, had been holding regular Sunday services at the Biltmore Theater, largest in downtown Los Angeles. About the time he relinquished the 5:30 evening time for the better 7:30 time, a dramatic or comedy show starring George Jessel was opening at the Biltmore.

This had forced Mr. Davies out of the Biltmore, and he had moved his Sunday services to an auditorium at the Ambassador Hotel.

Along in early July, probably close to the 10th, I heard that the Jessel show was ending its engagement and moving on to San Francisco. Immediately I went to the office of the manager of the theater.

The last Jessel performance was to be Saturday night. Would the theater be available on next Sunday?

"Why, yes, the theater will be available," he said, "but you couldn't afford to rent it."

"How do you know I couldn't?" I demanded. "How much will it cost?"

"Now look, Mr. Armstrong," he persisted. "Dr. Davies had been holding services here a long time. It took him years to build up a good-sized audience. He

56

took up *three collections* at every service—and he just
barely took in enough to pay the rent. You've only been
on the air down here about three months. You haven't
had time to build up a fraction of Dr. Davies' following
yet. Even if you took up *five collections* in your service,
you'd never get enough to pay for it—and besides, I'd
have to have the entire rent in advance. You haven't
been on the air down here long enough yet to fill a big
auditorium like the Biltmore."

"Well, that's what I'd like to find out," I replied.
"And I will not take up *any* collections at all! But how
can I tell whether I can afford it, unless you tell me the
amount of the rental?"

I think it was $175. And it was already Wednesday,
late afternoon.

I told him I would be back with the decision in a
few moments. The Biltmore Theater occupies one corner of the large block occupied otherwise by the large
Biltmore Hotel. I went to the hotel lobby and called
Mrs. Armstrong at our office in Eugene by long distance
telephone. Once again, we had just enough money in the
bank to pay this rental in advance, and the price of
postal cards for the Los Angeles mailing list.

I dictated over the telephone an announcement to
our secretary, instructing them at the Eugene office to
have the announcement mimeographed on the cards, all
addressed to those on the Southern California mailing
list, and get them in one big package into the air-express office addressed to me, yet that same evening. It
was then only about fifteen minutes before closing time
at the post office.

I dashed back into the theater lobby and up to the
manager's office and wrote him out a check for the
following Sunday's rental.

In those days, because of the war and fear of

Japanese bombing, we were having blackouts every night. I had been advised that people in Los Angeles would not come out to a religious service at night. Theatergoers would attend the theater for night performances—but for some reason people were afraid to attend a religious service at night. It merely demonstrated where people's hearts and interests were.

So the meeting had to be held on Sunday afternoon—I believe the time was 3 p.m.

Next day, Thursday, the large package of printed and addressed postcards arrived. I took them to the Hollywood post office. There was a vigorous protest about letting me mail them there. I had not bought the cards there. That post office lost the credit for the sale of the post cards, and objected to having the expense of handling charged to them. But I explained our emergency, and there was no other way I could have done it. They finally took them.

Then on my program, Wednesday, Thursday, Friday, and Saturday evenings, I announced the Sunday afternoon meeting at the Biltmore—and finally, again, on Sunday morning. People received the postcard announcements Friday and Saturday.

After the Sunday morning broadcast, Dick, Dorothy and I went back to our apartment very tense. Would enough people come to look like a fair-sized audience, or would the small crowd simply look LOST in that big theatre seating about 1,900 people?

"Oh BOY!" Dick had exclaimed excitedly, as soon as he had heard I had rented the Biltmore Theater. "I'm going to sit in a BOX! I've always wanted to sit in a box in a theatre. Now my Dad has rented *the whole theater.* Oh BOY! I'm going to sit in a box at last!"

We took a streetcar to the theatre, arriving about 2:15. A few blocks away I noticed the streets were

58

unusually crowded with people—especially for Sunday afternoon in downtown Los Angeles. I wondered what was going on!

We soon found out. It seemed all those people were going in one direction—toward the Biltmore Theater!

I thought it best that I not get involved in a handshaking experience until after the service, because I still had to prepare the sermon. So I went in through the rear stage door, while Dick and Dorothy entered by the lobby entrance.

I learned later what happened. All of Dr. Davies' former ushers were on hand, and it seemed they had gotten divided somehow into two divisions. There was no one in charge, and there was a dispute over which group of ushers was taking over. Confusion reigned.

Dick's experience in self-reliance and initiative now paid off. Immediately he—not yet fourteen—took charge. He called all the ushers to one side.

"I'm Dick Armstrong," he told them, "and I'm taking charge here."

Then he snapped out orders. He said he would use *all* the ushers, since the crowds were literally streaming in—and each would do whatever he assigned. He then, without any previous experience, organized the two groups, assigned stations to each man, directed everything, and from that moment there was order.

It had never occurred to me we would have a crowd large enough to need ushers—and I would certainly not have known where to turn to obtain ushers, anyway. But God worked that out, supplied the needed ushers, and used Dick to restore quick order and system.

No Collections

Although I had never taken up any collections in any public evangelistic service—and have not to this day, and never shall—I did have two things done hurriedly on Thursday and Friday of that week. I had a sign painter turn out large lobby signs for the theater, and I had two wooden boxes made, about the size of a shoe box, with a slot in the top of each. These were placed at each end of the inner lobby of the theater by Dick— to one side, and *not* in the direct path of the exits from the inner aisles.

Actually, Dick did get to sit in his box—but by the time service was to begin, all the boxes were crowded full. Nevertheless, he went into a box, told them who he was, and the people managed to squeeze a little closer and make room for one more.

The first floor and the balcony were packed solid, and the second balcony half or more than half filled. The attendance was 1,750!

I had decided to conduct the service just like a broadcast—precisely on time! At precisely 5 seconds before 3 p.m., I walked briskly to the pulpit in the center of the stage, arriving at the pulpit at 3 o'clock to the second. Before I could say a word, I was surprised by an uproarious burst of applause. I had never seen or heard anything like that at a religious meeting. But I learned later that this was common practice in Los Angeles, and ministers are commonly called "doctor" whether they possess any such degree or not. Up in the second balcony there was the blowing of a foghorn. A well-known Los Angeles character, who went along barefoot and with long, flowing white hair and, I believe, in a white robe, whom I heard called "Father Time," had come in. But there were no others of that type.

As soon as the applause died down, I started with the usual, "GREETINGS, FRIENDS!"—then another burst of laughing applause. I said, rapidly, that although I loved to sing hymns as much as any of them, that right now we were in a WAR, prophecy was being rapidly fulfilled, and I had things of too great importance to say to take up time with either singing, or taking up collections. I said that I knew some would be disappointed if they could *not* leave an offering, and for those who *wanted* to, there were the two offering boxes in the rear lobby—but that they would not see them unless they went out of the usual path to find them—that we never took up collections, never asked for contributions either in such services, nor over the air.

Then I got immediately into my message, and closed the service right on the exact second—I think it had been announced to close at 4:15—just as the broadcasts have to end precisely on the second.

Later, when we opened the two offering boxes, what do you suppose we found? Yes, I think you guessed it! Exactly, to the penny, the precise amount of the expense of hiring the theater, extra cost of janitor and electrician, the lobby signs, and the postcard announcements. That is, *to the penny*. THERE WAS EXACTLY ONE CENT MORE THAN THIS EXACT AMOUNT!

Dick's "Final Exam"

We engaged the Biltmore for the following two Sundays. We decided, for those two Sundays, to hold TWO services each Sunday afternoon. I'm not sure, now, of the exact time, but I think the first service started at 1:30, ending at 2:45, and the second service started at 3:30, ending at 4:45.

It was planned to have Mrs. Armstrong and young Garner Ted, then twelve and a half years of age, come down in time for the final Biltmore service, and our whole family would drive back together.

At each of these two services at the Biltmore, total

attendance was estimated at 2,000. There were 1,300 or 1,400 at each service, with several who attended the first service coming back for the second. For this reason I preached different sermons at each service.

But I had another motive in getting Ted down to Hollywood before returning to Eugene. I needed his presence for Dick's "final exam" in snapping him out of feeling inferior to Ted.

Our office secretary and her husband drove them down in our car, which I had left at home when we left in April. They were there three or four days, and it seems we started back to Oregon on July 31, after the final Biltmore service.

When they arrived, I explained to Dick that he would have to take Ted in tow.

"Now remember, Dick," I briefed him, "Ted is not as old as you, and he's never been to Hollywood before. He'll be pretty green. I want you to look after him— take him places—show him Hollywood and Los Angeles. Take him boating on the lake in Echo Park, but don't let him handle the boat—he wouldn't know how." During those few days, Dick was the complete leader. For the first time in his life he was made to realize that he was not inferior, but LEADER over Ted.

Dick passed this "final exam" with flying colors and a grade of "A." The feeling of being inferior to Ted was gone. And, it did no harm to Ted, for he did not realize, then, what was being done. However, it was some time after this that Ted went into his intensive "muscle-building" program.

But Dick was still human. And it is human to go from one extreme to the other. Once back in Eugene, far from feeling whipped and inferior, Dick now was suddenly a "big shot."

It was a glamorous thing to have been in Hollywood. Dick had spent most of the summer there. The other boys had not been there.

So now I had to go to work on him again, and get him back in the "middle of the road." And with God's help this was achieved, and later he came to have the supreme confidence that is FAITH IN GOD rather than confidence in *self,* and to have full assurance, yet in humility. That is a difficult state for any human to attain—but one of the supreme right goals of life!

44

Work Leaps Ahead— World Tomorrow *Heard Nationwide*

THE YEAR 1942 was by far our biggest year of progress up to that date.

The response to *daily* broadcasting on station KMTR (now KLAC) was an eye-opener to me. The effectiveness appeared to be *more* than seven times that of the once-a-week program. Response was immediate. And even though no request for contributions ever was made, voluntary contributions were sufficient, from the very first week, to pay the multiplied expense.

But after the three Sunday afternoon evangelistic meetings held at the large Biltmore Theater in downtown Los Angeles, the last three Sundays of July, it was necessary to return to Eugene, Oregon.

At that juncture I had to drop off the daily weeknight broadcasting. Recording facilities in Eugene were not adequate to carry on a seven-programs-per-week schedule from our home office in Eugene. Yet I had learned by this experience the tremendous POWER and impact of daily broadcasting.

Planning Expansion

Back in Eugene, after almost four months in Hollywood, our co-worker list had grown to at least double. In other words, twice as many or more were now co-workers with me, supporting God's work regularly with their tithes and offerings.

Although I was unable, because of lack of facilities, to continue the *daily* broadcasting at that time, it was most gratifying to be able to now make a big expansion in other directions.

As related earlier, that superpower station WHO, Des Moines, had offered me time. On our trip to Des Moines and Chicago, the summer of 1941, this tremendous opportunity had opened.

Of course, in 1941, this giant WHO was still completely beyond our reach. But by early August, 1942, with our income doubled, and with the very low rate offered by the manager of WHO, I felt ready to take this leap.

Before going to Des Moines, I decided to reinforce our radio coverage of the Pacific Northwest. Station KGA, Spokane, had offered us time at the early Sunday morning time of 8 a.m. In Seattle station KRSC had moved us to the earlier time of 8 a.m. from the better time of 8:30. Once again I employed the old Postal Telegraph lines for a network broadcast between Seattle and Spokane. We called it the Liberty Network.

I overlooked mentioning that, before leaving Hollywood, I had arranged to release the program Sunday mornings over station KFMB, San Diego. At that time the old KMTR signal was so strong in San Diego, more than 100 miles distant, that KFMB was able to pick the program out of the air and rebroadcast it at the same hour, 9:30 a.m.

And so now, with coverage on the Pacific Coast over stations in San Diego, Hollywood, Eugene, Portland, Seattle and Spokane, I took the train to Des Moines, Iowa.

And now NATIONAL!

On Sunday night, 11 p.m., August 30, 1942, for the first time in my life I was speaking, from the studios of WHO, *to a nationwide audience!* I have before me, now, the script of that program.

The announcer's voice—recorded, and I think it was the voice of famous network announcer Art Gilmore, as it is today—heard in all parts of the nation, was saying:

"The WORLD TOMORROW! At this same time every Sunday, Herbert W. Armstrong analyzes today's world news, with the *prophecies* of The WORLD TOMORROW!"

And then, for the first time heard nationally:

"GREETINGS, Friends! We enter the *fourth year* of this war next Tuesday. We entered the *ninth week* of the supreme CRISIS of the war *today!* In all probability the ultimate outcome is being determined right *now* on the Russian front!"

And then followed an outline of Hitler's "Thousand-Year Plan" for world rule by German Nazis. On this very *first* program heard *nationally* the coming UNITED STATES OF EUROPE was proclaimed. By that time it was already becoming apparent to me that Hitler would be defeated, and that this resurrected ROMAN EMPIRE would precipitate a *third* and final World War, at a later time after another recess between wars.

Then, in that first nationwide program, GOD'S

Thousand-Year Plan was explained from the Bible—the coming millennium! Hitler's plan was indeed a satanic and clever counterfeit, aimed at producing diametrically opposite results. Where Christ's millennial rule shall bring freedom and happiness, Hitler's would have produced slavery. Where Christ's reign shall give eternal life to multitudes, Hitler's would have brought torturous DEATH to enslaved millions.

Twelve-Page Plain Truth

Before going to Des Moines to begin the broadcasting over WHO, I had written and turned over to the printers in Eugene the articles for the August-September issue of *The Plain Truth*. We were not up to twelve pages, although it still was coming out bimonthly.

The leading article in that number revealed the amazing Japanese plan for conquering the United States. It was based on a Japanese *Mein Kampf,* called the Tanaka Memorial. This plan had been in process of development for *three hundred years*—growing out of an ancient document dated May 18, 1592. The great national hero of Japan, Hideyoshi, had set forth in this document the great national plan for world empire and setting the Mikado on the throne to rule the world.

This had been a Japanese national dream for three centuries. Then on July 25, Baron Tanaka, then Premier, presented The Tanaka Memorial as a definite blueprint for world conquest to the Mikado. This led directly to the bombing of Pearl Harbor December 7, 1941. It was based on the *religious* conviction that the Mikado is the direct descendant of the Mother of Heaven. Being, therefore, the SON of Heaven, the Emperor had to be established on the throne of the world to show that he is GOD. Thus even the Japanese attack had *vital* significance as another counterfeit of CHRIST'S

67

GOSPEL of the kingdom of God—and of Jesus Christ as the true SON of GOD, who is to RULE THE WORLD!

An article captioned "The WAR, at the Moment" said this:

"We entered the supreme CRISIS of this war the first of July. It came with the launching of Hitler's supreme gamble for the Russian Caucasus. . . . The situation is this: We do not *have* to WIN the war this year, but Hitler *does!* United States power is mounting fast. It is only a matter of perhaps ten to twelve more weeks until this nation shall be able to hurl such crushing power against the Axis that, with this power steadily increasing, the ultimate outcome will be assured, with victory for the Democracies. . . . It might, even then, take us until 1945 to end it, but the outcome would be predetermined. . . . From now on Axis power cannot increase, while Allied power will. . . .

"And so it is A RACE AGAINST TIME. . . . The Germans, to win, must win *before* we get set with the power we shall have by approximately November 1st. They must knock Russia out of the war. They must take Suez and drive the British out of the Mediterranean and the Near East. They must be ready to turn *west,* against the British Isles, without fear of attack from behind, free to hurl their WHOLE POWER against Britain in one supreme final victory, *before* we can launch the much-talked-of offensive against Hitler's Europe. . . . Hitler staked everything on his death-gamble that he could knock out Russia *before* the Allies can open the second European front."

There, in summary, was the analysis of the war as of August, 1942, as reported in *The Plain Truth.* Looking back in retrospect, the analysis was accurate. Hitler did take too big a gamble. United States' might *did* turn the tide before the end of the year. And it *did* take until the spring of 1945, just as predicted, to END it!

Now POWERFUL Pressures

The work of God was now really beginning to "go places"! The message for which Jesus Christ was crucified—the message the world has rejected ever since—was for the first time being heard in every state in the Union!

But if God now was granting us to grow in power, He also allowed the persecution, opposition, and pressures aimed at STOPPING God's work to increase in power. Never before had we felt any truly MAJOR-power opposition. But now we did.

Along about the end of January, 1943, I received notice of cancellation from radio station WHO. I was in Hollywood at the time, broadcasting daily again for a few weeks on KMTR.

Consternation seized me. To be thrown off WHO at this stage might prove fatal to the whole work. Even though the charge they made for time was exceedingly low for such a station—because of my uncle's local influence, I had been given a *local* rate—and a *religious* rate at that, which was, as I remember, just half of the local commercial rate—yet it seemed very large to us at the time. After five months we had spent quite a sum of money, *for us at that time,* as an investment in WHO broadcasting. We had not been on long enough, as yet, with only three programs a month, to have established the financial support from new co-workers hearing the program on WHO. Remember, we made no request, even indirectly, for financial support over the air. Nor was there any in the free literature we sent to listeners.

The WHO broadcast, our most costly so far, was being supported by Pacific Coast co-workers. It was not paying its own way—yet.

Immediately I obtained train reservations for Des

69

Moines. Then I wrote out a letter addressed to WHO listeners who had written me in response to the program. In the letter I told our listeners what had happened, and asked them, if they wanted the *World Tomorrow* program to continue on the station, to write the station and tell them how they felt. Then I dictated the letter to my secretary in Eugene by long-distance telephone, and asked her to mimeograph it and mail immediately to the entire WHO mailing list.

Tremendous Response

That list had mounted and multiplied into many thousands. By this time we had received letters from *all forty-eight states.*

I remember one WHO broadcast in particular. I had recorded it at the Studio & Artists recording studios at Columbia Square, Hollywood, on a Thursday night. I had been overworked, losing sleep, and was tired. I was not up to usual broadcasting form that night. I knew it, and felt very badly about it. I tried, but for a half hour of speaking into the microphone it just seemed the usual spontaneous enthusiasm wasn't there.

"Mr. Armstrong," said the owner of the recording studio after I finished, "you ought to remember that WHO is a *very* important station. You ought to take it more seriously. This broadcast we just recorded was not good enough. You usually do better."

Now I felt worse. I knew only too well how poor it was. But I had tried. I had done the best I could. I just was too tired to be at my best. But there was no time to do it over. I had to rush it to the airport.

But what I had lacked in that program, God more than made up. That Sunday night God caused the weather to be extraordinarily cold—all over the continent. In Iowa it was one of those twenty-below-

70

zero nights, without wind—cold and still! That is the kind of weather in which radio waves radiate with extraordinary sharpness. That very "poor" broadcast, as we thought when recording it, heard at 11 p.m. in the Central time zones, at midnight in the East, brought a total of TWENTY-TWO HUNDRED letters— 2,200!

I think that was some kind of a national record for response to a half-hour speech starting at 11 p.m. on *one station only!* That one program brought mail from every state in the Union!

After that phenomenal record-breaking response, my sorrow over having thought I did poor work was turned to real JOY!

Well, that was a record! It will give the reader some idea of the way the mailing list had grown from WHO broadcasts.

Many thousands of letters went out from Eugene to these listeners the same day I dictated the letter by telephone.

Door Stays Open

A few days later I arrived in Des Moines. The cancellation had come, not from Mr. Mailand, but from the sales manager. So I went first to his office.

He stared at me.

"Are you the man who has been flooding this station with all these thousands of letters of protest against cancelling your program?" he demanded— somewhat angrily, I thought.

"Why, I suppose so," I replied, rather startled. "Is that wrong?"

"WRONG? Why, man, don't you know that showering such a downpour of *'inspired'* mail on any radio station is the very *last* way to influence the station?

71

That kind of mail has no influence on us at all—but it is a mighty big NUISANCE!"

"Well, I didn't realize that," I replied. "I thought you'd want to know how our program was being received by listeners. I surely didn't mean any offense."

"Well, let me tell you, Mr. Armstrong, *I* certainly learned that lesson! A while back we were appearing before the Federal Communications Commission in Washington. Before I went down there, we put out an appeal on the air for our listeners to write to the FCC. They did! And the officials of the FCC didn't like it."

"Well," I asked, "if I had to learn by experience, the same as you, and if you made the same mistake I did, then do you think you ought to blame me?"

He had to laugh at that.

Nevertheless I found I was *really* on the spot—and in trouble. I had not met this sales manager before. Because my uncle had known the general manager and arranged an appointment for me, I had transacted business with him. I saw immediately that this sales manager was a very able and competent man for that job—undoubtedly very valuable to the station. But he did not like our program. He didn't say why. And I rather guessed that he felt I had taken matters over his head in going to the general manager of the station. Further, he explained that very powerful pressure had been brought on him from New York against selling time commercially for religious programming.

We went into Mr. Mailand's office. I learned that Mr. Mailand *did* like the program, and sat up Sunday nights until 11:30 so he could hear it. He was on my side, but his sales manager, a very aggressive man, was insistent the program go off.

I then explained to the two men our own position—how we were a very small church in Eugene, Oregon, and how hundreds of people, mostly very poor people on the West Coast, had made great sacrifice to finance our broadcasting on this powerful station heard nationally.

"Mr. Mailand," I said, "I signed a year's contract with you. All these co-workers have backed me in good faith. I signed the contract in good faith. I believed that *you* signed it *also* in good faith, and that when you opened the door of this great station to us, and signed a contract to keep it open for a year, that WE COULD RELY ON YOUR WORD BEING GOOD. All these co-workers have backed me for five and one-half months feeling that, in due time, a sufficient number of interested listeners would voluntarily join them as co-workers backing this work financially to make the broadcasting to all the rest of the nation self-supporting. You know we never request contributions over the air, or in any literature. If you cancel now, YOU WILL CAUSE VERY GREAT INJURY TO US! You have given us a YEAR'S contract in which we trusted, and have taken this hard-earned money contributed by all these poor people— and now threaten cancellation BEFORE we have had a chance to be on long enough to relieve those people of this burden. If you had told us you'd keep the door open only five and one-half months, we surely never would have signed the contract or started—or have spent any money with you. Would you want to INJURE a Church by breaking your contract?"

"Well, Mr. Armstrong, of course we wouldn't. The way you put it, you make it mighty hard for me. Would you mind if Mr. B. (the sales manager) and I talk this over privately a few moments, to see what we can do?"

I was shown to a reception room outside. I was alone there, and quickly knelt before a chair and appealed to the God of Heaven. He had opened this giant

73

DOOR. He had said no man can shut doors he opens. I asked Him to intervene and save His work.

When I was called back to Mr. Mailand's office, I was able to talk to him alone. He explained that he had opened that time and signed the contract in perfect good faith—that he liked our program and was himself one of our interested listeners—that he certainly didn't want to do us any injury—but on the other hand, he didn't want to lose a very able and valuable sales manager.

"Mr. Armstrong," he said, "if we compromise by letting you fill out your contract and complete the year, will that give you time enough to become thoroughly established, and possibly to get on other stations that will maintain your coverage?"

Well, of course, I could not be sure, but it certainly would be a lot better than stopping the broadcast right then.

"Well, if I leave *The World Tomorrow* on the station until the year's contract is finished, will you agree to go off then?"

There was nothing else I *could* do—I certainly had no contract beyond that time. Reluctantly I had to agree to this—and actually it was a tremendous victory, after all.

We Go on WOAI

I have mentioned that there were, at that time, only eight stations in all America that enjoyed absolutely *exclusive* channels. One other, which by its location I felt might have a better chance of being heard nationally than most, was 50,000-watt WOAI of San Antonio, Texas.

From my hotel I immediately called Mr. Hugh Halff, manager of WOAI. Did he have 11 p.m. Sunday

74

nights open—could he clear it if he found the program acceptable? He could, but would have to know more about the program and audition it.

I caught the next train for San Antonio. I think Mr. Halff might have called Mr. Mailand, when I told him we were on WHO. Anyway, he had no objection to the program after listening to a transcribed broadcast, and the doors of WOAI swung open to us. The expense of adding this station six and one-half months before going off WHO gave us a tight squeeze, but it seemed imperative that we get our listeners established to listening to WOAI *before* we went off WHO and lost them altogether.

And so, although through the years, the individual doors of *some* radio stations have closed to us, the general giant DOOR of TV, radio and the printing press has never closed—just as Christ has said that NO MAN CAN SHUT IT!

And every apparent setback has proved like the cocking of a gun—it actually results in shooting us *ahead* faster than ever!

There probably are no finer, higher-prestige radio stations in the United States than WHO and WOAI, and today the *World Tomorrow* telecast is also heard on *many* of the most powerful stations in the world.

45

More Opposition—More Growth!

I HAD GONE on WOAI sooner than we were financially ready. But when it became definite we could not continue on WHO after August 23 of that year, I felt it imperative that we become established on another station of such wide coverage so that our listeners would know where to find the program.

I thought we would, at last, be free from this kind of persecution and opposition. But we were not—have never been since—never will be, in *this* world, as long as we remain faithful in proclaiming Christ's own true gospel in its purity and in power! "All who will live godly in Christ Jesus shall suffer persecution," says the sure Word of God.

And from what source does persecution usually come? Jesus Christ was our example. He was persecuted. And from what source? Mostly from the source of *organized religion!* His true message from God was

76

different from the doctrines and ways of the organized religion controlled by Pharisees, Sadducees, and their ilk. They had strayed from, and perverted, the doctrines and ways God had given them. But their false teachings and customs were well established in the religious tradition of the time. They accused Jesus of being a false prophet, a deceiver, a heretic and of being subversive to Caesar's government.

It is hard to realize, but it is true—there are the modern Pharisees today, and they are organized. They, too, incredible though it may seem to some, maintain a well-established religious tradition which has, long before the living generation, departed far from the true gospel and the teachings and practices of Jesus Christ, the original apostles, and the original true Church of God! Human nature has not changed. The same hostility seizes them, toward Christ's truth, that inspired religious leaders to accuse, persecute, and to crucify Jesus Christ!

But, did you ever notice that God's ministers who faithfully proclaim His truth in the power of His Holy Spirit do not resort to personalities, do not impute motives or attempt to discredit specific persons, do not belittle or ridicule? Nor do we, either on the air, or in print, knowingly or intentionally say anything derogatory about any person, organization or group. True, Jesus Himself did tell the Pharisees in presence of others that they were hypocrites, liars, false leaders— He told his listeners what they were, and warned against following their false ways. But He was always straightforward and sincere, never using the psychological trickery of implication, designed to falsely discredit or belittle.

Anyway, the insidious forces of persecution followed us to WOAI. But the station liked the program—

the leading businessmen of San Antonio liked it, and made me an honorary life member of the Businessmen's Bible Class (not denominational, though men of many denominations belonged)—and the program remained on WOAI until after we obtained the earlier and prime time of 8 p.m. on the 100,000-watt clear-channel XELO. We had started on XELO in 1944, and continued on WOAI until some time during 1945.

Meanwhile, God had been moving to increase the radio power in the Pacific Northwest.

Portland Power Increase

During 1941, 1942 and 1943 I had been holding evangelistic services in the Chamber of Commerce auditorium in downtown Seattle, and also a few services in Everett, Washington. A small church had been formed there. Several local members in Seattle and Everett made it possible to release *The World Tomorrow* over the more powerful KVI, with studios then in Tacoma. This was a 5,000-watt station, but with its dial spot at 570, and its transmitter on an island in Puget Sound, KVI had a signal about equal to 25,000 watts at a higher frequency and average transmitter location. We did not drop KRSC, but used both stations by means of our Liberty Network wire at 8:30, Sunday mornings.

It must have been early winter, 1942-43, that I had taken a trip to Des Moines to put the program on WHO "live." It was necessary to do this frequently, on so important a station. Returning I stopped off briefly in Denver. We were not ready to expand on additional stations as yet, but I was then beginning to lay the groundwork for future expansion by making contacts with managements of stations we might desire to add later.

I called at the offices of the ABC network station,

KVOD, 5,000-watts. I believe the executive I contacted was the vice president. In any event, he was having a busy day with conferences, and was very abrupt in telling me bluntly they would clear no time for religious programming.

I never had been in the habit of taking a flat turndown, without a hearing, as the saying is, "sitting down." I came back at him with all the force and salesmanship I had ever had in my former advertising days.

I explained how different *The World Tomorrow* is from any other "religious" program, and demanded that he audition a program. Reluctantly, he consented, but offered no hope.

I had to return to my hotel room to obtain transcription discs, telling him I would return in ten minutes. I walked rapidly—almost ran—to the hotel. On the way I realized, belatedly, why I had met with such a negative reception. I had failed to take this call on KVOD up with the One I was working for. It had long before become custom to pray before any call or conference of any import, asking God's direction, wisdom, and to give me favor in the eyes of the man with whom I had to deal.

Christ's Commission is "Go ye into all the world" with His message. To go *to* the world with the gospel necessitates dealing *with* the world, and with some of its business organizations. Therefore God's servant ought to seek not only divine guidance in such dealing—but also, since God is able to make even our enemies at peace with us, to ask for favor with such people as we must deal. In all my years of experience, God has never failed to grant this request!

But this time, in my eagerness, I had gotten ahead of God. I had gone "on my own," without asking for either guidance, or favor.

And right here perhaps I may give the reader an example of what God's Word means by the admonition: "Pray without ceasing," or, as Jesus said, to "pray *always.*" He means we must be continually *in a spirit of prayer.* And he means to pray, constantly, over even little things that arise.

As I half walked—half ran—I prayed. There was no opportunity to kneel—nor was there, now, time. I prayed as a walked. I asked God to forgive me for negligence in not asking Him before I called. Then I asked Him, now, to change *this* man's attitude to one of favor toward me and toward the program. And I believed, and expected to receive it!

Returning to the KVOD offices, I found this official smiling. He introduced me to a couple other men. We went into an audition room. The discs were given to a technician who took them into an adjoining control room. Ordinarily, with a religious program, radio station men would listen to perhaps five or six minutes, then signal to cut it off. In those days of "electrical transcription" our half-hour program was put on two large discs, with fifteen minutes on each disc. In airing, the second disc was started so smoothly the listening audience never knew there was a change of records. I hardly dared hope that, after reaching the end of the first fifteen-minute disc, they would ask to hear the other. But the program was gripping their interest. The operator did not expect to play the second disc, but they signalled him to put it on. No one said a word. They just *listened,* intently.

When the half-hour program was ended, the only word spoken was "We can clear the time 8 to 8:30 Sunday mornings for you."

By now I was not timid—I was *confident!*

"No, 8 a.m. is too early on Sunday mornings," I said, "We have found 8:30 is O.K., but 8 o'clock is too early."

"But we air our star news program at 8:30," was the reply. "We couldn't move that."

By now I was superconfident.

"No," I came back, "I won't accept 8 a.m. on Sundays. It has to be 8:30 or nothing."

He weakened and agreed. Then it was that I learned that one of the men in the room was not a local Denver man, but a station representative who had just bought an interest in station KXL in Portland.

Now it happened that, after we had gone off KXL—and the reader will remember it had been a small 100-watt station on which we first started in Portland, going later on 500-watt KWJJ—that KXL, under new ownership, had gone to the increased power of 10,000-watts, at the splendid low dial spot of 750 kilocycles. I had tried to get on that station, but had been unable. Desperately I wanted on KXL.

This man was on his way out to Portland. At once I told him of our desire to go on KXL. But now I was in the driver's seat, and knew it—for these men had been really impressed—so I demanded 8:30 a.m. or nothing. He agreed. I was to contact him in Portland about three days later. We could not afford to go up to the more expensive KXL in Portland, and go on KVOD too—so I had to postpone KVOD.

The sequel is that actually we did go on KVOD, many years later.

46

A Talk to San Antonio Businessmen

ABOUT February 1, 1943, the *World Tomorrow* program started on the powerful WOAI in San Antonio. Later that year, after we had been on the station a few months, I went again to San Antonio to put the program on the station "live." It must have been the next night, Monday, that I held my first meeting in Texas.

This was announced on the air over WOAI on Sunday night. I had engaged a banquet- or lecture-hall on the ground floor of the St. Anthony Hotel. Every seat was filled. Several businessmen and their wives came.

On another occasion Mrs. Armstrong and I traveled to San Antonio, and on the Sunday night broadcast I announced we would be holding "Open House" through the following afternoon and evening in our hotel suite. It was encouraging and inspiring to receive a continuous stream of new Texas friends—some com-

ing just to meet us—others with problems for coun-
selling.

I was invited to speak before the Businessmen's
Bible Class of San Antonio. It was nondenominational,
and met in a club room of a leading hotel for coffee and
a short service before the Sunday School hour. Those
who were members of various denominations proceeded
on to their own Sunday Schools or church services after
this earlier Bible class.

As I wrote the above paragraph, I supposed this
talk to the Businessmen's Bible Class was a little later
that same year—1943. But I remembered that I have
with me the abbreviated notes from which I spoke to
that class of businessmen. I am a little surprised to find
it dated Sunday morning, November 9, 1944, toward the
close of the war. So I am now getting ahead of myself
by more than a year.

However, I felt our readers might like to read, now,
a very brief summary of what I said to these businessmen on that occasion. Remember, this was only about
a half year before the end of the war.

Talk to Businessmen

First I read from the 127th Psalm, verse 1: "Except the
Lord build the house, they labour in vain that build it."
"That," I said to that class, "is a basic truth that
applies to human activities generally—building a house
for a home, building a city, a nation, or a business. We
are prone to take things for granted—even this WAR, as
well as the economic system in which we find ourselves.
We've been in the war about three years now—we've
gotten used to it. You've been in this system of business
quite a while—and naturally take it for granted.

"But there is *tremendous significance* to world
events right now! They are fraught with meaning far

deeper than realized. Let's look at it from the standpoint of BUSINESS. Basic and far-reaching changes are occurring in the industrial, distribution, and commercial structure as a direct result of the war—and changes have been shaping during the past forty years unrealized by most businessmen.

"Back in the years 1912-1915 I was making surveys of business conditions for a national magazine, which brought these changes into bold relief. This country was founded on the basis of *de*centralization. Today there is a rapid shift toward centralization in all fields—not only business, but government. But even in those years the little man in business was being squeezed out.

"The big headache then, in retail circles, was the encroachments of the giant mail-order houses; and chain stores were beginning rapid development. World War I put impetus to the centralization trend. As an aftermath of that war the flash depression of 1920 shook America, economic collapse rumbled through forty other nations, finally producing our Great Depression of 1929-1936. All this time the MACHINE AGE was developing rapidly in America, making possible three to thirty times the output per man-hour as compared to hand labor. There was sufficient raw material in the ground to have provided luxury for all the people.

"Yet no economic utopia came. Instead, we've had troubles, wars, depressions. WHY? Unequal division of the proceeds of production is the reason. The profit system has been *selfishly exercised!*

Capital and Labor

"First, capital and management, being greedy, retained *most* of the increased wealth of mass machine production. Labor was not given its rightful share. Read the prophecy of this, in James 5:1-5: 'Come now, you rich men, weep and shriek over your impending miseries! You have been storing up treasure in the very last days. . . . See, the wages of which you have defrauded the workmen who mowed your fields [or worked in your factories] call out. . . .' Verses 2 and 3 show the final fate yet to come on businessmen guilty of this unfair practice.

"But, second, organizers appeared and began to organize labor, with the equally wrong philosophy that capital and management is the enemy of labor, and that by organization LABOR ought to exact more than its fair share.

"Meanwhile, World War I spawned the Soviet power dedicated to overthrowing every other nation, government, and economic system and ruling the world with atheistic Communism. Now we are fighting to stop the Nazi onslaught to conquer and rule the world with *National* Socialism. It all adds up to WORLD REVOLUTION—CHAOS—DESTRUCTION! They are producing the robot bomb and the rocket bomb—and working on constantly more powerful *destructive* forces. *Mankind cannot stop!* Mankind has now gone *past* the point of NO RETURN! Man will plunge on fanatically toward DESTRUCTION, unless God Almighty intervenes—which He PROMISES TO DO!

"WHAT'S WRONG?

"*God did not build this world's house!* Therefore they labor in VAIN that struggle to build it. They are reaping DESTRUCTION. This world is *not* of God's making. It is *basically* WRONG! It is built on principles diametrically opposite to those RIGHT principles and laws set in motion by the living GOD.

"The basis of God's law is *LOVE*. It is love *toward* God, and love *toward* neighbor. This is the principle of "GIVE" and "SERVE," not of "get" and "BE SERVED." This

85

world's business is based on the foundation of competition. The competitive system is the relentless effort to *take from* competitors—to get the best of a deal.

"Also, the SYSTEM underlying the world's whole civilization is based on concentration in CITIES. We are now beginning to see the *destruction of cities*. They are not built on God's pattern. God says He will destroy them—tear them down!" (Micah 5:14 and Isaiah 14:16-17 were quoted and expounded as prophecies, among many others, foretelling this.)

"God set apart 6,000 years to *allow mankind* to make their own choices—go their own ways—to write in human EXPERIENCE the lesson that only GOD'S WAYS can bring us the happiness, prosperity and joy we all want."

I then explained a little of God's economic laws, and gave a glimpse into the world tomorrow when Christ puts down this world's systems and establishes the WORLD RULE of the KINGDOM OF GOD.

The talk seemed to be well received, and I was presented with a card conferring honorary life membership of the Businessmen's Bible Class of San Antonio.

Also I notice, on the back of the paper on which my notes were written, the following, which I remember one of the men of the class wrote there for me: *"A city is an artificial development of an imperfect distribution system."*

The Work Grows

By late August 1943, our year's contract with station WHO was completed. We had then had six and one-half months of broadcasting on WOAI, in addition to WHO. By this time most of our regular WHO listeners knew that *The World Tomorrow* could be heard on WOAI, so that going off WHO gave us no noticeable setback or

86

loss of audience. However, at the time we went off WHO, or just before, I decided to put the program on one of the two leading local stations in Des Moines. Station KRNT had opened a forty-five-minute earlier time, at 10:15 p.m. Sunday nights. This was a 5,000-watt station.

Also, station KMA, a 5,000-watt station at Shenandoah, Iowa, had gained a reputation for having a very wide and responsive audience. This station cleared the same time—10:15 Sunday nights.

About this time, a smaller station, KNET, in Palestine, Texas, solicited the program. It was so unusual to have a radio station actually *come to us* with an offer of time, that I took it—at 9:30, Sunday mornings.

And so it was that the November-December issue of *The Plain Truth,* for 1943, listed a log of ten stations.

However, the three smaller stations, KRNT, KMA, and KNET, gave local coverage only, and we were not big enough yet to carry them long enough to make them voluntarily self-supporting. Remember, we never solicited contributions from the public—either over the air, or in any of our literature, which was always all FREE. After one or two years, these stations were dropped.

Coming into the year of 1944, Bulletins in old files show that mail response and other methods of checking indicated the radio audience had grown to between a half and three-quarters of a million in the war years. That was a big jump from our small and humble start ten years before.

The circulation of *The Plain Truth* had climbed to 35,000 copies, now reaching every state and province in English-speaking North America.

From the approximately $5 cost of printing the first issue of *The Plain Truth,* the printing cost in ten years had mounted to $1,000 per issue.

A short decade before, just starting in 1934, our cost of radio time was $2.50 per week. In early 1944 it had soared to one hundred times the original cost—an expenditure of $250 per week.

Fierce Wolves Enter

It was during these years—1943 and 1944—that we encountered another experience to teach us that the Apostle Paul was prophetically inspired of GOD when he warned the elders and ministers of the Church of God at Ephesus: "Take heed therefore unto yourselves, and to all the flock, over which the Holy [Spirit] hath made you overseers, to feed the church of God, which he hath purchased with his own blood. For I know this, that after my departing shall grievous wolves enter in among you, not sparing the flock. Also of your own selves shall men arise, speaking perverse things, to draw away disciples after them. Therefore, watch . . ." (Acts 20:28-31). The Moffatt translation renders it "fierce wolves."

During those years I made occasional visits to Hollywood to resume *daily broadcasting* for a period of two to six weeks each time, on station KMTR. Also, when there, I continued holding Sunday afternoon services frequently at the Biltmore Theater or other large halls in Los Angeles. A former minister frequently called at the studio. He continually assured me that he certainly did fully accept and agree with everything I was preaching. As time went on, we became well acquainted.

I shall not mention this man's name. He has been dead many years now, anyway. As a result of the broadcasting, *The Plain Truth,* and the personal meetings, a number of people were baptized in Los Angeles, and I formed them into a small local church. There were twenty-three at the start. I made this former preacher pastor of the tiny flock. This, I believe, was in the autumn of 1943.

Also our work paid his expenses up to Eugene, Oregon, and return, to assist me in an annual fall festival of meetings we were holding in our little church building in Eugene. This man had good personality, was friendly, flattered parents about their babies and children, and seemed well liked.

A year later I found the little "church" I had gathered together and turned over to his shepherding had disintegrated. I tried to follow up some of the people, but those I was able to contact had formed an extreme dislike for this "pastor" and refused to attend his services. Nevertheless, he came once again in the fall of 1944 to Eugene for our fall festival.

I have mentioned before that the Sunday night evangelistic services held beginning late 1941 in Seattle and Everett, and personal work Mrs. Armstrong and I did in that area, had raised up a small church group, which met in Everett. They purchased a fairly old small church building there. These Seattle and Everett people seemed to like the minister from Los Angeles, and during the 1944 festival, attended by this entire group as well as our local Oregon people, he succeeded in worming his way into their affections.

His wife, we learned just prior to this festival, had been supporting him. She told Mrs. Armstrong that he *would* condescend to water the lawn with the hose, *provided* he could SIT while holding the hose! Apparently she had given him an ultimatum to get a job preaching and support her, or she was going to refuse to support him longer. She had been professionally employed at rather good salary. So this man went on up to Everett, Washington, to become the pastor.

No sooner had he ingratiated himself in the affections of the "sheep" than he began "devouring" them. It began appearing he did not believe very much of the BIBLE truths I had been preaching, after all. One thing he had firmly believed—before going to Everett—was the biblical teaching on tithing. This Everett group were all tithers. They averaged considerably better incomes than the others who were co-workers with me, supporting God's work. In fact, about 25 percent of the entire income of the work was being supplied by them.

But, once established in Everett as their local pastor, this man did a reverse-twist in his doctrinal beliefs. Suddenly he did not believe in tithing any more. The proportionately big lump of income that kept God's work alive suddenly stopped. By now, of course, I only received news from there indirectly, perhaps not 100 percent accurately, but the indication was that the new "pastor" did another reverse-twist, and did once again revive the tithing system among these people—only this time it all went to him.

When this large portion of the financial support for the nationwide work was cut off, we suffered no pangs of consternation or fear. We did pray and commit the problem to the HEAD of our work, the *living* Jesus Christ. And, somehow, the income for God's work did not drop. It kept right on climbing—just as if we had never lost the Everett income.

This experience did cause Mrs. Armstrong and me real sorrow to see those we had come to love so dearly— among whom we had labored diligently for approximately three years—fall by the wayside—cutting themselves off from GOD'S PRECIOUS WORK and thus from His true Church, which is His instrument carrying on God's work.

47

Severe Financial Crisis

W E HAVE come, now, to the year
1944—one decade after the broad
casting and publishing work had
started, in 1934.

It had been a decade of hardship, persecution,
opposition and struggle. It was still a very small work—
compared to the world-girdling power of that same
work today. And even then—after ten years—at the
beginning of 1944, we faced the most severe financial
crisis up to that time.

Now NINE Stations

Yet, viewed comparatively, *remarkable* growth had
been made. One must remember the almost incredible,
infinitesimal beginning. Jesus Christ compared the
beginning and growth of the kingdom of God to a
mustard seed—which starts as the smallest of all, but
grows to become the largest of all herbs—just as, even-

tually, the kingdom of God will fill the whole earth. The kingdom of God will actually appear very soon—with the END of this present evil world, and the beginning of the happy world tomorrow. This very work of God is the end-time proclamation of it, going just before, preparing the way, leading up to it.

This work—GOD'S WORK—of necessity *had* to start infinitesimally small—smaller, in fact, than any sizable worldly work of a religious nature had for its beginning. But now, January, we were on NINE stations! Two of these were giant *exclusive*-channel *maximum*-powered 50,000-watt major stations heard in every state in the Union. In Portland, Oregon, we had now gone from 250 watts to a 10,000-watt station, and in Seattle we had added a 5,000-watt station which, like the Hollywood KMTR, on the identical dial spot of 570, actually put out the equivalent of about 40,000 watts!

The Plain Truth had developed from a hand-mimeographed little "magazine" of about 150 copies to a printed magazine of 35,000 copies circulated nation-wide—though limited to eight pages, and published every other month—*when funds allowed!*

We Sell Our Home

Actually, January, 1944, was a month when funds did *not* allow! The days of hardship and struggle were far from over. Instead, we now had come to the most serious financial crisis faced so far.

There was no January-February issue of *The Plain Truth* that year. It looked, at the moment, as if there never would be another.

A few months before, our supply of copies of the booklet *United States and Britain in Prophecy* had been exhausted. TEN THOUSAND requests had piled up, unfilled! TEN THOUSAND envelopes lay there in our

92

office, addressed, ready to enclose copies of the booklet and rush to the post office—but there were no booklets. There was not money for postage.

We were running behind in paying radio bills for station time. We were threatened with being forced off the air—having this whole work stop. Co-workers had failed to rise to meet this financial emergency. We had reached the point of desperation. If co-workers could not, or would not, make sufficient sacrifice to save the work, Mrs. Armstrong and I had to—even if it took our *all!* This work always has been a work of FAITH—relying on GOD. But God supplies needs *through human instruments* whose hearts are willing.

For eight years we had been making monthly payments on a small and very modest house, while we struggled along with financial burdens in general. It had been purchased as Church property, while still in the depression years when property values were at lowest levels. The purchase price had been $1,900, with $190 down.

One of the Church members had put up the $190 as a loan, to be paid back by Mrs. Armstrong and me. Although the property was deeded to four of the Trustees of the Church—my name among them—as officers of and trustees for the Church, the understanding was that I should repay the down payment, and meet the monthly payments of $17.10 per month. This was approximately the amount we had paid as rental *before* making it a purchase—and far less, by the year 1944, than paying rent. However, the Church board had agreed that, if I was able to keep up the payments, the property was to be deeded over to Mrs. Armstrong and me when paid out.

We had repainted and decorated the house not long before, and improved the property. Meanwhile, property values had risen. So the property was worth considerably more than we had paid, back in 1936.

In the dire predicament of the work, there seemed no other solution. We decided we had to give up our home, sell it, and put the money in the work. The three other trustees agreed to the sale, to save the work. We listed it with a real estate broker.

In February it was sold—at a real sacrifice according to current real estate values, though for quite a little more than the original purchase price.

The Work SAVED!

There was a March-April number of *The Plain Truth*. 25,000 copies of the booklet *United States and Britain in Prophecy* were printed. We stayed on the air! The work was, for the time, saved!

We were able to stay on in the house a few more months. But during the summer of 1944 we had to vacate. From that time, we had no home to live in until July, 1947, when we moved to Pasadena, California.

Our two daughters were married before we left our Eugene home—our younger daughter, Dorothy, very shortly before, on July 22, 1944; our elder daughter, Beverly, earlier, as recorded previously.

Living Without a Home

After we vacated our home in Eugene, we were not able to find a house to rent. The housing shortage was still acute in Eugene—had been since 1936.

At that time—1936—we had been renting for about a year the house we bought. We had been *forced* to buy it! The company that owned it gave us notice to vacate, at that time, saying the property was to be sold. They owned many houses and were putting them all on the market for sale. The salesman, in 1936, had grinned and said, "You'd better find a way to turn this into a *purchase*—or you'll have no place to live. You won't be able to find a place for rent, anywhere!"

We had first searched the city with the proverbial fine-tooth comb—and found the salesman did, literally, have us "over a barrel." But we found a way to make the purchase, as described above.

But now, eight years later, we had sold in order to save the work. We were out on the street, so to speak, and we found the rental situation was still the same.

So we put the small amount of furniture we possessed into storage, and moved into a motor court. Because of the housing shortage, motels and auto cabins were limiting guests to transients, and a three-day stay as a maximum.

Now began the troublesome, irksome, frustrating experience of having to move from one auto court to another every three days. In a very few instances we were able to stay for a week or two, but not many.

After we had, with our two boys, made the rounds of all the motels several times, the owners got to know us. Then they began to inform us that they had to keep their rooms open for transient guests, and since we were not transients, they began to refuse to take us again.

Fatherly Advice Backfires

It was while we were living in one of these motels that I noticed our two sons, then about ages fifteen and sixteen, each for the first time smoking a cigarette. How was I going to handle this situation? If I tried author-itatively to *command* them never to smoke again, I was afraid they would then smoke anyway, and the more—but in secret.

I thought I had a better way. At the time, it really seemed to me to be a foolproof way that couldn't fail.

95

I called the two boys into our one-room motel, and sitting on a bed, had a "man to man" talk with them.

"Boys," I said, "I could order you to stop smoking. I could try to stop you by force, but that would not build character in YOU. So I prefer to let you make your OWN decisions.

"But I want you to THINK about this problem, and *get all the facts,* before you make your decisions—for the result may affect your entire lives, and I don't want you to make a mistake. Now, if cigarette smoking is beneficial—really GOOD for you, and will help you to do good to others—then I'm sure God would want you to take up smoking, and so would I. But if it is BAD for you, harmful, then I feel you won't want to do it, and will stop right now, before you smoke a second one and develop a HABIT that's mighty hard to break."

You see, I myself still had a lesson to learn. These boys were still carnal—unconverted. In effect, I was actually saying the same thing to them, in principle, that God said to Adam and Eve. God allowed them to make their own decisions about taking the forbidden fruit.

"Now, boys," I continued, "here is what I want you to do. I want you first to check up—get the facts—get the TRUTH—and get it from the *voice of experience!* I want you to make a SURVEY, just as I have made many fact-finding surveys in business in the past. I want you to approach 100 experienced smokers—men of middle age or older who have smoked for many years, and *have the habit.* Tell each of these men you are a couple of young men who have thought of taking up smoking, but you want to know whether you *ought to,* or not. Ask each of these *experienced* smokers, who have had the habit for years, whether, as a result of his years of actual EXPERIENCE, he advises you to take up the habit, or leave it alone."

"Oh, Dad," chimed in young Garner Ted, age fifteen, "we don't need to make any such survey. I know right now, every one of them would tell us not to do it."

I felt secure. I felt sure, after that, that my boys would not start smoking.

Now GOD, in putting the proposition of the forbidden fruit up to Adam and Eve, *knew better!* He knew humans will choose the wrong—even when some *know* it is wrong!

Yes, God knew well, in advance, which choice Adam and Eve probably would make. He knew, too, that *YOU*—every one of you reading this autobiography—would probably do what you realized was wrong— ALL would *sin!* Nevertheless, God left every human mortal FREE to make his own choice. Not one of us ever *had* to sin! We just *did*—of our own volition—and we often KNEW we were doing wrong!

Well, other boys smoked. People, like sheep, follow others—seem to lack the courage to go against the crowd. Yes, my boys did start smoking—and I was terribly disappointed, wondering where my clever "psychology" had failed to work. Psychologists need to know a little more than most of them know about HUMAN NATURE!

Both boys, later on, came to themselves, and realized how cigarette smoking, among many other "minor vices," is, after all, NOT GOOD! Both had to undergo a terrific struggle with SELF *to break the habit* later on. But they both conquered the habit, instead of letting it conquer them.

Moving into a Rooming House

Finally, after many months moving from one motor court to another—still unable to rent a house—we did find two upstairs bedrooms in a rooming house for rent.

97

The one and only upstairs bathroom was shared with other roomers. These rooms were about six or seven blocks from our office.

We found it necessary to eat our meals out, at restaurants. This was neither good for our health nor our pocketbooks. With growing boys, reaching, now, from fifteen on up to eighteen, this was no right kind of family life! In fact it was not FAMILY LIFE *at all!* But for the time, we had to put up with it. One thing may be said in our favor. We did not complain, through all these years. We knew we were being given trials for our development.

But we had tremendous blessings spiritually. We rejoiced and were *happy.* We knew well that we deserved NOTHING! Yet we were privileged to be used in GOD'S WORK! That blessing outweighed all material acquisitions and enjoyments possessed by all the rich people of the earth combined! We thanked God for trials and tests—and for always carrying us through, and seeing every problem solved. Scores of times we thanked God that our trials and hardships had been physical and financial. My heart was no longer set on material acquisition. I had come to know its worthlessness. Instead, God had literally *lavished* upon us the TRUE riches—the *spiritual blessings!*

Electrical Transcriptions

March 24, 1944, I sent out a co-worker Bulletin from Hollywood. I was en route to San Antonio, Texas, for one or two live broadcasts over WOAI, and then to Des Moines, Iowa, for a special three weeks' *daily* broadcasting over station KSO, 5,000 watts. In those days most of the programs had to be aired by means of electrical transcription. The programs were recorded on large-size semisoft acetate phonograph discs—fifteen

inches in diameter. Each disc recorded fifteen minutes—or *half* of our thirty-minute program. The quality
was not equal to the present tape recording.

Nevertheless, we made every effort to provide
stations with the best quality we could. Most of the
recording was being done in Portland, where there was
one professional recording studio. We felt that the
recording obtained there was a shade inferior to that of
the best recording studios in Hollywood—the nation's
broadcasting capital. Frequently I made trips, through
those years, to Hollywood in order to get as many
programs as possible recorded where the very top
quality of transcriptions was available.

Often, however, in traveling, the program was
recorded in other cities—San Francisco, New York,
Washington, D.C., Chicago, Des Moines.

But in those days the Federal Communications
Commission, the government supervising agency, enforced the rule that announcers must always tell the
listeners that the program came via "electrical transcription," or was "transcribed." And when this was
announced, listeners universally felt they were listening
to a "canned" program—a mere record—not an actual
live *person*. For this reason, especially on our large
50,000-watt stations, we felt—and so did the stations—
that it was necessary that I visit these stations in
person and do the programs "live" as frequently as
possible. This necessitated a great deal of traveling.

At Hollywood on this particular visit in March,
1944, I learned of a new coast-to-coast network in
process of being formed—to be known as Associated
Broadcasting Corporation—or, for short, the ABC network. I received information that this new network was
going to be willing to accept religious programming. At
that time, only Mutual was selling any time for religious

99

programming, and the word was that even Mutual was soon going to throw off all religious programs. I was hoping that we might be able to go on the new ABC network. We were beginning to envision constantly bigger and bigger things as the living Christ expanded His work.

Meanwhile, we had virtually outgrown the facilities of the local printing company in Eugene for publishing *The Plain Truth.* I was beginning to check with the largest printing and publishing establishments in Los Angeles. This, and the need for top-quality recording to be obtained only in Hollywood, brought to my mind, about this time, the first thoughts of the approaching necessity of moving our headquarters to Southern California.

We Go on a 100,000-watt Station

In early August of that year, Mrs. Armstrong and I spent two weeks in fasting, as we did nearly every summer, at a cabin on the Oregon coast beach, near Waldport. Returning, refreshed, I heard of the possibility of securing a good night time on a superpower 100,000-watt station, XELO, at Juarez, Mexico—just across the river from El Paso, Texas.

This station had twice the power of any station in the United States, had an *exclusive* clear channel—no other station on the North American continent at that time on its wave-length—800 on the radio dial.

We returned from the beach about August 20. The following Sunday night, after the Sunday morning broadcast, live, over KXL, I was once again on the train for San Francisco, Hollywood, and El Paso.

At El Paso, I learned that this station had good coverage in every state, and even into Canada, after dark. It was managed by two men, partners. One, Mr.

Don Howard, I contacted in El Paso. He was interested in opening a time for *The World Tomorrow*, but I found it necessary to travel on to Del Rio, Texas, to consult his partner, Mr. Walter Wilson, before anything final was arranged.

Walter Wilson knew all the "ropes" in the matter of operating border radio stations, just beyond the American border, with a superpower that could reach a national audience over the United States.

I was not very happy about the company I was going to have to keep on this Mexican station—programming that never would have been acceptable on most United States stations—and religious programs of a nature I most certainly did not want to be identified with.

Nevertheless, knowing *The World Tomorrow* was a program of highest quality, and yet of power and tremendous listener-appeal, these partners offered me the prime, *most* desirable time of 8 p.m., every Sunday night.

We had been forced to take the very *poor* listening time of 11 p.m. over any large United States station—and we were able to be, then, on only the one—WOAI. This BEST time on XELO was going to cost quite a little more, but I know we would have many times the audience at 8 p.m., and 800 on the dial, that we had at 11 p.m. after most people had gone to bed. So I took the plunge.

Fantastic Response

Immediately the mail response was fantastic. Never did it equal the more than 2,000 letters from a single broadcast we had once received from a program on WHO, but it was sensationally heavy, and continued steady and increasing. *Plain Truth* circulation rose steadily.

101

More and more I was having to contemplate moving our headquarters to the Los Angeles area.

By winter, 1944, and perhaps about January, 1945, I was trying out an early-evening *nightly* broadcast on XELO, using discs recorded at KMTR, Hollywood, while doing live series of fifteen-minute programs on that station. I had frequently, since July, 1942, gone to Hollywood for about three weeks' continuous *daily* broadcasting of fifteen-minute programs.

However, these fifteen-minute programs never seemed to bring a large response. It was becoming evident that our type program was a full half-hour program. It was much easier to *hold* a listening radio audience to the *World Tomorrow*-type program for a full half hour than a short fifteen minutes.

These try-out fifteen-minute programs on XELO were aired, I believe, at 6 p.m. But after available recordings were exhausted, this series was discontinued—until we could afford to go on every night with a full half hour.

48

Historic San Francisco Conference—The United Nations Is Born

THIS *Autobiography* began with the year 1892. This chronicle of events has now covered almost fifty-three years, and we have come to the tremendous year of 1945.

What a fateful year of world history that was!

The Fateful Year

To say nothing of what developed in the very work of God that year, look at these pivotal world events of 1945:

February 3-11—The Yalta Summit Conference between President Franklin D. Roosevelt, Prime Minister Winston Churchill, and Premier Joseph Stalin—at which the Western powers were outmaneuvered into giving all, and getting nothing.

April 12—President Roosevelt died at Warm Springs, Georgia, and Vice President Harry S. Truman was sworn in as President of the United States.

Notice, now, how in quick succession, in this one fatal month, *three* of the world's top figures were erased from world power. The year 1945 was a pivotal turning point of world history—these men went—the war went—a NEW AGE, the *nuclear* age, was born.

April 28—Only sixteen days after Mr. Roosevelt passed from the world scene, Benito Mussolini was executed, after having been captured by partisans at Dongo, Italy, as he was trying to flee across the border into Switzerland. His body was strung up, upside down, in extreme disgrace.

April 29-30—Adolf Hitler was blotted out of this world's history, presumedly a suicide in his bunker underground beside the Chancellery in Berlin.

So notice—these three of the five world leaders, were all removed from world leadership during the *same month*—the fateful month of April, 1945.

Man's LAST HOPE of saving this world also *began*—doomed to failure—during that crucial month of April, 1945, at San Francisco. I was there.

But before we pass on to a more specific description of these tremendous events, let me impress upon the reader a truism we too often overlook. In February that year three of the world's top leaders met at Yalta. Two months later, the three of them were removed from power—their voices silenced, their activities ceased. It is TRUE—*you never know what an hour may bring forth!*

But to finish the listing of tremendous events of that one year:

April 25—The great San Francisco Conference opened, at which leaders of forty-six nations formed and adopted a Charter for the United Nations.

May 7, 1945—Germany signed unconditional

104

surrender, ending World War II in Europe.

July 17-August 2—Potsdam Conference in Germany, a summit conference with President Truman, Prime Minister Churchill, and Joseph Stalin—at which, once again, the Western powers gave all and Stalin took all.

August 6—First atomic bomb dropped on Hiroshima, Japan, destroying the city, and terrifying the world with sudden knowledge of the NUCLEAR AGE.

August 9—Second atomic bomb exploded on Nagasaki, Japan, destroying that city.

August 14—Japan surrendered—END of World War II—with the world now looking *fearfully toward a* nuclear World War III.

September 2—Formal ceremony of surrender by Japan to General MacArthur on board the U.S.S. *Missouri.*

WHAT a chronicle of world events for one single year!

Civilization's LAST HOPE

It was less than two weeks after the sudden death of President Roosevelt. The war was not yet over in Europe, but German resistance was crumbling fast. The nations outside the German-Italian-Japanese axis were planning a UNITED NATIONS ORGANIZATION, which was expected to end all wars—make future wars impossible.

A great conference was set to convene at San Francisco on April 25. This conference of nations was to draw up and adopt a Charter for this world organization of nations.

I decided it was advisable that I attend. Practically every hotel room in San Francisco was booked in advance before the world even heard the news of the Conference. But I had a few useful connections and was able to arrange a reservation for Mrs. Armstrong and myself for the duration of the Conference.

As editor and publisher of *The Plain Truth*, I was able to obtain full press credentials from the State Department, as a fully accredited press representative, and also associate press credentials for Mrs. Armstrong.

At the opening plenary session, on April 25, we were sitting in the forefront of the press gallery of the grand and famous San Francisco Civic Opera House. The seat next to us was occupied by one of the best known network newscasters.

We sat through a round of formal speeches. Secretary of State Stettinius for the United States, Foreign Secretary Anthony Eden for Great Britain, and one or two others delivered very serious speeches.

They said that we were gathered there, charged with the grave responsibility of producing a world organization that was *civilization's LAST HOPE!* They assured the delegates assembled that the survival of mankind depended on what they should do there.

I wondered whether they realized how true their words really were—so far as *man's* efforts to survive are concerned. Or was it merely window dressing, to be printed in the newspapers to impress the public?

Only STRIFE—Not Peace

Here were the *world leaders,* except for the Axis powers. They freely confessed—they put oratorical emphasis on the fact—that this world is DOOMED, *unless* the nations of the world can find a common ground for PEACE. The world had tried the Peace Conference of The Hague, the Pact of Paris, the League of Nations. Now it was going to try an organization of UNITED NATIONS.

The League of Nations failed, because it had NO TEETH in it. *Only* a world organization, or world government, wielding military power stronger than any nation bent on disturbing world peace, could PREVENT ANOTHER WORLD WAR!

So here, on the floor below us, under the same roof with us, were the leaders of the world's nations, trying once again to bring about world peace by human effort and organization! Truly, it was a spectacle!

The speeches certainly painted the grim picture. These men *knew* this was the world's *last hope!*

But what happened? At every turn, Mr. Molotov and the Russians balked, opposed, blocked, fought.

A few days after the Conference opened, a press conference had been scheduled for Secretary of State Stettinius. It was held in a special conference room in another building. Mr. Stettinius was some thirty or forty-five minutes late in arriving. When he came in, his face was white with fury. He literally blazed with indignation. He had been delayed by the Russian Molotov, in a meeting of leaders of the few major powers, which should have ended some time before this news conference was scheduled to begin. He explained to the newsmen how Molotov had blocked every move, fought and opposed every plan or suggestion, deliberately antagonized the other leaders, and started an intentional war of nerves.

I think that up until that moment the leaders of the United States government had naïvely *believed* that the Soviet Union was really our ally. President Roosevelt had felt that he could "convert" Stalin, by kindness—by giving him everything he wanted —by appeasing him. During the war I was not allowed to tell the public, over the air, the truth about Soviet plans, or to say anything that was not complimentary about them. I was given to understand this was "policy" which had gone out from the White House.

More than once I witnessed to my shame, in newsreel theaters, a mild and restrained clapping when President Roosevelt's pictures were flashed on the screen—and then, when Stalin's picture was shown, wild applause, shouting, foot-stomping shook the theater!

Even before Potsdam—when General Patton's forces were starting their drive toward Berlin after the Channel-crossing—academic psychologists convinced the Administration at Washington that the allies owed it to Russia to remove Russian fears of future German aggression by giving the Communists most of Eastern Europe. That is why General Patton's forces were halted on the drive toward Berlin and forced to draw back from territory already conquered!

The Dispatch That Never Came

It was about this time, possibly March, 1945, that I was waiting to go on the air one Sunday morning in the KXL studios in Portland. Broadcast time was 8:30 a.m. General Patton's forces were making good progress toward Germany on the west. Russian forces on the east had, the day before, come within a calculated half day of crossing the border into Germany. The first invasion into Germany itself would be big news. Customarily I covered the war news, with an analysis according to prophecy, on each program during those war years. It was already between 5 and 5:30 p.m.—or even an hour later—at the eastern front.

Arriving at the radio studios, I anxiously scanned the news teletype for a dispatch stating that German soil had been occupied by the Russian forces. No such dispatch had come in. I arranged with the station announcer to check every few minutes, and if the news came in on the tape, before my program ended, to shear it off and bring it in to me so I could put it on the air.

But no such news came. Not that half hour. Not

that day. Not for many weeks!

WHY? The Soviet rulers did not want to plow immediately through for a quick knockout of Germany. Instead, they left adequate forces just outside the German border and sent their invading divisions on south to conquer and occupy such eastern Europe countries as Czechoslovakia, Romania, Hungary, Yugoslavia and Albania, setting the Russian boot on those lands, as conquered satellite countries, *before* bringing the war to an end.

At the same time, the Kremlin, with the help of the theoretical psychologists, prevailed on Washington to send orders through to General Eisenhower to pull General Patton back—to prevent ending the war *until* the Soviets had occupied all the east European satellite countries!

Sometimes, I wonder how gullible statesmen and heads of government can get! I continually pray: *"Thy kingdom* come, THY will be done on earth, as it is in heaven." Well, we are, with this revision of the *Autobiography,* forty-one years closer to that happy world tomorrow than we were then!

The Strutting Molotov

But if the American Secretary of State had been altruistic about the Communists being converted—or being then, or ever becoming, our friends, Mr. Stettinius certainly was disillusioned now! He literally blazed with anger, after the closed-door conference with Molotov! This I saw, and heard, in that press conference.

One morning—whether the first morning of the first plenary session or later, I do not now remember—Mrs. Armstrong and I arrived early at the Opera House to get a close-up view of the celebrity statesmen arriving. One of the first was Mr. Anthony Eden of Great

Britain. Quite a crowd was gathered in front of the Opera House. Police guards kept a passageway up the middle of the crowd cleared, from the curb where the delegates stepped out of their cars on arrival. Mrs. Armstrong and I were standing very near the curb, just one or two steps up, off the sidewalk, and directly in front.

Mr. Eden stepped out of his car, smiled, took off his hat and waved warmly and in a most friendly manner to the crowd.

News cameramen rushed to him.

"Will you pose for us, Mr. Eden?" they asked. Smilingly he nodded. The cameramen decided they would like him on the very spot where Mrs. Armstrong and I were standing. Would we kindly move to the other side, just long enough for the "shot"? Sir Anthony smilingly thanked us, and stood while flashbulbs flashed, then briskly walked on up the steps and into the Opera House.

A little later, three big, shiny black Cadillacs pulled up to the curb. Out of the first and third of these cars sprang a dozen or more Russian bodyguards. They promptly and rather rudely pushed all of us back farther, to widen the path through the crowd up the steps to the Opera House entrance. Then, quickly behind them, out leaped about six more bodyguards from the middle car.

Last of all, out strutted Foreign Minister Molotov of Russia. Six or eight of the bodyguards completely surrounded him, and as he walked stiffly and haughtily up the steps, no smile or nod to anybody, more and more of his bodyguards closed in around him, marching up the steps with him.

WHAT A CONTRAST, between the British and the Russian foreign ministers! Mr. Molotov's haughty

110

behavior made Mr. Anthony Eden all the more well-liked by all of us there.

Mrs. Armstrong whispered to me, "Isn't Mr. Anthony Eden a handsome man?" I assented—and added that so was Mr. Stettinius.

During the Conference, I attended a few other press conferences held by outstanding delegates. Mr. Molotov gave one press conference, and I attended. It was stiff and formal. He spoke through an interpreter. He made himself thoroughly disliked and detested by all. We saw quite a little of him during that month-long conference—more than we enjoyed.

Meeting the Sheik

Very much in the news at the Conference were the Arab delegates, always noticeable by their flowing robes. They were headed by Sheik Hafiz Wabba of Saudi Arabia. I arranged for a private conference with him. We spent an hour together in his suite in the Fairmont Hotel and became good friends.

The sheik was in charge of all Arab negotiations on the Jewish-Arab controversy over Palestine. He explained to me, thoroughly, the Arab view, and why they felt the Jews had no rights whatever in Palestine. Of course, I also interviewed Jewish delegates, who gave me their side of the story. Each side had a most logical and convincing story.

I wondered if the Arab people themselves knew and believed they are the descendants of Ishmael, son of Abraham through Sarah's handmaid Hagar. I asked him. He did not mention Ishmael's name, but he said,

"Oh yes, Abram [he pronounced it A-*brahm*, with accent on last syllable] is our ancestor. We are children of Abram."

The sheik spoke very good English. Mrs. Arm-

111

strong and I met him again, in 1947, in London, when he invited us to a royal reception to be presented to a former king of Arabia, then the Crown Prince. And again, in 1956, in Cairo, he and his wife came to our hotel and spent an afternoon with us. These contacts will be described when we come to those years in the *Autobiography.*

I had another interesting full-hour's private conference with Mr. Constanin Fotich, former foreign secretary of Yugoslavia, who gave me a firsthand description of what happened in the Communist invasion of that country—and how farm owners had their farms taken from them.

One press conference attended was held by the former head of Latvia, or Estonia, or Lithuania—I forget which, but believe it was the latter of these three countries the Soviets had gobbled up. He gave us a lurid description of the Communist takeover.

On one occasion I chanced to meet the Admiral of the Chinese navy. He represented Chiang Kai-shek's Nationalist China. This was before the Communist takeover. The admiral was a gentlemanly sort. I met him in the elevator of the Mark Hopkins Hotel. He was in a glamor uniform—not even the Arabs in their flowing robes were more glamorous. On the uniform about every color of the rainbow was somewhere represented. There was only one unusual thing about the presence of the admiral of the Chinese navy—Nationalist China had no navy! Not a single warship! That may be one reason all the glamor was concentrated on the admiral's uniform.

A High Pontifical Mass

Also, during our stay in San Francisco I myself spoke a couple of times—not before Conference delegates, but

112

in halls before local radio listeners.

We also attended a Roman Catholic High Pontifical Mass held in the general civic area of the Conference, and attended by many hundreds of delegates. It was presided over by the San Francisco Archbishop, and the address was delivered by Bishop Hunt, of Salt Lake City, one of the two outstanding Catholic radio ministers at the time. Mr. Hunt was a powerful speaker, and his speech to those delegates—important officials and heads of state of many nations—actually carried prophetic significance.

He built his address around Psalm 127:1: "Except the Lord build the house, they labour in vain that build it." He stressed the seriousness of the world condition—how this effort to unite nations for peace was man's LAST CHANCE. These delegates were trying to build a "house"—a union of nations. Unless the Roman Catholic Church was put at the head of it—for of course he assumed that Church was the Lord's sole instrument on earth—it was doomed to failure. Since they claim the Pope is in place of Christ on earth—what he really meant was that no move to associate or combine nations together can succeed unless headed and ruled by the Pope. It was prophetic, because this is precisely what PROPHECY says *will happen* in the new European Union, now emerging in Europe, to resurrect the Roman Empire!

49

World War II Ends—Atomic Age Begins!

WHILE ATTENDING the San Francisco Conference, I spoke on Wednesday night, May 9, at the auditorium in Native Sons' Building, to an audience of listeners to *The World Tomorrow.*

What I said that night might be of some interest, in the light of subsequent events. I still have my notes on file. Here is a brief summary:

"This San Francisco Conference is the greatest, most important conference of heads of nations held in world history. Here the top statesmen of the whole world are gathered. And WHY? To build a HIGH TOWER— a super WORLD ORGANIZATION—man's nearest approach toward WORLD GOVERNMENT—an *armed* organization, with the power of armed force to guarantee world peace. But since world leaders do not know the WAY to peace, it cannot succeed.

"The war is over, in Europe—*or is it?* We need to

114

wake up and realize that right now is the most danger-ous moment in United States national history, instead of assuming we now have peace!

"Men plan, here, to preserve the PEACE of the world. What most do not know is that the Germans have *their* plans for winning the BATTLE of the peace. Yes, I said BATTLE of the peace. That's a kind of battle we Americans don't know. We know only *one kind* of war. We have never lost a war—that is, a military war; but we have never WON a conference, where leaders of other nations outfox us in the BATTLE for the peace.

"We don't understand German *thoroughness*. From the very start of World War II, they have considered the possibility of losing this second round, as they did the first—and they have carefully, methodically *planned*, in such eventuality, the *third* round—World War III! Hitler has lost. This round of war, in Europe, is over. And the Nazis have now gone UNDERGROUND. In France and Norway they learned how effectively an organized UNDERGROUND can hamper occupation and control of a country. Paris was liberated by the French UNDER-GROUND—and allied armies. Now a Nazi underground is methodically planned. They plan to COME BACK and to win on the third try.

"The Bible foretells that third round—and it spells DOOM for us, as God's punishment, because we, as a nation, have forsaken Him and His ways! The third round is termed, in prophecy, an invasion by "BABY-LON"—a resurrected Roman Empire—a European Union. I have been proclaiming that since 1927. For a while I thought Hitler might organize it—especially when he tied up with the Roman Mussolini. It wasn't done in this *second* World War. It *will* be done and provoke the *third!*

"This Nazi underground will introduce a new kind

115

of internal warfare and sabotage, *to divide and conquer!* It will stir race hatred, class prejudice, strife among ourselves, religious bigotry while professing to champion religious tolerance—especially toward the religion of the coming United States of Europe.

"Even at this conference, classes and races are demanding their 'rights.' This conference, and the United Nations Organization it is forming, must solve three problems to succeed. First, Big Three unity; second, the serious problem of what to do with Germany to prevent World War III; and third, solve the world's injustices against smaller nations, and the growth and tactics of Communism toward world domination. Can it succeed?

"These world leaders here in San Francisco are trying to build a HIGH TOWER of world organization to produce and preserve PEACE. Can it succeed? Listen to God's Word: 'Except the LORD build the house, they labour in vain that build it' (Ps. 127:1). Again, Christ said (Matt. 15:13), 'Every plant, which my heavenly Father hath not planted, shall be rooted up.'" (This first quoted *before* Bishop Hunt used it, at the Pontifical High Mass.)

"The Lord God is *not* building this house. These men have not sought His guidance. Their deliberations were not opened by prayer, but by a moment of SILENCE! The heavenly Father in heaven is not planting it. It shall, therefore, be rooted up!

"Once before, men started to build a high TOWER to reach to the heaven of world domination. And God Almighty intervened and broke up their building (Gen. 10:8-11, and 11:1-9). In the end, God Almighty will have to intervene with force, to break up what will grow out of this effort of nations to assemble themselves together—without GOD!"

Today, Many Years Later

How prophetic those words were! They are proving true—because they were based on the prophecies of God! This United Nations organization *started* the IDEA—planted it in men's minds—of *uniting nations* together. It paved the way for the prophesied resurrection of the Roman Empire—by a United States of EUROPE. Today there is talk of a South American "Common Market," and even a Southeast Asian "Common Market." Uniting nations together is in the air.

Before concluding events of the San Francisco Conference, one amusing little incident comes to mind. Mrs. Armstrong and I were having lunch one day in the Mark Hopkins Hotel. I noticed Walter Winchell, the New York newsman and broadcaster, rise from a table with two or three other men. At the hat rack, just inside the entrance of the dining room, I saw him pick up my hat and put it on. But it didn't fit apparently, for he removed it, looked at it, then put it back and found his own.

Deep-Sea Fishing—War's END!

After the UNO (as it then was called) Conference at San Francisco, we returned to the office in Eugene, Oregon. But by August the need of another period of fasting and rejuvenation physically was again imperative. In August we went, once again, to the Oregon coast, for a two-weeks' rest and opportunity to catch up on writing, while fasting in a cottage on the beach.

We started on Monday, August 6. Passing through Corvallis, seat of Oregon State College, we picked up a newspaper EXTRA. It was *filled* with sensational news. The first ATOMIC BOMB had been dropped that day on Hiroshima, Japan!

The newspaper was literally *filled* with sensational news and facts about nuclear fission. It was the first news to be given to the public about the perfection of ATOMIC ENERGY.

WE HAD ENTERED *A NEW AGE!*—the ATOMIC Age!

We were somewhat filled with awe! We knew this heralded the speeding up of events to bring this world to its END—and usher in the better WORLD TOMORROW!

On Thursday of that week, August 9, news came over radio of the wiping out of Japan's second city, Nagasaki, by the second atom bomb. The crescendo of events was becoming terrific!

The following Tuesday, August 14, I took our two sons, Richard David and Garner Ted, then ages sixteen and fifteen (Dick was almost seventeen), deep-sea fishing for salmon, off the coast of Depoe Bay. It was the first experience of the kind for all three of us. In fact it was my *only* such experience. Mrs. Armstrong, who has a tendency to become seasick easily, remained ashore at Depoe Bay.

At this point, as well as at Newport and other points, regular deep-sea fishing boats make regular excursion trips, lasting perhaps a couple of hours, taking a number of paying passengers on each trip. Proper equipment for salmon fishing is provided, with attendants to instruct and help the passenger "fishermen."

As we reached a good distance from land, lines were thrown out, and several if not all passengers began to bring in salmon, caught on the hook. These small fishing boats rock and roll (but not like Elvis Presley) considerably. Soon both Dick and Ted were *feeding* the fishes instead of pulling them in. I never told them, but I almost did as well. I did feel a little woozy, but managed by strenuous mental concentration to avoid contributing to the food supply of the hungry fishes.

■ *Herbert W. and*
Loma D. Armstrong
by their DeSoto
in front of Eugene
home that they
later sold.

■ *Top of page:*
Dorothy, far left,
and Beverly, and
far right, Richard,
in garden with
parents. Above,
Richard, in chair,
and Garner Ted,
with parents. Right,
Herbert and Loma
Armstrong on a
stroll.

■ *Eva Wright Armstrong, above, with sons Russell, left, and Herbert, center. Borrower's card for Eugene Public Library was often used by Herbert Armstrong. Left, the Armstrongs with their Chrysler on cross-country trip.*

■ *Stages in development of* The Good News. *First, the mimeographed* Our Co-workers' Bulletin, *then* The Good News Letter. The Good News *became a magazine in 1951.*

■ *Visiting ruins in the American Southwest during the 1946 cross-country tour. Herbert W. Armstrong and son Richard on one of numerous trips to Hollywood/Los Angeles area to record* World Tomorrow *program.*

■ *Belknap Hot Springs, Oregon, became the site of annual autumn festival of the Church of God from 1946 through 1951. Center, the members gather in front of the main lodge. Left, Herbert W. Armstrong in woods surrounding Belknap Springs.*

■ *Mr. Don Hunter cutting an electrical transcription for* The World Tomorrow *in his Eugene studio.*

Closeup of disc gives subject of broadcast, speed at which to be played, radio station call letters and date of

airing. San Francisco UNO meeting, right, with Loma Armstrong's visitor pass signed by Alger Hiss.

■ *Formal portrait of Loma D. and Herbert W. Armstrong, taken at time of passport photos, winter 1947. "Helenium" on the shores of Lake Lugano, Switzerland, with a closeup, lower left. Villa was patterned after the Petit Trianon, Versailles, France.*

In spite of their seasickness, the boys each got a nice large salmon, as did I—I believe one was the limit for each passenger. In any event, the fish were easily worth the small fare for the trip.

As we drew close to land, the boats sailing under a bridge on the Coast Highway into a lagoon harbor, we saw Mrs. Armstrong standing on the bridge, waving her arms vigorously and trying to shout something to us. We could not hear until we approached closer to the bridge, but we knew well what she was trying to say— word had just been flashed over radio of *Japan's surrender*—the END of WORLD WAR II!

I had received the news of the *start* of the war— that is, of United States participation—on December 7, 1941, while up in the air on my *first* airplane flight. And now that war was finally ended while I was on my first sailing on an ocean—the war in the PACIFIC sector ending while I was *on* the Pacific!

We took our fine fresh salmon to our cabin at Yakone beach. Mrs. Armstrong canned two of them, and one of them provided meals for us and guests. Mrs. Armstrong's girlhood high school chum and family were visiting us. Mrs. Armstrong served us baked fresh salmon in hot poured butter. It was delicious!

A New AGE Dawns!

Returning refreshed, with recharged energy, to the office in Eugene, I issued a special Bulletin for our co-workers. It summarized the momentous stage of history through which we were passing. It gave something of the "feel" of world events, as they appeared at that time.

I think it will be interesting, and pertinent, to quote here a few excerpts from that Bulletin:

"Since I last wrote you, May 28 from San Francisco, we have lived through the most momentous events of world history. At that time, we had entered the period which has been the most vital PIVOT in American and world history. President Roosevelt had died. The military war had ended in Europe. Mussolini had been ignominiously put to death and buried. . . .

"But even greater news has followed. World War II has come to its final end, and as I write, General MacArthur is preparing to go into and occupy Japan at the head of the most impressive display of military might ever beheld by mortal man—on land, on the sea, in the air. This is planned in order dramatically to convince the Japanese they have been completely whipped.

"But the most important news of all is the announcement, with the actual horrifying demonstration, of the atomic bomb and the age of atomic power. This, say scientists, will at once completely revolutionize both peace-time life and warfare upon earth.

"Within the past 400 years the world has passed through the age of exploration, and then the machine age. Now we suddenly find ourselves plunged headlong, without warning, into a new, totally unexplored AGE OF ATOMIC POWER. Adjectives have been exhausted in an attempt to describe the staggering magnitude of this thing. It's a NEW AGE—but one destined to be of extremely SHORT DURATION. It's an age fraught with horrifying, imagination-defying possibilities. Yet it's an age which at once opens to us marvelous new opportunities—and a most STUNNING challenge and RESPONSIBILITY in the work of Almighty GOD!

"Thousands of years ago men started the terrible scourge of war with elementary weapons—knives, swords, slingshots, bows and arrows. As a prominent military analyst expressed it, the most effective military weapons are those which can be used to strike at the enemy in the quickest time, at the longest distance, and with the most destructive power.

"And now, as World War II came to an end, the WEAPONS OF THE FUTURE put in an appearance—jet propulsion and rocket weapons, carrying missiles still faster and farther.

"And then, the tremendous CLIMAX! The best-kept secret of the war—the ATOMIC BOMB, suddenly *perfected,* and just TWO of these indescribable weapons of destruction and death dropped upon Japan, bringing the war to a sudden END!"

At Last—DAILY Broadcasting

Also it was announced, in this Bulletin of August 27, 1945, that, beginning October 1, the *World Tomorrow* program was to be broadcasted six nights a week, at the prime listening time of 8 p.m., at 800 on the radio dial, over the superpower 100,000-watt station XELO, Juarez, Mexico.

That station, then having an exclusive channel over the North American continent, could then be heard in virtually every state.

This was by far the biggest leap ahead of God's work, so far!

After this tremendous impact of *nightly* broadcasting got under way, the number of listeners of God's truth increased faster than ever.

Then, on the heels of this, GOD OPENED ANOTHER STILL BIGGER DOOR! Station XEG, with 150,000 watts, making it the most powerful voice reaching over the United States, opened its mighty doors—and at the prime listening time of 8 p.m., Central standard time, *and also six nights a week!* I do not, at the moment, seem to find records in the old files showing the exact date, but I believe we started on this station on October 1, 1945.

Apparently the additional expense of this tremendously powerful broadcasting, suddenly multiplying broadcasting effectiveness many times over, had prevented the publishing of an edition of *The Plain Truth* for three or four months. I do not find a copy in the files until March-April, 1946, after starting this powerful program. And that issue is Volume XI, Number 1—the first issue printed that year.

But circulation of *The Plain Truth* had taken a big flight upward. It is printed on the front cover, *"Circulation, 75,000 this issue."*

50

A Momentous Year

A S THE years sped along, each seemed to usher in more important developments than any preceding year in God's work. 1945 was a *momentous* year!—but, for the work, 1946 was even more important.

Actually, 1946 was the *year of BEGINNINGS,* as an organized major national and worldwide work.

This was the year in which our own printing department was started.

This was the *first* year in which the full impact was felt of three superpower radio stations, blanketing the entire United States and reaching even Canada and Alaska.

The was the *first* year in which we had the impact of *six-nights-a-week* broadcasting, at *an early prime listening hour,* coast to coast.

This was the year in which the *first* baptizing tour was taken. It covered the four corners of the United

States, and much of the middle sections of the country besides.

And this was the year in which the founding of Ambassador College was conceived, planned, and the *first* block of property for the new campus acquired in Pasadena. This college was to be the means of training of the growing personnel for the fast-expanding organized work.

Now notice the *startling significance* in the fact this all happened in *this particular year!*

The "Magic Number" Twelve

Looking back in retrospect, it is truly amazing to recall how many things, lifting this almost obscure *minor* effort to the dynamic worldwide FORCE God's work is becoming today, had their *beginnings* in 1946.

I have remarked before how certain numbers have significant meaning in God's plan. *Six* is the number of MAN and materialism. *Seven* is GOD'S number of perfection and completion. God made the material creation in *six* days. MAN was created the *sixth* day. But God *completed* the first week, and *perfected* it by creation of His Sabbath, on the *seventh* day. That *seventh* day typified the completed and perfect SPIRITUAL creation.

Thus God set apart *six* millennia for MAN to be allowed rejection of God's government, and to write the lesson of human rebellion, to be followed by the *seventh* millennium in which God will *perfect* and *complete* His SPIRITUAL creation.

But *twelve* is God's number of spiritual *organizational* BEGINNINGS. God's promises pertain to Abraham's children. His children *began* with the twelve sons of Jacob. God *began* His organized nation on earth with TWELVE tribes. Christ BEGAN His Church with TWELVE apostles.

124

But TWELVE is the number of *organizational* beginnings, not first beginnings. God started off the human race with ONE man, Adam. The first human "father of the multitude" that shall be converted and inherit salvation was the ONE man, Abraham (Gen. 17:5); and this same *one* man is the human "father of the faithful" (Rom. 4:16). The actual *first* beginning of the Church of God was the ONE man, Jesus Christ. But the *organizational* beginning was through the *collective* Body of Christ, empowered by the same Spirit, starting with the TWELVE.

This present *last-warning* work of God, officially, was started by the little Church of God in Eugene, Oregon. Yet I was the pastor and leader of that little Church, and most original members of that time showed little interest, and took no real part, in the work. To all practical effects, it started with one man, with the help of my wife—and, of course, a handful of co-workers.

The first conception of *The Plain Truth* had come in 1927. I had made actual dummies of the magazine that year. But it was only after *seven years* that the dream came to reality and *completion* as a fact. Even then it was a crude, home-produced, mimeographed "magazine." For the first *seven* years, from then, this whole work remained a crude, unprofessional, struggling little work. After seven years, the magazine became a *printed* publication, the work moved into a daylight, efficient office, we began to acquire some office equipment, and the work took on a more perfected and professional appearance.

But the year 1946 was *TWELVE* years after God's work began. And it was in 1946 that the vision of Ambassador College, the BEGINNING of the *organizational* activity of this great work first was placed in my

125

mind. But it was by no planning of mine that this first BEGINNING of an enlarged, world-girding, ORGANIZED work first entered my mind—and that the property for its beginning was purchased that year. The truth is, I never so much as realized that this all happened TWELVE years after the first starting of the work, until researching material for this *Autobiography!* But see now what happened in 1946!

START of Business and Printing Departments

During these first twelve years, there was no such thing as a business office to handle the finances. Through those years I, myself, was business manager of the work, as well as editor, printer, office boy and everything but windowwasher (there were no windows the first seven years).

But an organizational operation could not operate worldwide, as God's work does today, without a department of business administration.

We didn't know it at the time, but the first manager of the business office, in charge of handling all monies, paying all bills, keeping all financial records, and making all but the very top-level financial decisions (which I still must make), in regard to budgets, requisitions for purchases, etc., joined the "organization" (if it could then have been called that) in mid-February, 1946.

This was my son-in-law, Vern R. Mattson, husband of our younger daughter Dorothy. They had been married in our little church in Eugene in July, 1944. He was on brief furlough from the Marines after returning from the Marines' engagement at Guadalcanal, and having been in an Australian hospital. After their marriage, due to his record in action, he had been sent back to Quantico, to Officers' Training Camp. He graduated from officers' school with highest grades and honors, at the head of his class, and was commissioned a 2nd Lieutenant. He had been discharged finally from service in November, 1945.

In February he joined our small but growing staff, to become office manager. For some two to four weeks he did ordinary office work, working in every department, to learn our system—and making suggestions for improvements, preparatory to taking over the office management.

At that time we had a forelady, a secretary to me, one woman reading and channeling incoming mail, one girl cutting stencils for new names on the mailing list, three girls filing at the mailing-list cabinets, and two girls in the "co-worker department," keeping card records of all people contributing to the support of the work, with amounts and dates.

Later, after moving the headquarters to Pasadena, in 1947, Mr. Mattson became business manager of the work and controller of the college. His department developed into a sizable operation, with a competent staff.

The first START of our own printing department came about under unusual circumstances, by late May.

In early March, 1946, our other son-in-law, Jimmy (James A. Gott), husband of our elder daughter Beverly, met with a serious accident. He had been working in the Oregon woods east of Eugene for a lumber company. This was dangerous work. Employment was somewhat spasmodic. The pay was good—when they worked. We were glad, therefore, when he was transferred to a more steady and "safe" job, in the mill.

But it was on this "safe" inside mill job that the accident happened. Jimmy was working on the edger. At the time he was wearing a glove, which caught on the

127

teeth of the feed-roll. The spinning feed-roll gouged out the whole back of his left hand, even shearing thin the tendons and severing one or two.

He was in the hospital some six weeks or more. During the war, the doctors had learned to do some remarkable feats of plastic surgery on injured soldiers. A plastic surgeon, by binding the back of Jimmy's hand to his abdomen, grafted new flesh and skin from the abdomen onto the back of his hand. The operation restored most, but not complete, use of the hand.

We didn't want to see Jimmy go back either to the woods or the sawmill. At this time the Davidson offset printing machine was brought to my attention. I sought further details, obtained circulars and catalogs. The company offered special training to teach men to use the equipment. I found we could purchase this equipment on terms.

I took the printed matter and illustrations about it to Jimmy in the hospital.

"How would you like to get into the printing business?" I asked. "I think the time has come to start out our own printing department. I don't have in mind printing *The Plain Truth* ourselves, but we need many more booklets than we can afford to have printed at commercial printing establishments. I think this offset method of printing, in a department of our own, will pay for itself in a year's time or less. I was thinking you could learn this type of printing in a short time, and it would be a STEADY job, and a safe one. I can't pay you as much as you make in the woods—*when* you have work there, but this would be steady, and you'd make more per year than you have been making."

Jim liked the idea immediately. He read up on the Davidson literature, and by the time he was released from the hospital he was enthusiastic over it.

128

The equipment was installed in a room in the basement of the IOOF building in Eugene, and with a factory instructor teaching Jim the first few days, our printing department got under way late in May.

My Mother's Eightieth Birthday

My mother reached her eightieth birthday April 21, 1946. Although the biblical instruction of God shows that only pagans celebrated birthdays, and Mrs. Armstrong and I have not done so since learning this truth, my sister, who lived in Portland, was of a religious denomination that does follow this custom. She had planned a celebration for Mother at her home, and it was up to me to get Mother there.

My mother had never flown on a plane. I can remember very well, as a boy, hearing her use the expression often: "I could no more do thus and so than I could fly." I decided it was time she began to fly—and she was quite willing.

So, at Eugene airport, we boarded a United Airlines plane for Portland. I took "movies" of her walking out to the plane, ascending the steps, and standing on the platform in the door of the plane, waving. At Portland, I left the plane first, to take pictures or her getting off. In the doorway she waved, with a sort of triumphant smile that reminded me of the supposed expression of a cat that had just swallowed a canary. She flew frequently after that. My sister and husband were there to meet us.

It seemed that eighty was a very ripe old age—one that deserved honoring. But God granted my mother an additional fifteen and a half years after that—fifteen and a half years of *enjoying* life abundantly. In September, 1961, recovering from a deep-seated cold and semipneumonia condition, sometimes called "the old

129

people's friend," she simply seemed to lack the physical strength to continue recovery. In midafternoon, she smiled, said she felt a little tired, and thought she would lie back in her easy reclining chair and take a nap. She went to sleep, and, a half hour or so later, simply stopped breathing.

Only the preceding afternoon she had smiled at one of our favorite little jokes. I said, as I had done many times before, teasing her a little, "Mother, you're the best mother I ever had." As usual, though a little weaker and more tired than usual, she smiled and replied, "Herbert, you're *one* of the best sons I ever had."

No one grieved, though she was greatly missed. She had lived to the fine old age of ninety-five and a half, enjoying life to the last day. She simply went to sleep happily—no pain, no suffering, just peaceful, restful SLEEP. She will awaken, in the next second of her consciousness, in the resurrection of LIFE. Instead of grieving, we gratefully thanked God for giving her long life, in the happiness of the knowledge of His WAY, always loving her Savior.

She often talked of her joy the day I was born—for I was her firstborn. She bore me, and for Jesus Christ I baptized her.

But I have gotten fifteen and a half years ahead of the story. Back, now, to the spring of 1946. Back, now, to that year of *organizational* BEGINNINGS, when God's work began emerging from virtually a minor one-man work into a highly organized major worldwide power and influence.

The "Shirttail Shoot"

The first meeting of the Security Council of the new United Nations was scheduled to begin on March 25, 1946, at Hunter College in New York. And *that* marked the *beginning* of the END of man's efforts to rule the world.

The General Assembly of the United Nations was merely a debating body—a sounding board for rival propaganda. Only the Security Council was supposed to have the real power. If ever men were to be able to bring about PEACE on earth, this Security Council was their sole and last hope.

I decided to cover this first session of the Security Council in person for *The Plain Truth* and the *World Tomorrow* radio program. It was my first coast-to-coast flight.

This flight was made in a series of hops in the best air service of the time—DC-3s, or the equivalent. My first hop started from Portland.

I do not now remember whether I have ever told on myself about a certain proclivity. I think I have pretty well overcome it now, but I had not in 1946. I had developed a habit of always catching a train, bus, or plane at the very last minute. I suppose this tendency had been influenced as a boy, when parents, uncles and aunts always felt they had to arrive at the depot at least an hour or more before departure time for a train. This seemed to me a foolish waste of time.

Through the years I had caught many a train on the run, after it had started. My wife had a name for this habitual last-second dash. She called it a "shirttail shoot." She never approved of it. She preferred to waste the hour of waiting, rather than waste the following hour calming jangled nerves. I'm afraid I pampered and petted the habit somewhat, before I finally determined to overcome it.

Often, through my life, I had not been able to accomplish things I set out to do on the original planned schedule. Sometimes goals or objectives were

131

reached a whole year later than original schedules. But I took comfort and courage in being able to say: "... but I *always arrived"*—and, even if late, I could always say, "Mission Accomplished!"

It *was* a fault—and it *has* been overcome—but I always insisted it was better to have set the goal and to have achieved it, even a day or a month or a year late, than never to have tried in the first place; or having set the goal, to have started out with a flourish and then to have given up and quit.

I do now strive, with every pressure, to complete projects and to accomplish various objectives *on time.*

GOD DOES THINGS ON TIME! God is never a single second late. It took me years to learn that lesson, and I pass the experience on to you for what it is worth.

First Security Council Session

But on March 23, 1946, I had not yet overcome the last-second-dash tendency. Even when I started out on time, something always happened along the way, it seemed, to necessitate that final leap for the departing train—or, in this instance, plane.

I decided to drive the car to Portland airport. On this occasion, I believe we started in time. But we encountered tire trouble—or car trouble of some nature—along the way. After an enforced stop at a garage, it became doubtful whether I could reach Portland in time. Mrs. Armstrong went along to see me off on the plane, and both of our sons, one of whom drove the car back to Eugene.

It was a wild, nerve-shattering ride in the rain the remaining seventy-some miles. I don't think Mrs. Armstrong ever forgot it. But, as usual, I arrived at the airport at the last split second.

Sometimes we need to reflect back on events such

132

as this. We need to remind ourselves of the swift pace at which this world is traveling. This trancontinental flight was not flown nonstop in four hours in a big jet plane—as thousands fly the distance every day now. The best available then was this little two-prop DC-3. We made stops at Pendleton, Oregon; Pocatello, Idaho; Salt Lake City, Utah; Cheyenne, Wyoming; Denver, Colorado; Omaha, Nebraska; Chicago, Illinois; Detroit, Michigan; Washington, D.C.; and New York La Guardia Airport. This flight lasted all night and next day, arriving in the evening.

However, during that very week I was in New York, air transportation took a big leap ahead. The larger DC-4s were inaugurated. On my return flight, to Los Angeles, I enjoyed the thrill of what seemed then like a *huge* DC-4, with stops only at Washington, D.C., Nashville, Dallas, El Paso, and Los Angeles. It was an overnight hop!

As we flew over Manhattan after takeoff, it was 9 p.m. We arrived at Burbank Airport around 6:30 a.m. I shall never forget the exhilarating sensation I felt, walking up Hollywood Boulevard before 7 a.m.—before many people were out on the street, and thinking, "And only 9 o'clock last night I was looking down on the lights of New York!"

I thought of my first trip to the West Coast in 1924, in a Model-T Ford—eighteen arduous days from Des Moines, Iowa—just a little over half way across the United States. And now, only twenty-two years later, I had come all the way from New York just overnight! It seemed to me we were living in a tremendous age!

But think what has happened since then. Next came the DC-6s, and the 3-tailed Constellations; then the still larger DC-6Bs; then the DC-7s, when we felt planes had reached the ultimate. But soon even that

133

model was improved and enlarged into the DC-7Bs, and rivalling it was the Super Constellation. But then a little later we were gasping for breath when the 707 jets occurred.

I was a passenger on the first overnight jet flight from Los Angeles to New York—leaving Los Angeles International Airport about 1:30 a.m., after midnight, arriving in New York early morning.

And now there is the giant 747, besides the DC-10, and, in Europe, the manufacture of the SST! I suppose we soon shall be leaving New York in rocket planes, arriving in Los Angeles *before we start,* due to the three-hour difference in time. Already, with this time differential, jet planes arrive in Los Angeles only about three hours after leaving London, England, on polar flights!

Yes, *time flashes past*—and it is LATER THAN WE THINK!

But back, now, to New York, where I arrived the evening of March 24, 1946. Next morning I took the subway out to Hunter College. I had full access to the press room set up for the opening sessions of the Security Council, because of my press card from the State Department.

But, in these first deliberations of the BIG POWERS who were members of the Security Council, I found no moves toward peace, but only a continuation of the bickering, accusing, and struggle for selfish advantage I had witnessed at the San Francisco Conference.

Special Dispatch from the Security Council

The very START of the United Nations is summarized in the special dispatch I filed in the press room, sent by wire to Eugene, Oregon, and published on page 7 of the March-April *Plain Truth* of that year. It was short, so I reproduce it here:

134

"UNO Security Council, New York. *Special:* As Secretary of State Byrnes said in opening the first meeting of the Security Council of the United Nations Organization today: 'This is a moment of great importance in the history of the world. With this meeting the Security Council of the UNO begins to function permanently and continuously.'

"I write this from the press room of this temporary headquarters of the Security Council. The session begins today as all such conferences do, with speeches by important personages. Press men and women are milling around in the press room here, writing and filing, for their papers, thousands of words, reporting names and happenings.

"But what is being said in these opening speeches; and what is being sent out from here to be read in newspapers throughout the world is not of itself important.

"What is important is what is going on in the mind of Joseph Stalin, over in Moscow, Russia!

"What is important is what is still in the minds of multiple millions of Germans poisoned by Goebbels' propaganda, and for which poison our occupation forces have no cure!

"The world's LAST HOPE of preventing atomic annihilation lies IN HARMONY in this vital Security Council of the UNO. BUT THERE IS NO REAL HARMONY!

"An open break on the Iranian dispute this week would bomb UNO out of useful existence, make immediately imperative the British-American alliance advocated by Mr. Churchill and possibly lead to imminent war.

"Russia is not ready for another war now. Consequently the Iranian dispute will have been worked out in some way before you read these lines.

135

"The Security Council will continue to function for the present. But that does not mean the kind of harmonious unity between the Big Three IMPERATIVE FOR PREVENTION OF ATOMIC WAR!

"In the minds and hearts of the principals here, and in Moscow, London and Washington, there is not that kind of unity. THERE CAN NEVER BE PERMANENT WORLD PEACE UNTIL NATIONS AND THEIR LEADERS LEARN THE WAY TO PEACE. THAT WAY THEY DO NOT KNOW AND WILL NOT CONSIDER!

"There is a beehive of activity here though this conference is on a much smaller scale than the San Francisco Conference, a year ago: frankly, it all reminds me of the adages 'much ado about nothing' and 'tempest in a teapot.'

"The WAY to permanent peace I DO NOT FIND HERE!

"But what I do find here is the way men and nations will insist upon following until the *entire Babylonish world order finally topples to a self-imposed oblivion.*

"AND THAT DAY IS NOT FAR OFF! IT'S LATER THAN WE THINK!"

Work Outgrows Eugene

Even before this flight to New York to cover the Security Council opening, it had become painfully apparent that the work had outgrown Eugene, Oregon. We had started *daily* broadcasting, six nights a week, nationwide, on the two most powerful radio stations covering the United States. The program, beginning October 1, 1945, had gone *daily* on 100,000-watt XELO, Juarez, Mexico, just across the Rio Grande River from El Paso, Texas, at 8 p.m. on the clock (Mountain time) and 800 on the radio dial six nights a week. At the same time we had gone on 150,000-watt XEG, Monterrey,

136

Mexico, six nights a week at 8 p.m. Central standard time. Also the program started simultaneously on our first 50,000-watt West-Coast station, XERB, just south of San Diego, at 9 p.m., Sunday nights only. This station was heard from Mexico to Alaska up and down the coast, and reaching as far as Montana and Alberta.

I should mention here that none of these stations have more than a fraction of the effective coverage today that they had then, even though the power remains the same. The number of radio stations in the United States has increased rapidly, until there are several times as many now as then. For example, in Eugene, Oregon there was one station then. These hundreds of additional stations, on all frequencies up and down the radio dial, cut in tremendously on the superpower stations, so that they do not reach out as far or as effectively as they did in 1945 and 1946.

After October 1, 1945, when this superpower national-coverage nightly broadcasting began, our office staff at Eugene increased rapidly. The one office we had first occupied in the IOOF building expanded to four, with six times our original space, including one large general workroom. By this time I had an office manager in charge of the general workroom, and about nine girls. We had acquired equipment for mailing. Through the years, this type of equipment has been stepped up gradually, a step at a time.

Originally, the mailing list was handwritten on two sheets of paper. The first few years Mrs. Armstrong kept this list. All copies of *The Plain Truth* were addressed by hand. Then, about the time we moved into the IOOF building, we picked up an antiquated, second-hand, foot-powered addressing machine, with which we could use the Elliott stencils.

These stencils were cut on a typewriter.

But by the end of 1945 we had our first Elliott addressing machine. Later, as the work continued to grow, we stepped up to the Addressograph system, with metal plates. Today, of course, we keep our mailing list on IBM computer.

However, I was confronted not only with the problem of getting 75,000 copies of the magazine printed each issue, having outgrown local commercial printing facilities, but also with the problem of recording six half-hour programs each week.

By this time I was going to Portland for recording. I was having to spend an average of three days each week in Portland, away from my office. Even this meant recording two half-hour programs each day that I was in Portland. This was too strenuous an assignment, as a regular grind. When more than one half-hour of full speech is recorded in a day, the quality and effectiveness of the second one suffers. There is bound to be a physical letdown in the second program.

For a while, I avoided spending half the week in Portland by installing a regular telephone broadcast line, connecting my office with the recording studio in Portland. But this was not satisfactory.

Radio headquarters for the United States was Hollywood, with New York a sort of secondary headquarters. The best-equipped major recording studios were all in Hollywood and New York. It was becoming more and more necessary to have the recording done in Hollywood. So, by December, 1945, I was making trips as often as possible to Hollywood to do the recording, and to look for a location to move our headquarters.

Searching a Location in Pasadena

At first, I thought only of moving our office to the Los Angeles area, accessible to Hollywood, and to the larger printing establishments in Los Angeles for adequate facilities for printing *The Plain Truth*. The idea of a college didn't strike my mind until 1946.

Of all places, however, that Mrs. Armstrong and I did *not* want to live, Hollywood headed the list. Neither did we want to live in Los Angeles. It was too large a city, and we regarded it as the spawning ground of crackpot religions. We did not want to be identified with it.

So, needing to be accessible to both Hollywood and Los Angeles, yet desiring to live in neither, we turned to Pasadena.

We had first visited Pasadena in 1941. We knew it was totally different from either Hollywood or Los Angeles—or Beverly Hills. Pasadena was a cultural city, conservative, and a city of homeowners.

It must have been in December, 1945, while in Hollywood for recording, that I began making a series of arduous, patience-trying trips to Pasadena in search of office space and a place to live. At this time we had no home, as explained previously. We had lived in various motels in Eugene, and later in a rooming house.

Day after day I "tramped" afoot all over Pasadena, looking for a suitable location. Nothing suitable seemed to open. I would return to my hotel room in Hollywood at night dog-tired.

Idea of College Germinates

As the weeks and months sped by, an idea was begotten in my mind. As the work was growing, the need of additional trained help was becoming more and more apparent.

Up to this time I had been holding nightly evangelistic campaigns in various towns and cities in Oregon and Washington. Nearly always there had been enough

139

converts to organize a small church group. But there was no minister to pastor the little flock. Not one of them lasted longer than six months. I had to realize that sheep cannot endure without a shepherd.

In Eugene, one of the four larger churches conducted a school for training ministers. It became headquarters for a new denomination. I had noticed that once *they* established new small church groups here and there, their little churches continued to hold together and grow. They had ministers available to pastor each new church raised up. They had a school for training ministers.

If necessity is the mother of invention, perhaps God created the necessity to get through my thick skull the realization that God wanted a college of His own for the training of His ministers, as well as other trained personnel that soon would be required for His rapidly growing work.

What KIND of College?

And so it came about that, by the time of my flight to New York in late March, 1946, I was well aware of the need for a college. And I knew that college must be located in Pasadena, California.

As I thought and planned—*and prayed* for wisdom and guidance—the *kind* of school to be established gradually took shape in my mind. It must *not* be a "Bible School" or a theological seminary. There was a vital REASON!

The one profession no man is free to choose for himself is Christ's ministry. The true ministers of Jesus Christ are CHOSEN BY HIM—just as He chose His original apostles. Jesus said: "Ye have not chosen me, but I have chosen you, and ordained you" (John 15:16).

I had learned, by observation and experience of

140

others, that invariably if God *does* call a man to His ministry, that man will try to run from it—as Jonah did. I did the same, myself. But, if a man decides for himself that he wants to be a minister, invariably time and the fruits demonstrate that Christ never called him.

The students in this school *must not* come with the expectation of becoming a minister. Again, specialized BIBLE instruction alone would not be enough. In today's world of wide diffusion of education, only an *educated* ministry can adequately represent Jesus Christ.

The type of college soon became crystal clear. It must be a LIBERAL ARTS college, offering a general cultural education, with biblical and theological training offered as *ONE* of *several* major courses. And then there could be a Graduate School of Theology for those who, after four years of undergraduate work, appeared as possible or probable future ministers *chosen by the living CHRIST.*

Also, because we would need trained girls and women in the work, and because most effective development of character, personality, poise, and true culture is better achieved by social contact of both sexes, it became plain that the college must be coeducational, admitting girls as well as men.

With all this in mind, I planned to fly from New York to Los Angeles.

And that explains my cross-country flight to Los Angeles in one of the very first DC-4s, about the first of April, 1946. Arriving early that morning in Hollywood, I telephoned Mrs. Armstrong at Eugene, and we decided she would catch a plane that same day and join me in Los Angeles. That flight is one of the reasons she gave up flying, except when it was absolutely necessary. She had suffered a severe case of airsickness.

In Search of a COLLEGE Location

By that time I *knew* there had to be a liberal arts college. I knew what kind of college. I knew what its basic policies must be.

What I then had in mind was a small college of one building. There was no idea of beautiful campus grounds. The beautiful, spacious, magnificently landscaped campuses we now have were of GOD'S planning, not mine.

But I did not yet know CHRIST'S mind as to what constituted a suitable location. My conception was merely a building with three or four classrooms, and a small auditorium or assembly room. Of course there had to be office space for our growing mailing office. There was no thought, then, about dormitory space or housing.

After Mrs. Armstrong joined me, we remained for some two or three weeks recording the daily program in Hollywood studios, and spending all available time searching for a location in Pasadena.

It was a long, arduous, tiresome search day after day. Finally, I found a vacant lot west of the arroyo that seemed somewhat near my conception of a suitable location. It was in a residence section, where two streets joined like the base of a V at an intersection. This lot was triangular in shape, rather rounded at the base of the V. It contained perhaps a third of an acre of ground. I envisioned a triangular, V-shaped building to be erected on this lot. The idea of spacious campus grounds simply did not occur to me.

With this concept in mind, I consulted two architects in Hollywood who worked in partnership. They designed preliminary sketches of the building I had in mind. When laid out on paper, the building occupied

142

nearly the whole of the lot, leaving room only for a small patio.

We returned to Eugene, Oregon, with the problem of how to manage the purchase of the ground, and the financing of construction. This problem proved to be a real headache. We had the money for neither. The income for the work must have been between $50,000 and $75,000 per year at that time, but operational expenses of the broadcasting and publishing work had a habit of keeping equal with, and always trying to run ahead of income.

In June we returned to Hollywood, accompanied this time by our two sons. Dick was then approaching eighteen, and Ted was sixteen. I began to feel we needed more ground. I continued the daily trips to Pasadena. Finally I found a vacant plot of some four or five lots —perhaps 250 feet by about 100 feet, on California Street, on a corner. This site would at least make possible a larger patio.

I made preliminary plans to buy it. The money was not on hand at the moment. But I planned to set aside a definite amount each week, until enough for a down payment would accumulate. I hoped to have this within three months.

The First Baptizing Tour

Meanwhile, scores of letters had been received from radio listeners coast to coast requesting baptism. There were requests from all over the South, the Middle West, and even Florida. You've heard people speak of things tugging at their hearts. If ever anything tugged at our hearts these appeals did. Mrs. Armstrong and I felt they could be deferred no longer.

So we had planned a nationwide tour to visit these people personally and baptize all who were found ready.

We were still driving our 1941 DeSoto. It was one of the best cars ever manufactured in America, but it was now more than five years old. While recording in Hollywood, and searching further in Pasadena, we left the car for about a week in a Hollywood garage for a complete overhaul.

Meanwhile, I spent many hours in our hotel room sorting out many scores of electrical transcription discs that had been broadcast six months or more previously, for repeat broadcast during the weeks of our tour. These had to be sent to the stations so that the program would continue daily until our return to Eugene, when I would resume recording new programs.

I felt that by our return from the baptizing tour we might have enough accumulated in a special fund for a down payment on this Pasadena plot of ground. The hope was that we would be able to pay off the balance within a year, and then, with the ground paid for, obtain a loan with a mortgage on the ground for construction of the college building.

We started the baptizing tour one evening, so that we could drive through the heat of the desert to Las Vegas during the cooler hours of the night. It must have been near 2 a.m. when we arrived in Las Vegas. The car was now in good shape mechanically, even though five and a half years old—it was in good shape, that is, all except the tires.

Perhaps many of our readers will remember the scarcity—almost nonexistence of good tires after those war years. Our tires were mostly recaps. The rubber supply had been largely shut off during the war, and the tire makers had turned to synthetics. They were not yet perfected in quality as they are today.

I think it was the next day out of Las Vegas we began having our tire troubles. Time after time we had

144

blowouts. At one filling station a dealer sold us a recap tire that lasted just long enough to get us far enough away that we could not afford to turn back and demand a replacement. Finally, at a town in Texas, we found a man, whom I believe I baptized, who had ration coupons or some kind of priority for two or three new tires, which he insisted we take, at his sacrifice. After this we had little tire trouble.

Bathtub Baptizing

I think a few of the unique experiences of that first baptizing tour are worth recording.

Some time before this, I had obtained in Eugene a lightweight rubber wader's suit. The soles of the feet were of heavier rubber, and the suit came up to the body almost to the armpits. I used this rubber suit for baptizing. In nearly all cases we were able to find a local stream, or small lake suitable for the baptizing ceremony.

One night we had been delayed by previous visits by some hours in reaching Lake Charles, Louisiana. It was rather late in the evening—perhaps 10 o'clock—when we arrived. We had made appointment by letter to meet a number of people at this home. They were all patiently waiting when we arrived. But there was no available river or lake for baptizing. I do not remember the details specifically. But I seem to remember that there had been rains, and there was swamp water, and it was positively unsafe—either because of snakes or poisonous matter in the water.

I do remember these people said there simply was no available water anywhere for baptizing. The idea of using the bathtub was suggested. I had never done this, or heard of it—but the requirement was enough water to "bury" the candidate in the "watery grave," and so

145

I decided the bathtub could serve in the absence of anything else. It was a struggle to get the candidates completely "buried" in the water, but I succeeded.

We had to forego baptizing one man in Florida altogether. He said the swamp waters in the area were so dangerous he would not risk his life going into them. There was no bathtub!

On this tour we zigzagged up and down, going north from New Orleans through Mississippi as far as Memphis, back down through Alabama, into western Florida, up the Atlantic Coast through Georgia, South Carolina, North Carolina, Virginia, into Washington, D.C., New York, and as far as Portland, Maine. Then across New Hampshire and Vermont, and up to Montreal, Canada.

Then on to Ottawa and Toronto, with a side-tour by boat to Niagara Falls and return. Then across Canada to Windsor and Detroit. On to Chicago, Des Moines, then again south into Oklahoma, then west through Kansas and back to Canon City, Colorado, where I had held the evangelistic campaign a year or two before. Then northwest across the Rockies and on to Eugene, Oregon.

Led to GOD'S Location

By November, in 1946, I had again gone to Hollywood for recording, and was again making trips over to Pasadena in search for a location for the college.

I had not been able to save out the weekly amounts planned to accumulate a fund for the purchase of the site I then had in mind. And by this time I had learned that, being a nonprofit church, and not a commercial business, it would be impossible for us to borrow the money to construct a college building, even if we had the ground already paid for.

146

It seemed every door for opening the college was slammed shut in my face. Yet I knew God was leading me to start a college that would be His college. There was no doubt whatsoever of that!

It was discouraging. It was frustrating! But I was determined not to give up. One real estate broker I had contacted in my search was a Mrs. McCormick. Her husband had been a real estate broker, and after his death she carried on the business. I had found her to be an intelligent and experienced businesswoman in her field, who at the same time remained every whit a lady of culture and refinement. In going the rounds of real estate agents, I chanced to drop in once again at her office.

"Oh, Mr. Armstrong," she said, "I'm glad you dropped in. I have a property I'd like to show you. It isn't quite what you have in mind, but I think it might be worth your while to take a look at it."

I was taken to a small mansion of some eighteen rooms, on Grove Street just off of South Orange Grove Boulevard—Pasadena's "millionaire row" residence street. This was a two and a quarter acre place known as the "McCormick estate"—because it had been built by a Mr. Fowler who was vice-president of the International Harvester Corporation, and Mrs. Fowler was the daughter of the founder of International Harvester, Cyrus McCormick.

The property was on a hillside. It had been magnificently landscaped, although it appeared not to have been maintained in good condition for a few years. Beside the main building, there was a four-car garage with two servants' apartments. To the east of these buildings was a beautifully contoured slope to a balustrade, and then a six-foot drop of ornamental concrete retaining wall under the balustrade, dropping

147

to a long, level space known as "the lower gardens." This space was headed by an ornate concrete tempietto, and ended at the other end with a large square pool and a classic pergola.

I could not see how we could use the building which had been a residence, or the large garage, but it did seem that the lower level space might become the building site for the classroom building I had in mind.

Of course, this space was well grown up in weeds, but I knew we could clear that. Also there were two other fountains at either side of the tempietto, and built in as part of it.

But the price was $100,000, and the owner, a Dr. B., whom I will not name for reasons that will be obvious, wanted cash. I shook my head. Indeed it was *not* quite what I had had in mind!

The next day, however, I began thinking it over. The thought occurred to me that it might be possible to use the big house as a classroom building. After all, I remembered suddenly that it was not designed in residential character, but was a concrete building with flat roof, architecturally of institutional appearance rather than residential.

Of course I didn't have the $100,000 cash. Nevertheless, I called Mrs. McCormick on the telephone, suggested this possibility, and asked if I could inspect the property once more, viewing it from this new and different angle.

She arranged another inspection with Dr. B. I could see on this visit—I had hardly taken notice of the inside of the building on the first visit—that the large living room, about twenty-seven by thirty feet, could make a good library room, and even serve as an assembly room. The adjoining large dining room could serve as an additional library room. A small office room off the entrance hall could serve as a small classroom for ten or twelve students.

Upstairs there were three large bedrooms, of adequate size for classrooms seating from thirty to sixty-five or more students, besides other smaller rooms. There was a small three-room penthouse above.

Then I inspected the garage building again. The main garage room, intended to accommodate four automobiles (it had originally been horse stables, but had been rebuilt into a four-car garage and servant apartment building), was even larger than our main larger office room in Eugene, Oregon, used as the mailing room. The apartment rooms to the rear could house our printing department. That left a small office in front, and the living apartments on the second floor could supply the other administrative offices.

For the first time I began to envision GOD'S type of college location. Here were beautiful grounds to provide a small but, once cleared of weeds and relandscaped, magnificent campus with beautiful and majestic trees—palms, deodars, magnolias and other fine specimens.

I asked the two Hollywood architects to inspect the property. "Why," they exclaimed, "here is your college, already built, and with a small but outstandingly beautiful campus."

The Proposition

I telephoned a boyhood Sunday school friend at that time, Dr. Walter Homan, dean of student personnel at San Francisco State College. I had previously consulted him about the founding of a college. I described this property to him.

"Providential!" he exclaimed, "It sounds positively providential!"

149

I telephoned Mrs. Armstrong to come to Hollywood immediately, to have her opinion. She, too, felt it was just the place —and, if we outgrew it, perhaps adjoining estates could be some day acquired.

But how could we make the purchase without any money? That, you may be sure, was the REAL problem, now. Besides, I was not yet convinced in my own mind this was the location God had selected.

An idea came to my mind. It was already mid-November. The first college term would not start until the next September—ten months away. Why not submit a proposition whereby we would start making the largest possible monthly payments, but not take possession until nine payments had been made, by the following July 1. That would give time to prepare for a September opening.

I asked Mrs. McCormick who was the best attorney in Pasadena for the handling of a property transaction. She recommended Judge Russell Morton. I arranged an appointment and went to his office.

Judge Morton recommended, under the circumstances, that a lease-and-option contract would be more attractive as an offer to the owner. I had suggested that we would make monthly payments of $1,000 per month. That was certainly a maximum ambitious monthly payment for me to offer, in our financial circumstances.

But 1 percent per month was rather common practice, and I feared any smaller offer would not even be considered. If this was where God wanted us, I felt I could rely on Him to increase the income enough to cover it.

Judge Morton suggested we draw up a contract providing for taking occupancy the following July 1, continuing on a lease rental basis until the end of twenty-five months. Then the $25,000 so far paid would become the down payment on the purchase, and we would then exercise our option, be given the deed to the property, giving Dr. B. a trust deed until fully paid.

The "Catch" in the Deal

The proposition was drawn up in legal form, and I gave it to Mrs. McCormick to present to Dr. B., with my check for the first $1,000.

Then I prayed earnestly. I asked God to reveal His will respecting His college by causing Dr. B. to accept if that were God's will, but to cause him to reject it, if this was not the place God had chosen for His college. I realized there did not appear to be one chance in a thousand that a man who wanted $100,000 cash would let his property go for only $1,000 per month, with no down payment at the start whatever—and taking two whole years and one additional month to build up a 25 percent down payment.

I was not at all sure this was the place God wanted us—and yet it had begun to look more and more like the finest place we could possibly have. But I knew God would cause it to fall into our hands if that were His will.

I did not hear any answer for two or three days. Then Mrs. McCormick told me she had the contract all signed, sealed, and delivered! The date was November 27, 1946.

For the moment I was elated, grateful, thankful!

But what I didn't know was that apparently Dr. B. had no intention of ever letting us get possession. He was not a medical doctor. He was a doctor of law.

As time went along, it became evident that when July 1, 1947, arrived, Dr. B. had no intention of letting us gain possession. It appeared that his intention was to keep the $9,000 and keep the property too.

151

51

Planning a New-Type College—in U.S. and Europe!

WHEN THE idea of founding a college to provide the future trained personnel for the expanding work was first conceived, I thought immediately of my brother-in-law, Walter E. Dillon. My wife's brother had been a life-long educator. Those who have read the *Autobiography* from the beginning will remember the episode of the oratorical contests at Simpson College, in Iowa, back in 1922-1924. I had worked with him in oratory, when he was a college freshman. He won the state contest. Walter and I had been closer together, from that time, than with our own brothers.

He held a Master's degree in education from the University of Oregon, and had done additional work toward a Ph.D., or an Ed.D. He had started teaching school upon graduating from college, later becoming a principal, and finally principal of the largest public school in Oregon outside the city of Portland. Thus he

152

had had considerable executive and administrative school experience, in addition to being a natural-born and experienced teacher. He was thoroughly familiar with college and university life, methods and procedures. He had the technical experience for academic organization I lacked.

Choosing a President

Immediately when the conception of the college entered my mind, I had contacted my brother-in-law, asking if he would join me in the venture, as president of the college.

"I hardly think I could do that," was his first response. "I don't know much about the Bible. Administering a religious college, I'm afraid, is altogether out of my line."

"But this is not to be a Bible school, or religious college," I quickly explained. "It is to be a straight liberal arts college, although it will offer a course—as one of the majors—in Bible and theology. You won't need to have theological experience. Do you think I would be able to teach that course?"

"I think you have more Bible knowledge and understanding than anybody on earth," he smiled. "You know, I think we'd make a good team in getting this college started. With your business experience and ability, your religious knowledge and experience, and my academic experience—well, I'll think about it."

He did think about it. Often we talked about it. Of course it was a weighty decision for him to make—he had been established since his own college days in Oregon. Finally he decided he would come to Pasadena to help me get the new college started.

Before presenting the lease-option contract as an offer to Dr. B., Mr. Dillon had come to Pasadena to inspect the property and help me decide whether this was the right location. He had been immediately enthusiastic over it.

So now that we had the first segment of the future campus under contract, preparations began in earnest for organizing the thousand and one things required before it could swing open its doors as a going educational institution.

Special Magazine Edition

The very first thing to be done was to produce a special edition of *The Plain Truth*. The problem of recruiting students had been brought up by Mr. Dillon. That is a major problem of colleges and universities.

"The Plain Truth and the broadcast will provide us with students," I had explained.

The first thing to do was to let people know about it. *The Plain Truth* was still an eight-page bimonthly. The next issue was to be the January-February, 1947, number. With it we went up to sixteen pages. I made this a very special, more attractive edition. For the first time, it had a front cover, instead of starting the lead article on the cover. It showed a picture of the entrance to the new college-to-be. The center spread—pages 8 and 9—had a large four-column picture showing a portion of the new campus. The article announcing the new college began on that page, with a four-column headline: "And *now* . . . OUR OWN NEW COLLEGE!"

The article explained that "an amazing new setup has come into our hands that is unique, and, we believe, without parallel! Prospective students learning of the unusual program are thrilled!"

Policies were announced. The article said: "AMBASSADOR offers superior advantages in location, beauty of campus, nature of courses of study, high academic stan-

154

dards . . . advantages in our special recreational and social program, cultural advantages, physical education, *as well as in religious instruction.*

"AMBASSADOR is to be a general liberal arts institution—not a Bible school, ministers' college, or theological seminary. It will fit students for all walks of life, offering a general and *practical* basic education. . . . There is no other college like AMBASSADOR. It is, in a sense, a revolutionary new-type college . . . a forward-looking, progressive institution built on soundest principles, having highest goals and objectives, yet employing the best of proved methods of administration, and maintaining highest academic standards."

The reader will be interested in a little further explanation of the college, which appeared in that article.

"But why should we establish and conduct a college in connection with this, God's work?" the article continued. "The reasons are concrete and vital. . . . The work has grown to a scope where *called,* consecrated, properly educated and specially trained assistants, ministers and evangelists to follow up this work in the field, have become an imperative need. The time has come when we must lay definite plans for carrying the gospel of the Kingdom of God into *all nations,* in *many languages!* Never, until now, could we foresee just how this was to be done. But the time has come; God has given the answer, and moved miraculously to open the way before us. The only answer was a COLLEGE of *our own!*"

But why, then, was this not to be a Bible school or theological seminary?

The article, continuing, explained that:

"Yet, the active ministry is *different* from every other profession in one very important respect. No man ever should enter it of his own volition. . . . A true

155

minister of Jesus Christ must be specially *called* of God. And how may we *know* whether one is really called? Experience has shown human nature to be such that most who *think* that they are called are mistaken, and those who really are called invariably try to run from the calling! Jesus gave us the only test. 'By their fruits,' He said, 'ye shall KNOW.' But the fruits are worked out by experience, and that requires time. For that very reason, *our college cannot be a ministerial college —* though it *is* being designed so that, should we be fortunate enough to find one out of twenty really and truly called to the ministry, that one will have been prepared and properly trained. . . . These considerations led naturally to the policy of making AMBASSADOR a general liberal arts institution for all young men and women, regardless of future vocation, occupation or profession."

The article continued to show what is wrong with this world's education today—what has happened to it—how it has drifted into materialism. It showed that the revelation of God—in the Bible—is the very FOUNDATION of all true knowledge—the right approach to knowledge—the concept through which to view and explain what is seen, measured and observed. But in this world's education, the false theory of evolution has been substituted as that basic concept and foundation.

The article concluded with detailed, but brief, facts about the new college—its location, courses offered, tuition.

Planning College in Europe

It may come as a surprise to many readers, but the conception of a second college abroad actually was generated in late December, 1946, or early January, 1947.

I had gone back to Pasadena at the end of Decem-

156

ber, 1946. On New Year's eve, I spent the night as Dr. B.'s guest, in the building still occupied by him and his sister, which was to become Ambassador College. In these days Dr. B. was very friendly. About 4:30 a.m., New Year's day, I was awakened by crowds trudging up the hill in front of the building, carrying blankets, camp-chairs, and stools.

The world-famous Tournament of Roses parade starts each year just one block south, on Orange Grove Boulevard. This first of our college buildings is only a half block east of Orange Grove boulevard.

This was my first opportunity to see the fabulous Rose Parade. I found the excitement of the throngs lining up along the parade course, beginning on South Orange Grove, and then making a right turn into Colorado Street—the main business street of Pasadena—was even more exciting than the parade—if possible. In order to secure an advantageous position along the curb and parkway, vast throngs begin to assemble long before daylight.

It was during this visit that the idea of the second college in Europe came about. It was during a conversation with Dr. B. I was quite concerned about our future foreign language courses. I knew we had to have people trained in many languages, to get the gospel to all nations. I felt the average foreign language course, as taught in most colleges, inadequate. I wanted our young people to be taught to speak these languages as the natives of those countries do—without a foreign accent. This was almost impossible, as taught in an American classroom. I felt students needed to actually *live* in these foreign countries, learning the languages there.

I knew, of course, that Switzerland is peculiar in that it has no one native language of its own. In northern Switzerland the official language is German.

157

In central and western Switzerland, French is the official language; and in southeastern Switzerland it is Italian. Yet I knew most Swiss people speak all three, and a very large portion speak English beside.

In Switzerland, children are taught the official language of their district from birth. Then at age six most children start to learn a second language, and at age ten or twelve, a third—and often one or two more later.

As we were discussing this situation, Dr. B. mentioned that he had a very close personal friend, a Madame Helene Bieber, of German birth, the widow of a very wealthy Frenchman, who owned the newest, finest, most modern villa in southeastern Switzerland, at Lugano. Mme. Bieber, he said, had lost all her money during the war. It had been in Paris banks, and had been confiscated when the Germans occupied Paris. She had some money in New York banks, but wartime regulations, not yet released, apparently tied it up and prevented transmission of it to Switzerland. She was left with this ultramodern and superelegant five-story villa, facing on beautiful Lake Lugano, yet without funds even to employ a single servant.

"She still has all her fine clothes, dozens of mink wraps and coats, and her villa, but no money," Dr. B. explained. "Since you would not want to start your college over there for about three or four years, I believe you could effect a purchase—if you can stretch to it—on a basis similar to the one between you and me on this property here. You could begin making payments now, which would provide her with an income to live on. She could continue living in her villa for the next three or four years, with an income—sort of eating her cake and having it, too, these first few years. Then, when you take possession and start your school, you will have a very sizable payment made on the purchase.

By that time she will have her money from the New York banks, and will continue to receive regular sizable monthly payments from you for a few more years.

"I think she might be willing to make such a deal—and it would make it possible for you to acquire your second college without capital—just monthly payments, beginning now."

I was intrigued. I did not realize that the "good doctor" actually had designs on marrying the rich widow—surmizing that she probably would also get her money from the Paris banks some day—and that he probably had no more thought of allowing us to actually ever gain possession of the Lake Lugano villa than he did of allowing us to actually gain possession of this property in Pasadena!

I thought over the idea for some time. Finally, along about the tenth of February, 1947—or a day or two later—I talked to Dr. B. on the telephone from Pasadena about the Switzerland idea further. He suggested we go over and see it. He offered to go along. We decided to go immediately. There was a sailing of the Cunard liner *Queen Elizabeth* from New York on February 19. Dr. B. said he would meet me aboard ship.

There was no time to obtain passport or steamer reservations before leaving the West Coast. Dr. B. already had his passport. Under regular routine it required thirty days to obtain one by mail from Oregon. But I knew the Press Officer of the State Department, and felt confident he would be able to get my passport issued immediately, at Washington.

Mrs. Armstrong and I had discussed the matter of her accompanying me. But there not only was the added expense, she had such fear of the water, she felt afraid to sail.

As a young girl her grandmother, born in England,

had told her of a terrible shipwreck on her voyage to America. The grandmother was twelve years of age, when her widowed mother, with her eleven children, sailed to America. Some distance off the banks of Newfoundland, the sailing vessel was torn apart by a hurricane. Six of the children, lashed to a mast, were picked up by another vessel—but the mother and five children were drowned. Hearing the vivid, stark details of this tragedy while a very young girl had put fear of the ocean into my wife's mind. So she had decided not to sail with me to Europe.

Accordingly, on February 12, after my telephone conversation with Dr. B., I procured round-trip tickets and Pullman reservations to New York for myself alone.

I had decided to make the trip to New York this time via Portland, Seattle, and on the crack train of the Great Northern Railway—the "Empire Builder"—to Chicago, thence on the B & O line to Washington, D.C., then to New York. The cost and time was the same as going straight east from Portland on the Union Pacific.

52

Our First Trip Abroad

IT WAS the morning of February 14, 1947. At that very moment, the Shasta Limited was approaching the station at Eugene, Oregon.

Mrs. Armstrong, Mrs. Annie Mann (a later hostess of girls' student residences at the college in Pasadena), and I were in my office. I had my hat and coat on, my suitcase packed and beside me and was throwing last-minute papers into my briefcase.

Suddenly Mrs. Armstrong exclaimed, "I've decided I want to go with you!"

Mrs. Armstrong's *"Shirttail Shoot"*

"Well, *this* is a nice time to make up your mind," I said. "You couldn't possibly get ready in time, now."

"Oh yes I can!" she replied. "Grab your suitcase and typewriter, and *let's hurry!*"

We dashed to the elevator. On the street below,

one of our sons was waiting at the wheel of the car.

"Drive over to our rooms! HURRY!" I said. "Mother's decided to go with me."

At the time, the reader will remember, we were living in two upstairs rooms in a rooming house about five or six blocks from the office. We had sold our home nearly two years before. The work had needed the money.

We were whisked, as only a seventeen-year-old boy can whisk an automobile around corners on two wheels, to our rooming house. We dashed upstairs. Mrs. Armstrong first threw her suitcase out of the closet, asking Mrs. Mann to throw her clothes into it while she pulled them down off hangers and literally threw them out of the closet. In less than two minutes she had dresses, suits, and other things out of dresser drawers, thrown and jammed into her suitcase.

We dashed back downstairs, and the car careened around corners, pulling up to the depot about one minute before the train pulled out. Eugene was a division point on the railroad, and the train stayed there ten minutes while they changed engines and crews. But the train had pulled into the station just about the moment we were coming down the elevator of the office building.

I told my sons to put our luggage on the train, while I dashed across the waiting room floor to the ticket office, and asked for a one-way ticket to Portland. There was not time, now, to procure tickets to New York and return for my wife.

Many, many times I had made what my wife termed "shirttail shoots" for trains. This is one time she herself was guilty.

But the "shirttail shoot" was not over, yet. I now had to pick up her round-trip ticket to New York, while we changed trains at Portland. We had twelve minutes between trains at Portland. But, as usual in those days, there was a long line standing queued before each ticket window. At the very last second, I finally obtained her tickets, caught the train as it was starting.

We arrived in Seattle in the afternoon, and that evening started the long ride from Seattle. It was a rough, jerky ride across the states of Washington, Idaho, Montana, North Dakota, Minnesota and Wisconsin, into Illinois at Chicago. Our Pullman berth must have been at one end of the car, immediately over the wheels, where the riding is much more rough. It was even rougher on the B & O all-night ride into Washington, D.C.

How NOT to Plan Your Trip Abroad

Now ensued a series of exciting events which give the reader an example of how *NOT* to plan your trip abroad.

Arriving in Washington in the morning, we first checked in at the Statler Hotel. Before applying for passports, it was necessary to obtain passport photos of ourselves. We found a leading photograph studio in the hotel. The photographer tried to sell us a dozen larger photographs along with the passport photos.

I had not had my photograph taken for many years. I had never allowed my picture to be reproduced in *The Plain Truth* or any of our literature. I had, for years, even dodged and avoided all camera shots, except a few to be kept within the family. But just prior to this I had received a letter from a radio listener that convinced me I had been wrong.

This listener asked me what I had to hide. He asked me what I would think of a minister if I dropped in at his church, and the pastor hid behind the pulpit while he preached. Would I not think he had something to hide? Would I not become suspicious? He said character is written on one's face, and he always liked to see the faces of those he listened to. Of course, this was not possible on radio but, at least, he said, I ought to let listeners see my picture.

The thought came of using one of these photographs to reprint, but I was still hesitant about printing it in *The Plain Truth.* The photographer made a proposition. Why not place a bulk order for 500? He would make us a very special low price for such an order. He did it all the time, he said, for Congressmen and government officials, who thus sent these photographs to constituents.

So, it occurred to me it might be preferable to send real photographs to just those few who personally requested and wanted them, rather than publishing my picture for all readers to see. We placed an order, I believe, for some 400 of me and 100 of Mrs. Armstrong since most requests we had received were, naturally, for mine. Actually, I think we found later that we should have ordered them just the other way around, for there was a far bigger demand for my wife's picture than the supply. After our return from abroad, these were mailed out to those who had personally requested them.

Next I went to the State Department, but the press officer could not be seen until afternoon. Then I went to the ticket office of the Cunard Line, owners of the great ship the *Queen Elizabeth.* They had one cabin left, space for two, cabin class, on this particular sailing but that was the only space on the ship. We wanted to return mid-March. But there was no space whatever available on the west-bound voyage until August. I was told there might be some chance of a cancellation in the next two days, before sailing. The agent agreed to telephone their New York office, and I could contact them there, after arriving in New York. I purchased the ticket for the cabin on the east-bound passage.

In the afternoon I waited a long while in the office of the State Department Press Officer until he returned, about 4:30 p.m. He was glad to see me again, and immediately called the passport office across the street, asking them to process my passport at once. It was a few moments before closing time when we arrived at the passport office.

They told me our passports would be ready in the morning. I happened to show them my State Department credential card which I carried.

"If you had just shown us that," I was told, "we would have put through your passports earlier in the day, and you could have had them before now."

It was necessary to obtain visas to cross France, and to enter Switzerland, as well as to enter England.

The next morning, February 18, after obtaining the passports, we visited both the Swiss and French embassies, and had their visas stamped in the passports. However, we learned that the British visa had to be obtained in New York.

We had another very rough ride that afternoon on the train to New York—rougher than the others before it.

Arriving in New York, we went to the Ambassador Hotel, where I customarily stopped when in New York. I had wired ahead for a reservation the day before leaving Eugene. But even then my telegram had not arrived in time. The hotel was booked up solid.

"Mr. Armstrong," the desk clerk said, "we certainly try to take care of our regular guests, but we're simply filled up, and booked ahead for about two weeks. But we have arranged a room for you and Mrs. Armstrong in another very good hotel just a couple of blocks away. We were also unable to accommodate your United States Senator from Oregon. You'll see Senator Wayne Morse sitting over there across the lobby."

I was acquainted with Senator Morse. He had been dean of the law school of the University of Oregon, in Eugene, before his election to the Senate. Mrs. Armstrong and I walked across the lobby, and chatted with the Senator a few moments, then went on to the other hotel.

Immediately upon reaching our room, I telephoned the Cunard Line to see if a cancellation had turned up on the return voyage, sailing from Southampton March 15.

"Mr. Armstrong," said the man at the Cunard office, "I would say that your chances are absolutely hopeless. We are booked solid for all our ships—and so are all other steamship lines—until the middle of August. More than that, we have several hundred others on the waiting list—all ahead of you. There's absolutely no chance of so many cancellations that we can fill all of those ahead of you before tomorrow's sailing."

Hopeless or not, I do not give up easily. I determined to call the Cunard office again next morning.

But let me say right here, all this experience is an example of how *not* to plan your trip abroad—on a moment's notice, without passport, steamer or plane reservation, visas, or other preparations. Start planning at least a month ahead.

Out-Determining John Bull

Next morning I telephoned the Cunard office again. The same voice answered at their reservation office. It was the same story.

"I told you, Mr. Armstrong, there's no chance whatever," he said.

But I kept on talking. Soon we got into quite a conversation. I was telling him about a branch college in Europe. The idea was something new in education. He became interested, and so I kept on talking. After a while he said, "Would you excuse me a moment? I have to take a call on the other phone. I'll be right back."

In just about fifty seconds his voice came back.

"What lucky star were you born under, Mr. Armstrong?" he asked. "Talk about miracles! Do you know what that call was? It was a man cancelling a cabin on the March 15 sailing from Southampton, and just because you're on the phone at this moment, I'm going to forget all those other applications on the waiting list ahead of you, and let you have it!"

It was no "lucky star," but it probably *was* a miracle! Mrs. Armstrong and I walked hurriedly over to the closest subway station on Lexington Avenue, and caught the first express train to downtown Wall Street, and hurried over to the Cunard office, where we procured our return passage on the *Queen Elizabeth.* Without it, we knew we would not be able to obtain British visas, or even to board ship that night.

The actual sailing was set for about 5 a.m. next morning, but all passengers had to be aboard ship by 11 p.m. that same night, Wednesday, February 19.

Immediately we took a subway back uptown, and went to the British visa office in Rockefeller Center on 5th Avenue. A line was queued before the visa window. I waited in line. Finally reaching the window, I was told that no visas could be issued in less than thirty days' time. I could file my application now, but the visa could not be issued for thirty days.

"But I must have this visa immediately, today!" I

said, "Look, here is our ticket on the *Queen Elizabeth.* We have to be aboard ship before 11 o'clock tonight."

"That makes no difference, sir," replied the clerk. "We require thirty days to issue a visa. You Americans are always trying to do things in a hurry. But you are in a British office now, and we don't rush things through in such a mad manner."

"This may be a British office, but you're in AMERICA, now, Mister," I returned. "And here, we do things the AMERICAN way. I have tickets to board the *Queen Elizabeth* tonight, and we are going to board it!"

"My dear sir," the clerk said politely, "we British are quite determined, you know. Would you please step aside, now. You are holding up this queue."

"Well now," I smiled, "you may be Johnny Bull, and you may have bulldog determination, and stubbornness, but right now, I'm *more* determined. I will not move from here until you stamp the visa in my passport. If you want to make room for those behind me, just stamp it, here."

"But I simply *have* to clear the way for the others behind you. Would you continue talking, then, to one of the officers at one of the desks behind me, so I can get to the others?"

"That depends," I said. "Is the man at the desk behind you your superior? Does he have more authority to issue a visa than you?"

Assured that he did have superior authority, I agreed that if this officer would come to the window and agree to let me inside the gate to see him, I would leave the window and continue with the man higher up.

He asked me why I had not sent in my application thirty days earlier. I explained that this was an emergency trip, planned suddenly only six days before, out on the West Coast. I explained how we had picked up

168

passports on the run, as it were, and how miraculously space on the ship had opened up, and we had all the other required visas. Now all we needed was the British visa, so we could land at Southampton and pass through England on the way to Switzerland and return.

But he, too, was stubborn. He refused to issue the visa short of thirty days. It seemed very unjust. If he was determined, I was *more* determined. I kept talking.

"Mr. Armstrong," he said, finally, "I simply *must* ask you to please excuse me. I have much work to do."

"I will not leave until you stamp the visa on our passports," I said with finality.

"Well then," he compromised, "will you leave now and come back at 3:30 this afternoon?"

The office closed at 4 p.m.

"Will you promise to see me then, if I do?" I asked. He promised, and Mrs. Armstrong and I left. Promptly at 3:30 p.m. we returned. But this man avoided even looking our way. I stood at the gate, waiting. He did not keep his promise. He refused even to glance my way, and I was unable to open the gate and go to him.

Finally, at five minutes to four, he walked into another room. A moment later, another man, who sat at another desk, after cleaning up his desk to leave for the day, saw me waiting at the gate. He came to the gate, asking if there was something I wanted before the closing time.

"Yes indeed," I replied. "Mr. Blank asked me to return at this time for my visa. We are boarding the *Queen Elizabeth* tonight. But Mr. Blank just went into another room, and didn't seem to know I was here."

"Oh, I'll take care of it for him, then," he smiled. "Will you step in?" We walked over to his desk, and he stamped visas in our passports. I got out quickly, before Mr. Blank returned.

The Floating City

With nerves almost shattered, we walked up the gang-plank of the *Queen Elizabeth* about 9 o'clock that night, looking forward to five quiet days aboard ship.

But there was no quiet until after 11 p.m., when all visitors had to leave the ship. The letters Mrs. Armstrong and I wrote our children tell the story:

Wednesday Night, 11:39 p.m.
February 19, 1947

Hello, kids!

We are on board—mail leaves in ten minutes—must be brief.

Visitors all have just left. This is the largest passenger liner ever built—*tremendous!* It's been like an exaggerated movie premier—mobs throng all over—fourteen decks—blocks and blocks long—everyone dressed up—many in evening clothes—everyone happy—crowd surrounding Mischa Auer getting autographs (he's going to Europe on the Queen)—now it's quieting down. This ship carries 3,500 passengers—a city *floating!* One gets lost on it.

At last we're really going to England—Europe! We have a nice small private stateroom to ourselves.

Dick and Ted, prove you are grown up and worthy of being trusted and taking responsibility. That's the way to get more privileges. Ted *dress warm.* That's all the time I have.

Keep the home fires burning. They say there's no coal for fires in England or Europe. We'll probably freeze and starve—but *here we go!*

Love,
Dad

Dearest Children all of you,

It's a quarter of midnight. We are aboard and lack a whole lot of having seen the ship. It's immense. We are going to bed.

Ted if only I knew you were taking care of yourself I would be much happier. *You must not* go out in a "T" shirt when you are accustomed to a sweater. Now take care of yourself.

I can't realize that I'm at last going to see England. I've always wanted to. This is a *beautiful* ship. We'll get pictures of it.

We wish we could see all of you. We send a world of love to our dear family.

Mother

The *Queen Elizabeth* was 1,031 feet long—almost a quarter mile. It had fourteen decks; its gross tonnage was 83,673 tons—about double that of a large battleship; it carried 3,500 passengers.

I was much amused at a cockney elevator operator aboard ship. Of course, actually the ship did not have elevators—the British call them "lifts." In calling out the various decks, he would say: " 'C' Deck next—'C' for Charlie." Then, " 'R' Deck next —'R' for Restaurant." Then, " 'B' next—'B' for Bertie." Then, " 'I' Deck next—'I' for Albert."

We had the smoothest crossing ever experienced by members of the crew—so some of them told us. We had prayed for it. Nevertheless, Mrs. Armstrong spent two days in bed with seasickness.

Aboard ship, at the reservations office, reservations were made for us at the Dorchester in London. At Southampton, the boat train to London was waiting in the Customs shed at the docks. I had obtained Pullman car reservations. This does not mean sleeping cars in

171

England—just first-class coaches. The tickets had been obtained at the reservations window aboard ship. In the Customs shed, an officer examined our tickets, and told me we were in Car 'I'. So we walked almost the length of the train, past cars 'C', 'D', 'E', and on down to 'I'. Then we learned that we had encountered another cockney—and we had to trudge back to car 'A'.

Arriving London

We docked at Southampton on Tuesday, February 25. Thursday morning, the twenty-seventh, a reporter from the *Daily Graphic* called on the telephone and asked for an interview. He arrived at 12:30, so I invited him to lunch in the Dorchester Grill Room. The idea of a college with one unit in America, and one in Europe, with a number of qualifying students transferring from the one on scholarship to the other was a new idea in education.

"A *wonderful* idea," he exclaimed. I did not get to see his story in the paper about it, since we left early the next morning for the Continent.

Our first real look at London was on Wednesday morning, February 26. In some respects it was like a dream. To us, it was a different world. Some of our first impressions were recorded in letters to our children. Here are brief excerpts:

From Mrs. Armstrong: written Wednesday: "It's *so different* here in London. Cabs, buses, everything— never saw such a conglomeration of buildings, so many twists and turns in the streets. We went to Somerset House today. I thought I would look up Grandma's birth record, but couldn't find it. However, I don't know just the year or place of her birth. We have a nice room, but cold. Lights all go off and elevators (pardon me— "lifts") stop running from 9 until noon, and from 2 to

4 p.m. Scarcely any heat in the coldest winter England has had since 1840, around two years before Grandma was born. The sun shone brightly today—first time since five weeks ago. We've seen Buckingham Palace, Parliament buildings, etc.—of course, so far only a very small part of London, for we slept till almost noon."

We had not arrived in London until after midnight.

A portion of my letter, written same day: "Dear Kids all, at home: We have spent our first day in old London town. As mother told you, because of a strike, and due to coal shortage, we were kept on board the *Queen Elizabeth* until 7:30 last night. Our train didn't get started until 9 p.m. We almost froze. We're almost freezing now. The temperature in the hotel room and lobby is about fifty-five degrees. It's a different world. Old buildings—many in ruins, all originally nearly white, and of stone, now almost black—coal smoke."

Attending Royal Reception

Just before noon on Thursday, I received a telephone call from the private secretary to "His Excellency, the Ambassador and Plenipotentiary Extraordinary of Saudi Arabia, Sheik Hafiz Wabba." She said that His Excellency had heard that I was in London—I had an hour's interview with him at the San Francisco Conference, in 1945—and wished to extend a very special personal invitation for Mrs. Armstrong and me to attend a royal reception to be held that evening in the ballroom of our hotel, the Dorchester.

I wondered how the sheik had come to know we were in London. Then I remembered that the day before I had seen some Arab officials in their flowing robes in the lobby of the hotel. I had gone to the reception desk to inquire whether Sheik Hafiz Wabba was in the hotel. He was not, but I was informed that

173

he did frequently come to the hotel. I had mentioned that I knew him. I supposed the reception office had made our presence known to the sheik.

This royal reception was in honor of H.R.H., the Crown Prince, Emir Saud. He later became King Saud of Saudi Arabia. The Sheik's secretary said that His Excellency would like to have another chat with me, and this reception would be the only opportunity, since he was leaving with the Crown Prince the next morning.

We had planned to leave London for Zurich that afternoon. We had an appointment to meet Dr. B., and Madame Helene Bieber in Zurich that evening. When I expressed regret at being unable to attend, due to this appointment in Zurich, the secretary urged me to postpone the Zurich appointment and stay over for the reception. It would be, she said, the most glamorous and important social event held in England since the war, and again reminded me it was the only opportunity for another interview with the sheik.

I said that I would telephone Dr. B. in Zurich, and if I could postpone our appointment, I would call her back. The appointment was postponed, and I notified the ambassador's secretary. A little later a specially engraved invitation arrived at our apartment by private messenger.

Perhaps excerpts from a letter written to the family at home immediately after returning from the reception will best describe the experience. This is what I wrote:

"Just this second we returned from the royal reception held by Sheil Hafiz Wabba and H.R.H. Emir Saud, the Crown Prince of Arabia. It was very colorful. About 200 invited guests—earls, dukes with their monocles and flashing decorations, admirals, commodores, dozens of ambassadors—we saw those from Turkey, Chile, Albania, etc. We entered in couples. A brightly uni-

174

formed page announced each couple in a very loud voice, as 'Lord and Lady so and so,' 'Admiral and Mrs. so and so,' 'The Turkish Ambassador,' and so on. We were announced as 'Mr. and Mrs. Herbert W. Armstrong.'

"The Arabs, in their flowing robes, stood in the receiving line. Mother advanced first, then I—since this was the customary way. First we were greeted by His Excellency Sheik Hafiz Wabba. In turn he introduced us to the tall and very handsome crown prince, whom they addressed as 'Your Royal Highness.' Then the remaining five or six top Arab officials. Then the crowd mingled around, munching on tiny sandwiches, French pastries, while being served tea. The dress was not formal. The people over here have been through a *war*, in a way we Americans have no conception, and they simply don't have many fine clothes over here right now. There were very few in evening clothes. The clothes of several were becoming a bit threadbare. Yet the titled ones wore their glittering decorations. Mother was the nicest-looking woman there.

"We had a very nice, brief, private talk with the sheik, and got a statement for my article on the Palestine situation for the next *Plain Truth.*

"We were seated at a table, when the royal party approached. Immediately we arose, and took seats at another table. The Crown Prince sat at the table we had vacated, but before doing so smiled and motioned for us to be seated beside him at the table. He does not speak a word of English. I felt we should not accept his invitation, since it was apparent that table was intended for the royal party. He was merely trying to be cordial. Twice he smilingly motioned a welcome to us, but I smilingly and apologetically shook my head and refrained."

That Crown Prince later became the king, when his father, old King Ibn Saud, died. That experience was the first time we had ever come into personal contact with royalty.

While I was writing the above, Mrs. Armstrong was writing the following about the reception:

"We just returned to our room from the royal reception. I felt just like Little Lord Fauntleroy. It was all so interesting. We were announced in a thundering voice to all. Presented to Sheik Hafiz Wabba (His Excellency), who in turn presented us to the Crown Prince (His Royal Highness), and on down the receiving line. We were among the lords and ladies, dukes and earls, and admirals and ambassadors of many countries. They are all *just folks*. We were so interested in it all—tables everywhere—you could sit or not. In the center of the ballroom were large banquet tables with different kinds of food and drinks. One just walked up anywhere and helped himself. There was beautiful music—violins and piano. The Palestinian announcer for the BBC branch there introduced himself to me and then to two ladies, and I later introduced him to Dad.

"It's March 1 now;" (this part evidently written later) "I'm all packed. We leave soon for France. It's bitter cold, no heat at all in the rooms. I fill the bathtub with hot water and get in until heated through, and then jump into bed. Last night the maid brought me a stone hot water bottle that kept me warm. Poor Britain is suffering even worse, it seems, than during the war. Everything but water is rationed."

And Now—the Continent

The evening of the first of March I was writing a letter with my portable typewriter on my lap, in my upper berth in a compartment on the sleeping car of a French train from Calais, bound for Zurich. Mrs. Armstrong occupied the lower berth. This is part of what I wrote:

"Here we are in France. Just boarded this train a half hour ago. It's now dark. At 4:30 this afternoon we were on a boat crossing the English Channel, and the sun not far from the horizon sinking in the west. I looked at my larger watch, which is still set Eugene time, and it was 8:30 a.m. I did a little quick calculating and discovered that at that hour, you were looking at the same sun, same distance from the horizon, rising in the east, while we were looking at it setting in the west. We are one-third way around the earth from you. In other words, you people are walking almost upside down. I know you are, because one of us is, and it isn't us over here.

"Calais is quite a little town. We've seen many bombed and shattered buildings. OUR bombs probably did that. The Nazis had this town. Seems strange, like a dream, to think we are actually over here where the war was fought, in territory that was occupied by the Germans. I don't see any Germans here now. The people here are French. And I mean FRENCH! At the dock and depot, which are joined together, the officers or attendants, or whatever they were, had typical French caps, like French army officers, and flowing capes. The porters, seeking opportunity to carry luggage for the tips, yelled out, 'Por*teur!* Por*teur!* Por*teur!*" with accent on the last syllable—or equally on both. The train porters can't speak a word of English. They say 'Oui!' (pronounced 'we').

"It's now 8:45 p.m. Just at that last paragraph we were called to dinner. A Frenchman walks through the cars ringing a cute little bell. We weren't sure it was a call to dinner, or whether there was even a dining car on the train. We were in the rear car, so we started

177

forward. After going through all the sleepers, and about four day coaches (European type, six to a compartment), we came to what looked like the baggage car, decided there was no diner and turned back. Two cars back a porter stopped us. He couldn't understand us; we couldn't understand him. We tried by motions to make him understand we were looking for the dining car—*if* any. Mother suddenly remembered that the word 'cafe' is a French word, but probably we didn't pronounce it the French way—at least he didn't understand. I pointed to my mouth, then my stomach, and finally a light dawned on his face, and a smile. He pointed back up front. We opened the 'baggage car' door and found it was a diner. We sat by two Englishmen, one of whom travels over this railroad every two weeks or so, and speaks French. He steered us through the meal. First a waiter came by and served something supposed to be soup. (Right here Mother says we are entering Amiens—this town figured prominently in the war—remember?) After the soup, another waiter came along with a great big dish of spaghetti, with meat balls stuffed in deviled half-eggs. There is no water—unfit to drink. Everyone drinks red wine. The Englishman told us we could have fried chicken, not too bad, at extra cost, but by that time we had eaten enough spaghetti. Then a course of potatoes, then 'ice cream,' made with, apparently, water and skim milk. I paid in English money, about 14 shillings and some odd pence.

"Wish you could see this funny French sleeping car. These French cars are larger than the British—about the size of an American car. We had to climb up a steep ladder to get on the train. It's rather crude compared to our Pullmans—still, not too bad. Altogether different, though. Seems funny to us. We have a private compartment. There are no sections—all private rooms. It has private wash basin, but no toilet. All use the same public toilet—both men and women.

"Mother has seen some of those French farms we've heard of—house and barn for livestock all in one building. The ground is covered with snow—has been, all over, since we landed at Southampton. We are to arrive at Basel about 8:10 a.m. There are no railroad folders, timetables, or maps. Those are luxuries only Americans enjoy."

I have quoted the letter at some length. Most books or articles about foreign travel do not mention many of these little things that an American notices on his first trip abroad. I felt those reading this *Autobiography* might find it interesting.

The Vision of the Future

A portion of a letter written on the train next morning may be interesting—and prophetic:

"The English tell us that we Americans are just now starting to go through the stage of development they did 200 years ago—that we are that far behind the times. They really think they are ahead of us! They are smugly ahead of what they *suppose* us to be—yet they know nothing of America, actually. I was particularly impressed by their pride. They feel they are superior, morally, to all people of the earth. Yet it is quite apparent that their morals have hit a toboggan slide since the war! They are surely *a long way* from realizing their sins, nationally and individually, and of repenting of them—and they don't even dream, and would never believe, that they are to be punished and conquered, and then rescued from slavery by Christ at His Second Coming—so as to bring them to salvation. In some manner, I know now that I must warn them, *and will,* but it will be difficult—no use of radio there, as it's

179

government owned and operated. YET, THEY MUST BE WARNED.

"I think it can be done by purchase of advertising space in newspapers and magazines, getting people to write for *The Plain Truth*. I've been making plans, while in London, for our coming campaign to reach England. The newspaper reporter said the advertising idea could be used. We will have to either send *Plain Truths* across, or have them printed in England, which is what we undoubtedly will do—a European edition. The college over here will probably become a European headquarters for carrying on our work all over Europe. WE MUST REACH EUROPE AND ENGLAND, as well as America! Our work is just STARTING! I see, more and more, why we have been simply *led* into taking this trip, and why the way opened so miraculously and suddenly before us at every turn. Before the coming atomic war, we have much work to do."

As I wrote then, the prophecy has been fulfilled. The college was established some years later than I then expected—it was established in Bricket Wood, near London, instead of in Switzerland.

General Eisenhower and Channel Invasion

On Thursday, February 27, I had written this to our children at home: ". . . Today I tried to purchase a pair of gloves. It is cold, around freezing, and will be colder in mountainous Switzerland. I walked almost the length of Bond Street, stopping in all men's clothing shops on the right side of the street proceeding north, and on the west side of the street returning south back to Piccadilly. Finally, at the last store, I found a pair of dark tan kid gloves. I engaged the shopkeeper in conversation. Why were gloves so scarce, in so cold a winter?

"He explained that a large percent of everything

manufactured in Britain is exported. I asked why. 'Because,' the merchant replied, 'England would *starve*
otherwise. We must import nearly all our food, and we
can't get a credit exchange to enable us to buy food in
foreign countries unless we export to those countries an
equal value in manufactured products.' You can buy
'made in England' gloves, luggage, leather goods, china,
woolens, etc., easier in the United States than here.

"After finally finding a shop that had a pair, I
didn't get my gloves after all. After he had removed the
price tag, he couldn't let me have them because I had
no ration book.

"This morning we finally spotted some lemons in
a fruit and vegetable shop. My liver really needed some
citrus juice, after the kind of food we had been getting.
Quite a crowd was queued up before the stand. After
standing in line ten or fifteen minutes, I asked for a
dozen lemons. The woman asked for my ration book.
No ration coupons, *no lemons!*—and only ½ pound to
a customer, then! I'm starving for fruits, juices, and
leafy vegetables. You don't realize what we have to be
thankful for, on America's Pacific Coast. We have the
best of everything in the world—and yet we *grumble!*
What we are seeing here is next best. Every other
country (except Switzerland) is worse right now.

"As we were leaving the lobby of the hotel this
evening, the hall porter, who looks more like an impressive, important business executive, told us this hotel
(The Dorchester) was Gen. Eisenhower's headquarters
prior to the Channel Invasion. Marshall, Patton, Brad-
ley, and all our top generals stayed here. They were all
well liked. This porter saw a lot of them, talked to them,
and arranged many things for them. He said they were
quiet, but simply *oozed* with personality, and he rated
Eisenhower as the ablest, strongest personality of all,

even over Marshall, and thinks he is one of the strongest men in the world. . . .

"Do you know, the Channel Invasion that defeated Germany might have been planned in this very hotel! It could have been in this very room where I'm writing. When the invasion zero hour came, the porter said Eisenhower and all other top military men came down one morning smiling and happy, and said they were off for a two or three day rest in the country. They were good actors—appeared happy. They said they could throw off all restraint and heavy responsibility a few days, and get in some needed rest and a vacation in the country. They were not a bit tensed up. No one suspected a thing. They didn't check out of the hotel. They left their things in their rooms. If any Nazi spies were in the hotel, they would have been thrown completely off. Then next morning—BANG! The great invasion smash was on—and doom for Hitler! No one in this hotel suspected anything was up."

53

Impressions of Switzerland and France

WHAT a difference between France and Switzerland! On the French train, no breakfast was served that Sunday morning, March 2, 1947. The reason: the train was running two or three hours late. Our sleeping car had been scheduled to be transferred to a Swiss train at Basel in time for breakfast.

We Arrive in Switzerland

Our French train finally dragged itself up to the depot at Basel, Switzerland. The minute we crossed from France into Switzerland, everything suddenly seemed refreshingly *different!* France was then in a state of lethargy and discouragement. People in Switzerland appeared more alert, better dressed, cleaner. The French, so soon after the war, seemed whipped, beaten, run down.

Our car was hooked onto the Swiss train at Basel.

There was a light, airy, clean Swiss dining car on the train. After Immigration and Customs officials went through the train, we finally made up for the lost breakfast with the best meal since we had left the U.S.

Dr. B. was stopping at the Hotel Storchen in Zurich and had made reservations at this hotel for us. Arriving in Switzerland's largest city, we took a taxi to this hotel. I did not have any Swiss money, so I asked the taxi driver to come into the lobby with me, where I transferred $20 into Swiss francs, out of which I paid the taxi fare. Dr. B. happened to be out somewhere with Madame Helene Bieber, who was staying at another hotel. Mme. Bieber, the reader will remember, was the owner of the newest and finest villa in southeastern Switzerland, Heleneum, on Lake Lugano, in Lugano-Castagnola.

Switzerland, by the way, was at that time so much more prosperous than France because Switzerland was not involved in the war. Switzerland had profited from both sides. The Marshall Plan and United States' billions of gift dollars had not yet put France in her present state of Common Market prosperity.

An hour or so after our arrival at the hotel in Zurich, we located Dr. B. and Mme. Bieber. We joined them at tea in one of our hotel lounge rooms and were presented to the owner of Heleneum. She was accompanied by her big full-blooded chow dog "Mipom."

Next afternoon we were riding through the Gotthard tunnel through the Gotthard Pass. It and the Brenner Pass are the only two passes for travel between Germany and Italy. During the war, the Swiss managed to remain neutral and hold the Germans off from invading them. They did this by threatening to blow up the Gotthard tunnel, and destroy these two passes if the Germans attacked. That is how this little

184

nation of Switzerland held powerful Nazi Germany at bay.

We found the lofty Alps all that had been claimed for them—*breathtaking*—MAGNIFICENT!

At Zurich, we noticed that the style of architecture was almost wholly German. But the minute we emerged from the tunnel, on the Italian side, the architectural design was all Italian.

The same would, of course, be true of the French-speaking area.

Yet there is really no language barrier between these three sections of Switzerland. Customarily, babies and children are taught the official language of their section until age six. Then Swiss children are taught a second language beginning at six years of age, and a third language at about age ten or twelve. Most better educated Swiss speak four or more languages.

I Am Not the Boss

At Lugano we inspected what was the object of our whole trip—the site of a possible future Ambassador College in Europe.

Often I have to stop and realize how many proofs we have been given that we have been called to the work of GOD—that neither I nor any man plans and guides it.

It is not our work, but GOD'S and the living Jesus Christ is HEAD of His Church and the real Director of this work. He has not allowed it to be of my planning.

Christ, through the Holy Spirit, said to the prophets and teachers of the Church at Antioch, during fasting and prayer, "Separate me Barnabas and Saul for the work whereunto I have called them." Saul's name was then changed to Paul. He and Barnabas were ordained apostles. They were called to GOD'S WORK.

They did not choose it as a profession—Christ first struck down Saul with blindness, converted and called him. Christ ordered his ordination for THIS WORK.

But even though the Apostle Paul was put in charge of God's work to the Gentiles, Paul was not allowed to plan it or make the real decisions.

In A.D. 50, Paul and Silas, "After they were come to Mysia [western part of Asia Minor—Turkey today], they assayed to go into Bithynia, but the Spirit [of Jesus] suffered them not" (Acts 16:7).

Paul *planned* to go EAST, along the north shores of what is Turkey today. But Jesus Christ, HEAD of His Church and God's work, planned otherwise! By a vision at night, the resurrected living CHRIST showed Paul that they were to go the very OPPOSITE direction, carrying the gospel for the first time to the continent of EUROPE!

This was a MOST IMPORTANT decision. In obedience to orders from Christ, by this vision, Paul and Silas went immediately into Macedonia IN EUROPE, holding their first meeting at Philippi (Acts 16:7-13).

In like manner, on this trip to Lugano, I tried to plan to start operation of GOD'S WORK for these last years either immediately, or within three years IN EUROPE—and to establish a branch Ambassador College in Lugano. That was MY planning and intention — just as Paul's was to travel east into Bithynia.

Here is what I wrote to those at home, from Lugano, on March 3, 1947: "I have decided DEFINITELY and FINALLY on the Swiss branch of Ambassador. The idea is right. But the PLACE is still open for investigation."

But I was to learn, later, that CHRIST had decided DEFINITELY and FINALLY otherwise! He had decided that the great DOOR of radio would open for me to preach His Gospel to EUROPE on the first Monday in 1953. And

186

His COLLEGE for Europe was to open later—SEVEN years later; in 1960—and in ENGLAND just outside London, not in Switzerland!

In ways that often seem astounding, CHRIST shows repeatedly that it is *HE* who is guiding and directing this great worldwide work of God!

Inspecting Potential College Site

I was much impressed with Lugano. On Tuesday evening I wrote:

"Dear Family at Home:

"Today we have seen Lugano! Partly. And what a place it is! It's all so different—so strange. It's ITALY with Swiss prosperity. A BEAUTIFUL, prosperous Italy. It's the most intriguing place we ever saw. It's certainly OLD-WORLD. It's the perfect place for the European unit of Ambassador College."

So I thought. But CHRIST thought otherwise!

Mme. Bieber remained in Zurich until Tuesday. We did not have an opportunity to inspect Heleneum until Thursday. That evening I wrote to my brother-in-law, Walter E. Dillon, who was to be the first president of Ambassador College at Pasadena. This, in part, is what I reported to him:

"We have been here since Monday night. Tuesday we took a boat trip down the lake, east, to the very end of Lake Lugano. About two miles east of here is the Italian border. Most of our boat trip was in Italy. We were within five miles of the place where they shot Mussolini. He was caught trying to get across the frontier into Switzerland, and they say he was heading for Lugano. I talked to a man who was then a Swiss Army captain, in charge of the frontier at that point. He knew Mussolini, talked to him. Mussolini was caught at Dongo.

"The trip on the lake was a life-time experience. The majestic Swiss Alps rise on either side. The Alps really surpass our Cascades, or the Rockies—even the Canadian Rockies. Just now they are snow-covered—look as if they are miles high, in fantastic shapes. Lugano is the Swiss Riviera. It's *different* from our mountain or lake scenery. The very atmosphere is different.

"What I started to write tonight is this: This afternoon, for the first time, we saw what we have come 9,000 miles to see—'Heleneum'—the possible future seat in Europe of AMBASSADOR COLLEGE. . . . We were invited to 4 o'clock tea. On arrival, we stepped into the most beautiful and elegant interior we had ever seen. It *far* surpasses what we expected! It is the ideal home for Ambassador College in Europe. It is adequately designed to house forty or fifty students, besides supplying six classrooms, library, lounge, and dining hall. Its atmosphere would automatically breed culture, poise and refinement into students. Mme. Bieber appears to want us to have it. She thought the kind of deal we have discussed very splendid. She knows little about business, and probably will be guided by her lawyer. But it's the only way she can eat her cake and have it too—that is, sell it, live off the income from the sale, and still live *IN* it for the next three or four years. And it's the only way we can purchase such a property without the capital for a large down payment. We make it during these three years while she would retain possession. I have made every check. I am now convinced we must have our European branch. Switzerland appears the only place for it."

Better Things Opened Later

So, you see, I was planning for it—but Jesus Christ was

planning otherwise—and HE, not I, guides and directs GOD'S WORK. In HIS due time, He opened the DOOR (see II Cor. 2:12-13) for His END-TIME work of *our day* to start in Europe.

And, the living CHRIST did open miraculously and unexpectedly what we ourselves had never planned— His Ambassador College overseas. He opened in England a place we never dreamed of finding—not merely one building with mere residential-size grounds, but several buildings, with magnificent gardens and landscaping, spacious grounds, and a total of approximately 200 acres! And instead of a maximum of forty or fifty students, we had the capacity for many more.

Surely GOD'S WAYS ARE BEST! How happy and GRATEFUL I am that Christ Jesus does not leave the real master planning of His great work to me. My ideas would not have been best—but what HE plans is always just right. It is a wonderful thing to KNOW we have the SECURITY—of GOD'S GUIDANCE. It's a wonderful feeling of absolute trust, faith and confidence, with no worries!

Leaving Switzerland

We left Lugano with Heleneum still uncertain, but hoping to close the deal by mail later.

We traveled by train from Lugano to Geneva on the following Sunday, then back to Bern where we caught the night sleeper for Paris. In purchasing our tickets, I noticed we had only twenty minutes to make a connection at Bern. Based on American experience, I was a little uneasy.

"Suppose our train is late arriving in Bern tonight," I suggested. "Is twenty minutes sufficient time for that connection?"

"*SIR!*" came the indignant response from the ticket

agent. "A Swiss train is *never late!* You can set your watch by it!"

There is another saying Swiss people like to quote: "It's impossible to get a bad meal in Switzerland." We have since eaten in many restaurants and hotels in Switzerland, and have never been served an unsatisfactory meal. There is a third saying in Switzerland: "We raise our children from the *bottom* up." And they are well-behaved!

En route from Lugano, our electric-driven train retraced our route through the Gotthard tunnel, but turned westward to Bern some distance north of the tunnel. On the train I opened my portable typewriter, and here is part of what I wrote to our children at home:

"Here we are again in the world-famous Gotthard tunnel—the pass high in the Alps between Italy and the north of Europe. It's a Sunday morning, 8:07 a.m. For two hours we have been thrilling to the most marvelous scenery! Yet it's only 11:07 Saturday night in Oregon. Seems funny. It's been daylight two hours, here. Yet you may not have gone to bed yet last night!

"Now we are headed back toward home, speeding northward through these awesome, spectacular Alps. An hour and a half ago I got some good color movies (I hope) of the pinkish rising sun shining on the snow-capped peaks of the Alps, still darkish gray of dawn below—only the sun-drenched peaks illuminated with a yellowish pink.

"Now we have emerged from the tunnel, on the German side. There is much more snow. All limbs of trees covered with snow. It's fantastically beautiful. Mother exclaims that this is the most beautiful scenery in the world. She will hardly let me write. 'O LOOK, Herbert!' she keeps exclaiming. 'You can write some

190

other time. But LOOK, now, *LOOK!* Those trees on that mountainside are *green*, underneath, but they're WHITE, now! Isn't it EXCITING? O, *come over here*, QUICK! Oh, you're so provoking—it's too late, now—we've passed it! etc. HOW CAN A MAN WRITE? Ha! Ha! In the middle of that sentence I got some marvelous camera shots. (I hope). However, no matter how good they come out the pictures won't show it to you. You have to *be here* and EXPERIENCE it!"

At Bern we changed trains, and continued south from there to Geneva, arriving about noon or somewhat before. I remember we were especially inpressed with the baby carriages, or "prams." Thousands of people out walking on a beautiful Sunday afternoon, many pushing these elegant baby carriages.

Also we were impressed with young people on dates. It seems the American young people have LOST the art of dating. The automobile has changed everything. But in Switzerland, instead of the degenerating custom of driving out on a lonely and secluded road to "neck" and arouse passions while minds were dulled, or letting their minds drift in a ready-made daydream in a darkened motion picture theater, hundreds of couples were seen sauntering afoot along the two sides of the lake, which in downtown Geneva narrows like a river— with many bridges across at each block.

We saw the League of Nations buildings. We found Geneva a clean, beautiful city. It, too, offered many advantages as a potential seat for a European branch of Ambassador College.

It was late afternoon or evening when we took a train and returned to Bern. I had telephoned long distance to a man in the educational division at the U.S. Embassy in Bern. He met us at the railway station. I spent the twenty minutes layover there discussing educational advantages of a branch college in Switzerland. (Yes, our Swiss train was precisely ON TIME!)

First Visit to Paris

Our sleeping car delivered us to Paris in the early morning. Everybody has heard of the beauty of Paris. We were introduced to it, so it seemed to us, by way of the back door—entering through a dilapidated blighted area. It was a drizzly, dreary morning. The railroad station though which we entered was in an unattractive wholesale district.

I checked our luggage, expecting to leave it there until boarding the noon train to London. I walked up to the ticket window to purchase 12 o'clock tickets to London, which would leave us time to see Paris until noon.

The mademoiselle ticket agent could not understand a word I said. After some five minutes of trying to speak by gestures, she sent for a man from the other side of the railway station. He could speak English.

"These foreigners can't even speak plain English," I exclaimed to my wife. She reminded me that WE were the foreigners! *That* realization gave a funny feeling.

The English-speaking man explained that the train to London departed from a different station. Paris has several railroad stations. So we were obliged to return straightway to the checkroom and reclaim our bags. Our obliging French friend said he would help us into a taxicab. He asked Mrs. Armstrong to wait inside and watch our luggage. I found that getting a cab on a rainy morning in Paris in 1947 was not like a big-city American depot, where one finds dozens of cabs lined up and waiting, as rapidly as incoming passengers can be piled into them. In fact, I learned that finding a taxi in Paris on a rainy morning is a superb accomplishment—*if* one can do it!

Taxi Hunting in Paris

Fifteen long minutes dragged by at the taxi entrance, and not a cab in sight, except those with passengers, and one or two whose drivers shrugged their shoulders, saying "Nothing doing!" in French motions. My French friend asked me to wait there and ran bare-headed out into the street. In five minutes he returned, shaking his head. Another fifteen minutes. Then again he left, saying he'd go over on the boulevard, a block away, in search of a taxi. He explained that the Nazis didn't leave them many cabs in good repair, and besides, depleted the petrol supply. So taxicabs were a scarce commodity at that time. As time slipped by, Mrs. Armstrong and I were becoming more and more hungry. There had been no diner on our train. Finally, at 9 a.m., our friend came back triumphantly in a taxi. We wanted the cab until noon, but this driver was soon due in at his garage. He would have time only to drive us to the George V hotel for breakfast.

Breakfast took a whole hour. Service came with great flourish, much style, and very leisurely. We ordered orange juice, toast and coffee. The waiter brought four oranges to his service table, and started laboriously squeezing them on a little hand lemon-squeezer. Then he served the two small glasses to a couple of ladies at an adjoining table. Then he walked to the kitchen and returned in no time at all with *our* "orange juice" which was NOT orange juice but some sort of artificial orange crush, with artificial flavor and sugar and water. The toast was cold, dry, packaged melba toast. The coffee was black, strong and bitter— no milk or cream. The cost was 400 francs—$4.00.

Foreigners Seeing Paris

After another ten minutes delay the English-speaking doorman got us a taxi. The driver could not speak a word of our foreign language. I asked the hotel doorman to instruct him that we wanted to see the Eiffel Tower, the Champs Elysées, stop at a shop to purchase an umbrella for Mrs. Armstrong, who had left hers at Lugano, and then to our railway station.

At the Eiffel Tower, even in cloudy rain, I got one good picture with my Plaubel-Makina German camera—only picture I was able to take in Paris. We saw many ornate and beautiful buildings, though they were dark and dirty, and gloomy in the rain—much gorgeous statuary. The driver drove around and around in the shopping district—but all stores were closed. It was a Catholic holiday. He did find one small shop open. But their ladies' umbrellas were a new style with long handles, and Mrs. Armstrong was afraid one would look freakish in America, so she didn't buy one. (When we returned to New York, we found all stores selling the same style there!)

By now we had to go straight to our railroad station. I tried to instruct the driver, but he couldn't understand. I tried to tell him our train left at noon, by pointing to 12 o'clock on my watch. He immediately smiled knowingly, nodding his head that he under-stood—and drove us in fifteen or twenty minutes to a jewelry store—which, of course, was closed! I tried to make him understand I'd like to buy some film for my camera—and he drove us to a photographer's studio. Somehow, in desperation, I finally got through to him that we wanted to go immediately to the railway station, where he deposited us at 11:30 a.m.

We boarded the famous crack Golden Arrow for London.

194

54

Mid-Atlantic Hurricane!

STREAKING northward on the crack Paris-London Golden Arrow, we saw much of the desolate ruins left by the war that had ended only a year and a half before.

In America, we had heard and read about the war daily. We had seen pictures and newsreels. But now my wife and I were *there,* where it happened. Here was the actual devastation of war all around us. Now it suddenly became *real!*

The Marshall Plan and American dollars had not yet made progress toward restoration. Europe was laid waste, many of its cities in ruins. Almost no one believed, then, that Europe could ever rise again. Yet I had been persistently proclaiming for two years, over the air and in *The Plain Truth,* that Germany would once again come to economic and military power, heading a ten-nation resurrection of the Roman Empire.

Desolate, Hopeless Europe

Have we forgotten what bleeding, war-torn, disheart-
ened Europe was like, immediately after World War II?
That is, all but prosperous Switzerland. Switzerland
kept out of the war, by means described previously.
Switzerland did business with both sides and prospered
during the war years.

We need to be reminded of the condition of pros-
trate Europe before United States dollars went to the
rescue. These dollars did a sensational pump-priming
job. German and Dutch industry did a phenomenal job
of rebuilding. Then the Common Market produced the
almost unbelievable prosperity that is Western Europe's
today.

I was seriously impressed with this wretched postwar condition in France and Italy. From Lugano I had
written our family at home:

"This afternoon we were in Italy. Took a boat trip
down the lake, east, to the end of Lake Lugano. Half
way we crossed the Swiss-Italian frontier. Immediately
we noticed a difference. The style of architecture was
much the same—all Italian—but as soon as we were on
the Italian side, everything was run-down, dilapidated,
gone to rot and ruin.

"There are seven or eight little towns along the lake
shore, and the boat is like an interurban railway by
which people from all those towns come to Lugano to
shop. We docked at every town. The Italians were so
very shabbily dressed. Some of the women had no
shoes—they wore a sort of flat wooden sandal, strapped
to their feet with string or ribbon. Most of the Italians
looked defeated, hopeless.

"Once they were a proud, prosperous, world-ruling
people. But ancient Rome became prosperous, as the

United States is today. Then they went in for soft, luxurious living, idleness and ease, entertainment, lax morals.

"Rome fell.

"The United States is starting that same toboggan slide to DOOM, today.

"This afternoon, along the five or six Italian towns where we docked, we saw the result of going the way of ancient Rome. We saw their 20th Century descendants, poor people one looks on with pity. Yet the Italians are emotional, and Mussolini took advantage of them, played on their emotions, whipped them up to a fanatical frenzy for Fascism. Then Hitler took them over. Then the Allies invaded the peninsula. And now they are a dejected, discouraged, helpless, hopeless people! Even worse than the French we saw."

And Mrs. Armstrong wrote this about our boat trip:

"Italy is in terrible shape. We were up and down the shores of Lake Lugano, in Italy. It was a cold day in winter, but women, old and young, were on the lake shore on their knees leaning over into the water, washing clothes in the cold lake water on flat boards—not washboards—no soap, just pounding and rubbing, some using a brush on their sheets, men's pants, sweaters and everything—big baskets of clothes, grey and dingy looking. They hung them along the lake front or on buildings, balconies—anywhere."

Back in London

Arriving back in London, I found letters and reports from the office in Eugene, Oregon, awaiting me. The news from the office was not good. Receipt of money was way down. The office was in a tight financial squeeze.

I wrote the office staff: "Since receiving your letters and reports today, I have had to decide we will not, at this time, obligate the work to payments on 'Heleneum,' the villa we went to Lugano to see. Madame Bieber is anxious to sell it to us on the terms we had in mind when we came over. I received a letter from her here this morning, enclosing a complete list (in German language) of the rooms on every floor, and assuring me she would send a blueprint of floor plans if I still wanted them, which I do. . . . It is offered to us at a fraction of its cost (it is a replica of the 'Petite Trianon' at Versailles) and on terms we could handle, once out of this financial slump, with about 8 percent increase over present income. There is no down payment whatever required. Just monthly payments three or four years, before we take possession—while she still lives there. . . . God will direct us and show us His will, and His selection, in due time.

"I have been shown a fine large building (large for us, that is)—right on this fabulous Park Lane boulevard, just a half block from our hotel—The Dorchester—here in London. I am advised that the price is very low, right now. It was used as the officers' club by United States Army officers during the war. I was advised that we very likely could purchase, with use permit for a college, and very likely get local support for such a college here that would pay half the costs, because Britain is now *very* anxious to encourage everything she can in good relationships with the United States. They feel here that an American college in London, sending American students here to study, would bring here some of our very best young men who will become leaders, and would better international relations between the two countries.

"If it were not for the foreign language angle, I

believe I would prefer to have it here. . . . It might ultimately work out that we would have TWO European units—one in London, one in Switzerland. We are the *first* to have the vision of such a college. It is something entirely new in the world of education. It's something BIG! It will be accomplished. But it will take time. I know we are being led by the hand of God into things never before done. They will be done, and in time—and there is not too much time."

How *PROPHETIC* were those words, written March 13, 1947!

God did guide and lead—*not* the way I then planned. But He *did,* in His due time, which was the year 1960, establish His college overseas. He did not establish it in Switzerland, but on the outskirts of London. NOT in that fine but very old stone building in congested downtown London, but just outside, in the scenic Green Belt, with a 180-acre campus, beautiful and colorful gardens and lawns, adequate buildings. The building on Park Lane was finally torn down in 1962— probably to be replaced with a modern skyscraper.

A Prophetic Occurrence

In view of an event that occurred March 10, 1963, it becomes pertinent to quote another paragraph from the above letter to our office staff, written March 13, 1947 from London:

"But after visiting Geneva, we are somewhat in favor, now, of Geneva as the seat of the European unit of AMBASSADOR. The city and buildings are more beautiful at Geneva, but the natural surrounding scenery and mountains are more beautiful at Lugano. Both are on lakes. Geneva is the number one education center, with great libraries, the large university, and it is a world political capital in international affairs. We will never find another place as modern and elegant as 'Heleneum' but for extracurricular advantages, great libraries, and international atmosphere, and a center for world affairs, Geneva would be preferable."

Was that, by coincidence, prophetic?

On March 10, 1963, I gave our French Department approval for signing a five-year lease for a suite of offices in Geneva!

Mr. Dibar Apartian, at the time of this writing, is professor of French language at Ambassador College in Pasadena. Also he is director of the French work, and the voice on the air of the French-language version of *The World Tomorrow*. Our French Department is now well organized, with offices and a staff at our headquarters Pasadena campus, and also an office and French-speaking staff at the college in England.

Many of our booklets have been translated into French. And, of course, we have a full-color French language edition of *The Plain Truth*.

Sir Henry's Gripe

Our 1947 trip to London, Lugano, Geneva and Paris did pave the way for important developments that have followed.

In the lobby of our hotel in London, The Dorchester, I met a baronet—a "Sir Henry," though I do not remember his family name. He was indignant at us Americans, and candidly told me so. That morning, the London papers carried a story of Herbert Hoover's recommendation that the United States appropriate a few hundred million dollars to feed starving Germans.

"Why, hang it, Sir," he sputtered in exasperation, "they ought to use those millions to feed us starving Britons before they feed those Germans who *caused* all this starvation. Do you know, sir, what I get to eat for breakfast? I haven't been able to get an egg for six months, and just two little slices of bacon a week. The nearest we can come to eggs is some kind of dried powdered synthetic stuff, sir! And it isn't fit to eat! We get almost no fruit, or fresh vegetables, or milk, butter, or sugar."

Sir Henry may have been griping, but we found this allegation true. Actually we ourselves fared better than English titled people in their homes. Leading hotels and restaurants were allowed to serve more and better food than was obtainable by private citizens. But even so we subsisted primarily on potatoes and cauliflower at every meal, along with soups thickened with flour but no milk, and a limited amount of fish.

Spencer-Jones—Guide Extraordinary

On Tuesday, after returning to London, we spent an eventful day on a tour, afoot, of the royal and government sections of London.

We had been standing that morning before the entrance gate to Whitehall Palace, watching the mounted King's Guards. A guide came up to us and began to give us an interesting explanation. He showed us his credentials as an accredited guide. Spencer-Jones was a real character! We decided to engage his services, for a foot tour beginning at two that afternoon.

He met us at the entrance of The Dorchester. After three hours of seeing some of the most interesting things of our lives, he asked so little for his services I paid him double, and then wondered if I had not underpaid him. He knew his London and British history.

He took us through places closed to the public. He seemed to know all the guards and officials, and they would smile and let us through. He told us that the then Queen Mother, Queen Mary, knew him, and always

201

gave him a smiling, friendly nod when he passed her. He had acted as guide over this same tour to General Eisenhower, and at the end of their tour he said the General said to him, "I wish I had your memory, Spencer-Jones." We could understand why. He gave us a whole college education on British history.

On our tour we walked through the court of what had been the palace of Britain's kings 400 years before. It was so dirty and shabby I asked why they didn't clean the place up.

"Oh that would never do, Sir!" the guide assured me. "We are proud of its *age,* Sir, and it must be left just as it was 400 years ago. But it's very beautiful inside, Sir."

Spencer-Jones' wife and two daughters were killed one morning at 11 a.m. in a daylight raid by German bombers during the war. But he wanted no pity. He was proud.

"Imagine," he said, "a dark night, a complete black-out, a thousand planes screaming overhead, bombs exploding like deafening thunder here and there around you, the incessant fire of our antiaircraft guns, and people screaming. I've walked right past here," he said at one point, "and watched hundreds of planes overhead—Germans desperately trying to bomb this royal and government section—our boys up there shooting them down. A Nazi parachuted right into that tree you see there, Sir, and would have been torn to bits by the women who rushed at him, but the guards reached him first and took him prisoner. Dozens of planes crashed right in this park, Sir!"

This guide lived in a humble "pensioner's home." He drew a pittance of a pension from World War I. His clothes were worn and frayed.

But Spencer-Jones was English, and the English

are PROUD. He asked if I would convey one message from him to America. This was his message: "Tell America, *please,* DON'T EVER EXPRESS ANY PITY FOR US BECAUSE WE'VE GONE THROUGH A WAR AND ARE NOW HAVING A HARD TIME. THAT, WE JUST COULDN'T STAND, SIR!" He had lost home, family and prosperity. But he still had his pride!

Mid-Atlantic Hurricane!

We sailed from Southampton on the return voyage, again on the mighty *Queen Elizabeth,* at 4:30 in the afternoon of March 15.

On our eastbound crossing, we had prayed for a calm sea. Stewards and stewardesses had told us it was the smoothest crossing in their memory—and in mid-February at that. But somehow we must have taken calm crossings for granted by the time of our return voyage. At least we neglected any petitions to the God who controls the weather. And we learned a lesson!

In the early afternoon of Tuesday, March 18, I wrote the following from the middle of the Atlantic:

"Dear Everybody at Home: *What a sea!* Today we're seeing something you never see at home—a real rough sea in the middle of the Atlantic. Mother isn't seeing any of it. This is her third day confined to bed. A rough sea greatly encourages her penchant for seasickness. We've had three days of choppy sea, but today the waves are far bigger and higher than before.

"This great Lady (the *Queen Elizabeth*), who is no lady, lurches, and heaves, and tosses back and forth, and groans and literally SHUDDERS! The doors and walls creak. Out on deck the high gale whistles and *screams!* And the great giant waves sink way down the depth of the ground from a fifteen-story building on port side, as the giant ship swings and dips over to starboard, and

203

then we roll back to port side just as a massive wave swells up alongside, it seems only two stories below.

"It's a SENSATION—but, unfortunately, one of those things one must experience, and cannot be really understood by a word's eye view. So you won't really know what I mean. Right this second this ship is shuddering like a dying man. She groans, and then amid her rolling, swaying motion just shivers, and shakes, and *shudders*—and then sways on! A while ago 'Her Majesty' got to heaving more than usual, and I rushed to the aft main deck, just as she sank way down. Then the rear deck tossed high, and a wave that seemed as high as a ten-story building rolled over and broke into a beautiful white spray, dropping like a cloudburst on the deck. In the excitement I shot the last ten feet of movie film. I think I caught the most spectacular film of all—waves rolling like mountain peaks—then the break—and the stiff gale blows spray like boiling steam.

"Most of the ocean is dark muddy green in color—almost black, but covered with white caps as these gigantic waves break about every 750 or 800 feet. Then, in the wake of the ship is a trail of light, bright, turquoise-blue in the sunlight—when the sun flashes its brilliant rays down between clouds.

"It's real stormy weather—yet there's no rain today, though there was yesterday and Sunday. But, in spite of the intermittent sunshine playing hide-and-seek behind spotty billowy clouds, we are today heading into the stiffest gale so far. And, although I hope I have shot some more or less thrilling pictures of it, *you'll* never know what I mean. No picture can give you the third dimension—the *feel*—the *motion*—the lurch and sway, the sounds, and the EXPERIENCE of it. Poor Mother! She's *experiencing* it in seasickness, but not *seeing* any of it! They say we won't dock in New York until Friday or Saturday, now. We've had to slow down to five or six knots."

But the worst was yet to come—and I had not realized, when the above was written, that we were in a hurricane! Actually I did not realize how serious the storm was until we docked in New York, as I shall explain below. But the storm became more wild toward evening. Early next morning I added a postscript to the above letter. Here are excerpts from it:

Storm Worsens

"Mid-Atlantic, Wednesday a.m., March 19, 1947. Dear Folks at Home: Just a little early morning P.S. to yesterday's letter about the storm. Yesterday, toward evening, the sea became wildest and most thrillingly exciting. Finally there were tremendous swells, about 1,500 feet apart, farther than the length of this ship that is 1,031 feet. They became like mountain ridges. Sinking down in between the towering ridges the sea was like smooth valleys. The gale was so stiff that, while the 'valleys' in between liquid peaks or ridges were quite smooth, yet spray was being whipped along like a sandstorm on the desert. It actually looked more like a desert sandstorm than a sea—in between peaks, that is.

"The sea seemed wildest about dusk. I had shot all my movie film, but I still had seven shots left on the Plaubel-Makina. It was becoming too dark for most cameras, and I was thankful for the f.2.9 Makina. There was quite a little haze, too—and the fierce gale raised a continuous spray above the water surface (like a sandstorm). So I used a haze filter, opened the shutter all the way, set it down to 1/25 of a second. My light-meter showed the necessity of this, although I should have liked to have taken these shots at 1/200th of a second. I hope the fast-whipping spray doesn't turn out to be a blur." (These pictures were developed by Associated Press, New York, immediately on landing.)

"At times it seemed the stern of the ship lifted fifty or seventy-five feet out of the water. As I stood on one of the aft decks, as low as we were allowed to go, it seemed we sank way down into the water, then lifted up clear out of the water as the prow plunged down. After some time, I decided I had all the good pictures possible to get. I had closed up the camera, and started back inside, when, suddenly, the deck below seemed to leave my feet, as if I were left in mid-air. It was a sensation!

The Climax

"Instantly I realized we were taking another of those superdips. As soon as I could get traction under my feet, I rushed back outside on the deck at the stern to catch the thrill of the next dip. We usually got about three in succession before those extreme tilts dissipated themselves. This had been the most sudden and extreme dip I had experienced, so I tried frantically to pull out the tin shutter in front of the film pack and get the camera set for action as I ran. In the excitement I failed to get the camera set and adjusted in time, but I did reach the open deck in time to SEE the one most thrilling dip of all!

"It was the sight of a lifetime! The stern of the gigantic ship rose high above the water, as the prow plunged down into it. Then we on aft deck seemed to lunge down deep into the water, just as a huge liquid mountain peak rolled up behind us. It seemed almost as if the ship were about to stand straight up in the water—we on the bottom, the bow pointing straight up to the sky. Of course, we didn't sink quite that far down—but we experienced the sensation of being about to do so. A big portion of that stupendous wave rolled up behind us, broke, sprayed up into the air like an explosion, and came like an avalanche full force down upon the lower deck just below us at the complete stern of the ship! Then the flood of water rolled off the far-stern deck like the torrent of a river, as once again *we* mounted up toward the sky.

Mrs. Armstrong Collapses

"For an hour I kept running intermittently down to our cabin on "C" deck to urge Mother to come up and see the thrilling sight. I knew that in an hour it would be too dark to see it, and it might be the last chance in our lifetime to witness anything like it. I was more excited now than she was on the train ride through the Swiss Alps. I learned later it was the angriest, most furious sea in twenty years—with the highest waves and greatest swells, and mountain-peak waves forming a jagged and uneven horizon as far as the eye could see! Every now and then—perhaps a half mile—perhaps three or four miles away—a great aqua-peak would suddenly rise up, towering above all else on the horizon, only to sink rhythmically back down again.

"The sea was almost half WHITE with the white caps in sandstorm effect in the screaming gale—half, ugly dark green-brown, almost black, forming the most weird and fantastic shapes as giant waves surged up toward high heaven, broke, then sprayed down to sink below other heaving waves surging up in front of them. I was as excited as a twelve-year-old boy!

"I guess a stewardess outside our cabin door overheard my almost frantic urging of Mother to try to come above with me to see the exciting spectacle, and she must have thought there was going to be domestic trouble if she didn't get Mother up there. Anyway, she went into our cabin, and took the covers off Mother and insistently marched her out to the lift, and on up to the main deck lounge.

"But there Mother almost completely collapsed. The stewardess (all stewardesses are trained nurses) finally found me and brought me to Mother, slumped over in a chair, pale-white. Together we got her back to our cabin and to bed. It was just after this that the above-described most exciting scene occurred.

In Mortal Danger

"The motors of the ship were stopped down to around six knots. I did not realize until after the above-described incidents that the big ship actually was in danger. We were in *desperate danger!* I was told then, at late dusk last evening, that the ship might break in two, in the middle, if the full speed were put on, or if, at any time, Captain Ford failed to keep the ship headed straight into the wind in that furious storm. Regardless of direction, we had to keep headed straight into it. It was the worst storm the Queen ever fought through.

"When I learned from a steward that we were actually in mortal danger, I went to our cabin and prayed. Suddenly I remembered how we had failed to ask for God's protection on this voyage. Now I realized we were in the plight described in the 107th Psalm, verses 23 through 30:

'They that go down to the sea in ships, that do business in great waters; these see the works of the Lord, and his wonders in the deep. For he commandeth, and raiseth the stormy wind, which lifteth up the waves thereof. They mount up to the heaven, they go down again to the depths: their soul is melted because of trouble. They reel to and fro, and stagger like a drunken man, and are at their wit's end. Then they cry unto the

Lord in their trouble, and he bringeth them out of their distresses. He maketh the storm a calm, so that the waves thereof are still. Then are they glad because they be quiet; so he bringeth them unto their desired haven. Oh that men would praise the Lord for his goodness, and for his wonderful works to the children of men!'

"So now I prayed, in real earnest—and also in real FAITH. I knew that those words of God were not idle words—they were the very PROMISE of Almighty GOD. He is no respecter of persons. Here was the largest ship, so far as we know, ever built by man—in mortal DANGER!

"Until now, I had looked on the whole thing as an exciting experience to be enjoyed. Now I was sobered. I knew the eyes of God were on that great ship and its thousands of passengers. I knew that if I asked Him to do what He promised in that 107th Psalm, He would do it. He is no respecter of persons. Those lives on that ship were as precious to Him as any.

"So Mrs. Armstrong and I very soberly and earnestly prayed to the Eternal to calm the storm. We claimed this Psalm as His PROMISE that He would. We thanked Him for doing it. After that we had a good night's sleep.

"So I awoke early this morning, and before breakfast I went up on the main deck to see a *calm sea!* Not yet completely, but relatively calm and quiet. It was cloudy and began to rain while I was up on deck. The rolling movement of the ship is now caused by the forward motion—the motors are now opened full blast, and we are plunging full speed ahead. What a changed ocean from last night! No whitecaps this morning, except those created by this floating city."

209

Safe in New York

We had smooth sailing the rest of the way. The big Queen arrived in New York two days late. When we docked, excited newsmen were allowed to come on board before anyone could disembark.

I attended the news conference in Captain Ford's quarters. The captain said it was a "storm of hurricane force," and the worst of his entire life's experience. It was BIG NEWS. The world's largest ship had been in mortal danger.

I had the only good camera shots of the storm. The Associated Press men asked if they could have the films, promising to develop them immediately and turn them over to me, with prints, the next morning.

Mrs. Armstrong and I were allowed to disembark from the ship immediately, ahead of other passengers, with the AP men, and Customs waved us through with very scant inspection, on learning that the AP wanted to get our pictures by wirephoto to all papers coast to coast immediately. I left the film-pack at Associated Press headquarters.

Next morning I returned to Associated Press offices. An angry official said that some "dumb cluck" around there had mislaid or misfiled my films, until too late to get them into print while it was still fresh news. He apologized profusely, and handed me the films and prints.

So they were never published in the newspapers across the United States, after all.

55

Strategy to Gain Possession—Birth Pangs of the College

THE *Queen Elizabeth* docked in New York on March 21, 1947. It was good to be back on solid ground.

We returned to Eugene, Oregon, March 25. Immediately I plunged into preparations for establishing the new Ambassador College in Pasadena. All thought of the European branch of the college was of necessity shelved for the time being. The financial situation dictated that.

Appointing a President

I have recounted, earlier, how I had first approached my wife's brother, Walter E. Dillon, as prospective president of the college, when the conviction to found the college was first conceived.

At first mention, he had only laughed.

"Me become president of a Bible college?" he had exclaimed. "Why, I know almost nothing

211

about the Bible. That would be out of my field."

But I had hastened to explain that Ambassador was *not* to be a "Bible college," but a straight coeducational LIBERAL ARTS institution.

"Do you think I could teach the theological classes?" I had asked.

"Why, I think you know more about the Bible than anyone living," he replied.

When I explained that there would be a course in theology, along with other usual liberal arts courses, and that I would personally teach the Bible classes, the whole idea began to make sense to Walter.

"You see," I explained, "you are an educator—I am not. You've devoted your life to education. You are head of the largest school in Oregon, outside Portland. You have a master's degree from the University of Oregon, with work toward a Ph.D. You are familiar with academic requirements, organization, and procedures. You are an experienced academic administrator. You have proved your ability to direct teachers. In these things I am not experienced. I will organize and teach the Bible courses, but I need you to help me plan and organize the college as a whole, and supervise the academic administration. You've had the academic experience. I've had the business experience. Don't you think we'd make a good team?"

"I certainly do," he replied, after hearing my explanation.

We talked over all the details, and policy plans generally. I explained that I was bent on founding a NEW KIND of college, consistent with tried and sound organizational and administrative practice. Ambassador, I said with emphasis, was *not to be a rubber stamp.* I was well aware that colleges had fallen into a dangerous drift of materialism. He agreed. I also realized that mass-production, assembly-line education in universities of five to forty thousand students resulted in loss of personality development and much that is vital in student training. To this he also agreed.

The Foundational Philosophy

I explained how the Bible is, actually, the divine Maker's instruction book He has sent along with His product—the human individual. It reveals the PURPOSE of life—the purpose for which the human mind and body was designed and brought into being—the directions for operating this human mechanism so that it will perform as it was designed to do, and fulfill its intended purpose, reaching its intended goal.

In other words, that the Bible is the very FOUNDATION of all knowledge—the basic concept as an APPROACH to the acquisition of ALL KNOWLEDGE—whether academic, scientific, historic, philosophical or otherwise. The Bible provides the missing dimension in education. Therefore, it must be the BASIS for all academic courses.

The Bible does not *contain all* knowledge—it is the *foundation* of all knowledge. It is the *starting point* in man's *quest* for knowledge, and equips man to BUILD on that foundation.

The Bible, alone of all books or sources of knowing, reveals basic PURPOSES. It *alone* reveals the inexorable, yet invisible LAWS that regulate cause and effect, action and reaction—that govern all relationships—that produce happiness, peace, well-being, prosperity. The Bible is a guide-book of vital *principles,* to be applied to circumstances, conditions, and problems.

God has equipped man with eyes with which to see; ears with which to hear; hands with which to work; minds with which to reason, think, plan, design, make

213

decisions, and will to act on those decisions. Man has capacity to explore, investigate, observe, measure. God enabled man to invent telescopes, microscopes, test-tubes and laboratories. Man, of himself, is enabled to acquire much knowledge. But without the BASIC knowl-edge—that FOUNDATION of *all* knowledge, revealed *only* in the Bible—man goes off on erroneous tangents in his effort to *explain* what he discovers.

Only in the BIBLE can he learn the real PURPOSE being worked out here below. Only through this revela-tion from GOD can he know the real *meaning* of life— what, exactly, man *is*—or THE WAY to such desired blessings as peace, happiness, abundant living—the *spiritual* values.

The biblical revelation provides man with the true *concept* through which to view and *explain* what he can observe.

HOW Ambassador Was to Be Different

But the educational institutions of this world have rejected this FOUNDATION of knowledge. They have built an educational structure on a false foundation. They left God, and His revelation, out of their knowledge. They have built a complicated and false system com-posed of a perverted mixture of truth and error.

Ambassador College was to *correct* these ills and perversions in modern education. That was to be its basic policy.

The board of trustees of the Radio Church of God, of which I was chairman, would set all policies until the college could be incorporated in its own name with its own board of trustees. Until that time, it would be operated as an activity of the Radio Church of God. Mr. Dillon would administer these policies.

To this he agreed. But I was to learn later that, not

214

possessing a real grasp or understanding of the Bible, he apparently never did really comprehend what I meant by this basic concept of education.

Mr. Dillon was the product of this world's education. He was imbued with its concepts. He never did quite grasp the real meaning of my continuous emphasizing that Ambassador College was definitely *not* to be a "rubber-stamp college." I assumed he was in complete harmony with our basic purpose. I feel sure *he* thought he was.

Had I, too, been indoctrinated with the prevailing educational concepts, there would be no Ambassador Colleges today—but God saw to it that I came up through different channels.

Starting Active Preparations

The special January, 1947, number of *The Plain Truth,* announcing the future college in Pasadena, brought applications from both prospective faculty members and students.

One application came from Dr. Hawley Otis Taylor. He was chairman emeritus of the department of physics at Wheaton College. Dr. Taylor had a Ph.D. from Cornell University; had taught at Cornell, Harvard, and MIT; had been a consultant of the Navy in the war; had been a member of the U.S. Bureau of Standards. His scientific publications were voluminous. And he was a professed Christian.

This all seemed too good to be true!

Dr. Taylor had reached Wheaton's retirement age—seventy. He had once lived in Pasadena and wanted to spend his retirement years here. He felt he had several active years of service left, and Ambassador College offered the opportunity to add his salary here to his retirement pay from Wheaton. After due correspondence, and, I believe, a personal interview in Pasadena, we appointed Dr. Taylor dean of instruction and registrar of the new college.

Other applications arrived. Mr. Dillon and I were anxious to get on the job in Pasadena immediately. The very next morning, early, after our return from Europe, he and I started the long drive from Eugene to Pasadena.

We stopped off at a small town in southern Oregon to interview a woman, a Dr. Enid Smith, teaching English in a high school. She had Ph.D. degrees from two universities. One was from Columbia University— the other from the University of Oregon. We had received an application from her. We hired her as our first instructor in English.

We Buy New Home

We arrived Pasadena Thursday night, March 27. Things now were moving into high gear. Friday morning I contacted Mrs. C.J. McCormick, the real estate broker through whom the purchase of the college property had been made. I had been looking at a number of places, before the trip abroad, for a home. She had said she would try to have a few places lined up for me to inspect on my return from Europe.

She said she had three places for me to see, which she felt might fit the requirements. Chief requirement was the fact that I lacked even enough money for a down payment. We were going to have to manage to purchase a place, as we had the college, with no down payment.

Mr. Dillon went with me. The first place she showed us was an ill-arranged, two-story Spanish home.

I didn't like the second place. The third place was three miles from the college, in the California Institute

216

of Technology district. At first glance from the street, I said: "That place exactly reflects the character of Mrs. Armstrong. She'd like it."

But on the entrance sidewalk, I stopped.

"Look, Mrs. McCormick," I said. "It's no use looking at this place. It's the most homelike-looking place I've seen—but we could never afford a place like this. What we're looking for is a *small,* modest-type house— something inexpensive. This place is sufficiently modest in appearance, but it's too big."

"Mr. Armstrong," she promptly replied, "this is the only kind of place you *can* afford. That's why all three of these places I had chosen to show you are larger places. You can't afford to buy a small place. If it is a new tract place, the company selling it will demand a down payment which you don't have. If it's an older place lived in by the owner, such people are selling because they need the money, and they would have to have a sizable down payment. These people are financially well-to-do. They don't need the money. If they like you and Mrs. Armstrong, and you like the property, they can afford to let you have it without a down payment.

"These people love their home. The only reason they want to sell it is that Mrs. Williams is unable physically to walk up and down stairs any longer, and doctors have told her she must move to a place of one floor only. They have found a lovely one-story place in South Pasadena. They paid cash for it. I've already briefed them on your financial position, and how you are starting a cultural college, and that you are people of the character that would take the best of care of this property. That's important to them. They do love this place, and want to be sure the family moving in will take the best care of it."

We went on inside.

The home reflected character and charm. It seemed even more homelike inside than out. It was a fourteen-room house, fourteen years old, but of quality construction and had been well maintained. It was a frame colonial house, two stories, and a half-basement of three rooms in clean, excellent condition.

We examined the construction from underneath, in the basement. It was substantial. Mr. Dillon had spent a summer selling real estate. He had learned how to appraise the quality and value of a house.

"This place," he whispered to me, "is so desirable that if you don't buy it, I will. Don't ever let *this* place get away from you."

Of course I wanted Mrs. Armstrong to see it. And the Williams wanted to see her, before deciding whether to sell to us. After we left, I called my wife long distance. She had just an hour to catch the evening train for Los Angeles. The next evening she arrived—or, more probably, it was Sunday evening.

On Monday morning I took her out to see it. It was love-at-first-sight with her. It had seemed to me that this home and my wife simply belonged together. It was just her type—her character. It had quality, charm, character. Yet it had simplicity. It was not a showplace, not ostentatious. Just quiet, modest, with charm, beauty and character. The Williams, we learned later in the day, fell in love at first sight with Mrs. Armstrong. Immediately they felt she was the woman who would take good care of the place.

Mrs. McCormick contacted us in the early afternoon. "It's like a miracle," she said. "They want you to have it. They will sell to you at just half the price the property has been listed for, for over a year. They will sell it to you on quarterly payments, no down payment, *no interest,* and will give you possession and the deed,

218

taking a trust deed (mortgage), in ninety days when the second payment is made."

We couldn't believe our ears! I did some quick figuring. We had been living in motels, forced to eat at restaurants. The money we were spending at restaurants for ourselves and two sons was almost exactly the amount of the payments. Mrs. Armstrong is a *very* economical cook, when we could have a home where she could do the cooking. With her management over grocery buying, I figured the food would cost no more than we were spending for motel rent.

In other words, IT WAS GOING TO COST US ABSO-LUTELY NOTHING to step into this beautiful home and start owning it! It would involve no increase in our cost of living!

I went immediately to the office of Judge Russell Morton, our attorney, asking him to draw up the agreement. When I told him the terms, he looked at me with a strange look.

"I never heard of such a deal," he said. "Why, I ought to refuse to write up the agreement! That's the second important property that has come to you without even a down payment.

He did write up the agreement, and the next day, Tuesday, April 1, 1947, the Williams, Mrs. Armstrong and I, signed, and I gave them a check for the first quarterly payment. We were to have possession and the deed July 1, the same day we were to take possession of the college property.

First College Office

Mr. Dillon was anxious to get into an office, and get started with the preliminary work of organizing the new college.

There were the two buildings on this original prop-

219

erty we had purchased for the college. One was the present library, which we then called "the college," for the simple reason that it housed all classrooms, library, music department, assembly—everything, except business office. And, besides this was the former garage. It was a four-car garage, with apartments occupying the second floor and each end of the ground floor, and filled with tenants. We managed a deal, at a premium cost, by which the people in the apartment at the rear upstairs and the rear downstairs vacated. The center of the downstairs, garage space for four cars, already was vacant. The building originally had been stables—way back in B.C. years—*before cars!*

In the rear ground-floor room, later to become our printing shop until 1958, we opened the first Ambassador College office. We purchased desks and office equipment and supplies. Mr. Dillon employed a secretary—a Miss Ruth Klicker. He began work of planning a curriculum.

One day he said a man had walked in, while I was out, and applied for the job of professor of French. He was Professor Emile Mauler-Hiennecey, French-born and educated, with degrees from a university in Paris. He had moved to New Orleans and done private French tutoring, and in recent years had lived in Pasadena. He had taught in high schools, and continued private tutoring. Mr. Dillon wanted me to interview the professor— even then a year or two past seventy.

After my interview, we appointed him our first instructor in French.

We employed two other women teachers—Mrs. Genevieve F. Payne, with an M.A. from Colorado University, and graduate work in history at other universities, as instructor in history and Spanish; and Miss Lucille Hoover, with a B.M. from Chicago Musical

College and considerable additional study in America and abroad, as head of our music department.

And then, about June 20, after Mr. Dillon had gone to New York to study at Columbia for the summer, Mrs. Lucy H. Martin came in for an interview. She was an experienced librarian—had served on the staff of the Library of Congress at the nation's capital. I did not know until later that she had degrees in music equal to or higher than Miss Hoover. I employed her as librarian. It was then a part-time job. She was teaching in another private school in Pasadena.

We also appointed a Mr. Krauss, with an M.S. from the University of Southern California, who had been officer in charge of the Navy physical fitness program, as director of physical education.

All in all, we felt our new college faculty rated very well in degrees and previous experience.

I had wanted Mr. Dillon to earn a Ph.D. from Columbia University. He already had graduate credits from the University of Oregon. So he and his wife departed, about mid-June, for New York City for summer work toward his degree.

Dr. B. Balks

After signing the papers for purchase of our new home on April 1, 1947, I began to think about how we would furnish such a large house. Of course we had some furniture in storage in Eugene, Oregon. But most of it was old and worn, and there was not enough to furnish even a small part of our new home.

The main building we had purchased, as "the college building" from Dr. B., had always been used as a large residence. It was, however, more institutional than residential in appearance. Dr. B. and his elderly sister were living in it. The building was completely furnished.

Most of the furniture and furnishings were somewhat old, but of the character usually found in larger mansions. He probably had bought it all second-hand at one of the auction markets. We were not going to be able to use this furniture in the college, when we turned the rooms into classrooms.

I approached Dr. B. about moving the furniture and furnishings to our new home on July 1. Immediately he refused. For tax reasons, he had itemized the purchase price, segregating the furnishings from the real property. By placing a higher value on the furnishings, he avoided a portion of the capital-gains tax on the real estate.

But the wily, scheming Dr. B. suggested that, for a separate cash payment, he would agree to removal of the furniture. I think his price was $2,000, to apply on the last two months' rental on the twenty-five-month lease. The reader will remember that we purchased this first college property on a lease-and-option basis. We were to pay $1,000 per month rent on a twenty-five-month lease. At the end of twenty-five months, the $25,000 thus paid was to become the down payment on the *purchase.* The contract included an option to purchase at that time, with the $25,000 down payment thus accumulated, and $1,000 payments per month, plus interest.

So Judge Morton drew up a legal contract, by which, as a result of *advancing* this last two-months' rental under the lease part of the contract, Dr. B. agreed we might move the furniture and furnishings to our new home address—but to no other location.

We became convinced before July 1, however, that Dr. B. had no intention of ever giving us possession of the property. Our contract called for nine months' rental payments at $1,000 per month, *before* possession.

After this $9,000 had been paid, we were to take possession.

It had been a real headache of a problem to raise that extra $2,000. It probably took some thirty days, but I think it was managed by mid-May. But as July 1 approached, Judge Morton, his associate attorney, Mr. Wannamaker, and I had become convinced that Dr. B. did not intend to give possession—that his intention was to keep the money we had paid—which now would be $11,000 by July 1, and to keep the property too! We went into a huddle at the law offices about strategy for peacefully taking possession.

Dr. B. had always made me a welcome guest, personally. Mrs. Armstrong and I had spent the night there on New Year's eve, so we could view the 1947 Tournament of Roses parade. This world-famous parade starts just one block south of this property, on South Orange Grove Boulevard—and this original property is less than a half block off Orange Grove.

We worked out a strategy.

So on the morning of July 1, Mrs. Armstrong, our two sons and I parked our car, filled with our luggage, a block away—out of sight from the Dr. B. building. Then I walked over to the front door and rang the bell. Dr. B. came to the door, and, as I suspected, looked carefully to see that no luggage or other members of the family had come with me. Seeing no one, he allowed me to step inside, as I had so frequently done.

We went inside and chatted. Nothing was said about our taking possession. Then, after about ten minutes, the front doorbell rang. I beat Dr. B. to the door, opened it, and before Dr. B. grasped what had happened, in walked Mrs. Armstrong, and our sons, carrying our luggage. We were inside.

But so was Dr. B. and his sister!

We took over two bedrooms. We planned that not more than one or two of us would ever leave the building at one time—always keeping at least two of us inside, to admit any who left.

Some two weeks went by. Dr. B. and his sister made no move to leave. We were in. But *so were they*—and they seemed to have no intention of moving out or turning over possession.

Of course, he was violating his signed agreement. We could possibly have taken it to court and forced them out. But that was the last thing we wanted to do. We wanted to keep the peace.

So we had another strategy conference at the attorneys' offices. We remembered the legal paper he had signed agreeing to removal of the furniture and furnishings to our new home on or after July 1.

It was decided to inform Dr. B. we had set a date for removing the furniture, and that on that date, set about three days ahead, house movers would come and remove the beds on which they were sleeping—and in fact all, except the one Mrs. Armstrong and I were using. Dr. B. protested, when I informed him.

"I have a piece of paper here," I said, "which you signed, which says these beds are going to be moved on that date. You have three days to get your own things packed, and to vacate and turn complete possession over to us. I don't want to have to resort to legal means or force."

"Oh, well," he answered gruffly and angrily, "All right! All right! We'll get out!"

The strategy worked. We had possession. But Dr. B. still thought he was not beaten. He still thought he could outsmart us and keep the property. We were to learn that, when the time came to exercise our option to turn it into a purchase, in December, 1948.

224

56

A Supreme Crisis!—Now Forced to "Fold Up"?

NOW CAME the *real* troubles! We reached the crossroads. This was to be the real test.

Ahead, now, was the possible transition from a small, struggling, virtually one-man work to a major-scale organization exerting a powerful influence on humanity the world around! Ambassador College was to provide the only possible means. It was to be the recruiting and training center, integrating into effective organization those whom God would call to surround me—to become this Christ-led and Spirit-powered organism.

But lying in wait, poised to spring at us in satanic fury, was a succession of such seemingly insurmountable obstacles, diabolical plots, persecutions and oppositions as I never dreamed of facing. As I think back, now, I realize, as I did not then, how these efforts to thwart the founding of the college seemed to come from

225

all directions—and from within as well as without. Yet in actual fact all were instigated from one source—the same that had always sought to destroy the work of God.

It seemed, however, as if the irresistible FORCE met head-on with the immovable obstruction.

"The $30,000 Headache"

The wily Dr. B., possessing the highest law degrees in the land, and living by his wits had tried to prevent giving us possession of "the college" on July 1, 1947. We called the building that is now the library "the college" in those days.

Then, in August, the city building inspectors came around to inspect our proposed college building. Dr. B. had assured me it was of solid concrete, fireproof construction. I had had it examined by two architects. They, too, said it was a solid concrete building. But the building inspectors bored inside the outer layer of hard concrete. It was a frame building, after all. It did not come up to codes to qualify as a classroom building!

They slapped on us what proved to be—as we then called it—a $30,000 headache. That's a real costly headache!

Before we could be given official occupancy for a college building, they informed us, all walls and ceilings must be torn out and replaced with one-hour-fire-resistant construction!

Once we began tearing out walls, the inspectors condemned all the electric wiring system and the plumbing pipes. New electric conduits were required throughout, and all new plumbing pipes!

I engaged a contractor, highly recommended by our next-door neighbor who then owned "Mayfair," later to become our first girls' student residence. The contractor agreed to do the job—on $4,000 weekly progress payments.

But *where* was I to get the $4,000 per week, *on top of* regular operating expenses? Our income at the time was perhaps $2,500 per week—all obligated in advance for the operational expenditures of the work. Now I had, somehow, to raise *an additional* $4,000 per week!

I sent out a desperate emergency letter to church brethren and co-workers. I made personal long-distance calls to those I felt might be able to help with larger sums.

A peanut and watermelon farmer in Texas sent in most of his life savings—a few thousand dollars. His education had been neglected. It was now too late for him, but he wanted to help others still young enough to obtain the higher education he lacked.

A doctor in Missouri sent a few thousand dollars, and then more later. He later became a trustee of Ambassador College, and the first director of its Bible Correspondence Course. Although he had had nine years of college education and a doctor's degree, he came to Ambassador and earned an additional master of arts degree, in theology.

A radio listener I had never known before, in northern California, mortgaged his own new home for $5,000 and loaned it to me—without security. I was six months past the allotted year in paying it all back, but I made a business deal with his mortgagee, paying him a cash bonus, to extend the time six months on the unpaid balance.

The final week, early October, the contractor came up with a $12,000 bill and demanded immediate payment. I had planned for only $4,000, and had gone through a dozen nightmares to raise that.

The pressure was almost unbearable.

Everyone—except my wife and I—*knew* the college had "folded up"—before it even opened its doors to students. And, of course, the living HEAD of His Church, Jesus Christ, knew it hadn't!

How I finally raised that additional $8,000 within a few days' time, I don't remember, now. I think that was the week when this $5,000 loan came in. But, somehow, God saw us through.

The Lesson in Faith

It became almost impossible to sleep nights. I never lost faith—really. I never doubted the outcome. Yet I had not yet learned the total, implicit, trusting faith that can RELAX and leave it quietly in God's hands. I was under terrific strain. It was literally multiple nightmares condensed into a super ONE!

On one occasion, I almost snapped. I weakened to the extent that I actually prayed, one night, that God would let me die through the night, and relieve me from the almost unbearable agony. But next morning, I was deeply repentant for that, and prayed earnestly for God's forgiveness. Twice I did give up, on going to bed at night. But next morning was another day, and I bounded back, repentant for having given up—if only momentarily.

Yet this "$30,000 headache" was only the *beginning* of troubles. Others were yet to come—from within and from without. It was not until early 1949 that things eased up. By then I had come to the place that I had to pray in final desperation for "six months' grace" from this constant harassment. I humbly asked God to consider that I was human, with human weaknesses, and PLEASE to give me six months' rest from the terrible ordeal.

He did. And during that respite I finally learned

how to RELAX in faith, and shift the weighty BURDEN of it over onto CHRIST! And, at least up to the time of this writing, God has enabled me not only to trust Him for the final outcome, but to let faith remove the strain of anxiety.

When troubles or emergencies arise, we *should* be tremendously *concerned!* We should not take these things lightly or nonchalantly. We should be "on our toes" to DO whatever is *our* part, but trusting God in relaxed FAITH to guide us and to do HIS part which we *cannot* do for ourselves. We should be freed from destructive strain and worry.

This lesson of faith does not come easily. Sometimes it is achieved only through punishing experience. We need to learn that God does not do all things *for* us. He does many things *in,* and *through us.* We have our part to do. But there are some things we *cannot* do, and which we must rely on Him to do, wholly, *for* us. It takes wisdom to know which is which.

We had received some forty applications for prospective college students. But this reconstruction program had delayed the college opening. I had been compelled to notify all applicants that I would advise them when we finally were ready to open.

College Finally Opens

Ambassador College did finally swing open its big front door to students October 8, 1947. But by that time nearly all applicants had gone elsewhere. Besides our son Dick (Richard David), there was only Raymond C. Cole, who came down from Oregon where his family had been in the Church for years; Herman L. Hoeh, who came from Santa Rosa, California; and Miss Betty Bates from Tulsa, Oklahoma—four pioneer students— with a faculty of eight.

Did ever a college start so small? Or with a ratio of two professors to each student? But the things of God, through human instruments, always start the *smallest,* and grow to become the BIGGEST!

Ambassador College had *started!* It was not born without agonizing birth pangs! But, as a mother is soon over the pangs of childbirth, so we are not suffering them today.

Yet the trials and troubles, oppositions and satanic plots to *stop* the college and the work, did not end on October 8, 1947! Even the worst was yet to come!

But in the end, even Satan will be forced to bow to the TRUTH that GOD'S PURPOSE *STANDS*—that Satan can do no more than God *allows*—and that, though Satan's power is far greater than that of us humans, God's power is *infinitely* greater than Satan's.

God has said HIS GOSPEL *SHALL* BE PREACHED AND PUBLISHED IN ALL THE WORLD! Satan has *tried* to prevent it. Had this not been the very WORK OF GOD, it would have been stopped long ago. But the living CHRIST has said He would open the DOOR for the proclaiming of this message, and that *NO MAN can shut it!*

In His power and strength HIS WORK *continues* to GO FORWARD!!

57

Surviving the First Year of Ambassador College

WOULD you really say it was a *college* that finally swung open its door to students the eighth of October, 1947? There were only four students!

There were no dormitories—no place for students to be in residence on the original little "campus" of one and three-quarter acres. We had some books and encyclopedias on shelves in the one room that served as music room, assembly room, library, study room and lounge—but no real college library. There was no gymnasium, no track or athletic field.

WHY Smallest Beginning

I suppose many people would laugh at the idea of dignifying that by the name "college." But there is a reason why it *had* to begin that small.

When the Great God, Creator and Ruler of the vast universe, does something by Himself, He demonstrates

His supreme power by doing it in a stupendous awe-inspiring manner. But when it is actually GOD who is doing something through humans, it must start the smallest. Like the grain of mustard seed, the smallest of herbs, which grows to become the largest, God's works through humans must start the smallest—but they grow, and grow, and grow, until they become the biggest!

Had Ambassador College started big, with several hundred or a few thousand students, a great campus filled with large college buildings—an administration building, classroom buildings, laboratories, music conservatory, large ornate auditorium, gymnasium, a fine quarter-mile track and football field, a large library building with 500,000 volumes, dormitories, dining halls—everything complete, then I could certainly have no faith in accepting it as GOD'S college.

Ambassador started in a building that had been a private residence. True, it had been built in an architectural design more institutional than residential in appearance. But it had been a residence. Then there was the garage. As I mentioned before, it had been originally stables—way back in the years B.C.—*before cars*. It had later been converted into a four-car garage, with apartments upstairs and apartment rooms at both ends.

We had turned some of the living rooms into business offices, and the central garage space into our general mailing room for the radio work. Our small printing shop, with a Davidson duplicating machine, occupied the rear ground-floor room. We called this building the administration building. Since then it has undergone successive remodelings, and served as the administration building until our modern new four-story administration building was completed in 1969.

And, again, I have explained before that God's

number for *organized beginnings* is TWELVE. His original beginnings always start with ONE MAN. God started the human family with one man, Adam. His nation Israel started from the one man, Abraham. That nation's government and leadership started with the one man, Moses. The Church of God and GOD'S WORK started with the one man, Jesus Christ.

But God's own nation on earth had its *organized beginning* through the TWELVE tribes. The Church had its *organized beginning* with TWELVE apostles.

God started the original planning and founding of His college through myself. I had no help from our church in Eugene. The members were too poor to give financial aid. One or two offered disapproval and criticism. But, on that morning of October 8, 1947, the actual *organized beginning* of the college numbered TWELVE persons in total—four students, eight faculty members, myself included. The property had been purchased, as previously explained, TWELVE years after the start of the work.

No Dorms

We had no facilities for housing students. Our own son, Richard David (Dick), lived with us in our new home (new to us, that is). Betty Bates had rented a room out in the east end of Pasadena, some five miles from the college. She used the city bus service for transportation. The other two students, Raymond Cole and Herman Hoeh, rented a room together some two and a half miles from the college. They used less expensive transportation—shoe leather. They managed to prepare their own food, somehow, in their room.

Those pioneer students had to "rough it" in a way I am sure our students of today do not realize. They certainly did not live in luxury. We did manage to employ these pioneer students for part-time work, at $40 per month. But they had to pay $31.50 room-rent— per *each!* In order to have enough to eat, they often picked lamb's-quarter—in place of spinach—where it grew along certain sparsely settled streets and in vacant lots, then prepared it after returning home from school. Many times, they simply went hungry. They were more hungry for an education than for physical food.

Yet they never mentioned any of this, and I didn't learn of it myself until much later.

They heard talk from others about "when this thing folds up." But there was no thought of the college "folding up" in their minds—nor in mine. They had faith. They were there for a *purpose!* It was a mighty serious purpose! It was the one goal of their lives, and they concentrated on it and worked at it with all their energies!

The part-time work these pioneer students did was janitor work.

Opposition from Within

Previously I have mentioned the opposition faced in getting the college started. There had been plans, plots, and schemes to stop the broadcast work before it started, and to kill it after it started. Not from lay members, either at Eugene or up in the Willamette Valley—but from jealous and coveting ministers. There were "temptations" to drop it—offers of something *"better"*—financially. Only these didn't really tempt me. There had been seemingly insurmountable obstacles to hurdle over.

But there now was opposition, whether intentional from those who brought it or not, from within the faculty.

Remember, I had set out to found a NEW KIND of

234

college—GOD'S college. Not a Bible school. Not a "religious" school. A straight liberal arts co-educational institution—but BASED bon God's revealed knowledge actuated by God's Spirit.

But where was I to find teachers and college professors, at the university level, who taught courses on the very FOUNDATION of God's revealed knowledge? Such instructors simply did not exist. I had to start with those reared and schooled in this world's type of education.

And I have explained before how educators, long ago—from the days of Nimrod—from the days of Plato who founded the curricular system—from the days of the University of Paris which started the present universities in the 12th century—had not retained GOD in their knowledge. The world had inherited education, not from God's teachings, but from PAGANISM.

Since I could do no other, I was forced to choose instructors trained in the prevailing system of education. But I sought those of outstanding qualifications and adequate degrees. I wanted the best!

There was the woman professor of English. She had at least two Ph.Ds.—some eight degrees altogether. This surely sounded like the best. She had taught many years in India. I did not know, when Mr. Dillon and I employed her, that she was saturated with eastern philosophies and occultism. As time went on, it became evident that our English professor was not at all in harmony with the real objectives of Ambassador College.

Later on in the year we learned that Professor Mauler-Hiennecey did not really believe in God, but had strong agnostic views. However, he was a lovable old fellow, and a very fine French teacher, as well as a good instructor in Spanish. Under him my son Dick learned to speak French without even an accent. When he went to France, in 1952, he was accepted often as a native Frenchman.

We found M. Mauler-Hiennecey to be pleasant, friendly, kind-hearted. He was with us several years, but finally resigned. But, he was then getting pretty old. We did love him, and he rendered service for some six years.

But in Dr. Taylor I felt we had a sympathetic Christian believer. Dr. Taylor, in spite of his illustrious academic record, which included faculty membership at such institutions as Harvard, Massachusetts Institute of Technology, Cornell, and Wheaton, strongly professed Christianity.

It had seemed too good to be true. The application I had received for a professorship on the Ambassador College faculty from a man of Dr. Hawley Otis Taylor's record in education and science appeared positively providential.

In today's world of materialistic higher education and science, God has been virtually thrown out the window. The Bible has been relegated disdainfully to the scrapheap of medieval superstition.

Of course much if not most of the doctrines of traditional Christianity might well be put in the category of superstition.

I should have known Dr. Taylor's Christianity was this traditional variety. But somehow I didn't realize this until after he arrived in Pasadena.

It seemed indeed a rarity to find a man of Dr. Taylor's illustrious scientific status professing fundamentalist Christianity. And I was overjoyed. Dr. Taylor was appointed, as previously explained, as dean of instruction, and registrar.

Before the college was scarcely more than started,

I was somewhat disillusioned. I soon learned that Dr. Taylor's religious beliefs were, indeed, those of traditional "Christianity." Of course, he was sincere and unalterably confirmed in his convictions.

These basic differences of belief produced a certain friction, but later were resolved in a spirit of happy cooperation.

Bible Course Minimized

In planning the curriculum, class schedules, and the purely academic matters of the college, I left arrangements in the hands of Mr. Dillon and Dr. Taylor. In preparation of the college catalog, I wrote merely the introductory pages describing the *kind* of college, leaving all technical data, description of courses, curriculum, credits required, to Mr. Dillon and Dr. Taylor. I was not experienced in curricula-planning.

The catalog was not printed until after classes were started. But after they were actually in progress, and class schedules set, I discovered to my great dismay that my own course in theology—the real foundation course of the college—had been reduced to a two-hour *minor* subject!

By then classes were under way. All students' schedules were fixed—all records set. It was too late to change them—for that year.

Sensing this undercurrent of hostility within the teaching staff, I immediately decreed that faculty members, as well as students, must attend all my classes. I taught entirely by the lecture method. I did this, not so much as a retaliatory measure, but as a means of getting the new college off to a start as the very *kind of* college God was building.

Since the BIBLE is the very *foundation* of all knowledge, I was determined to see that this approach to

237

knowledge permeated the entire institution. This class provided me with a forum as a sounding board. It enabled me to keep constantly before both students and faculty the biblical FOUNDATION of knowledge, and the scriptural *approach* to understanding.

I was quite conscious of the materialistic educational backgrounds of faculty members. I was well aware of the evolutionary concepts most of them had imbibed. I kept my lectures on a reasonably dignified plane, and I constantly used the four gospels to demonstrate that the current teaching of traditional Christianity was at total variance with the inspired record.

I took great pains to make my lectures so rational and factual as to leave no room for refutation. And none was voiced!

I was reminded of a church service I had conducted back in Eugene, Oregon, a few years before, when a converted former atheist brought an atheist friend. After my service she asked her visiting guest what she thought of the sermon.

"Well," the visitor answered curtly, "I can't refute his statements, but I'm simply not interested in accepting them."

No one knows better than I that it is impossible to cram truth down unwilling and obstinate throats. But I did want the satisfaction of making the truth SO PLAIN that faculty members had but two choices—to accept it, or deliberately reject it in which case it became a witness *against them,* for which they alone were responsible, and for which they would answer in the judgment.

I have been called merely to *proclaim* Christ's message *as a witness.* I am not sent to force conversion on the world, but to be a witness of the TRUTH, made plain, to those willing to receive it. And, of course I realized that unwilling minds can shut the door from allowing it

238

to enter. I am sure that first school year was a bit uncomfortable to some of the faculty members attending my lectures.

But it did establish the educational FOUNDATION for Ambassador College. And it became very convincing to all four students!

At the beginning of the second year I compromised. I saw to it that the theological courses were three-hour majors that year—that is, three hourlong class periods per week. One of them I designated as my own forum period, at which attendance of all faculty members was required. The faculty was excused from further attendance at the other two periods from that time onward.

I was determined that the AMBASSADOR POLICY was going to be inculcated thoroughly in faculty and students alike. Ambassador was to be GOD'S college—not another rubber stamp of the educational institutions of this world! But, with a faculty trained in this world's scholarship, I found that it required determined dominance on my part, plus vigilance, to assure it.

By the third year, I felt sufficient progress had been made to this end that I could safely dispense with the requirement for faculty attendance at biblical lectures. Besides the three hours per week in theology, however, I continued the forum one hour a week, which continues to this day, attended by students and faculty alike.

The Broadcast Dilemma

But now, back to the main thread of the story. The most traumatic crisis of all was to come in the second school year.

This "$30,000 headache" I have described, in being forced to convert our main college building into a fireproof structure, played havoc with our financial situation generally. I was forced to get farther behind with our big radio station.

We had been forced to drop off XELO, the 150,000-watt clear-channel station at Juarez, Mexico, altogether. We had been on both XELO and XEG, the other superpowered 150,000-watt station. In those days these two stations could be heard over most of the United States, and even in central Canada. They had built a tremendous audience for us.

While the cost, per half hour, seemed very high to us, it was only half to two-thirds as much as many major-city 50,000-watt stations in the United States. And although the listening audience to those stations was not a concentrated metropolitan audience such as major-city American stations enjoy, it spread over most of the United States. The total audience, in those days, was much larger than that of any United States station.

We had means of checking and arriving at a close estimate of the number of listeners. I was able to say, then, that every radio dollar reached 2,000 people with a powerful half-hour message!

We can't make that claim any more. Already at that time, 1947-1948, more and more small radio stations were being licensed. Where there had been one small 100-watt station in Eugene, Oregon, in 1934 when we started, there were, in 1961, some five or six, and at least two of them 5,000-watt stations. The number of radio stations multiplied all over the country, in small towns and in major cities. Power increased also. And all this brought more and more interference over the airwaves, constantly reducing the coverage and clarity of signal of such superpowered stations as XELO and XEG.

Up until March, 1948, we were on XEG at 8 p.m. nightly except Saturdays, and 5:30 a.m. daily except

240

Sunday. This was our only southern and midwestern coverage, but it was the most powerful and effective single station existing for a widespread coverage of all that vast area. In addition, we were then using five stations on the Pacific Coast—XERB, 50,000 watts, Sunday only, Saturday and Sunday coverage in Portland, and Sunday only in Seattle. What a far cry that was from the television and radio coverage of today!

But, before the close of 1947 we were getting further and further behind in paying our bills with XEG. The management told me very pointedly that they were not in business for the purpose of financing the start of a college for me. If we were going to use our money to operate the college instead of paying their bills, we would have to go off the air.

It was a frustrating dilemma. I *knew* God had opened the way for the college. I knew the Eternal wanted the college. I knew the work of God could not continue to grow without the college.

But I knew also God wanted us on the air. He had called me to proclaim Christ's gospel.

Thrown Off the Air!

Of course it will be easy for the "armchair quarterbacks" to say that the college should not have been started under these circumstances. Plenty of them *did* say that. Anyway, I was now *into* this dilemma, and I had to face it.

Of course I prayed—continually and fervently. But if God had had a better way, perhaps He found my head so thick He couldn't get it through to me any faster. Now, however, I asked for deliverance out of the trouble. And it came—*later!*

By the first of March XEG carried out their threat to throw us off. They allowed the program to stay on

Sunday nights, *only,* provided I began to make progress in paying off the back indebtedness, and that this progress be continued.

Other bills were pressing. I was being hounded on every side for money by creditors. Many around me continued to harp about "when this thing folds up." But I was determined it was not going to fold up!

We were off XEG with the week-night broadcasts until the following October. Somehow, we weathered the storm.

Loyalty of Co-Workers

One very precious lesson was learned by that experience. Our family of co-workers who regularly support God's work with their tithes and voluntary offerings, remained loyal, even though we were off the air except for Sunday nights. I had learned that it was the *every night* broadcasting that was really effective and resultful. One might have expected that the money to support the work would have stopped when the listeners no longer received the broadcast.

But they had accepted Christ's teaching from my voice, that it is more blessed to GIVE than to receive. Their hearts, as well as their tithes and contributions, were in the work of God. When they no longer *received* the broadcast, they DID NOT STOP *GIVING!* There was scarcely any lag in the income. But the expenses were greatly lessened.

This allowed us to make progress in paying the accumulated XEG bill sufficient to induce them to put us back on the air in October that year, 1948. Nevertheless, it was a harassing spring, summer, and fall—and the frightful agony of it rose to a climax by October and November.

We had been forced to get behind even with the

242

faculty payroll. Now of course that was a thing regarded among teachers generally as the unpardonable sin of an educational institution. One particular teacher tried to injure us legally.

But the Labor Relations Board—or whoever it was that the matter came before—allowed us to distribute the back pay over several months of time. So *that* attempt to put the college out of business failed.

It surely is needless to say, however, that experiences of this kind were a living nightmare to endure.

Reducing to Half-Time

During the summer of 1948 I was faced with a frightful situation and a tough decision. Everyone seemed to think I ought to simply give up, close the college down, and try to build back up the broadcasting work. But somehow I knew God wanted neither dropped. I had supreme and abiding FAITH that He would see us through. True, I had not yet learned to have *relaxed* faith. I continued to allow the strain of this situation to punish me. The following year I was to learn the secret of *relaxed* faith—but I will come to that in due course.

After counsel, meditation, prayer, and much thinking, I made the decision of what to do. I decided to reduce the college schedule to *half-time* for one year. I could only pay *half*-salaries. And I could not continue to pay all of those. We would have to suffer through *one* year with a pruned-down faculty.

Just one of our women teachers remained with us—and she is still loyally with us today—Mrs. Lucy H. Martin. Of course Mr. Dillon remained on, and Dr. Taylor and Professor Mauler-Hiennecey. I found that Mrs. Martin was well qualified to teach English.

And then Mrs. Martin really surprised me.

"Perhaps I had not made it clear to you before," she

said, "but I happen to have degrees in music just as high as the former teacher—and I can make them higher by going on, during summer vacations, to complete work at Juilliard [America's highest-ranking musical college in New York], for my master's degree in music. I'll be happy to take over the music department if you'd like, besides teaching English and being librarian."

And so we started the second year of Ambassador College on half-schedule, with classes only three days a week. It was that or let the college die.

Three New Students Arrive

No effort had been made to recruit any additional students, due to this situation. However, one student showed up—a fellow from Wisconsin, named Kenneth C. Herrmann.

A very few weeks after the 1948-49 school year had started, the front doorbell of our home rang one morning while I was shaving. My wife told me that two young radio listeners from Arkansas were there to see me. I hurried down.

They introduced themselves as Marion and Raymond McNair. They had been working in the apple harvest up in Washington, but wanted to swing by Pasadena and see me on the way home.

We had a nice talk, and I was surprised to learn how much they knew about the Bible. I was intensely interested in hearing of their experience leading to this biblical knowledge, and how they came to listen to *The World Tomorrow*.

These boys had not had Sunday school or other *religious* training. They had never been taught anything about immortal souls, or going to heaven when one dies. Their very *first* religious training began with the Bible. They studied it daily before they were teenagers.

244

Some years later, they happened to hear a religious broadcast on the radio. "Why," they exclaimed in surprise, "that fellow is not preaching what's in the Bible! He's telling people just the *opposite* of what the Bible says!"

This aroused them to tune to other religious programs on their radio set. They were astonished and disillusioned! It seemed that all the "radio preachers" were preaching a "Christianity" that was very contrary to the Christianity of Christ, of Paul, and of the apostles which they had been receiving out of their Bible!

Then one day they heard a program coming in from a Mexican station. They were startled in happy surprise.

"Why," they exclaimed, *"that* fellow is preaching exactly what we have been getting out of the Bible!" That program was *The World Tomorrow!* They became steady listeners.

This experience was just one more example of what I have always said: Give a Bible to someone who has never had any religious teaching, and let him study it diligently, without any of the popular teachings of "Christianity," and he will believe precisely what is proclaimed on *The World Tomorrow.* Yet those who *do* believe and proclaim the PLAIN TRUTHS of the BIBLE will be branded today as "false prophets."

"Well, I hope you boys will come to Ambassador College when you've finished high school," I said.

"Oh, we're older than we look!" came the quick answer. "We've already graduated from high school."

"Well, how does it happen you're not in Ambassador College, then?" I asked.

"Well, we supposed we couldn't afford it," they replied.

"Well, look!" I said. "This is Friday morning. Can

you boys find a part-time job before tonight?" I explained that college was in session only three days a week.

"Yes, Sir, we can," came the immediate and decisive answer.

"Well, you go find that job, and report to Ambassador College Monday morning," I said.

They left. And they did find jobs.

Today Mr. Raymond F. McNair is an ordained minister and Deputy Chancellor of the Pasadena campus of Ambassador College.

Crisis with Dr. B. Approaches

I have previously explained the difficulties we experienced in dealing with Dr. B., from whom we purchased the college property. He had continued to harass us. He never had intended to let us obtain permanent possession of the property. But, as the fall and winter of 1948 approached, with the college now in its second school year, the wily Dr. B. had still one more card to play—his trump card!

We had been off the air in our daily broadcasting from March until October. We had been forced to operate the college on a half-time schedule for this second school year. We had been all but knocked out.

But there were a number of conditions that now loomed as the supreme crisis of all.

While we had paid the $25,000 as rent (to be converted into a $25,000 down payment via the lease option), we had, of course, paid no interest. Neither had we paid the taxes or insurance. These accumulated amounts were all to come due on December 27, 1948. They amounted to several thousand dollars. Taxes had to be paid, retroactive for the twenty-five months. Also interest on the unpaid balance, starting at $100,000, less

246

San Francisco, January 3, 1947

Dear Uncle Frank:

I have about twenty minutes before leaving for the train home, so thought I'd get off a short account of happenings since I saw you last summer.

Sorry my call at your office was so brief and full of interruptions. We had a good trip home, arriving on schedule.

Did I tell you I planned to start a college in Pasadena? This work has grown to the place it needs several Herbert Armstrongs, and so far it has had only one. It needs a follow-up—a personal follow up—I haven't been able to give it. So far I've been able to get clerical help, and shift about all that kind of detailed responsibility to others, but I need several who can do some of the things that, so far, only I can do. Another thing, I'm not getting any younger and the work so far has been built solely around me, and if I dropped off it wouldn't continue long. Only thru a college, where we can educate and train men to do some of the things I do, can the work expand much bigger, and be sure of continuing on—and even with the college going I realise I'll be lucky if I'm able actually to use one in ten or twenty of the students.

■ *A letter to Uncle Frank Armstrong, leading advertising writer in Iowa in* *his day and mentor of Herbert W. Armstrong. Ambassador College expanded significantly in* *1956 with the acquisition of the Merritt estate.*

■ *The first four students of Ambassador College at entry to main classroom building, now the Library, left above. Snow remained all day on campus in February 1949 in second year of the college, left. There has been no snowfall of such magnitude in Pasadena since that date. Students of the fourth year, top. First commencement, center. Richard David flanked by Mother and Father.*

■ *Mr. Armstrong in his first office on Ambassador College campus in what is now the Library annex. A lovely sunlit room of Mayfair, now a girls' dormitory, acquired in the third year of the college.*

■ *Faculty and students at a weekly assembly in the fifth year of Ambassador —1951-1952. Area is now a reference room in the library. A graduate seminar in the library.*

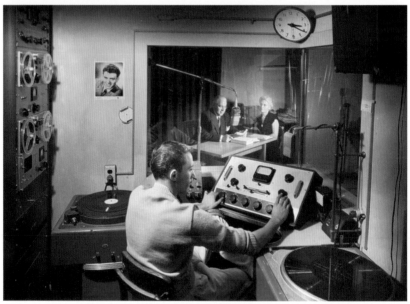

■ *The radio studio from which emanated* The World Tomorrow. *Early broadcasts had a music interlude, here being sung by daughter Beverly. Richard Armstrong at the controls.*

■ *Office wall map with radio stations carrying the* World Tomorrow *broadcast flagged. Strolling across the Big Sandy, Texas, festival site, later to become another Ambassador campus. At the typewriter preparing a script.*

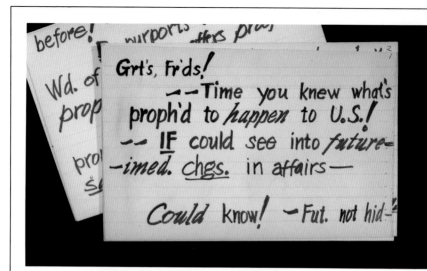

Grt's, Frds!
——Time you knew what's proph'd to *happen* to U.S.!
—— IF could see into *future*—
—imed. chgs. in affairs—

Could know! —Fut. not hid—

The first attempt to go on television in 1955 with The World Tomorrow. *Right, Herbert Armstrong often stood in the set. Above, handwritten cards, to prompt speaker, have long since been replaced by the teleprompter. Introductory scene used Ambassador campus as background. The Armstrongs at a desk in a set.*

■ *At the tent west of Cairo, Egypt, in 1956, with the pyramids of Giza in the background. Near Megiddo in the Galilee. The surviving wall of the Temple Mount, Jerusalem.*

■ *The passports of Herbert and Loma Armstrong and son Richard David. In the 1956 trip the Armstrongs toured throughout the Middle East and much of Western Europe, providing new insights for future articles and broadcasts. On tour in Cairo.*

■ *At the microphone following the extensive 1956 trip abroad. Ribbon-cutting as the* grounds of *Ambassador College, Pasadena, take on their present configuration. The first four-color* Plain Truth, *with Sir Winston Churchill on the cover.* The Plain Truth *matures over 30-year period.*

The

PLAIN TRUTH

The Coming

World Super-Government

The

PLAIN TRUTH

A magazine of understanding
dealing with the great truths of life

VOL. III.   NO. 6   JULY–AUGUST 1938

PROPHESIED EVENTS

Speed on In Europe !

The

PLAIN TRUTH

A magazine of Understanding

WHAT IS
Prophesied from NOW ON !

The

PLAIN TRUTH

A magazine of understanding.

RUSSIA

at the

The

PLAIN TRUTH

a magazine of understanding
JANUARY–FEBRUARY, 1947

the

PLAIN TRUTH

a magazine of understanding

the

PLAIN TRUTH

a magazine of understanding

the

PLAIN TRUTH

a magazine of understanding

■ *The office in Sydney, Australia, is visited by Mr. Armstrong, who approves of its character and quality. Richard David Armstrong, in the London office, keeps in touch with Pasadena headquarters.*

■ *The Yule estate in Bricket Wood, Herts, England, at the time of its purchase. The main residence was renovated and became Memorial Hall, in memory of Richard David Armstrong who died in 1958.*

■ *The Loma D. Armstrong Academic Center, Ambassador College, Pasadena.*

Ambassador Hall is flanked by the new Fine Arts and Science buildings. A painting of Loma D. Armstrong in

Ambassador Hall. Groundbreaking for the academic complex.

$1,000 each month for the twenty-five months. Insurance for the twenty-five months also became due in one lump December 27.

HOW, in our strained circumstances, were we going to raise that large sum of money by December 27? It was a frightening dilemma.

A MIRACLE Happens

Altogether it was going to require something like $17,000. It seemed an insurmountable obstacle.

I began making plans for every means that I could think of that might help raise that money. But I realized fully that *nothing* I could plan or do could accomplish that apparently unattainable goal. I knew I had to rely on GOD. Nothing but a miracle could now save God's college.

Somehow, I knew we would be delivered from this crisis—though I could not see how. I relied primarily on fervent, continuous prayer. I decided to do everything *I* could plan or think of, and then trust God with the result.

It must have been along about early November that our auditor, Mr. Bolivar O'Rear, and I, found it necessary to make a trip to Washington, D.C., to apply for a tax-exempt status as a nonprofit corporation. Mr. O'Rear had been an attorney in Washington for several years. While there, we had one long conference with a former friend of his—an attorney—in this lawyer's office. He was sympathetic in trying to help us come up with ideas that might raise the necessary funds.

Of course, I had written a letter to all our active co-workers acquainting them with our great problem and spoken of it to our radio audience.

Then, suddenly, about November 25, a miracle really did happen!

About $3,000 came in, through the mail, in one day. Our normal daily income for the work in those days was about $500. The $3,000 that came in one day was like a fortune being rained down from heaven.

The next day, to our utter amazement, another $3,000 came in. And then the next—and the next—and the next. This almost dumbfounding downpour of money continued until December 15. Our total income for that December exceeded $50,000! We could hardly believe it!

WHY did it come in? We could not account for it on the basis of anything we had done. No plans or ideas or efforts of ours had brought it. There was only one explanation—GOD SENT IT!

It seemed like God had sent us a great deal more than we needed! But we were soon to see that He had not. The college could not have been saved, had there been less. It turned out we needed considerably more money by December 27 than we had realized. Dr. B. had a $17,000 mortgage on the property that he had to pay off in order to transfer the deed to us. He was several years behind in paying taxes. Under the circumstances, the way he acted—and considering that he was planning to prevent allowing us to exercise our option—unless we had some $15,000 to $20,000 to temporarily loan him, IN ADDITION to the money we had to pay him, he could have beaten us and we should have lost the property, after all!

But GOD knew precisely what we NEEDED—and He SENT IT!

Dr. B. Holds Out

We still owed a few thousand dollars in back teachers' salaries we had as yet been unable to pay. By December 15, when we were assured of having enough money to pay off Dr. B., we paid these back salaries. And I was human enough to *enjoy* paying FIRST those who had been loyal and were still with us—even though we did send out the checks to the others *later* that same day!

We took no chances on coming up late in paying off Dr. B. We put the full amount due him in escrow on December 15. But he made no move whatever toward signing the papers for the transaction.

As the days passed, and it began to appear that he was going to try to avoid signing, we began to take action. Through the escrow company we learned that there was a mortgage against the property. It was past due—long past due. I contacted the man who held the mortgage. I told him the situation.

He was sympathetic.

"If Dr. B. refuses to sign, and tries to block our exercising the option," I asked, "will you be willing to SELL that mortgage to us?"

"Yes, I certainly will," he said. "And I'll tell you what you can then do. Since he is so far in arrears with unpaid taxes, once you own the mortgage, you can foreclose and take the property away from him."

I did not want to take the property in that manner. But it was reassuring to know that God had now put me in position to do so.

Finally, Dr. B. said he would sign if we would loan him a few thousand dollars, *in addition* to the money we had deposited to pay accumulated interest, taxes, and insurance. We arranged to do this, and then pay him $750 per month in payments instead of the full $1,000, for the next year or two—until in this manner he had paid us back.

Dr. B. thereupon signed—but he was still tricky. The property was held as a joint-tenancy between him and his aged sister. His signature was not sufficient without his sister's also.

FORCING Dr. B. to Sign

That year, December 27, fell on a Monday. On Wednesday, the 22nd, we were having another conference in the office of our attorneys, Judge Morton and Mr. Wannamaker. They suggested that Dr. B., knowing every trick of the law, might contend that our option had to be exercised at least a day *before December 27, in order to have been* exercised ON December 27. Probably no judge would so interpret it, but they advised against taking chances.

Therefore, they advised that we force Dr. B., if possible, to have his sister's signature on the papers before 1 p.m. on Friday, the 24th, or we should start suit against him in Superior Court promptly at 1 p.m. on Friday, withdrawing all the money out of escrow and depositing it in the Superior Court.

They began a feverish activity of preparing the legal papers to file suit, working late Wednesday night, and almost all of Thursday night, to have everything ready by 1 p.m. Friday.

Friday morning came. By 11 a.m. Dr. B. had made no move to have his sister sign. We had the papers she was to sign, and decided to go to their home with the papers.

About noon, or a little after, on that Friday, Mr. O'Rear and I drove out to the home of Dr. B. He claimed his sister was upstairs in bed, too ill to be disturbed.

I knew he was not telling the truth. It was now less than an hour before Mr. Wannamaker would be on his way to Superior Court.

The chips were down. This was the final crisis MINUTE!

250

"All right, Dr. B.," I said. "Either your sister signs in the next thirty minutes, or I'll tell you what's going to happen. I have exhausted my patience on you. I have suffered your harassment now for two years. I'm going to end it HERE AND NOW!

"Unless I telephone my attorneys that your sister has signed, before 1 o'clock, it will be TOO LATE— they will be on the way to file suit in Superior Court. All the money will be withdrawn from escrow yet this afternoon, and placed with the judge. We know you NEED that money to live. We will then seek for every delay the law allows. My lawyers tell me we can delay action on the suit for years. Meanwhile we remain in possession of the property. The college will go right along. You will receive NO PAYMENTS whatsoever.

"But that is not all. I have negotiated with Mr. Blank to purchase the trust deed on this property which you owe him. I have the money on hand to purchase it. Then, because you have violated the terms of the mortgage, by not paying taxes, I shall immediately FORE-CLOSE on you. In that manner we will take complete ownership of the property by paying only the amount of this mortgage. We will freeze you out completely. Once this is done, we can withdraw our suit, and recover all the money.

"Dr. B., you are a smart lawyer. You know I can do this—and *I WILL!* It's absolutely ridiculous, but here I am now, PLEADING with you to let us go on PAYING YOU for this property, instead of foreclosing on you and taking it away from you—but we are now in position to do just that. It's almost 12:30. At 1 o'clock it will be too late!"

Dr. B. was BEATEN!

"MARTHA!" he called at the stairway, "come on

251

down right away! We've got to HURRY! We have to hunt up a notary public to witness your signature before 1 o'clock."

His sister was already dressed and ready. She had not been in bed, or ill, as he had said. We drove quickly to a neighboring business street and found a notary public.

At 12:30—just thirty minutes before our attorneys would have left their office to file the suit—I telephoned them that I had the papers all signed, sealed and delivered!

And so ended Dr. B.'s efforts to have his cake and eat it too—that is, to take our money for the purchase of the property, and then keep the property too!

There were a few minor harassments from him after that. Had we ever been one day late in making any payment, he would have filed suit to reclaim the property immediately. But we were never a day late.

Some years later, he sold the mortgage to a bank, and long ago it was paid out and we have owned the property, CLEAR, ever since.

In due time both his sister, and then Dr. B., himself, died.

Ambassador College was over its first hump.

58

Ambassador Begins to Grow!

Ambassador College had been saved. The property originally acquired was now secured—as long as we kept up the monthly payments.

We were "over the first hump" in the struggle to establish and perpetuate this forward-looking college of TOMORROW! The nerve-shattering intense *ordeals* were behind us. Continuous problems were to be encountered in the path ahead—but we would cross each of these bridges as we reached them.

Half-Time Operation

The decision, born of necessity, to operate the college on a half-time schedule through the 1948-49 school year proved a blessing in disguise. It was one of those occasional self-imposed temporary setbacks.

This half-time operation reduced the college budget by almost half. Together with the miraculous fifteen-day in-pouring of income in December, we were off to a comparatively good start by January, 1949. Of course that providential downpour of funds of the first half of December did not continue. After December 15, the financial income was back to normal.

During 1948 we had been able to print *The Plain Truth* only twice, prior to September. We had gotten out an abbreviated eight-page issue in March. But then we were put off the air on our one BIG station, and we managed only one more—a June number—prior to September.

By holding publication down to eight pages, we were able to issue a *Plain Truth* every month for the remainder of that year—September, October, November, and December.

In 1949 I felt we should get back to the 16-page size. This was possible only by combining the first issue as a January-February number.

It still was a tight financial struggle through 1949 as evidenced by the fact that I was able to print only two more editions that entire year—one in July, the other in November.

Part of the difficulty, however, was due to the fact that more and more duties were demanding my time. I had no editorial help whatever. Up until this time, and even another year or two in the future, it had been necessary for me to do 100 percent of the writing of *The Plain Truth.*

Our Second Land Purchase

During those first two school years of the college we had no dormitory facilities. The seven students enrolled that second year—1948-49—were obliged to rent rooms around town. But in May, 1949, the first addition to the original two and one-quarter-acre campus came our way.

254

Adjoining this original bit of campus grounds, on the north, was the stately 28-room Tudor-style building called "Mayfair," with 200 feet of frontage on Terrace Drive. It added about one and three-quarters acres, giving us a campus of four acres, with magnificently landscaped grounds.

The Mayfair grounds were not in the most desirable condition. Soon after acquiring them, we completely relandscaped them. Most of the work was done by our students, using a rented bulldozer to completely recontour the sloping grounds, bringing them into harmony with the original plot.

For some two years Mayfair had been used as a rooming house. Most of the tenants had leases running another year. We were able to obtain only partial possession during 1949.

But by that autumn, after two years of rooming off campus, our students were able to take up residence ON CAMPUS! We began to feel like a *real college!*

That autumn the student enrollment increased to TWELVE. I have said quite a little heretofore, about TWELVE being the number of organized BEGINNINGS. For one thing, that was the first year the college had an organized student council. The first student body president of Ambassador College was my son Richard David (Dick).

Among the five new students that fall was Roderick C. Meredith. Although he was a new student with us, he was a transfer from a college in Missouri, and consequently rated as a sophomore.

Our men students took up residence on third floor Mayfair in September, 1949. We were not yet prepared to feed students. During that school year the men really "roughed it," preparing their own meals in a dark, depressing, foreboding basement room in Mayfair. It had been painted in a conglomeration of deep yellow,

255

dark green, red, and black. In a later year, that room was modernized into a new-looking office, and served as an editorial room for *The Plain Truth* for some years.

Mrs. Annie M. Mann, who had moved to Pasadena from Eugene, Oregon, had been preappointed to become our House Mother for girls. She had been awaiting the time when we would have girl students and a girls' student residence. During the 1948-49 school year she and Betty Bates, our only girl student the first three years, had roomed together off campus. Now, however, they took up residence in one of the vacant ground-floor rooms in Mayfair. Most of the other Mayfair rooms still were occupied by lease-holding guests.

During 1949 we continued on our one superpower station, XEG, the program beaming out over most of North America at 8 p.m., Central Standard time, seven nights a week. We had also added another border station, XEMU, with the time of 6:30 p.m. every night. But though this station had a splendid dial-spot, 580, it never brought much of a response. But by November that year, the program had gone on a good 5,000-watt Chicago station, WAIT. It was only once a week—10 a.m., Sundays, but the response was good. The rating agencies showed *The World Tomorrow* the second highest rated program in Chicago during our half-hour.

During 1949 *The World Tomorrow* was still being heard over only nine stations. Yet the work as a whole continued to grow that year, its usual 30 percent over the year before.

1950—Still Tough Going

Although we had gotten over what I called "the first hump" by January, 1949, the upward climb of this work of God was still "TOUGH GOING." It was not easy. Jesus Christ never promised "easy going."

Through 1950 I do not remember any crises so severe that the very existence of the work hung in the balance. I had, at last, learned the lesson of RELAXED FAITH. I no longer let the problems we met put me under such an ordeal as I had gone through previously.

Now I was able to cast the burdens on the *living* CHRIST, meanwhile leaping to action to pray intensively for guidance, and to energetically *DO* whatever was in my own power to do—but in a FAITH that was relaxed and confident, trusting God with the results.

During 1950 I was able to publish only FOUR issues of *The Plain Truth*—in February, March, April, and August. As an evidence of the tight financial squeeze of the year, all four editions had to be reduced to a mere eight pages once again. Or course, as stated above, part of this was due to the heavy load on my shoulders of doing all of the writing, in addition to the many other responsibilities, now fast increasing.

For those first three years of the college, I taught all of the Bible and theology classes—and that meant three classes the third year!

And Now, FOURTH College Year

When college classes began, early September, 1950, ten new students had enrolled. For the first time, we had a full FOUR-YEAR COLLEGE. The first year we had only a Freshman class. The second, a Freshman and Sophomore; and the third, we added a Junior Class. There had been the pioneer FOUR students the first year. There were seven the second, and twelve the third.

September, 1950, brought five new girl students. Until then, we had had only the one girl student—Betty Bates. Now we had six girls and sixteen men. Now we had an enrollment of TWENTY-TWO!

And that autumn, for the first time, we had a real

257

student residence on the campus. Yes, the college was growing up! To officials of any other college or university it would have seemed still to be smaller than almost any college had ever been. But to us, with only four the first year, and only an even dozen students the third year, the twenty-two—with, at last, six girl students—seemed like we were becoming a real college!

Now Mrs. Mann was our full-fledged House Mother, with six girls under wing. We had brought down from Oregon a "nutritional cook," as we called her. Now we had FULL POSSESSION, for the first time, of Mayfair.

We had closed off the rear stairway so that it bypassed the second floor, and proceeded from ground floor to the third. All our men were housed that year on third-floor Mayfair. It was like a separate building altogether from the second floor. Our six girl students, and, in addition, the apartment we had done over for Mrs. Mann, occupied the second floor. The ground floor was dining and lounging.

Since we had operated on half-schedule in the 1948-49 year, it had been made virtually impossible for students to graduate in four years. However, by taking a heavier-than-normal load the last two years, both Herman Hoeh and Betty Bates graduated in June, 1951—completing their college work in four years.

First Graduation

That was another milestone attained. Our first commencement exercises were held, in our beautiful Garden Theater, on the last Friday of May, in 1951.

In order to qualify to confer degrees, the college had to be separately incorporated, show a minimum of $50,000 invested in college facilities, equipment, and library, and be officially empowered by the State of

California to confer degrees. This, too, was hurdling another major milestone.

Until this time, Ambassador College had been operated as an activity of the Radio Church of God. But by May, 1951, we had managed to meet all of the state's requirements, and to be approved, and empowered by the state to confer degrees.

Small as we really were, we ourselves began to feel that our college was GROWING UP! It was a real THRILL!

Athletic Field Acquired

In November, 1950, our third property acquisition was achieved in a rather dramatic manner.

For some time, we had had our eyes on a camellia nursery, across Terrace Drive to the east of our original campus plot. I had visualized it as some day becoming our athletic field.

Meanwhile, Mr. Hulett C. Merritt, the multi-millionaire capitalist who owned the second estate north of Mayfair, had been moving onto several properties he owned in our immediate vicinity, a number of large old houses.

Several large houses, or frame apartment houses, along the right-of-way then being cleared for the new Hollywood Freeway, were being condemned. Mr. Merritt had been able to buy them at a very low sum. For some months large-scale housemovers had been moving several of those monstrous frame structures to Pasadena, setting them on these vacant lots. In one or two cases, the structures had been actually cut in two, moved, and then joined back together again.

I think that Mr. Merritt had not counted quite the total cost. He probably obtained the houses for almost nothing. But he was not able to simply put them down on his vacant properties for nothing. He ran up against the very stiff Pasadena building codes. By the time he had constructed solid foundations under them, and brought plumbing and electric wiring and other services up to Pasadena codes, he probably had a lot more money invested in them than he had expected.

In any event, I learned that the owner of the camellia nursery was receptive to selling. Immediately we almost shuddered at the thought that possibly Mr. Merritt might purchase that plot of ground and move more of those old houses on it—thus wrecking our hopes of an athletic field.

One Sunday morning I happened to be in our administration building, and a real estate broker, who had a listing of the camellia nursery, came in. The afternoon before, he said, he had been informed that a $50,000 check had been deposited with another real estate broker who also had the property listed, as full purchase price for the nursery plot, plus four other houses and lots. Three of the houses were over on Green Street, just across Terrace Drive from Mr. Merritt's fabulous mansion. One was on Camden Street to the east of Terrace Drive.

This $50,000 cash was to be put into escrow at a bank on Monday afternoon. The real estate broker said he would like to see the college acquire it if we were able. However, if we needed terms, and lacked the cash, we'd have to pay a higher price, and move fast.

"I'll pay you $60,000," I said at once, "with $5,000 now, to go into escrow tomorrow *morning, as soon as the bank opens,* and the balance on terms we can work out. Is it a deal?"

"It's a deal," he said. "I'm sure the owners will accept."

"All right then," I said, "let's move fast. I will have a quorum of our board of trustees here in this office by

260

2 o'clock this afternoon, and I'll have a $5,000 check ready. Can you have the necessary papers drawn up to put the deal into escrow by that time—and can you get the owner and his wife here to sign?"

He felt sure he could.

He did. In our hurried special board meeting the transaction was approved. The owners signed the papers with us.

Next afternoon, when the other broker went to the escrow department with his $50,000 check, he found the property had been bought right out from under him.

I was expecting a furious call from Mr. Merritt.

I was not disappointed.

Late that afternoon he was on the telephone. "Now you look here, Mr. Armstrong," he said. "You're the first man that ever got the jump on me and beat me in a business deal. I'm glad you got that nursery property, because I know you wanted that for an athletic field. But what in blazes do you want with these lots down here on Green Street?"

"Why, it was simply just one complete package deal," I said. "We had to take the whole thing to get the athletic field."

Mr. Merritt wanted me to come over to see him.

"Those fellows charged you too much for these Green Street properties," he said. "Now I'll take them off your hands. You paid $30,000 for them. You shouldn't have paid over $25,000. So, tell you what I'll do. I will DONATE to your college $10,000, and my wife will donate $10,000. We can deduct that on our income tax report. Then you sell me those four properties for $10,000 cash. That way you get your entire $30,000 back, and you've paid only $30,000 for the athletic field."

"I'll consult my tax attorney," I replied, "but I'm

261

sure the Internal Revenue people will not approve a $20,000 deductible donation from you, when, in actual fact, the entire $20,000 reverts back to you, in the form of this property.

But Mr. Merritt remained adamant.

This was in November, or December. Along about the following March or April, a real estate salesman came into my office.

"I understand you own those houses down on Green Street," he said. "Would you be willing to list them? I think maybe I could find a buyer."

Immediately I deduced that Mr. Merritt sent him.

"No, I wouldn't sell them," I replied. "We need them for college dormitories. And besides, if I ever sold them to anybody it would be to our neighbor Mr. Merritt."

"Well," he said a little sheepishly, "to tell you the truth, it was Mr. Merritt who sent me here."

For years we used those houses for men's dormitories, then we tore them down. They were getting too old for use. Today those properties form a beautifully landscaped entrance to our new four-story Hall of Administration.

59

First "Fruits" of Right Education

AFTER THE purchase of the camellia nursery, and the Green Street properties, we felt that Ambassador College was really *on its way!*

The camellia nursery would give us an athletic field. It was small—there would not be space for a quarter-mile track, a stadium, or football field. But there was sufficient ground for an eighth-mile running track, and two new tennis courts. There was also room for the pole vault and broad jump, and space for the high jump, and the shotput.

Then the Green Street houses could be converted into men's dormitories. Mayfair could be made exclusively a girls' student residence.

We felt that, with a classroom building, an administration building, both men's and women's residences on campus, and an athletic field, even though small, we were coming to have a college campus.

First "FRUITS" of College

During 1950 I had been able to issue only four numbers of *The Plain Truth*—and they were all reduced to mere eight-page numbers. I have stated before that one reason was my personal inability to fully execute all the fast-growing responsibilities of this expanding work in mere twenty-four-hour days.

By the autumn of 1950 I was having to teach FOUR different classes in theology, and now three hours each class. That meant twelve hours of teaching each week.

Up to this time I had written *every word* that went into *The Plain Truth.* I had been doing a half-hour broadcast seven days a week.

The early years in Eugene, Oregon, had resulted in the raising up of several small churches in the Pacific Northwest, through evangelistic campaigns I had conducted. But there were no pastors to minister to those churches. Only two remained—in Eugene and in Portland.

All these years the broadcasting work was expanding. By the end of 1942 it had grown to a national audience. This necessitated my absence from Eugene and Portland much of the time beginning with 1943, and all of the time after April, 1947, when we moved to Pasadena.

The whole work was a one-man ministry in those years. In my absence, attendance at Eugene dwindled from around one hundred to about thirty. You know what the Israelites got into when God called Moses away from them for just forty days at Mount Sinai; the people abandoned God and made for themselves an idol.

". . . As for this Moses," they said, ". . . we wot not what is become of him." And then, in effect, "Come on, let us make an idol god of our own to worship."

264

At Eugene, three would-be leaders said, in effect: "As for this Herbert Armstrong, we wot not what has become of him. Come on, let us make an idol god of our own to worship in the form of a local social club, like all the worldly churches." And so even the thirty members remaining were split into two differing camps.

The Portland and the Vancouver, Washington, churches had consolidated into the one church at Portland. And even that had diminished to eleven or twelve members.

A one-man ministry could not maintain several local churches, an expanding broadcasting work, editing and writing all the articles for a fast-growing magazine, teach four college classes, and act as executive head of a growing college, without something slipping backward somewhere.

But 1951 was the year that produced the first "fruits" of the new college.

In April of that year we began the first activity toward an enlarged *Plain Truth*. I was still unwilling to publish, in *The Plain Truth*, articles written by students. Yet something had to be done.

A new idea was born. The *Plain Truth* circulation had grown to more than 50,000 copies, and it was too costly to publish every month on our income of that period. That, combined with the fact I simply could not find time to write the entire edition every month, by myself alone, forced the new idea.

I decided to completely scrap the entire mailing list!

We would start building a *new* mailing list from scratch. That would solve half the problem—the lack of funds to publish a sixteen-page magazine every month.

Twelve years before I had started a second magazine, called *The Good News*. It was to have been a church membership organ, edited exclusively for baptized church members. *The Plain Truth* was to continue as the general magazine for as many of the general public as would request it. But at that time—February, 1939—I had been unable to continue publication of *The Good News* beyond the first issue! The reason? Same reason—lack of funds, and inability of ONE MAN to do so much.

But now, twelve years later, I decided to bring *The Good News* back to life. It would circulate, at the start, only to co-workers whose tithes and offerings made this growing work possible.

If we could no longer afford to offer *The Plain Truth* to the entire radio audience, it seemed to me imperative that we provide, at least, a regular monthly publication for those who voluntarily financed God's work, and Ambassador College. And our students could share with me the burden of writing the articles.

Consequently, in April, 1951, *The Good News* was reborn!

Now, for the first time, our students began to make active contributions to the activities of this expanding work!

The New GOOD NEWS

The leading article, beginning on the front cover of the April, 1951, *Good News,* written by me, expressed the situation.

Here is a condensation of what it said:

Quote from that article: "A new idea is born! *The Good News* is *re*-born!

"With the turn of the war in Korea world events *speed up* in the chaotic plunge to oblivion! And beginning now, the all-important work of God also must speed up! The pace must be accelerated! It must expand now to *dynamic* WORLDWIDE ACTIVITY!

"It is later than we think!

"When God first started Ambassador College, many brethren and co-workers lacked faith. They couldn't see God's hand in it. Some felt your pastor's duty was solely to preach the gospel to the world—not realizing that one man *alone* can't do it all!

"They had forgotten that Jesus, Peter and Paul surrounded themselves with specially God-*called* men whom they *trained* to assist them in their great mission.

"Some said, 'Why, there isn't time! It will be four years before the first students graduate, and even then they will still be just youths without maturity or actual experience.'

"But there was, *and still is,* enough time—though there is not a day to lose. The end of this age *can't* come until this very gospel of the kingdom has been preached and published in all the world as a witness to all nations (Matt. 24:3, 14).

"Students Now Ready"

"Our students have been gaining actual experience *during* their college years!

"By their fruits we *know* they have been called of God for their important parts in this great commission of Christ. They are trained and ready. They are consecrated and Spirit-led.

"Already more than one hundred and fifty, brought to repentance and conversion through this work, have been baptized by these competent disciples (and the word 'disciple' means student, or learner).

"It is already ably demonstrated that God made no mistake when He started Ambassador College!

267

"The New Idea"

"And now, with this issue, A NEW IDEA is born. Through Ambassador College students, *The Good News* is re-born! With this issue, our students launch a new activity in Christ's ministry—and at the same time, a new college activity.

"It was back in February, 1939—twelve years ago—that with only Mrs. Armstrong's help, from a little stuffy inside office without windows or ventilation in Eugene, Oregon, the first issue of *The Good News* was printed—on a second-hand mimeograph. . . .

"But the commission to 'feed my sheep' is second to the great commission, *'This gospel of the kingdom shall be preached in all the world.'* One man alone could not carry on a campaign of evangelism then expanding from local to national, and conduct a personalized ministry to so many at the same time. And so no other issues of *The Good News* were published—until now.

"But now, at long last, *The Good News* is re-born, *as one of the first fruits of Ambassador College*—one of the *evidences* that this college was necessary."

But, even with the editorial help of students, finances permitted the publication of only four sixteen-page issues during the remainder of 1951—plus one sixteen-page *Plain Truth,* issued October, 1951—written wholly by me.

Still Struggling Upward

All this history, in retrospect, about the struggle to publish *The Plain Truth*, will remind the reader, once again, that it has been a long, hard, and persevering upward struggle to bring God's work to its present position of worldwide activity, power, and influence.

But back, for a moment, to this April, 1951, *Good*

News. In it appeared the very first article by Herman L. Hoeh we had ever published—and even this was not—*yet*—in *The Plain Truth.* Its caption sounds, to me today, rather tame compared to many he has written since. It was "Are Good Manners Good?" It had to do with the right or wrong of etiquette.

The radio log shows that, at that time, *The World Tomorrow* was being broadcast on only seven stations: XEG, seven nights a week; a local Pasadena station, KALI, at 7:30 seven mornings a week; and all others were Sunday only—stations WAIT, Chicago; XERB, Southern California; KXL, Portland, Oregon; KVI, Seattle; and XENT, Mexico, just below the Texas border.

In the second issue of this reborn *Good News* appeared the very first article we ever published under the by-line of Roderick C. Meredith. It was the lead article starting on the front cover: "College Atmosphere at Ambassador."

In the November, 1951, number, my picture appeared—for the first time in the eighteen years of this work. The caption at the top of the page was "You Asked for It —" followed by this sub-caption: "Ten thousand of you have demanded Mr. Armstrong's picture. For the first time in the 18 years of this work, he has finally consented. Here are four pages of pictures of Mr. and Mrs. Armstrong, faculty and students, and the campus of Ambassador College." There were thirty separate pictures—mostly of faculty members, students, and campus scenes.

Why Picture Finally Published

I remember how it came about that my picture appeared. For many years I had not even permitted a picture to be taken of me. If anyone came around with a camera, I ducked, dodged, or ran. But when Mrs. Armstrong and I went to Europe in 1947, it was obligatory that passport photos be taken.

We had arrived in Washington, D.C., one morning. We had to obtain passports and visas, and take the train next afternoon for New York. We hurried, first thing that morning in Washington, to a photograph studio for passport photos. We had to have these before applying for passports.

Those photographs were more than four years old by November, 1951. But they were all I had, except a few camera shots I had finally allowed to be snapped after our first college commencement exercises on June 15 of that same year.

WHY did I refuse, prior to this time, to be "shot" by a camera—or to have my picture published? No scriptural reason, certainly. It was merely my own personal feeling in the matter.

I reasoned this way: God had called me to preach His gospel—not show off my person. It was Christ's MESSAGE I sought to focus attention on—not myself. In my preconversion years I had been vain, egotistical, conceited. I knew full well that God had brought me low, especially in an economic way—to crush out the ego, and to bring humility. Consequently, from the time of conversion, I did my best to keep down the SELF.

But WHAT, then, changed the attitude—induced willingness to allow pictures to be published? It was a letter I received from a radio listener. I can't quote that letter word for word—but it said, in effect: "What have you got to *hide,* Mr. Armstrong? Why do you refuse to let us listeners know what you look like? Are you trying to cover up something? Suppose you attend a church service, and the pastor HIDES behind the pulpit. Suppose he lets the congregation hear his voice, but he hides his face. Wouldn't you get suspicious? Wouldn't you think he was covering up something? When I go to church, I want to SEE what the preacher looks like, as well as to listen to his sermon. A man's character shows in his face. Are you ashamed of yours? WHY WON'T YOU PUBLISH YOUR PICTURE?"

THAT DID IT!

I simply could not answer that man's argument any way except to let him—and all our readers—know what I looked like. So, in this November, 1951, *Good News,* I came "out of hiding," so to speak!

AT LAST! Publishing Monthly

The results of the college were beginning to show. Without it the work never could have expanded much beyond its status in the forties.

In 1952, for the first time in our history, we were able to publish a sixteen-page magazine every month— twelve full issues! The rapid development of students— and, now, our first graduates—made this possible. Ten of these issues were of *The Good News.* But the June and August numbers were *The Plain Truth.*

The very first time that any articles, written by someone other than myself, appeared in *The Plain Truth,* was the issue of August, 1952. Reporting from London, articles were published under the by-lines of Richard D. Armstrong and Herman L. Hoeh.

In a sense, that was the very BEGINNING of the larger, regularly published *Plain Truth* of today.

The following month *The Good News* was published. The lead article, starting on the front cover, was by Richard D. Armstrong, written from Paris. This number contained also an article written from Frankfurt, Germany, by Herman L. Hoeh.

This was the first tour abroad taken by Ambassador graduates. It was the high-spot of Dick Armstrong's life, up to that time.

Speaking Like a Native

For years, seeing Paris had been the great dream of my son Dick's life. He had taken his preliminary work in the French language while in high school at Eugene, Oregon.

One policy I had been determined to set for Ambassador College had to do with teaching foreign languages. I wanted them taught so thoroughly that a student would learn to speak the language he pursued precisely as that language is spoken natively in its own country—without any accent whatever.

French has always been taught here by men who grew up in France or French-speaking Switzerland. Dick took to French as a duck takes to water.

Actually we have learned that some students have the "knack" of adapting themselves to a foreign language. Others have no such aptitude, and probably could never learn to speak such a language natively—unless they had started learning at about age six.

Under old Professor Mauler-Hiennecey, Dick became very proficient after his four college years. It was the fulfillment of his life's dream when, near graduation time, 1952, he learned he was really going to be sent to Paris after graduation.

Dick still had enough "boy" in him to want to see if he could pass himself off in France as a native Frenchman. In Paris he bought a beret, dressed like a Frenchman, and sallied forth to see if he would be accepted as a native.

He was! It was a great thrill to him.

Later, in 1954, Mrs. Armstrong and I were being

driven by Dick in his British Hillman-Minx car from Paris to Luxembourg to visit our radio station there. It was a hot afternoon. Mrs. Armstrong and I were thirsty, so we decided to stop at the next town for a Coca-Cola. Dick drove us up to a soft-drink parlor. He needed to fill the fuel tank with petrol, so he let us out saying he would join after gassing up.

In the soft-drink parlor we had a terrible time making the proprietor understand what we wanted. Coca-Cola may be "everywhere," as their commercials and advertisements say, but this Frenchman simply could not understand our way of saying it. Finally I pointed to a Coca-Cola sign I found on a wall. He nodded assent and served us.

In five or ten minutes Dick drove up, parked outside, and strolled in. He began talking to the proprietor.

"I don't understand!" said the proprietor, in French. "You are a Frenchman; these people seem to be your parents—but they are Americans; and your car is English with a British tag on it. It's all confusing!" he exclaimed with a French shrug.

He was SURE that Dick was a Frenchman! Then how could Americans be his parents? All this gave Dick very great satisfaction. And me, too—for here I had EVIDENCE that Ambassador College taught French so students could speak it natively, without accent!

60

A Giant Leap to Europe!

W E NEED, now, to go back a few years, to fill in some interesting parts of the story concerning the opening of Ambassador College in Pasadena.

The reader will remember that a few of the church members at Eugene opposed the founding of the college. When I signed the lease-and-option contract to purchase the first two-and-one-quarter-acre block of our college campus, they screamed "Armstrong extravagance!"

SAVING by "Extravagance"

And yet, we were actually *being paid* $100 per month for the privilege of becoming owner of this $100,000 estate!

Here is how it worked out. Our office staff had finally enlarged at Eugene to a payroll of fifteen people. The office space had expanded until we were paying $350 per month rent. Also I was having to spend money for

274

the broadcast line between my office and Portland—and also for the frequent trips then necessary to Hollywood for recording. But, most of all, the fees for recording were running up to several hundred dollars per month.

When the new college was opened I went, for a few months at first, from Pasadena to Hollywood to record the program. But within a very short time we had remodeled the northwest corner of the second floor of our library-classroom building into our own radio studio. We purchased two secondhand recording lathes. My son Dick became our first radio studio operator. We began making our own recordings. The only cost, now, was the slight amount of electric power, and the cost of the blank acetate discs.

The savings—actual reductions in necessary expenditures for the operation of the broadcast work—amounted to $1,100 per month! That figure I do remember—definitely!

Out of that saving we paid the $1,000 per month payments on the property, and came out $100 per month to the good!

It was one or two years after we began doing our own broadcast recording in our own studio that tape recording came along. The more cumbersome electrical transcription method was made obsolete. We purchased two good quality tape recorders at the start. Later we installed the large top-quality Ampex recorders—the same equipment used in large network headquarters. Gradually, as the number of stations increased, more and more of these had to be added.

The radio studio served also as a classroom for students.

Plain Truth *Resumed Monthly*

During 1952, you will remember, for the first time in

the history of this work, we had been able to publish a sixteen-page magazine every month. Ten of those were *The Good News,* which had been introduced as a temporary stopgap, written and edited by students as well as myself.

The radio log published in the January, 1953, issue shows that we were by then on eleven radio stations. We had gone back on two more of the superpower border stations—XELO and XERB, beside XEG. The number of stations was growing gradually. Every phase of the work was growing.

During the year 1953 we were able to publish a 16-page magazine every month except December. The first five issues were all of *The Good News.* However, by this time Herman L. Hoeh, my son Dick, Roderick C. Meredith and others had graduated, and had sufficient experience writing articles that I felt there was no need to continue *The Good News* as a college magazine for co-workers, substituting for *The Plain Truth,* any longer.

Beginning the June number, 1953, I began once again to offer *The Plain Truth,* over the air, to all listeners. I now had the editorial help of a handful of college graduates and advanced students. So, it might be said that the present subscription list of *The Plain Truth* actually began with the issue of June, 1953.

Broadcast to Europe

But some very tremendous leaps of progress were taken with the broadcasting program during 1953.

Beginning the first Thursday in that year, which was January 1, *The World Tomorrow* leaped to EUROPE. The door of the most powerful radio station on earth swung open. The *same* gospel Jesus Christ taught His disciples went to Europe with *power* for the first time in eighteen and one-half centuries!

That gospel was first preached by the Apostle Peter on the day of Pentecost, A.D. 31. Nineteen years later, A.D. 50, "A DOOR" was opened to the Apostle Paul to preach that gospel in Europe for the first time.

Just as a DOOR was opened for the gospel to go to Europe, in the first century, after nineteen years, so a DOOR was opened for the same gospel to go to Europe in our time, after nineteen years!

For the past few years, as I now write in January, 1964, I have been assuming we started on Radio Luxembourg on the first MONDAY in 1953. Looking into the radio log of *The Good News* for February, 1953, I am reminded that we did not get to start on the medium wave band, known as 208, on Radio Luxembourg at that time. That came later. We started on a long-wave band, and the time was 4:15 to 4:45 p.m., Thursdays.

The lead front-page article in that February number was captioned "NOW ON THE AIR—OVER ALL EUROPE!"

Another article reported that on the preceding December 20 (1952), five young ministers had been fully ordained.

Then it was reported in the next paragraph, that two more of our young ministers "will be fully ordained following their graduation from the college January 30, 1953."

When it was written only five had been ordained. But, before the magazine was printed and reached its readers, the other two also had been ordained.

Was I crazy to start a liberal arts coeducational college? There was no fund of several million dollars for such a project. There was no fund of even several hundred dollars. For this purpose, there was no fund— period! *At all!*

277

What There Was—and Wasn't

There was no endowment. There was no sponsoring philanthropist.

There *was* opposition. There *were* obstacles. They piled up mountain high. There *were* problems, seemingly unsolvable.

But there was something else. There was vision. There was clear and definite realization of the imperative need. And there was faith and determination; a sense of mission, a fired-up zeal and energy that refused to be defeated or to quit.

I think most anyone would say that a man would be either crazy or a fool to attempt to found a college under those circumstances. It costs money to operate a college. No college can finance its operations by income from tuitions and fees. These pay for only a part—and often a small part—of the costs of conducting a college.

State colleges and universities are financed by the taxes of the people. Privately owned colleges are financed by large endowments, and contributions from successful and prosperous alumni, by foundations, and commercial or industrial corporations who have an interest in what such colleges can do for them.

We had to *pay* taxes, not receive them. That is, until the college was established, incorporated, and recognized by the state a few years later. Then we were granted tax exemption on properties used exclusively for college educational purposes. We had no endowment or hope of any. We had no alumni, wealthy or otherwise. No large business corporations had any interest in supporting our kind of college.

We had a radio broadcast—but that *cost* money. We had nothing to sell, made no appeal for contributions. Rather we constantly offered absolutely FREE

278

literature. We published a monthly magazine—whenever funds permitted, only it was *not* coming out monthly then, because funds did *not* permit! There was no subscription price—no advertising revenue.

Here we had no visible source of income. No one owed us anything. We had no accounts receivable. We were on the *giving* end, with no assurance except faith there would be anything to give.

You might try this experiment. Go interview one hundred college or university presidents. Briefly state the circumstances given above. Ask each what he would think of any man who would attempt to found a new college—especially a man who was devoid of any experience whatsoever as an educator—under those conditions. I'm quite sure every appraisal—if each college president did not call *you* a fool for even asking such a question—would be that such a man would be either an idiot, a fool, or insane.

WHY the College Succeeded!

But, of course, there is one other factor. One I'm equally certain none of these college presidents would grasp.

This is the WORK OF GOD! And the work of God required a college.

That statement, too, would, of course, be foolishness to such men. I knew there *had* to be the college or GOD'S WORK could not grow. Therefore I knew it was God's will. And if it were His will, *I had the power of the limitless* UNIVERSE *back of it!* I had the assurance of FAITH!

During our first college year, early in 1948, I attended a convention of the college and university presidents of the nation, in Chicago. Beside general plenary sessions, there were morning and afternoon special group meetings most days, during the convention. I attended the meetings of the group devoted to study and discussion of college financing—attended mostly by presidents, with a few controllers or business managers, of privately owned institutions.

I already knew that most privately owned colleges faced extreme financial difficulties. These sessions put loud emphasis on that knowledge. Many of these college heads were desperate. All or nearly all wanted federal government aid, and devoted most of the discussions to ideas and methods for obtaining it. For several sessions I remained silent and listened. In the end, however, I think I convinced them they didn't really want government help after all. It would mean, inevitably, government supervision, regulation and interference as well. When government, big business, or foundations put large chunks of money in a college, they first assure themselves that they are buying policy-making prerogatives. The institution is no longer free.

Ambassador College never has, and never will, sell out to such influences. Ambassador College is not a Bible school. The campuses are not "religious colleges." They are straight educational liberal arts institutions. But they are guided by GOD's principles as those principles apply to general cultural education. And they rely solely on GOD ALMIGHTY, in living faith, as their sole source of financial support! Of course, we are well aware that, if GOD sponsors and finances us, HE is going to insist upon directing our policies—just as human government, corporations, or foundations see to it that they pretty largely direct the policies of institutions *they* finance. We know well that if Ambassador College departs from GOD's ways and policies, God's financial sponsorship will stop forthwith.

But that's precisely the way we want it! And that is the real reason for the miraculous, almost incredible

SUCCESS of these institutions! God Almighty will back financially—to an extent almost beyond human belief—any person or institution that will place himself or itself unreservedly and vigorously under His direction!

Now, of course, there have been problems—obstacles—oppositions—persecutions—setbacks. It hasn't been EASY! God doesn't *make* it easy to go His way. Jesus Christ taught us to *count the cost!* We have to learn that God does most things *with* us, and *through* us as His instruments. He only does *for* us what we are utterly unable to do ourselves.

We have had to fight the way through! We have had to *think,* to apply ourselves energetically, to drive ourselves on to the limit of our capacity. In this sense, God has let us *do* it—He merely *directed us!* But He also *empowered* us where necessary, and He brought about *circumstances.*

God has never rained money down from heaven. While HE financed us, He has always done it *through human instruments* willingly yielded, even at great personal sacrifice, to serving Him —and voluntarily—with their tithes and offerings. Yet GOD financed us! He did it *through* those He could use!

That is the secret of our success. It's the way to success for anybody and everybody—whether individual, or group, or organization! And it has developed *not only* these campuses—it has developed *those of us* —and in constantly increasing numbers —who are dedicated to this great WORK OF GOD!

The College Develops

I have already covered student participation in producing *The Plain Truth* and *The Good News,* which became its temporary substitute, from April, 1951, through

281

May, 1953. This was the real *firstfruits* of the college in the growing WORK OF GOD.

The growth of the GOSPEL work has directly paralleled the development of Ambassador College! Without the college, the work of thundering Christ's GOSPEL around the whole world could not have been possible. It could never have gone *around the world.*

It was the development of the college in Pasadena that made possible the growth of the whole gospel work!

The college in Pasadena started, remember, in October, 1947 with just four pioneer students. There were eight professors and instructors. The second college year, 1948-49, there were seven students. That was the half-time year. It was operate half-time or give up and quit. Never would we do the latter.

The third school year, 1949-50, there were twelve students—eleven men and one girl. We felt we were now large enough to organize, for the first time, a student council. This was our first student organization.

For the year 1950-51, there were twenty-two students. The fifth college year, 1951-52, there were thirty-two students. The college was growing!

First Yearbook

At the close of the 1950-51 year, the students produced their first "annual," or "yearbook," *The Envoy.* It contained thirty-six pages—counting the cover. Of course it was pretty thin, compared to the "annuals" of larger, older, established colleges. But it was a beginning. Today *The Envoy* is one of the finest published by any college-grade institution anywhere—a fine book with heavy stiff covers, and printed in full color.

Where there is *life,* and *spirit,* and constant GROWTH, small beginnings mean only a START. It was

282

the same with *The Envoy* as with every other phase of this dynamic, fast-growing work!

The 1952 *Envoy* did not grow in pages, but improved in quality. Just as *The Plain Truth* had its struggle through the early years, so did the student publication, *The Envoy*. The 1953 book was a BIG improvement, but we had to skip 1954 altogether.

However, the 1953 edition came out with a thick, heavy cover for the first time. It was all black and white—that is, black ink only. But it contained sixty pages beside cover, and was a much improved production. The 1955 edition went to sixty-eight pages, and improved contents, especially the photography and art work. The 1956 *Envoy* continued the improvement, with seventy-six pages, but still black and white. By 1961 it reached two hundred pages, a much finer cover, much improved photography and design, and we were getting into color pages.

The Foreign Language Clubs

By the 1951-52 college year, extracurricular activities were getting organized. That year three foreign language dinner clubs were organized. These are dinner clubs, at which no English is spoken—only the language of each specific club. There was the French Club, the German Club, and the Spanish Club.

They were initiated at Ambassador College in order to give the students of each language the experience of speaking and hearing that language outside of class—in actual continuous conversation—to help them learn to express themselves fluently in that tongue.

We in GOD'S WORK are commissioned to proclaim Christ's original gospel to ALL NATIONS. We knew, then, that this would require much printed literature in various languages, as well as called and trained ministers experienced in *speaking* and *broadcasting* fluently, and without broken accent, in the various languages. This training began the very first college year—but the language dinner clubs began in 1951.

Other languages were later added to the curriculum at Ambassador College.

The Ambassador Clubs

In February, 1953, Mr. Jack R. Elliott, then dean of students, asked me if I would go with him as a guest to visit a businessman's "Toastmasters' Club." These clubs are, I believe, worldwide. They are evening dinner speech clubs. First, several men are called on without advance notice to stand and discuss, in one or two minutes, some topic assigned by the "table topics chairman." Later there are a number of prepared speeches, usually limited to about six minutes.

Mr. Elliott wanted to introduce speech clubs into Ambassador College activities, patterned after these clubs, but with a few variations adapted to our needs. We saw at once the value of such an activity at Ambassador.

In February, 1953, the first of these clubs was organized and under way. Our adaptation was called the *Ambassador Club.* Soon there were two such clubs on the Pasadena campus, then three, then four. In 1954, there were seven at the Pasadena campus.

These clubs have done more to develop public-speaking ability than any other activity. They are a most effective addition to our regular courses in public speaking. They teach men to think on their feet, develop personality and familiarity with world events and many important topics.

Soon the first women's club was formed. These, too, have continued to expand. I'm quite sure they are

284

different, at Ambassador, than any other women's clubs. They have a very definite effect in the cultural development of our young women.

Campus Paper

About November, 1951, the students started the first campus paper. It is called *The Portfolio.* It contains college news, personal items about students, news of the progress of the work, and a certain sprinkling of campus fun. It gives students training in writing.

The Portfolio started crude and small—mimeographed. In due time it became a real printed campus paper of quality.

Comes the Ambassador Chorale

In the college year 1951-52 we had thirty-two students. In the spring of that year, Mr. Leon Ettinger, director of the voice department in the school of music, decided to organize the students into a singing group, train them secretly at his home, and then spring the whole thing on me as a surprise!

How they all kept the secret through many weeks of rehearsals I'll never know. But they did.

At the annual spring concert of the music department—consisting of piano and vocal solo numbers by students—the whole group stood together, and to my amazement, sang the Fred Waring arrangement of "The Battle Hymn of the Republic" like veterans. Actually there was not a trained singer among them—but they had put their whole hearts and energies into it through many weeks.

As Mr. Ettinger later wrote about it: "At that time we scraped the bottom of the barrel to find talent. If you could put two notes together on an instrument or sing a little song in tune, you were on the program.

285

When we gathered together all our resources, we had twelve singers for our little chorus.

"We practiced faithfully for several months, always at Ettinger's to keep it quiet, and at last the great day arrived. At the end of the evening Mr. Ettinger announced that a new musical organization had been formed, called the Ambassador Chorale; and that, with Mrs. Ettinger at the piano, they would sing 'The Battle Hymn of the Republic,' and that they were dedicating this first performance anywhere to Mr. Herbert W. Armstrong. The years have smoothed away any slight imperfections, and we only remember that it was an absolute smash."

Actually, I remember, I was overcome with surprise, rather choked with emotion, and unable to speak.

That was the beginning of one of our outstanding activities at Ambassador College—the Ambassador Chorale. From that small beginning it has grown into a musical organization that I feel would do credit to any college or university ten to twenty times our size.

At Last! ABC Network!

In autumn, 1953, a new door was opened—a national radio network. For nineteen years the vision of broadcasting coast-to-coast over a great national network had been a dream—and a hope. At last it was realized!

The November, 1953, *Plain Truth* carried this big-type, full-page announcement:

"*And now* . . . ABC NETWORK!"

The article said: "GOD now opens another door—*a very great door!* Perhaps this is the greatest news we have ever been privileged to announce! Beginning Sunday, October 25, *The World Tomorrow* went on one of the great major networks, ABC, transcontinental! This means millions of new listeners every week. It means tremendous prestige. It means approximately ninety additional radio stations. THINK OF IT!—ninety additional radio stations—including the great basic 50,000-watt ABC stations in New York, Chicago, San Francisco, Buffalo, and other major cities." There followed the log of the ninety stations, taking the remaining two thirds of the page. There was a two-page map showing the location and area of coverage of each station—blanketing the United States.

Of course, this network broadcasting was *Sunday only!* We had learned by experience that it was the DAILY broadcasting that was really effective. Of course, that was impossible over a network. But the network was a TREMENDOUS step forward.

61

Our First Experience with Television

B Y 1955 television had become the popular craze in the United States.

That year there were some forty-three million television sets in the United States. That year the manufacture of television sets hit an all-time peak in the U.S.—7,800,000 sets manufactured.

Suddenly we became frightened. Almost in a panic, we decided to make a frantic dash to put *The World Tomorrow* on television—before radio went completely dead.

Rise of Television

Television has been referred to by the term "one-eyed monster." Millions of people spend four, six, or eight hours a day looking into a television screen.

I first remember radio in about 1920 or 1921. I was still in the advertising business in Chicago, then. But the primitive radio sets of that time that come vaguely, in blurred focus, to my memory were little "wireless" sets heard only through earphones.

My earliest memory of radio, as it is today, however, dates back to 1932. At that time I was advertising manager of a daily newspaper in Astoria, Oregon. It was the very depth of the Great Depression. It had become necessary to trade advertising space for merchandise. Money, as a medium of exchange, was too scarce. I had traded advertising space for a portable radio set. It was rather large in size, for a portable. But it would receive stations from greater distances than any I have ever had since.

When we moved back to Salem, Oregon, in February 1933, and I reentered the ministry, I began, for the first time, to listen to some radio religious broadcasts.

At that time I never even remotely contemplated going on the air myself. But when I heard that time was open on our little local station in Eugene, in October, 1933, I seized the opportunity. That led to the broadcasting of *The World Tomorrow,* starting the first Sunday in 1934.

How SUDDENLY have these inventions sprung up! WHAT A *DOOR* Jesus Christ has opened, that HIS MESSAGE may go boldly to the world for the first time in 18½ centuries!

Even in the year 1930 there were comparatively few radio sets in America. But by 1934 most United States homes had radio.

And *THAT VERY* YEAR that we started on the air—1934—TELEVISION WAS INVENTED!

Think of it! Television, so common everywhere today, was not even invented until the very year *The World Tomorrow* STARTED ON RADIO!

My first memory of television was at radio station KNX, the CBS network headquarters in Hollywood, in

1942. The CBS network was giving a rather elementary demonstration of television—still in the experimental stages. They then hoped to be broadcasting television after the end of the war.

We moved into our home in Pasadena in July, 1947. There were very few television sets in use then— but television was in operation on the air.

The sets at that time were mostly little nine-inch screens. I bought one because I knew it would be developed, and felt I needed to keep abreast of progress. If it became popular like radio, I felt we might need to put the program on television.

At that time there was no network television. There were two local stations in Los Angeles—KTLA (still on), and one other, which was then difficult to tune in at our home. The KTLA programs were all local programs. There was local wrestling, and other purely local programs.

The BIG shows, then, were still on radio over the national networks. Actually the image orthicon pickup tube was not developed until 1946 by RCA. The first network television, transcontinental, was inaugurated September 4, 1951. By 1952 we were getting several of the so-called BIG SHOWS, with the top radio talent now on television, coast to coast via the networks.

With the advent of these big-time network shows, television began to sweep the nation. In 1950 there were seventy-four million television sets in the United States. But the one year of 1955 saw the record production of 7,800,000 sets.

We Race to Television

By 1955 the big-name network shows had all left radio for television and were almost monopolizing nighttime entertainment in America. The motion picture business

290

was on the skids. The first of the notorious big-money quiz shows, *The $64,000 Question,* attracted television audiences above sixty million people.

This, and one other circumstance, conspired to give us the jitters. We had learned that it was the EVERYNIGHT, or *daily* broadcasting, seven days a week, which proved really effective. We were spending BIG MONEY, now, on coast-to-coast network radio—Sunday only—one program a week. This once-a-week radio was *not* producing results commensurate with the DAILY broadcasting over the superpower stations. At that time we were on superpowerful WLS, Chicago, seven times per week. Also on the equally powerful WWVA, West Virginia, and we had been for some years broadcasting EVERY NIGHT on the superpower Mexican border stations. The mail response from the Sunday *ONLY* network broadcasting, per dollar spent, was very low by comparison with the DAILY broadcasting on these super-power stations.

There were two reasons for that. One was the fact of the DAILY broadcasting—the other the fact that MOST of the ABC stations we were using were comparatively small-powered stations. I had found that a BIG-powered station, while it may cost two to four times as much, will bring a mail response from ten to fifty times greater than small stations.

But the main cause of our fears was the fear of television. It seemed that everybody was turning to television. It began to look like radio would soon be a thing of the past.

All these factors caused us to decide to plunge, quickly, into television. I issued advance notice of cancellation of the Sunday network broadcast.

Our advertising agent of that time brought in an associate, who was some kind of production manager at the new Television City plant of CBS, Hollywood. He was engaged as our director-producer.

Today television is using TAPE for TV recording. But at that time it had to be on FILM.

Suddenly I found that I was IN THE MOVIES!

So, "We're in the Movies, Now!"

The campus paper, *The Portfolio*, for April 21, 1955, carried a front-page story about our sudden rush to get on television.

It stated: "The nation is going crazy over television! Millions of viewers are sitting hunched in their TV chairs *for many hours each day.* They're forgetting about God's message—forgetting about the rocking, reeling world they live in—DRUGGING their minds with lethargy.

"And so," the story continued, "the truth of God will be THUNDERED at them right from their own TV sets!

"Mr. Armstrong announced that the first *World Tomorrow* program will be seen over channel KLOR, Portland, Oregon, within a few more weeks."

Continuing, the campus paper stated: "Planning far in advance, Mr. Armstrong said production will begin within a very few weeks, with other TV stations being added as fast as God provides the way.

"The supreme, *all-important turning point* has been reached! God's work must make a shift from one medium of circulation to another. It will be no easy task."

And it certainly was NO EASY TASK!

The programs would have to be filmed at a Hollywood motion picture studio. There would have to be "sets." First, under direction of our producers, an artist was engaged to sketch a picture, and draw plans for these sets. We decided on two sketches.

292

First was a sort of stage, with a podium, and a large globe of the world suspended from the ceiling, hanging in the background. This would be emblematic of the world tomorrow! The second stage setting would be that of a private study, with bookcases, and an office desk. For this we used the same desk I had used as my desk in my office in Eugene, Oregon—and was still using in Pasadena.

For the first set, we transported one of our semi-concert grand Steinway pianos from the college music department.

After receiving and approving the sketches, the sets were constructed in Hollywood. Meanwhile I began work on planning the type of program, and the format.

As we got into production on the first three or four programs, we began to use more and more "film stock"—that is, news-events motion picture film obtained from the NBC film library in New York, to illustrate the speaking message, and after the first few programs, we dropped all singing from the program.

A Lion on the Campus

Our original idea for a format to put the program on the air was to show one or two views of our magnificently landscaped campus, as the announcer's voice announced "From the beautiful campus of Ambassador College, in Pasadena, California, its President, Herbert W. Armstrong, brings you the real meaning behind today's world news, with the PROPHECIES of the WORLD TOMORROW!"

Then, as the announcer's voice moved into the words "with the PROPHECIES of the WORLD TOMORROW," the scene was to shift to another picture on our grounds, showing a little girl leading a big lion and a

293

little lamb—as a picture (Isa. 11:6-7) of tame animals in tomorrow's world.

Later we discarded this beginning, too. But we did start out with it.

But HOW were we going to show an actual motion picture of a big lion, being led by a little girl, and with a lamb alongside? THIS HAD TO BE PHOTOGRAPHED! And there are no tame lions, TODAY. There will be, tomorrow. But we had no time-machine to project ourselves into the future, take motion pictures, and then come back to the year 1955!

Immediately I thought of the famous MGM lion, so often shown in motion pictures. Our producers were able to obtain the use of this lion, for a fee, of course. He was big, powerful looking, kingly. And he was *almost* tame—ALMOST, but we dared not trust that he was *altogether* tame!

This lion—a real lion, in the flesh!—was brought by his trainers over to the Ambassador College campus, and allowed to walk out of his cage in his big truck, and on the grounds, in front of Mayfair, one of our girls' student residences. He surely *seemed* tame. But his trainer explained that he was neither tired nor altogether tame—he was just LAZY!

We had to obtain a permit from the City of Pasadena to have him there.

But, in planning this, we had to decide HOW we could photograph a helpless lamb beside this big beast, and a little girl leading. We decided not to risk it. Our motion-picture producers said we could do it with trick double-photography.

The producers decided the little girl must be a professional child actress. I think union requirements had something to do with this. They obtained the girl and the lamb. We photographed the lion, coached by his

294

trainer to move slowly toward the camera. Then, after the lion was again safely in his cage, and with the camera securely locked in the same exact position in its tripod, we had the little girl and the lamb walk toward the camera, and a foot or two *beside* the spot where the lion had walked. Later the film editor blended the two together, so that, when it appeared on the TV screens in broadcast, we had the picture of the little girl leading the ferocious lion and the gentle little lamb.

Yes, WE WERE IN THE MOVIES, NOW!

By the time we had the first few telecasts finished, on motion picture film, sound track and all, we managed to obtain time on TWELVE television stations. So, once again, our organized BEGINNING on television, like so many other beginnings, started out with TWELVE. *We didn't plan it to be twelve.* It just *happened* that was the number of stations, coast to coast, in the cities and areas we wanted, which opened to us. Also, by the time we obtained that number, we hit the limit of our budget!

Later we were on thirteen stations—adding Hawaii—but we *started* with twelve.

Camera Jitters

I think I should record, here, something of my personal experience in performing in front of professional motion picture cameras.

Emphatically, I *did not* take to it as a duck takes to water.

Trying to preach a sermon before a cigarette-smoking Hollywood crew of about nineteen people—cameramen, electricians, sound men, script girl, directors, helpers—a full crew, with two television cameras trained on me—well, it proved a NIGHTMARE!

Actually, once the bright klieg lights were turned on me, I was almost blinded, and I could see little in front

295

of me except blackness. The powerful lights were shining straight into my face!

On our first day of "shooting" in the Hollywood studio, we were scheduled to go through three whole programs on the one full day of "shooting."

When our announcer, Art Gilmore, announced me, I walked out to the podium. I began to try to talk. I *did* try! But it was no go! Just before this I had been made nervous and a little irritated by the fact our director brought a make-up man into my dressing room, and announced I had to wear make-up.

"What!" I exclaimed, indignantly, *"Me* wear make-up? Never in a million years!"

"You'll have to, Mr. Armstrong," replied the director soothingly. "Everyone does who appears on motion picture film."

"Let movie actors wear all the false faces and make-up they wish," I replied defiantly. "But I'm not a movie actor, and I won't wear make-up."

"But, Mr. Armstrong," pursued the director, "this is only to make you LOOK, on the television sets, perfectly *natural.* Your face won't look natural, as the cameras show it, unless we do put on make-up. We only do it to make you *look* as if you DID NOT have anything on your face."

They simply were not going to start shooting until I gave in. Finally, on promise I could try it later *without* make-up, I consented to let the make-up man start chalking up my face.

But I was nettled by it. The whole thing was a totally NEW experience to me. I felt that every one of that television crew in the studio was naturally hostile to what I was going to say. I decided I would talk to THEM, and challenge them as my skeptics! Finally I did, and found afterward that, far from being hostile, many

296

of them were quite interested in what I had to say. They had never heard anything like it before. But it didn't happen *that* day.

A Nerve-shattering Experience

I made false start after false start. Through the morning I struggled with it. The director tried to help me concentrate and get going. But nothing seemed to help.

During noon hour there was no time to drive back over to Pasadena. The producers had arranged an apartment in a nearby bungalow-hotel for Mrs. Armstrong and me, where she could prepare a lunch that would help quiet my nerves and leave me alert for the afternoon's work. I had lemon juice, I remember. I also tried to get in a brief nap.

The afternoon was no better. By day's end, we had shot and wasted a lot of expensive film—out of which the film editor was able afterwards to piece together enough usable footage to make the first half-hour telecast. I never did think it was any good—but it brought a huge response from listeners.

I do not now remember details of these events as well as I do those happenings when I was a boy. But it seems to me that we had to engage these movie crews, and the studio, for three straight days at a time.

It was frightfully expensive. We were trying to reduce this production expense by shooting three programs per day. I had to have the first NINE programs all ready—in brief notes, and other material—before we even started this actual production.

But that first day we salvaged just ONE program out of a hard and nerve-shattering day's work. As I remember it, we did a little better the second day—I think we completed TWO programs, and got to our quota of three on the third day.

297

High Cost of Television Production

I suppose most of my readers know little or nothing about the cost of PRODUCING a half-hour television program. At that time—1955—the average half-hour evening show on any one of the three big networks was costing between $30,000 and $35,000 for production. That means JUST TO PUT IT ON FILM. Then the purchase of station time for broadcasting came extra. That, also, on a major network, averaged about $35,000 for the half hour. Total cost, about $70,000 for each weekly half-hour show. That is what the sponsors of the big shows were spending.

We had estimated that, by shooting three programs per day, we could produce *The World Tomorrow* for television at around $900 per program. But that was mere wishful thinking. That first program cost over $2,500 to produce. Later we did get production costs down to around $2,000.

Of course the heaviest item of expense on the big entertainment shows is the high fees paid the stars. Many television stars were paid $6,000 for their acting in just one half-hour show. Lesser stars and supporting actors and actresses were paid from $500 to $3,000 —depending on how big a name they had. Of course, they go in for very expensive "sets"—with often several sets for a single show.

Perhaps the lowest-cost production of all was a show like *The $64,000 Question,* and similar quiz shows. There were no stars, except the master of ceremonies, and staff members, none of whom drew down the fabulous fees of the big stars.

We had succeeded in obtaining reasonably good times for *The World Tomorrow* on a number of very fine stations. In New York we were on the ABC net-

work station, WABC, channel 7. The hour was late—
11:30 p.m. But that does not seem so late, in New York,
as it would be for viewers in Kansas City, where people
go to bed earlier. Later we switched to WPIX in New
York—a station which had a very big viewing audience.

In Chicago we were also on the ABC network
station, WBKB, channel 7. Our time there was not so
good—9:00 a.m. Sunday. In Los Angeles we were on
KTLA, channel 5, at 10:30 p.m.

It was impossible for our type program to obtain
time during the "PRIME TIME" hours of 7:00 p.m. to
10:00 p.m. But we did obtain the 10:30 p.m. spot on
KLZ, channel 7, Denver; KOVR, channel 13, San Fran-
cisco-Stockton; KTNT, channel 11, Tacoma-Seattle,
Washington; KMBC, channel 9, Kansas City; KGMB,
Honolulu; and KCMC, channel 6, Texarkana.

We had even a better time, 9:30 p.m., in Portland,
Oregon, on KLOR, channel 12. Also we were on KPRC,
channel 2, Houston, Texas, and on stations in Tyler,
Texas, and Hutchinson, Kansas.

Our ratings, as shown by the principal rating
agencies, showing approximate size of viewing
audiences, were extremely HIGH.

Most religious programs on television were rated,
on the regular rating systems, below one point. Ratings
were 0.3, or 0.7, etc. The best known prime-time big
network entertainment shows had ratings averaging in
the 20s and 30s. A rating of, say, 32, was excellent and
considered well worth $70,000 to the sponsor. It meant
approximately *32 million people* viewing the program.

Programs like "Meet the Press," though probably
much more worthwhile, did not have as many listeners as
Bob Hope, Jack Benny, Red Skelton, and big-time entertainment shows. Even at our late hour, we had a higher
rating in some cities than "Meet the Press." On stations

299

like Portland, Seattle, and Kansas City, we had ratings of around 10 and 11, indicating ten to twenty times as many viewers as most religious television programs.

In Kansas City, at the time, the Steve Allen Show, then at the height of its popularity, was shown at 9:30 p.m. and *The World Tomorrow* at 10:30 p.m.—a much poorer time. Yet we slightly topped it in ratings.

Our mail response was big, considering the number of stations—only 12. It was bigger than from similar radio broadcasts—but television was so much more costly, we felt it *had* to bring a much heavier mail response, to justify its heavier cost. Actually, even with only twelve stations, *The World Tomorrow* was being viewed by a million or more people—perhaps two or three million. We were delivering a dynamic message in power to a *huge* audience, who were not only *hearing*—but also *seeing*—for a full half-hour.

If I told you the total cost, including the production of the master film (low-cost *copies* were sent out to each station) and the charge for station time, I suppose some of our readers would think it was EXCESSIVE extravagance. *But it was not!*

Stop a moment and figure. If, in 1964 you sent a message to someone on a 4¢ (in the U.S.A.) postal card, you would never have called that extravagance. If you sent a million postal cards to a million people, just figure the cost—*forty thousand dollars!* And *that* is lowest-cost ECONOMY!

A near as I remember, without checking 30-year-old records at our accounting department, we paid about an average of $300 per station for the half-hour broadcast—a total of about $3,600, plus about $2,000 for production cost—total, *NOT* $40,000, as postal cards would cost, but ONLY $5,600—less than one seventh as much as those small postal cards!

300

62

The Crossroads—TV or Radio?

T HE YEAR was now 1955. *The World Tomorrow* was on television, coast to coast in the United States—and in Hawaii (it was not yet a state). But it was a harassing experience.

Actually, this whole work had reached a crossroads.

Shift to Television

I have related how, by the spring of 1955, television had made such a leap in popularity in the United States that we became frightened. It began to look as if radio was going dead. Unless we shifted immediately to television, it began to appear that this work of God would go dead.

The decision was made. We entered a crash program to get on television—*QUICK!*

But we were to learn as the weeks passed by that we were still at the crossroads. Television was not the road to take. Three factors became distressingly plain about television broadcasting. The cost was greater than we were really prepared to meet. Second, it was only a ONCE-A-WEEK telecast. And third, this telecast was absorbing almost 100 percent of my personal time and energy. It was a nerve-shattering experience to keep up with the type of programming we were doing. I was having to neglect other top-level responsibilities—and, if this kept up, it threatened the future growth of the entire work.

But at the same time, another factor developed. As the weeks and months sped by, during that latter half of 1955, we began to realize that radio was *not* dead, after all.

Of course, the big-time network shows had all left radio and gone over to television. But people *were* still listening to radio. We checked and found that radio sets were being sold in greater volume than television. In 1955, about 14,500,000 radio sets were manufactured, and 7,800,000 television sets.

Many people were beginning to buy two, three, or four radio sets per home—placing sets in bedrooms, kitchens and other rooms, while the average home had only one television set.

The trend has been maintained since.

The Crossroads Solution

Yes, in the work of God in broadcasting Christ's own gospel to the world, we had reached a crossroads.

Once-a-week network radio, paying for so many small-power stations with only one broadcast per week, had not proved effective. Believing television was totally replacing radio, we had made the plunge into television. But it was too costly for our income at that time; it was once a week only and we had learned that we had a type program that needed to be aired *daily;*

we were on only thirteen television stations; it was, under the type programming we were doing, proving too strenuous for me and monopolizing all my time.

And, on top of all these points *against* continuing on television, we were learning that RADIO WAS NOT DEAD AT ALL.

We *had not* gone *off* radio. We had canceled out the once-a-week network, and a few of the once-a-week 50,000-watt radio stations we were using in addition. But we were still broadcasting *The World Tomorrow* on a *daily* basis on superpower WLS, Chicago, WWVA, Wheeling, West Virginia, the powerful border stations XEG, XELO and XERB, besides daily broadcasting in Los Angeles, Portland and Seattle.

And we learned that about 99 percent of the income to pay for all this costly television programming was coming from RADIO listeners—not television. Of course that was to be expected. There is never any appeal for money on any *World Tomorrow* program. There is no charge for any literature. There is no solicitation for contributions, except to our own inner family of co-workers who voluntarily, on their own initiative and without original solicitation, have become co-workers.

Only an infinitesimal percent of listeners—either radio or television—ever become co-workers and start sending in tithes and offerings for this work the first few months after they begin listening. This we well knew. We knew it would be three or four years before any sizable number of newer viewers and listeners to the television program would become co-workers—for we would never solicit this.

Truly, we had reached a crossroads decision. We had leaped to television, but we soon learned that was *not* the road to go from there.

The decision became obvious. Go back onto radio —but concentrate on putting *The World Tomorrow* on the major POWERFUL radio stations, and ON A DAILY BASIS.

That was the road we took until the radio audience did change listening habits.

As the weeks sped by, we found ways to improve the remaining television programs. Our advertising agent, production director and I flew to New York to arrange for the use of NBC film stock.

The one complete film library was owned by the National Broadcasting Company. They had gotten the start on this even prior to the earliest days of telecasting, and had developed a film library so complete that other networks did not try to build one of their own. It was less costly to rent what they wanted from the NBC library.

We found the manager of this library very sympathetic toward our problem. Arrangements were made so that we could have virtually unlimited use of film stock from NBC.

Thus, if I were speaking about Hitler, the viewers would see on the television screen pictures in motion of Hitler, while hearing my voice. If I were talking about the alarming rise of crime, the viewer would see motion pictures of a crime being committed. After each of these sequences, the picture would flash back to me, as I talked. When I read a passage of Scripture, a portion of a page of a Bible would flash on the television screen, with the passage I was reading underlined, and enlarged big enough so viewers could read along with me as I read it.

Toward the end of our twenty-seven weeks of telecasting, I began bringing certain men from the East to appear on television with me in conversation, or as an

304

interview. One was Montgomery M. Green, a World War II intelligence officer in the United States Navy. I interviewed him on the program about Russia's super-secret weapons.

Another was Joseph Zack Kornfeder. He was an American, born in Slovakia. Mr. Kornfeder had been a charter member of the Communist Party in the United States. The Party sent him, in 1928, to receive special political education at the University of Moscow. Later he became disillusioned with communism, defected, and supplied United States officials with a great deal of information about Communist secret plans. His wife and son were held in Moscow as hostages, in retaliation. He gave our television audience some startling facts about communism.

Leaving the Crossroads

But early in 1956 we left the crossroads dilemma behind. The road to take was that of *daily* broadcasting on the more powerful major radio stations in the United States.

We were still on Radio Luxembourg, world's most powerful commercial station, at 11:30 p.m., Mondays. We were on the three superpower bands of Radio Ceylon. From this we received considerable mail from far-off Burma, Malaya and Singapore. Also from India, Ceylon, and portions of eastern Africa. We were broadcasting once a week over Radio Lourenço Marques, at the border of the Republic of South Africa. By March, 1956, we were broadcasting once a week over Radio Formosa.

April, 1956, saw a big improvement in *The Plain Truth*. It was the first issue to come out with a real front cover. Until then, the leading article always had started on the front cover. That first pictorial cover was

305

all black and white, and showed a picture of the Library of Ambassador College. This front cover design has been further improved since, beside adding color and a heavier cover paper. Also that issue made another BIG jump ahead—it went to twenty-four pages. Until then, the *Plain Truth* magazine had never gone beyond sixteen pages.

By August that year, we had made our first advance along the new road of *daily* broadcasting on major radio stations. The ABC network originating station in New York—the 50,000-watt WABC—opened a *daily* week-night spot for *The World Tomorrow*. The time was very late, 11:15 p.m., Monday through Saturday. But it gave us one of the major big-power outlets in the United States' biggest population center. The total listening area had a population of some fifteen million people.

A month later we started on KARM, Sacramento, California, with a good listening time nightly. This was the first *daily* broadcasting in the central California area. By November, we were back on the air in our original home-base city, Eugene, Oregon—and on the best local station, 5,000-watt KUGN, at the prime listening time of 7:30 every night.

Also by November, 1956, we had started broadcasting in Australia. At that time we had started on a small Australian network of eight stations, including Sydney but none of the other major cities. This was only once a week, at the start.

Another Plain Truth *Improvement*

With the February, 1957, issue, *The Plain Truth* made another important advance. For the first time it came out in two colors! In size, it continued with twenty-four pages. We were then beginning to announce booklets in the Spanish language, preparatory to Spanish-language broadcasting.

Progress was not rapid in adding important stations for *daily* broadcasting. Daily broadcasting of a religious program had never been done by the major top-ranking stations. It took time to break the barriers of precedent and convince station managers that *The World Tomorrow* was really top-quality programming—and that it was a top-rated program that would *build* a listening audience, rather than lose listeners. But we were diligently working on this new policy. By this time we had a large, more aggressive advertising agency.

By July, 1957, we broke ice in St. Louis, Missouri, with daily broadcasting for the first time there. We were now, also, on the air on a network in the Philippines.

With the September number, that year, we published the first installment of this *Autobiography*. At the time I expected it to run for some six months to a year. But the response was such that I continued the series for several years—ultimately publishing these volumes.

By September, 1957, *The World Tomorrow* took a really BIG leap ahead. Only one more station was added at that time—but it was to prove our most responsive station—the superpower WLAC, Nashville, Tennessee. This great station cleared for us the valuable time of 7 p.m., week nights. Then by December, 1957, came the break-through in Denver. Station KVOD opened a good time for *The World Tomorrow*—seven nights a week.

New Policy Leaps Ahead

Beginning 1958, we added Radio Tangier International, and we were broadcasting into Franco's Spain. We were now on Formosa's powerful station beamed into China *twice* a week, and on Radio Bangkok five times a week.

Also on Radio Goa in India five times a week. We now added Radio Okinawa, and two stations in South America in the Spanish language, at Lima, Peru, and Montevideo, Uruguay. At last the new broadcast policy was leaping ahead, all around the world! By this time the radio log was taking a one-half page in *The Plain Truth*.

In March, 1958, the giant Radio Luxembourg opened up to us TWO broadcasts a week, and our British audience grew more rapidly. During the summer and early fall of that year, *daily* broadcasting was begun in Tulsa, Oklahoma, Pittsburgh, Pennsylvania, and Springfield, Missouri. Eight more stations were added in Australia, making sixteen—but still once a week.

But by October, 1958, another *major* radio station, San Francisco's great KGO, began broadcasting *The World Tomorrow every night.*

The November, 1958, issue of *The Plain Truth* took another leap ahead. With the first installment of *The Bible Story* by Basil Wolverton, the magazine was enlarged from twenty-four up to thirty-two pages.

The beginning of 1959 saw the work of God gaining momentum *fast. The World Tomorrow* was now broadcast worldwide, on five million watts of radio power weekly.

This was the 25th anniversary of this work. It was now expanding everywhere as a major work, constantly multiplying in power and scope. Its impact was being felt around the world. By the end of 1959 the radio log was occupying nearly a full page in *The Plain Truth.* From that time the policy of *daily* radio broadcasting multiplied rapidly.

I have pursued the progress of the radio broadcasting and the growth of *The Plain Truth* to the beginning of the decade of the sixties. But this has brought us considerably beyond other phases of this life story.

63

First Evangelistic Campaign in British Isles

N ow I should like to get back once again to the year 1952. In recent chapters I have been covering the development of Ambassador College, the growth of *The Plain Truth*, the progress of the broadcast up to the ABC network transcontinental, on through the television program, and the policy of *daily* broadcasting.

But, after all, this is my autobiography—the story of my life. Of course, this great work of God into which the living Christ plunged me actually *is* my life. The progress of the college, the broadcasting, and the publishing are the activities to which my life is devoted. But then, there is also the more *personal phase* of these activities.

Getting to Europe

The second commencement at Ambassador College was held on Friday afternoon, June 6, 1952. Our elder son,

Richard David, whom we always called Dick, received his B.A. degree that afternoon, along with others.

Dick was a devout student of the French language, and a great life-dream in his mind had been to travel in France and to visit Paris. I had told him that I intended sending him there after graduation, but somehow that seemed so impossibly distant I don't think he ever let himself accept seriously the idea he would really go.

Then one day in my car, probably in February 1952, driving home from the college, I told him I was planning for him to go to France as soon as he graduated. I remember how startled and elated he was. For the first time, he realized that his dream of seeing France was actually going to come true. Immediately he was on Cloud Nine!

Then a week or so later it seemed as if the trip might have to be called off, due to finances. But in the campus newspaper, *The Portfolio*, dated March 13, 1952, the big headline across page 1 said: "Herman and Dick Will Take Trip." It had, by then, been planned for Dick and Herman Hoeh to go together for a summer in Britain, France, and Europe, to look into possibilities of expanding the fast-growing work into Europe.

This story in the campus paper announced that tickets had been purchased on a steamship line sailing from Quebec, Canada, for Liverpool, England. Each of the young men had made the trip possible by managing to pay two thirds of the fare out of his own pocket. Dick would take a portable tape recorder along, to send back important interviews to be heard on the *World Tomorrow* program. The graduation date had been advanced from June 8 to June 6, so these two men could leave in time for the sailing, June 11, for Liverpool.

Dick Drafted

Then something happened! The trip appeared to be canceled after all! Dick received "greetings" from "Uncle Sam." He was ordered to report for induction in the Army!

Our other men students had been given the classification of 4-D, as theological students. But Dick had not been converted when the college started, and he had registered as a major in electronics and in French. He had been in charge of the radio studio when first installed. He had taken the full theological course required of all students, but had not registered it as his major. Consequently his Selective Service Board had not given him the 4-D, but a deferred classification as a student.

Now he was about to graduate, his draft board sent him an induction notice. Immediately I contacted the chairman of his board. I learned that the matter had passed completely from this board's jurisdiction the moment the induction notice had been sent. During his college years Dick had been converted, baptized, and was about to be put into the ministry full time, on graduation. The board chairman said the board would have, under those conditions, changed his classification to 4-D, but it was now too late. It was out of their jurisdiction. The only possible official who could now cancel the induction was the state chairman of Selective Service at Sacramento.

The next day I was in Sacramento. I explained the circumstances, and that passage had been purchased to send Dick to France in the full-time ministry of the Church. I explained that he was our only minister who could speak, read and write French fluently. The Church had been waiting for his graduation to open its work in France. Serious harm would come to the Church if he were prevented from going.

Also I explained the unique, yet most thorough theological training provided ministerial students at Ambassador.

On hearing the facts, the State selective headquarters not only telephoned Pasadena to cancel Dick's induction and reclassify him 4-D, but also sent notification to all other state chairmen that Ambassador College in their judgment qualified according to the meaning and intent of the Selective Service Act as a recognized theological institution.

It was an eleventh-hour reprieve from the death of the trip to France. Dick was to have appeared for induction the very next morning. As it was, he was reclassified 4-D, and given draft board approval to be absent from the United States and take the trip to Britain and Europe.

They spent some time in London, both in educational and theological research, and in checking every possible avenue for expanding the work to Britain and Europe.

I do not know now whether it was in London, Paris, or at Luxembourg, but they learned of the possibility of getting the program on Radio Luxembourg, most powerful commercial radio station in the world. On hearing this, I went immediately to New York to contact the New York representative of this giant station. And that, truly, was the beginning of getting the gospel, which Christ Himself brought and preached, into Europe and Britain!

While in London, they became acquainted with two brothers, William and John Cordas-Cousins, manufacturers of machine tools, whose sister we knew in Pasadena. In later years these brothers were a great help to Dick in getting established, and the work started, in London.

In Paris, where Dick spent a month of the summer, he found that his French was very good—without "foreign" accent. They traveled through Germany, where they wrote articles on the phenomenal upsurge postwar comeback of Germany. They also visited Italy, and traveled as far as Belgrade, capital of Tito's Yugoslavia.

Returning to Pasadena, Dick became associate instructor of French at the college.

Radio Luxembourg Opens Door

In the fall of that year, time did finally open to us on Radio Luxembourg. But it was altogether different from broadcasting to an American audience. Luxembourg is a small country sandwiched in between Germany, Belgium, and France—and its powerful signal heard in several other countries. Their very commercial life depends on being careful in what NOT to allow to be said over their powerful facilities. They allow NO political propaganda not even any ALLUSIONS to anything political. And, in accepting religious broadcasts, the station obviously enforces strict rules that no offense is given to any religion or religious belief.

In speaking on biblical prophecy, dealing with today's world events, we soon learned we had to become *very* familiar with their policies, lest our analysis of today's world news be construed as an allusion to things political.

November 22, 1952, was a historic day for us!

On that day I recorded the *first* broadcast for Radio Luxembourg!

I have written many times about how Christ opened the giant DOOR of Radio Luxembourg to proclaim HIS gospel to Europe precisely nineteen years—one time-cycle—after the beginning of the work in 1934. The door of radio first opened on the first Sunday in 1934. Our first broadcast to Europe occurred the first Thursday in 1953—the first week in January both times!

BUT WE DID NOT PLAN IT THAT WAY! *GOD DID!*

My November 22 recording was rejected by the station. A second try was rejected. The third time I had finally come to comprehend clearly the station policies—and it was accepted! It went on the air the first week in January, 1953!

Dick Returns to London

Our broadcasting on Radio Luxembourg, at first, was a 4:15 p.m., Thursday afternoon time. It was on a broadcast band that reached almost all Europe, but did not bring a big response from England. An English-language program could be understood by only a small minority of the people of Europe, where so many different languages are spoken.

Nevertheless, it did bring letters from listeners. And soon we were shifted to the 11:30 p.m. time on the well-known "208" beamed directly over the British Isles.

Now it became necessary to make plans to handle the mail response. Dick planned to return to London. First, we purchased a car for him, through the British Rootes motorcar corporation. Through their branch office in Beverly Hills, we purchased a little compact car—a Hillman-Minx—to be delivered to Dick upon arrival in London.

So, in February, 1953, Dick flew, alone, to London. There he arranged for a London mail address, at that time known to thousands all over Britain—"BCM

314

(British Crown Monomarks) Ambassador, London, W.C.1."

He remained in London, handling the mail, until September, when he returned to Pasadena. Old Professor Mauler-Hiennecy had retired, and Dick now took over the French-language department at the college.

The British Monomark office forwarded the mail direct to Pasadena. Dick then began organizing the British and European mailing list in our mailing office. *The Plain Truth* and all requested literature had to be mailed to European listeners from Pasadena. This was very unsatisfactory and had to be remedied as soon as possible. But Dick was required in the classroom for that college year, until a new French professor could be appointed.

In the spring of 1954, the British mail situation was becoming desperate. We needed to establish an office in London. We placed a request for a teacher of French with the teachers' placement bureau in Los Angeles, and I appointed Dick to make the selection.

Under most unusual circumstances Mr. Dibar K. Apartian, who had been reared in French-speaking Geneva, and spent much time in France, applied. Dick interviewed him.

"He's *just* the man we want," Dick told me. He was—*and still is!* Under Mr. Apartian the French department has grown into a big operation. He became the "voice" of the French-language version of *The World Tomorrow*. He is also editor of the French-language *Plain Truth*.

On April 2, 1954, our dean, registrar, and professor of science, Dr. Hawley Otis Taylor, died. He had completed seven years, lacking two months, as head of the faculty at Ambassador College. With Professor

315

Mauler-Hiennecy also gone, our own graduates were beginning more and more to fill up the faculty. Dr. Taylor was seventy-seven years of age when he died. His last seven years were devoted to helping establish the highest of academic and scholarly standards at Ambassador.

We Revisit London

While Dick had been in Pasadena during the 1953-54 year, his little Hillman-Minx car had been left in England with the Cordas-Cousins brothers. In May, 1954, plans were laid for Dick to return again to London—this time with Roderick C. Meredith. They sailed on the *Queen Elizabeth* June 16, to handle the British and European mail and further the work overseas.

It was now time that I personally inspected that situation abroad, where the work had now secured such a firm foothold. Mrs. Armstrong and I sailed, August 5, 1954, on the new, fastest ship in the world, the S.S. *United States.* We had now been on Radio Luxembourg a year and a half. A large listening audience had been built up. The mailing list had grown.

Our son Dick, with Roderick Meredith and the Cordas-Cousins brothers, were standing on the dock at Southampton to greet Mrs. Armstrong and me, as we debarked from the giant steamer *United States.* We had made reservations at the Dorchester Hotel where we had stayed on our 1947 visit. The Dorchester representative at the Southampton docks arranged for transporting our steamer trunk via the boat train to the hotel.

We loaded our hand luggage into the automobiles. I think Roderick Meredith rode back to London with the Cousins brothers. Mrs. Armstrong and I crowded

316

ourselves into Dick's little Hillman-Minx and Dick drove us to London.

A short distance out of Southampton Dick stopped at a small teahouse where we partook of the British custom of late afternoon tea.

Planning Meetings in England

Arriving in London I thought it well to make personal contact with as many of our radio listeners as possible. To arrange for booking halls for meetings, and placing some newspaper advertising I decided to engage a London advertising agency. I contacted the advertising managers of a couple of leading London newspapers on Fleet Street. They recommended the Frederick Aldridge, Ltd., agency. I contacted Mr. Philip Aldridge at the agency offices.

This agency had handled the Billy Graham evangelistic campaign in London, which had gained world attention. Mr. Frederick Aldridge had handled this account, and so his brother and partner, Mr. Philip Aldridge, was engaged as the *World Tomorrow* advertising representative for Britain. He handled our account for several years.

From our mailing list we knew our largest groupings of listeners centered around London, Manchester, Birmingham, Belfast, Northern Ireland, and Glasgow, Scotland. We planned meetings in Belfast, Glasgow, Manchester, and London.

The halls were booked, beginning September 14. Then announcements were mailed to those on the mailing list within those areas, and announcements arranged to go out on the program on Radio Luxembourg at the proper time.

Meanwhile we were free for other things.

My wife wanted to go to King's Lynn, north of

London on the sea, where her maternal great-grandfather had been a Methodist minister. Dick drove us to King's Lynn in the Hillman-Minx. En route we passed through Cambridge where we stopped for lunch. It was interesting to have our first view of one of these famous English universities. The various colleges scatter over most of the city of Cambridge. We walked through one of the halls, visited the cathedral, and enjoyed the beauty of the stretches of lawn alongside the river bank.

Also we stopped off a short while at Ely, to visit the huge old cathedral of Ely. It was then mostly or altogether in disuse, and sadly in need of repair if it were to be maintained at all. This is one of the very large cathedrals built by the Roman Catholics during the Middle Ages, now reeking with age. It has since undergone considerable repair. It is, of course, now one of the Church of England cathedrals.

At King's Lynn we searched out the little Methodist church where Mrs. Armstrong's great-grandfather had been pastor. A much larger addition had since been added since he died more than a century ago. We searched for his grave. Actually the graveyard where he was buried had been destroyed, for the building of a structure of some kind, but all the tombstones had been piled in an adjoining lot. We were just about to give up our search when one of us stumbled onto the great-grandfather's tombstone.

Later we drove in the Hillman-Minx on the Continent, crossing the English channel on a ferry.

We were taken all through the station at Radio Luxembourg. Then we drove on to Germany. Dick showed us the incredible recovery from the war, everywhere evident. Even the progress since his visit in 1952 was unbelievable—yet it was there in plain sight. After visiting Frankfurt, Bonn, Cologne, and Düsseldorf, we drove into Holland.

As a boy I had read stories about Holland—*Hansel and Gretel* and others. I had read of Haarlem, and supposed it to be a little village. I was amazed to find it a big city—and Rotterdam as big as San Francisco—with Amsterdam as big as Cleveland, Ohio, and bigger than Pittsburgh, or Boston, or many major American cities. We also drove through The Hague, about as large as Rotterdam. Then back through Belgium, and another ferry across the channel to the white cliffs of Dover in England.

This was the tenth of September. It was good to rejoin Roderick Meredith in London. We had enjoyed, and profited from, the trip on the Continent. But always, after being on the Continent, it seems just like coming *home* to be back in England! After all, the British and Americans are the SAME PEOPLE. Certain *national* differences have developed through the last two centuries, but we are the same people—and both nations ought to remember that.

And NOW! U.K. Speaking Tour

Late Sunday afternoon, September 12, Mrs. Armstrong, Dick and I started driving north in the Hillman-Minx. Over the weekend, our then advertising agent from Beverly Hills, California, Jack Parmalee, flew in to London. He wanted to attend the meetings on the speaking tour. He and Roderick Meredith met us in Belfast on Tuesday morning. They had driven from Dublin in a rented car after, it seems in a not-too clear memory, having flown to Cardiff, Wales, and then to Dublin.

We stopped off Sunday evening for dinner at a hotel in St. Albans. Little did we dream, that Sunday evening in September, 1954, that we would, within a few years, have a college already larger than the Pasadena College was then, with a St. Albans mail address!

After dinner we drove on north, bypassing Birmingham, and arriving in Manchester around midnight. Next morning we continued north. It was the first opportunity for Mrs. Armstrong and me to see northern England, and we found it a very interesting experience. We stopped at Carlisle for lunch. As a boy I had often visited a small town in Iowa named after this northern England city. It was just twelve miles south of Des Moines where I was born and reared. An uncle and aunt lived there, with a son—my cousin—just a year younger than I.

Carlisle is only a few miles from the Scottish border. Soon after lunch we were driving westward in Scotland. In the late afternoon we reached Stranraer. There was considerable excitement—and no little suspense—concerning our ability to get passage on the evening ferry across the north channel of the Irish Sea. We had dinner in a hotel near the docks while anxiously awaiting the verdict. If we failed, I might have missed the following night's meeting at Belfast entirely. We finally persuaded an official to let us on. There were more cars and passengers than they could accommodate.

It was interesting watching the cranes pick up Dick's car, swing it from a cable through the air, and drop it down onto the ship. But soon we were steaming the thirty-six-mile distance to Larne, Northern Ireland, where we had hotel reservations for the night.

Next morning, we drove the short distance down to Belfast, and met Roderick Meredith and Mr. Parmelee. We visited the hall that had been engaged for our meeting—one seating about a thousand or twelve hundred people. We found everything would be in readiness for the meeting. Then we went "sight-seeing" around Belfast and vicinity.

We had heard of a very old historic place of ancient Druid worship a few miles outside Belfast, known as The Giant's Ring. We drove out to it. Then we proceeded to the giant shipbuilding yards at Belfast. The size of this operation was truly astonishing. Belfast is a major port.

Evening came, and time for the meeting. Arrangements had been made for ushering in people at the hall, so we did not appear until five or ten minutes before time for the service. The large hall, located in the very heart of the city center business district, was well filled. We found approximately 750 people waiting for us.

There had been a small advertisement in the newspaper giving notice of the meeting, but no attempt had been made to draw any audience beyond our own interested radio listeners. So an audience of 750 was a very, very warm welcome to Belfast. People had come from miles around. One had pushed another interested listener a great distance in a wheelchair to a bus, in order to attend. My message that night was on "What's Prophesied for Britain."

The message was not intended to be for entertainment. This was my first opportunity to speak in person before an overseas audience. The time was serious, and the message was serious.

I said: "Last week, and part of the week before, I spent five days in Germany. And what I saw in a Germany only eight years ago almost shattered from the war, was emphatic evidence that the WORLD WAR *is not yet over!* We are now merely in the second recess of the war.

"What is *prophesied* for the United Kingdom, and

321

for the United States? I have crossed America and the Atlantic Ocean to tell you things I *can't* say on the radio. What I'm now going to say is not popular! But it is as *certain as the rising and setting of tomorrow's sun! Yet on beyond it all, after* our peoples have been PUNISHED as no nations *ever* were before, WORLD PEACE is coming, *in our time!"*

The audience showed tremendous interest!

After the service our two cars were driven on a boat. We all had sleeping accommodations on the boat for the night. Next morning we were docked at Glasgow.

That night another good audience, equally warm and friendly and interested, assembled in a hall in downtown Glasgow. The crowd there was smaller—perhaps 450 or 500.

Thursday we drove down to Manchester. The hall there was on the third or fourth floor of a building. There was only the one lift (elevator to our American readers). The hall here was smaller, but we had an overflow crowd, much to the displeasure of the lift operator. Extra chairs had to be brought in to the auditorium, and several had to stand. I must have spoken about an hour or a little over, but after about forty-five minutes the lift operator came in, interrupted the service, and wanted me to stop talking so he could close up the lift and go home.

But I had come a long distance to deliver a super-serious life-and-death message to hundreds of my radio listeners, and I was not going to cut that message off to please a disgruntled lift operator. The hall had been engaged for the entire evening. A good many had to hear more of this man's bad attitude before everybody had finally been taken to the ground floor, after the meeting was dismissed. And I was so thoroughly disgusted with his uncalled-for ill behavior, I expressed

322

myself rather sharply to him as I descended in the final trip of the lift for that night.

The crowd there was slightly smaller than at Glasgow, but still an overflow crowd.

First Convert Baptized

On Friday we drove back to London. We had a request from a lady at Crewe, home city of the Rolls-Royce factory, for baptism. So we drove by way of Crewe. She was Mrs. Edna Palin. We found that she operated a beauty shop for women, in front of her home. We also met Mr. Palin and talked to him. We were satisfied that Mrs. Palin really was ready for baptism. She knew of a river—or, I believe probably more properly, an irrigation stream—some few miles from town. We drove there. And my son Richard David performed the very first baptismal service resulting from this work on this side of the Atlantic. Later, after the work was better established in Britain, Mr. Palin was baptized by one of our other ministers.

Returning to London, we had meetings scheduled in a very nice downtown hall for the following Tuesday, Wednesday and Thursday, September 21 to 23.

While in London, a certain coincidence reminded us very much of the Ambassador College campus in Pasadena. Mrs. Armstrong and I were staying at the Dorchester Hotel, and Dick and Roderick Meredith at the Cumberland, only a few blocks away. But when we called them on the telephone, their hotel was on the AMBASSADOR exchange; and when they called us, the Dorchester was on the MAYFAIR exchange. And, as I think most readers know, Mayfair is the name of one of our principal girls' student residences at Pasadena.

We returned to the United States on the S.S. *America,* a very beautiful ship.

64

First Middle-East Tour

MY TIME was almost completely absorbed, after our return to the United States, with the coast-to-coast broadcasting over the ABC network, the television scare, and intensive preparations to leap from radio over to television.

Our original telecasting experience lasted twenty-seven weeks. By January, 1956, we had become satisfied that radio was *far* from dead. Radio had been forced to change its format—true! Radio had adapted itself to a different type of programming. But it had survived! People were actually buying more radio sets than ever!

Planning Our First Middle-East Tour

I had used a great deal of "film stock"—that is, motion-picture footage—to illustrate whatever I was talking about on television. I felt we needed some very *special* motion-picture film of Palestine, the ancient area of

Babylon, such places as Tyre and Sidon. Also I had for some time felt the need of a personal visit to those lands, to obtain material for articles and broadcasts. I knew that if I visited the ancient Bible lands, got the *"feel"* and experienced the very atmosphere of these lands, my preaching, lecturing, broadcasting and writing would be far more effective. The places I would be speaking about would be far more *REAL* to me, and therefore I could make them more real to listeners and readers.

We were now well along on our new road of DAILY RADIO. I was no longer tied down with the furious night-and-day grind of intensive television production. And I really *needed* a change of scenery.

So we began making plans for a tour of the Middle East, and an every-night evangelistic campaign in London.

Our son Dick, with George Meeker, an Ambassador graduate and ordained minister, had sailed back to Britain and Europe on June 29, 1955. A considerable mail response was coming from the broadcasts on Radio Luxembourg, and the broadcasts on Radio Ceylon, and into South Africa. Those men were needed in London to handle much of the response, although the general mailing list was still maintained at Pasadena headquarters.

But it was becoming impossible to process, answer, and handle this increasing volume of mail from Pasadena. We needed an office in London.

Late in August, 1955, Dick obtained occupancy of a small suite of offices he had located on Cranbourn Street, Leicester Square, in the very heart of downtown London. He had returned to Pasadena for some three weeks in October, 1955, speaking on the television program while here.

Once it was decided that Mrs. Armstrong and I would take the Middle-Eastern trip, to be followed by the nightly evangelistic campaign in London, Dick began planning the itinerary through American Express in London. He was to accompany us.

But at that time the Middle East began to sizzle as the world's trouble spot. Nasser was soon to seize the Suez Canal. Trouble was brewing between Jews and Arabs. War seemed imminent. Russia had been supplying Nasser with arms and planes. The Suez crisis might result in British intervention. That might result in Russian intervention against Britain. World War III *could* suddenly flare up out of this crisis.

Then, suddenly, the crisis quieted down along about February. The way was opened for us to proceed with plans for the trip. The war scare remained quiet until our tour was finished. Then, on our return to America, the crisis boiled hot again. Nasser did take over the Suez Canal on July 26. I wrote an article on it for the September *Plain Truth*, immediately on our return.

That article said: "The war clouds that have hovered over the Middle East were cleared just long enough to permit Mrs. Armstrong, our son Richard, and me to visit Cairo, and the capitals of the Middle East—Baghdad, Amman, Damascus, Beirut, Jerusalem and Tel Aviv.... Now that we have returned to America, our mission accomplished, the crisis explodes all over again—this time over the seizure of the Suez Canal! It was quieted just long enough to allow God's emissaries to complete their visit."

Mrs. Armstrong and I left Pasadena during the latter half of March, 1956. We stopped off a few days at what is now the site of the third Ambassador College Campus (opened September, 1964) near Big Sandy, Texas. We traveled by train to New York. One of our

Ambassador graduates drove our car to New York, loaded with the entire mailing list for Britain, Europe, Africa—which we were then transferring to the new London office.

We boarded the *Queen Mary,* sailing for Southampton, England, on April 11, 1956.

Mrs. Armstrong kept a diary of this trip. Her comments, written on the spot at the moment, are far more accurate than anything I could now write from memory.

Mrs. Armstrong's diary was published in *The Plain Truth* in three installments, in the October, November, and December, 1956, issues of *The Plain Truth.* They evoked a tremendous interest among our readers. Many exciting and interesting things happened. I feel that her diary belongs as a part of this record, so I shall reprint it here—breaking in, as I may, from time to time, with comments of my own.

PART I
by Loma D. Armstrong

WE arrived in New York after our train ride from Longview, Texas. We encountered varied weather conditions on the trip: dust storms in Texas, Missouri, and Illinois; rains, of almost cloudburst intensities, in Indiana and Ohio; and heavy fog in Pennsylvania, New Jersey and New York.

The weekend, in New York, was very windy and today (April 8) we awakened to see several inches of snow on the ground. It is still snowing. We hope that the weather will clear soon and allow the sun to come out.

Arriving in Europe

We arrived in Southampton on Monday, April 16, at

327

2:45 p.m. Our son Dick and George Meeker were on the dock to meet us. Dick was so glad to see us that he whirled me around until I was almost dizzy. When our car was unloaded at the dock it had three flat tires, but they held air when inflated. George Meeker drove Dick's car to London and Dick drove our car, with us.

The drive from Southampton to London, in the bright English sunshine, was beautiful. Our drive was interrupted with a stop at a quaint little tea room for tea. We arrived in London after dark. Dick took us first to the apartment where he and George live; then we went to our hotel. After our baths we enjoyed a good night's rest.

Tuesday, April 17

We had to completely repack our trunk and pack our suitcases as lightly as possible for our trip by airplane to Zurich, Switzerland, on our first lap to the Middle East.

Wednesday, April 18

We arrived in Zurich, Wednesday afternoon. It was a cold, rainy day—rain mixed with snow. In places the ground was white with snow.

In London, we were told that we would not need coats, and that it would be very hot over the whole area in which we would be traveling; so, before leaving London, at the airport, we gave our coats to George to take to their apartment until we returned. As a result we were damp, soggy, and shivering before we were in Zurich many minutes. Mr. Armstrong bought a Bolex movie camera for our motion pictures.

We left Zurich by train for Rome, having to sit up until midnight. When we arrived in Milano we changed trains for the remainder of the trip, Mr. Armstrong left

328

his hat on the first train. So we arrived in Rome with him bareheaded. He remedied that soon after we arrived, however, by buying a new hat.

We were in Rome only a few hours. The nearer the time came to fly across the Mediterranean Sea the more tense I felt. I do *not* like to fly.

Our flight was in the bright sunshine and the sea was beautiful. We flew along the Italian coast over the Bay of Naples—near Mount Vesuvius, over the Isle of Capri, across the boot of Italy, over Stromboli, then out to sea. In the middle of the Mediterranean we saw an American aircraft carrier and several cruisers.

Destination Egypt!

Though trouble had quieted down between the Arab Egyptians and Israel for a while, military ships were in evidence—standing by—in a number of places.

It was dark when we reached the shores of Africa. We flew over Alexandria and the delta of the Nile.

We arrived in Cairo at 9:30 p.m., April 18, to a strange and different world. At the airport, an Arab and a Nubian checked our passports. Because we were Americans, we were held up until our names were checked against a list they had of spies or political undesirables.

The friendliness of the personnel at the English and at the Swiss airports was sadly missing here. We were looked upon as sympathizers of the British, who are hated in Egypt.

We were taken to our hotel in a bus driven by an Arab dressed in robes—in fact, all people, here, dress in robes. It was a long drive and so surprising. We saw block after block—mile after mile—of large, *modern* apartment buildings, four to twelve stories high.

After arriving at the Semiramis Hotel, we had

329

baths and brushed our teeth in water from the Nile (along its banks, Moses was hidden in the bulrushes when he was a baby). It flows deep and wide, just outside our window and across the street. Ex-King Farouk's yacht is anchored just below and is used as an annex to this hotel. A young lady from Long Beach, California, a school teacher, was on our plane and has a room on the yacht.

It was 1:40 a.m. when I finally got to bed.

Friday Morning, April 20

A guide from the American Express office—a young Arab named Sayed, who speaks English very well, dressed in a red robe and red fez—came to the hotel after us. He had a nice car—a Chrysler—and an Arab driver who could not speak English.

What Egypt Is Like

We drove all through the native quarters where we saw the narrow streets filled with donkeys pulling carts of hay or vegetables; donkeys being ridden by men who were like giants on them (the men were so long-legged that their feet almost dragged on the streets); cars, mostly American, being driven by Arabs; and people wearing dirty and so often ragged robes. In the midst of it all there were children and dogs. Our driver used the horn on the car to drive through. All other cars were doing the same. Horns honking incessantly. The drivers of the donkey carts were yelling; people chattering; dogs barking; and the *smell was awful*. The motion pictures we took could not bring back with us the sounds or the smells. Actually, no one paid any attention to the honking of the horns. We had to wind our way slowly though the whole mess. The streets were as filthy as the people.

Some of the shops are crude holes in the wall where

different craftsmen are plying their trades. We saw one man carving large copper and brass trays by hand. These trays were intricate with beautiful designs—very beautifully done.

We were taken to the "City of the Dead." It is a place outside, or in the outskirts of the city. It is the place where the poor are buried. When we arrived, a pickup truck was unloading a body, merely wrapped in cloth, to be put in a hole which they dig in the clay banks and afterwards close up.

There were many caves in the hillsides. We found many people living in some of these dirt caves, sitting on the ground outside their openings in the dirty, dusty streets, even though they were in the midst of the "City of the Dead."

We were then taken to a large mosque. We were told that it is the largest in the world. When we entered the courtyard of the mosque, we had to don canvas slippers over our shoes. No one is allowed inside in shoes. All Arabs remove their shoes and go in either barefooted or in socks. In the center of the courtyard is a large fountain, around which the Arabs sit and wash their hands and feet before entering the mosque.

As we entered, we were surprised at the beauty of the place. Its only furniture was a high altar reached by an ornate stairway from which the Koran is read. The floor was completely covered by a beautiful red carpet on which a number of Arabs were sitting or lying down. They were scattered over the large room, not in groups. We tried to take pictures inside the mosque but the lighting was too dim.

We have never in all our lives seen so many diseased eyes. Many people are blind and deformed—especially with twisted feet.

After seeing Cairo, we left in the evening by train

for ancient Thebes, now called Luxor—450 miles south, up the Nile.

As the train pulled slowly through the city, we saw how the people live. There were mud or adobe apartments—just a conglomeration of rooms placed anywhere, one on top of the other. There was no plan, but they were placed as if they had been blown together by a strong wind and stuck just as they happened to light. The Arab women and children sit on the ground wherever they take the notion. It makes no difference what surrounds them.

After we were no longer able to see the country through which we were traveling, we went to bed in our tiny compartments only to awaken in the night choking with dust. The only way a person could breathe was by holding the sheet over the face. The dust was thick in the air.

Daylight came very early so we were able to see the country through which we were passing. A canal, beside the track, seemed to provide water for use in their homes and huts as well as for irrigation. The black-robed women were dipping the water in huge pitchers or bottles which they always carried on their heads.

We would also see people in water up to their waists and water buffalo wading. A highway ran along the opposite side of the canal, and, early as it was, early dawn, we could see many men and women walking briskly along. Some of the men rode small donkeys—with their feet almost touching the ground, while the women carried baskets or jars on their heads. Others rode camels. Children were driving goats or water buffalo. There were people scattered over the fields working with their hands in the soil. A few had crude hoes. Once in a while we saw a donkey and camel yoked together pulling a crooked stick or a plow. Their agricultural methods were primitive. But the soil appeared rich.

Ancient Egypt's Grandeur

We arrived in the early morning at Luxor and were taken to our hotel in an antiquated motor-driven hack. There was no room for Dick so he was driven in a horse-drawn buggy.

This was Luxor, built on the site of the ancient city of Thebes, capital of the ancient Egyptian domain when Egypt was at the zenith of its splendor. Luxor, today, includes also the village of Karnak, six miles from the main village.

All the wealth of war, the booty, and the shipments of goods from other countries were once hoarded in Thebes, the capital. Today, we saw the remains, only a number of rich monuments, and supporting columns of temples and tombs. Once they were overlaid with gold, silver, alabaster, or marble; now there is nothing but time-worn stone. The temples had been connected with one another by courtyards and lobbies. Now, however, the massive columns are all that remain of the former splendor.

Our guide, an elderly and scholarly Egyptian, walked over the ruins hour after hour with us, explaining the history and the religion of the people who worshiped at the temples. It was all worship of the sun-god Ra.

We were there during the Muslim fast called Ramadan. Although our guide was in his seventies, he carried on all day through the hot sun, with no food. The fast lasts a month and no food can be eaten from sunrise until sunset; however, they eat during the night.

After a long day we sat on the large veranda of the hotel overlooking the Nile. The moon was full and the stars seemed so near and so very bright. It was a beautiful evening.

Our beds in the hotel were covered with high canopies with curtains of mosquito netting. We did not pull the netting over us when we went to bed, but we soon found it was impossible to sleep without it, after being bitten a number of times by mosquitoes.

The food was terrible. I could not eat any breakfast, so I drank some hot tea. At least the water had been boiled.

King Tut-ankh-Amon's Tomb

This morning we crossed the Nile River in a felucca or sailboat built as they used to build them thousands of years ago. A driver with an old Ford car met us on the other side and we rode over hot dusty roads to the tomb of King Tut-ankh-Amon. His tomb was discovered in 1922. He is said to have died at the age of eighteen. His tomb was the last of the pharaohs' tombs to be found.

The tomb is deep underground, down a tiled and decorated passageway, past a false entrance and thence to the real entrance where the inner coffin lies. In the room were images of the history of some part of his life. These images were in the tile on the walls.

The contents of the tomb filled one whole wing of the museum at Cairo. It took several years to move all the contents from the tomb. The mummy is in a museum. The wealth buried or stored in the different treasure rooms of the tomb was fantastic.

After leaving the king's tomb, we entered the tomb of Ramses the Sixth. I did not go to the end of the passageway down into the tomb, but Dick and Mr. Armstrong did. I felt that the long climb back up was more than I wanted to try. I did, however, go into the tomb of Seti.

334

After our visit to those tombs we were taken to the temple of Queen Hatshepsut, which was carved out of a mountainside. She is said to have ruled Egypt from 1503 to 1483 B.C. She reigned like a king and the large figures or statues at her temple have been made with false beards. She claimed she was the daughter of the sun-god himself. The story of her birth and of her reign is depicted on one of the terraces of the temple ruins.

After returning to our hotel we packed our bags for our return through the night to Cairo. Once more a dusty trip.

Cairo Again

When we reached Cairo our guide who had previously taken us over the city was at the station to meet us with the same Chrysler car and chauffeur. He had planned a trip to the Pyramids and a camp out in the Sahara Desert.

Our next visit was to the site of the ancient city of Memphis, where Moses and Aaron pleaded with the Pharaoh to let the children of Israel go. Only a few ruins which have been excavated remain now of the ancient city.

We drove from there to the Pyramids at Saqqara which, we were told, were the oldest of the Pyramids. There were also, in this area, a number of tombs over 2,500 years old.

We then drove through the city of Giza, out into the Sahara desert past the Great Pyramid where we found our camp.

We were quite surprised to find it really *just* our camp. We expected to find others there, but the four tents were just for us.

Mr. Armstrong's and my tent was quite large. It

335

was white on the outside but very colorful on the inside with each panel of the tent a different design. The sand had been smoothed out level and covered with oriental rugs. There were two cots nicely made up with sheets and wool blankets (it is very cold on the desert at night). There were also a table, large pitcher of water, wash bowl and soap; and hung on the center pole were towels and a mirror. A large bouquet of flowers adorned the table. Dick's tent was like ours but smaller. Another large tent we found was our dining room. It also had a rug over the sand. In it was a large table with a centerpiece of flowers. There was a table for serving, and chairs with cushions. A short distance away was another tent—the cooks' tent. Here was a cook, assistant cook, and a waiter.

Sayed had brought his little seven-year-old son, Mohammed, out to spend the day and the night. They slept out under the stars on cots.

We arrived at the camp before lunch time.

After lunch, three camels with their leaders were outside our tent. We were helped aboard and had our first camel ride. We really enjoyed our camel ride to the Great Pyramid of Giza.

We went into the pyramid through its long, low passageway to the King's Chamber. It is a marvelous building and although the King's Chamber is in the center of the huge pile of stone, it is ventilated by built-in shafts.

I waited while Mr. Armstrong and Dick walked stooped over in the shorter low passageway to the Queen's Chamber.

When we once more mounted our camels we rode back across the desert to our camp, where the cooks had prepared a huge dinner which none of us could eat, because of the size of the lunch they had served before we left for the Pyramids. Our guide told us that he had asked some Arab entertainers from the village to come out that evening to put on a show for us.

We saw them coming by foot across the dunes in the moonlight. Then the dining tent was made ready for the entertainment. Although it was bright and beautiful out in the moonlight, the wind was cold.

There were six entertainers, all men, in their Arab robes. Four with strange musical instruments which they played with rhythm and not much music. The other two were dancers and the dances were weird imitations of animals. Finally, one danced the dance of a demon. Our guide stopped him before he danced himself into a frenzy because he noticed that I was shocked by it.

After they left we tried to eat some of the huge meal that had been prepared for us. Then we went to our tents for a night out on the Sahara Desert. The air was so clear we could hear the Koran being read over the loud speakers from the minarets of the mosques of Cairo.

When we awoke and had our breakfast, the car came to take us back to Cairo. We first visited the Sphinx again, then on in to Cairo.

We then went to the museum where we saw room after room of the fabulous furniture, vases, jewelry, and other material taken from Tut-ankh-Amon's tomb.

Sheikh Hafiz Wabba

During the afternoon, we returned to the hotel to pick up our bags that we had checked there while we were on our trek to the desert. We found that Sheikh Hafiz Wabba had called and had left us his telephone number.

He and his wife and three daughters came later in the afternoon to see us. While Mr. Armstrong and Dick

337

talked to the sheikh (whom Mr. Armstrong had met in San Francisco at the first meeting of the United Nations and later in London, England), I had an interesting visit with his wife. They had lived in London while the sheikh was the Ambassador Extraordinary from Saudi Arabia to Britain for twenty-five years. His wife was very irked to have had to dress in the black robe and veil of the women of the Middle East, and to be forced to walk several paces behind her husband. She was quite well educated and her daughters had been educated in London. All were dressed in Western clothes when they came to see us.

After our visit with them we went to bed early and were called at 3 a.m. to go to the airport for our flight over the Dead Sea and the Jordan River to Jerusalem, our first stop.

The airport at Jerusalem was so far from the city that we could see nothing of it. After a thirty-minute stop we flew to Amman. That was a rough flight and for the first time on the trip, I became air sick, or perhaps it was flight sick.

When we arrived at Amman airport, U.N. Secretary-General Dag Hammarskjöld's plane was there. He was sent by the United Nations to quiet matters.

Now to Babylon!

We were delayed in Amman about an hour, while some repairs were made on our plane. Then we flew on to Baghdad, where we arrived in the early afternoon. For some three or four hours we flew over nothing but desolate, waste, desert land. Our American Express guide met us at the airport and took us to our hotel. The hotel was a modern, air-conditioned building, opened only five months before. It is surprising to find, all over the Middle East, very new, modern apartment

338

buildings and hotels. Our hotel was on a narrow side street just a half block off the main street of Baghdad.

I was too tired to look at Baghdad but Mr. Armstrong and Dick walked a mile or so through the main street but came back to get away from the swarms of beggars. Everywhere children and grownups besiege one every few steps begging and blocking one's way, following along determined not to leave until they are given money.

We went to bed early and were called at 6 in the morning. After a breakfast of tea, toast, and orange juice our guide met us and we drove sixty-five miles by car over the roughest, dirtiest roads to the site of ancient Babylon.

A very small part of Babylon was excavated by the Germans prior to World War I. We saw the Ishtar gate with the dragons and bulls in the brick walls. There was also the lion's den into which Daniel had been thrown. A picture, or rather a brick form of a lion, is still on the wall (den). The inscriptions identifying this very pit as the lion's den, into which Daniel was thrown, were taken to Berlin by the Germans.

The "Processional Way" from the Ishtar gate to the ruins of Nebuchadnezzar's palace have been excavated. The paving stones are just as they were when Daniel and the three Hebrew children were there, but the palace is in ruins and a stork had built its nest on top of one of the ruins. The owls were there just as is prophesied in the Bible. We also saw the ruins of the hanging gardens, one of the seven wonders of the ancient world. Miles of the ancient city is still under fifteen or twenty feet of sand, soil and rubble.

It was so strange to realize we were walking over the same paved street that the prophet Daniel, with Shadrach, Meshach and Abednego, walked over. To be

339

in the place where Daniel had been thrown into the lion's den and the other three into the fiery furnace and to realize that one "like the Son of God" had been there too, and delivered them all from death, was awesome. All of those events seemed so real to us even though the proud old city is now in ruins.

On our way to Baghdad we passed through two villages. How any of the babies there ever grow up is a mystery to me. The villages are very unsanitary.

We were covered with dust when we returned to our hotel and after a good bath had naps until dinner time.

Although it was only April 26, the heat was terrible and our air-conditioned room was such a relief.

On the next day our guide took us all over the city of Baghdad. Our first trip was through the streets to the Gold Mosque. None but Muslims are allowed in the mosque.

There Are Dangers, Too

As we took movies of the open door of the mosque, a crowd began gathering around us. Their manner plainly told us we had better move from there *fast!* Our guide took us through the crowd and into a building where we climbed three flights of narrow, *very* steep stairs to the roof and had a good view of the Golden Dome. We took movies from that vantage point unmolested.

After leaving the mosque we were taken to the market, or bazaar (as they are called there). There were narrow streets packed with people—in discolored robes. There were open shops on both sides of the streets. A number of times in the crowd we were separated from our guide and from Dick. There were many square blocks of these shops—mostly filled with sandals, or cloth goods, Arab head-dress materials, or copper and

340

brass wares. We finally came to a wider street or passageway where men and boys were pounding out pans and other vessels from copper. It was a regular bedlam, but we stayed long enough to take movies of them and their handiwork.

We were so surprised to see on the main street of Baghdad men selling their wares outside the buildings. Along the curbs there were men with trousers or jackets for sale—with tape measure over their shoulder to measure the prospective customer. There were baskets of bread for sale, put upon the dirty sidewalks, covered with flies and dust.

Many of the people are diseased and blind and crippled or deformed. It is a miserable existence, but they know of nothing better.

We drove out of the city several miles to the southeast to the great Arch of Ctesiphon, built by King Kisra of ancient Persia, long after the days of Alexander the Great. It was an *immense* arch! We also saw a part of the king's palace. This palace of King Kisra had been excavated by the Germans. We took pictures of the storks on the ruins.

When we were returning from the arch, we passed a tribe of gypsies—some of them riding on donkeys. One woman was nursing her baby as she walked along. All their tents and equipment were carried on donkeys.

At Baghdad we were eleven hours sun-time from home—almost halfway around the earth.

Our flight back west to Damascus from Baghdad over the Euphrates River, and the desert, took several hours.

We saw the green trees surrounding Damascus from the air and they were a welcome sight after the wasteland of the desert.

65

The Holy Land
Part II
by Loma D. Armstrong
(Written February, 1965)

THE CITY of Damascus is a mixture of beautiful modern buildings in the new city and dilapidated, old structures of the old city inhabited by Arabs. The fine apartments are the foreign embassies and the residences of English, American and other businessmen.

Our American Express guide here in Damascus looked like ex-King Farouk of Egypt. He met us at the airport and took us to our hotel. The building was beautiful and modern, but the dining room was so filled with fly spray that it was difficult to breathe. We still had Arab food, some of it very strange. We were served licorice leaves in the hors d'oeuvres.

We went to bed early and arose early the next morning to see the city. Damascus is said to be the oldest continuously inhabited city on earth. And early as it was, the streets of this ancient city were crowded—as they were in Cairo—with people, donkeys, carts, dogs and cars. The car horns were continually being honked.

We first went through the market place with its narrow streets packed full of people as were the streets in Baghdad. Then we went through the Arch of Jupiter to a large mosque. This mosque has an intriguing history. Centuries ago, after the worshipers of Jupiter were driven from it, the Romans made a church out of it. When the Turks took over, it was changed to the present mosque. It is a large building with many, many beautiful oriental rugs completely covering the floor. On or along the east wall were niches to show the people which way to face Mecca when they pray. Many of the people were sitting on the floor in scattered groups bowing with their heads touching the floor. Many beggars were also among them.

We Visit a Harem

We were then taken to the former palace of the early Turkish rulers and also to the harem of the sultans. In their different rooms were life-size wax figures dressed in their native costumes and representing the different uses that each room was put to. In one, a woman was portrayed rocking a baby in a low cradle. In another the seamstresses were fitting a bride for her wedding dress.

Each room was beautifully furnished. There were many pieces of furniture inlaid with mother-of-pearl and camel bone with ivory. There were also Persian rugs covering the floors and one room contained the usual Turkish coffee pots in five sizes. They have five pots for this reason: First, the coffee is put into a large pot, then boiled down to the size of the smaller and so on until there is just enough remaining to fill the smallest pot. By that time it is thick and black and very strong!

343

In the courtyard of the palace was a beautiful fountain and pool, surrounded by porches and couches where the women of the harem used to lounge. This courtyard is enclosed and kept from view from the outside.

Street Called "Straight"

Later, we were taken to the street called "Straight" where Paul, on his way to persecute the Christians, entered Damascus after he was stricken with blindness by Christ. The old street Paul walked on and the gate through which he entered was fourteen feet below the present street and only the gate and a small part of the street have been excavated.

Our guide took us from there to a place underground which he called the house of Ananias where Paul received his sight. It is obviously a fake, for it is only a cave twenty-one steps down. It is now a very small religious shrine with the usual idols and the usual hands held out for money.

Leading off from this was a smaller, darker cave called the Confessional. It made me think of an evil bird's haunt—and if one were able to see clearly, he surely would have seen bats on the walls!

We were then driven by an Arab to a refugee camp—the most miserable place we had yet seen. We saw one hundred thousand Arabs living in huts made from old oil cans or anything else they could find. The dust was thick under our feet and the people were sickly and ragged. They were covered with flies. Most of them were beggars.

America had an "Atoms for Peace" display in Damascus while we were there.

We drove by the old wall of Damascus to the possible place where Paul was let down in a basket and escaped from those who plotted to kill him. After seeing the old part of the city, we were driven up winding streets to the top of a hill. Along these high winding streets were beautiful apartment buildings where the American and English businessmen, oilmen and others, along with ambassadors, live. This area was such a contrast to the part of the city we had gone through.

Easter Eggs at Baalbek

On April 30, we left our hotel at 9 in the morning with another guide who had driven down from Beirut in a car. He was sent to take us through Syria to Lebanon.

It was a beautiful drive through the mountains and fertile plains of Lebanon. We were surprised to see the fields of grain and other lush growth. We drove through a large and well-watered valley where the streams came down from Mt. Lebanon.

We arrived at Baalbeck, a city dating from the 3rd to 1st century B.C. It was the site of the ancient temple of Jupiter, built by Phoenicians, destroyed partially by the Greeks, rebuilt by the Romans, destroyed by them, then rebuilt again, and finally destroyed by God, with far greater devastation, through an earthquake.

Everywhere from Cairo, Luxor, Baghdad, Damascus, and now Baalbeck, we found eggs carved in the architectural embellishment of buildings and temples. The guides all call them the symbol of fertility. We have close-up pictures of eggs on the ruins of Babylon.

After lunch we drove back through part of the beautiful valley, then drove into the mountains where we came to a view of the seaport city of Beirut and the Mediterranean Sea.

When we reached the city of Beirut, capital of Lebanon, we found that most of the people were dressed in Western clothes and not in the robes of most Middle

Easterners. Very few women were wearing veils over their faces. The streets were crowded by now with hundreds and hundreds of cars. Most of the autos were American.

We Visit Tyre and Sidon

Our first day there, we drove along the Mediterranean Sea to the site of old Sidon and old Tyre. We found old Tyre completely gone and the city the Romans tried to rebuild on the island (now part of the mainland which Alexander joined to the mainland by filling in the channel between with the ruins and topsoil of old Tyre) in complete ruin. We walked over the fallen columns and the walls or foundations of the ancient buildings excavated many years ago by the Germans. We found among the ruins pieces of shattered pottery which our guide, who lived nearby, let us take with us.

We were not able to take pictures of Tyre, for it is in a military zone and the guards on the highway leading to Tyre took our cameras until we returned from having visited the place. We were very near the Israeli soldiers' machine gun nests.

We drove past great banana, loquat and orange groves. On our return to Beirut, as in all Middle Eastern cities, we saw the usual beautiful apartment buildings and homes. The most outstanding ones were especially near the city of Beirut.

We were so hungry when we arrived at our hotel that we were ready to eat anything. And we did!

The evening before, when we first entered our hotel at Beirut and asked for mail, we found a telegram from our son-in-law, Vern Mattson—our daughter Dorothy's husband—saying that our little granddaughter had arrived and that the baby and mother were just fine. He also said that their seven-year-old daughter Carol's only

346

comment was "Shucks!" She wanted a baby brother!

It was quite a relief to us.

We had expected the baby a whole month before and looked every day on the ship from New York to London, and in every place we had been since then, for a cablegram. Now it had arrived and everyone was all right! We were happy and very grateful to finally receive the news.

That evening, Mr. Armstrong and Dick went down to the office of the American Express to check up on our trip, for we had advanced our schedule several days.

Had Dick Met With Violence?

Around 6 o'clock, Mr. Armstrong came back to the hotel alone. I asked where Dick was and he said that he was remaining downtown to see the city and that he would be back by 8 p.m. for dinner. Then Mr. Armstrong, worn out from the trip, took a nap.

Eight o'clock came and Dick had not come! Mr. Armstrong was still asleep. I was not worried then, but kept waiting, thinking that Dick would arrive any minute. I was going to let Mr. Armstrong sleep until then.

Nine o'clock came, and 10, and still there was no sign of Dick. Mr. Armstrong was still sleeping. By this time, I could stand it no longer. I was really worried. So I called Mr. Armstrong and told him that Dick had not come back. He was startled. Our room was directly above the hotel entrance, five floors up. He leaned out the window, looking down, and began to listen for and watch for cars as they drove up to the entrance to see if Dick were arriving by taxi. The window ledge was so wide it was difficult to stretch over it far enough to see.

Around midnight, although I had had Dick paged in the lobby with no results, Mr. Armstrong walked

347

down the five flights of stairs (the elevator was not running) to see if he could possibly be in the lobby. I had kept our room door open and had made dozens of trips to look down the stairwell for Dick, but Mr. Armstrong's trip down to the first floor was fruitless.

I had called at Dick's door, adjoining ours, a number of times and knocked, but there was no answer. I had them to ring his room but still no answer.

Mr. Armstrong finally called a bellboy to come up and let us in Dick's room. He was unable to unlock the door. By this time it was 1 a.m. Three bellboys came up. One came into our room and again phoned or tried to get Dick's room. Still no answer. Had Dick been attacked in downtown Beirut? Had he met with foul play or violence?

The other two men decided to walk out on the window ledge from our window to Dick's window. His room was next to ours but it was quite a distance to be walking on a window ledge five stories above the street. One fellow reached Dick's open window and yelled and came backing hurriedly to the other fellow. Both came quickly crawling back into our room saying, "There is someone in there all right! He threatened to shove me off the ledge!"

All of us, with that news, ran quickly down the hall to Dick's door and pounded hard on it.

It was Dick! He called out, "What's going on around here?" His father said, "Open the door, Dick," and a tousled, sleepy, but startled Dick opened the door to ask again, "What's going on?" He had come to the hotel before 8 o'clock and had gone directly to bed. He was as tired and exhausted as his father, and so sound asleep that he knew nothing of the excitement he had caused until he saw and heard the two men at his open bedroom window standing on the ledge high above the

348

street! Dick was startled to see a prowler peeking into his room from outside and said, "Shove off!" The bellman on the ledge thought he had said, "I'll shove you off!"

Prior to coming to the hotel, Dick had met a man in downtown Beirut with whom he had talked about conditions in the Middle East. This man told him that if he really wanted to know, he would take him where several men were meeting.

Dick, being an American, was not too welcome. They expressed their views and evidently Dick expressed how he felt about their views of America.

When he saw these two men at his open window late in the night, he thought for a moment they were men who had followed him from that meeting and were there to do him bodily harm. We then learned why they so hurriedly scrambled back through our window into our room. Because Dick was so suddenly roused from his sleep, he sprang up in bed and yelled, "Shove off!"

They saw that he was startled and that he sounded as if he meant business, so, like scared rabbits they tumbled back through our windows. After all the excitement was over, we finally got to bed and to sleep—but not Dick. He said he got no more sleep the rest of the night.

On Wednesday morning, we went through the museum at Beirut. All the museums in all the ancient cities are an education. Although we saw them all, the most outstanding in our memory is the Cairo Museum with its immense amount of loot taken from King Tut-Ank-Amon's tomb.

We left Beirut after lunch to fly to Amman, the capital of the kingdom of Jordan. Our plane stopped for twenty minutes at Jerusalem, at the airport on the Arab side of the city.

It is not a long flight from Jerusalem but after all the

flying we had done. I still gave a sigh of relief when I felt the first bump of the wheels of the plane touch the runway.

Again, an American Express agent, named Yasser, met us at the airport and took us to our hotel. Then came a surprise.

American Tourists

When we were in Baalbeck, a number of tourists were there walking over the ruins of the temples and among them was a tall, austere, gray-haired American lady with a cane, traveling alone. A guide was showing her around—and receiving such *a torrent* of complaint! She scolded him because there was no railing built on the steep stair leading to a lower level and she criticized the people and everything else she could think of.

When we reached the hotel in Amman, *here was the same woman.* She came up to us and our guide and loudly complained about the staff there in the hotel. Yasser asked her what they had done to displease her. She replied they had heckled her.

All the clerks were sullenly listening to her and we had felt the antagonism to Americans in a most direct manner. We noticed this in a number of places. We became quite concerned listening to her tirade, but all we could do was to walk away and leave her.

On to the Rose-red City of Rock

Yasser soon followed us and we made our plans for the next day—our longed-for trip to Petra.

Yasser told us we would leave the hotel at 6 in the morning by car. We went to sleep until 3 a.m. when, from the minarets of the mosques of the town, the Koran was read over loud—and I mean *loud*—speakers.

Why at that time in the morning they read the Koran, I'll never know. I got no more sleep.

350

On our way to Petra, I asked Yasser if anyone ever listened to the reading at 3 a.m. in the morning. He said that the Koran used to be read by the priests, but now it was on recordings and was automatically read every so often and sent out over loudspeakers from the minarets.

We were ready to leave, with our lunches all packed, by 6 a.m. Our driver was also an Arab in robes and a cloth over his head. Yasser was dressed in a suit.

It was quite cool when we started out at sunrise, but as the sun grew higher, it warmed up as we drove over the plains of Moab.

We drove almost due south from Amman, along the plains to the east of Mount Nebo. This whole area east of the Dead Sea is a hilly plateau. Here the Israelites camped before entering the Promised Land. It was in this locale that King Balak ordered Balaam (Num. 23:13) to curse the advancing Israelites and where, instead, God caused him to give them blessings rather than cursings.

I do not remember the order of all the towns through which, or around which, we passed, but all were on the ancient trail of the Israelites, where Moses, as their leader, suffered their grumbling and rebellion against God and against him.

However, one of the towns was Madeba. In this small town there was a Greek Orthodox church that was built in 1896 on the site of an ancient Byzantine church. On the floor, which was a part of the ancient church, was a map made in mosaic. It covered a large area and depicted biblical Palestine as well as the northern regions of Damascus and Byblos; Memphis and Alexandria in the south; the Mediterranean Sea in the west; and in the east were Amman and Petra. It is said to be the oldest map of Jerusalem in existence. (I believe they

351

said it was constructed in the 6th century.) Also on the map were depicted vegetable and animal life. Among the animals shown were lions, which prove that these animals were inhabiting the region of Moab until that late date.

This land was where Moab and Ammon, the sons of Lot's daughters, settled in the days of Abraham. It was so level, here, that the grain waving in the wind could be seen for miles. However, the grain fields thinned out as we neared the Wady Arnon.

Actually, the Wady Arnon is a river at the bottom of a deep canyon. As we approached the fords of Arnon by way of the flat plateau country to the north, we could not see the Arnon until we arrived at the canyon rim. It looked like the Grand Canyon as it had a sudden drop of 4,000 feet.

We descended to the bottom over the narrowest winding road we had ever been on. No car could possibly have passed us.

Looking down on my side of the car, it seemed as if we were in space. It was hours, it seemed, before we reached the bottom of Arnon. Yet, on that lonely barren road, which was very high and miles from an inhabited place, we would meet a lone Bedouin walking. A few miles later there was another one riding a donkey.

We had passed many Bedouin tents before we reached the fords of Arnon. All of their tents are made of black goat hair. They are open on one side, and all are surrounded with herds of black goats and camels.

We also passed many herds of camels feeding on the hillsides and along the road. Our car had to slow down to make way for them in many places.

The gorge of the Arnon, however, was barren until we reached the bottom. There we found a small stream with the most beautiful and luxuriant oleanders lining its banks. All were in full bloom. We took color pictures of them.

After a few minutes rest, we started on the long climb up the opposite side. When we reached the top, we passed through another area of green fields. Feeding in one of the fields was a flock of eight storks. We tried to get pictures of them but they were startled and flew away.

When I expressed how thankful I was that all that climbing was behind us now that we were on level ground, our guide informed us that we would have still another deep canyon to cross.

Between these two canyons we drove up to the ancient city of Karak to refill the gas tank of the car. Karak was built with adobe or mud on top of a dry, desolate, dusty hill, inside the ruins of a high, ancient wall.

The agricultural lands surrounding Karak are rich and green; but the city itself, with a population of 5,000, is desolate, dirty and built of stone and adobe. We saw the green trees and fields below the city and we marvelled at the choice that the people had made for their city and their homes. The guide, however, explained that the city had been built on the hill as a protection from other tribes; and that the people used to leave their homes and work in the fields, always returning to the safety of the city in the evening.

This city is the ancient city of Kir-Moab of the Bible (Isa 15:1); also called Kir-Haresh (Isa. 16:11) and Kir-heres (Jer. 48:36).

The people of the city today seem about half Roman Catholic (or Greek Orthodox) and the rest Muslim.

We reached the bottom of the next canyon safely, however, and found a larger stream flowing across the road. We had to drive through this one.

It was now noon and we ate our lunch under the ancient fig trees that grew along the banks. Nearby was a Bedouin camp and, as we walked up the stream to eat, there followed several children, peeking shyly from behind large boulders or trees.

Our guide handed each of us a sack which contained a sandwich of hard coarse bread with beef, also one of cheese, and one with butter. There was also an orange and a tiny banana. I gave part of my sandwiches to a little Bedouin girl, but I felt safe in eating the cheese, a hard-boiled egg and the fruit. I had learned by this time to eat only what I could peel or to drink only what had been boiled.

Approaching Petra

At the small town of Shaubak built within the walls of an ancient fortress, we descended to Ain Musa, a spring, where there was a green and cool garden.

From Ain Musa the road descends to Wady Musa and to the police station at Eljy. When we arrived, we found all arrangements had been made by our guide for our horses to ride into Petra. It was mid-afternoon when we arrived—dusty and tired. What a relief it was to leave the car and mount the horses.

Our bags were piled on a small donkey (poor thing—he was almost hidden, with luggage for four people). I wondered if he would ever make the trip, but he did—allowing only one suitcase to fall.

A bridle path leads from Eljy to the entrance of the siq—the narrow ravine leading into Petra. It was rough going over rocks and rills to the siq. Then we entered the winding path of the ravine itself. It is a dry stream bed of rocks and boulders with sheer cliffs of 200 to 300 feet in height on each side. At no place in the ravine is it wider than ten or twelve feet. The walls are of fantastic shapes and colors and in places appear almost to meet high above. We often brushed by oleanders in full bloom growing in the siq in every crevice. It was such an inspiring and interesting trip through the siq. My horse stumbled several times and I lost my hat a time or two but it was recovered by the Arab boy who led my horse. We had to go single file all the way and the little overloaded donkey plodded along behind.

It is impossible to express the feeling that one receives from going on the trip to Petra. It was a different world altogether—as if someone had turned back thousands of years and we were living in history.

Suddenly we came to the end of the narrow part of the siq and there before us, carved out of the mountainside, was the immense Khazneh—a temple to Isis. It is called the Treasury of Pharaoh by the local people, and is the best preserved temple in Petra. Some believe that it was hewn out of the rock by some Nabataean king.

As we passed the Khazneh, the valley widens a little with great tombs or caves on either side. Further, on the left, were the remains of an ancient theater—a sort of amphitheater cut out of the mountainside. There were half-circular rows of stone seats for the audience. We could see how the Romans had sliced away many tombs in constructing this amphitheater.

From here on, the valley widens and we soon saw the ruins lining an ancient paved street. As we started to go north on this street, I could hardly help but think of some of the history of this great city.

This was the ancient city of the family of Esau and later of the Nabataeans. Five hundred years before Christ, this place, now in ruins, was occupied and was a hustling, thriving city. Then came the Romans who built some of the buildings and constructed some paved streets. (One of these streets we later walked on.)

Along the way we saw the walls of the only real building standing in Petra. It was formerly a Roman temple to a pagan god. We also viewed hundreds and hundreds of caves and facades of temples carved out of the mountains, but not a one of them could be called a building.

As we came to the north end of the ancient street, we saw many white tents. It was a camp for tourists that was called Nazzal's Camp. In the center was a large dining tent. On the north side of the camp and sheltering it is the great rock mountain el Habis. The whole side of this mountain is dotted with caves.

We had the choice of a tent or a cave in which to sleep. Because a cold, stiff wind was blowing, we chose the shelter of one of the caves. It looked as if the tents would not be able to stand in the wind. So we climbed up a stairway cut in the side of the mountain to a large cave. It was sectioned off into rooms by canvas sheets. There were two cots in each section and a large room in the center space.

I was so thoroughly chilled that I went right to bed. Soon, though, I found that I had to get up and put on part of my clothes and call for an extra blanket.

The Arabs cooked for the other guests in a cave below our tier of caves and served the food in the dining tent. I had learned by this time what *not* to eat, so I tacitly ate an orange that our guide had given me before and then went to bed. With hunger and cold I began to see that Petra was no bed of roses but a place to really *rough* it.

I had gone to bed quite early and despite the hunger and cold was sound asleep when suddenly I was awakened by a crowd of twenty-eight people who had just arrived from Eljy, who had come into the cave to hear a lecture by an English woman archaeologist who was here from the English Antiquities Society. She, with a number of Bedouins, was carrying on excavations in Petra. It seems it was too cold in the dining tent to hear the lecture so she brought them to the large cave where we were. It must have been after ten o'clock when she completed the lecture and all was quiet in the cave again.

Soon after everything had settled down, I heard other occupants of the cave, including my husband, Dick and our guide come in and go to their cots. Once more quietness prevailed until all in the cave were sound asleep, except me.

Suddenly I was startled by frightening sounds. A number of dogs began barking, which startled a number of donkeys so that they began to bray. That, then, started the jackals and the hyenas to yelping and screaming. I never heard such bedlam before. I was certainly thankful that I was in the cave and not in a tent.

Next morning I learned that the animals were scattered over Petra and not near the camp. In fact, as we walked throughout Petra, we saw none of them save the donkeys.

After having tea and an orange, we started the climb to Petra's famous "high altar." We began the climb behind the ruins of the ancient Roman temple.

Soon we came across a little Bedouin girl about ten years old, herding a flock of black goats. I gave her some money to have her stand beside me and have her picture taken. She was dressed in black robes with a piece of black cloth over her head, a ring in her nose, beads around her neck and bracelets on her arms. All were made of cheap materials.

After she had stood for her picture, she called in an ordinary tone of voice to someone way across the valley, and in her Arabic tongue told them of the coin she had received. The incredible acoustics of Petra carried her voice as if by a super loudspeaker. She held her hand high, with the coin, to show it as she called. I am sure that their sight is not as clear in Petra as the sound, for many of the Bedouins have diseased eyes. But we were amazed at being able to hear sounds so clearly over great distances.

One evening Dick was across from our cave on another hilltop quite a distance from us. Mr. Armstrong tried out the carrying power of his voice and in a quiet tone asked, "Can you hear me, Dick?" Dick answered, "Very clearly."

There are very few of these Bedouins in Petra. Children were more in evidence than adults. They are the ones that herd the black goats over the hills and even up the sides of the mountains. We were surprised to see them no more than nine or ten years old skipping around from rock to rock on a steep mountainside as nimble, almost, as the goats.

After getting the little Bedouin girl's picture, we continued on our climb to the "high altar." The going became more difficult and we had to stop and rest often. It was quite frightening to look down and we began to wonder whether to go on further. Our guide told us that it would be dangerous to try to descend now. He said if we would just keep climbing we could go down on the other side of the mountain. The climb was difficult. In some places we had to crawl on all fours.

As we ascended, we came face to face with a sculptured lion cut in the face of the rock. We rested here and took pictures of this beast which had been carved out of the stone many centuries ago. It was not in the best of condition for the weather had almost erased his head.

At last we reached the top. Here were two giant obelisks. They had been made by hewing away of the whole top of the summit of the hill. These were two of the gods of the ancient Nabataeans.

Ascending to another high point we came to the ruins of a temple situated high above the whole rock city of Petra. A wonderful view!

Yet still higher up was the "high altar." By this time Mr. Armstrong and I were perfectly willing to sit and rest by the temple ruins and let Dick and Yasser, our guide, who had been with us all the trip, and the native Bedouin guide, go on up to the "high altar."

The "high altar" is a platform with an altar hewn out of the rock. It is forty-seven feet by twenty-one feet. On one side, a bench was cut in the rock for those who brought their sacrifices.

As we sat on the mountain top, we looked across to a mountain called Jabel Haroun.

When Dick and Yasser and the Bedouin rejoined us, we started our precarious descent to camp. The going was not too difficult, that is, until we came to a large boulder much taller than any of us, down which we had to go. The Bedouin hopped down to a ledge below. Yasser, too, hopped down but not too easily — the Bedouin had to help him. There was not too much room left for us on the ledge, but I was finally lifted down by two of them and was placed at a little distance away. Now the problem was, how was Mr. Armstrong going to get down?

On the sheer side of the rock there was nothing to hold onto. If he slid down and did not land on the narrow ledge, he would fall a great distance. Dick had gone on far ahead of us. We called to him but he was too far below to return. Finally, the Bedouin bent his back and encouraged Mr. Armstrong to step on him.

359

Yasser stood near to steady him. We spent some time getting out of this predicament and were very thankful when we got out without accident.

The descent was not so difficult from this point.

Dick had waited for us and we stopped often to view the city of caves, temples and tombs. Far across we could see Bedouin children here and there with their herds of black goats. We marvelled at their ability to climb around on the steep places with seemingly no difficulty at all, while we had to be so careful.

We continued down, finally coming to a narrow stairway hewn out of the rock. Here we saw and photographed an exquisite blue lizard with the most beautiful amber eyes. I hope that the picture comes out good.

We finally emerged near the Roman theater and then walked back to camp.

Dick explored much more of Petra than we did—at least in the higher mountains. One mountain climb was enough for us.

We spent the afternoon in the lower hills, photographing a number of the colorful natural caves as well as many that were man-made.

We were rather weak from lack of food, most of our stay in Petra. We drank tea because the water had been boiled. Perhaps the water as it came from the spring was good, but it was brought to camp in square tin cans slung over the back of a donkey that was led by a very dirty Bedouin.

We could not see far into the "kitchen" cave, but what we saw did not look too clean. However, Mr. Armstrong and Dick both ate dinner. I stuck to the tea and as a result spent the night in wakefulness. Even without the tea I would have not been able to sleep because the same bedlam of the night before broke loose. The blood-curdling sounds of wild animals seemed to continue for hours.

Early the next morning, we arose and found that our horses had already arrived from Eljy and along with them had come our faithful little pack donkey.

We left the camp before sunup and soon reached the Khazneh. It was still too dark to take pictures so we waited until the sun began to shine on the marvelous carved temple. We obtained some clear pictures of it.

Once more we mounted our horses and bade farewell to Petra. We rode single file through the siq on our way back to civilization—that is, Arabic civilization.

66

At Last!—Jerusalem

I'M SURE every true minister of Jesus
Christ has dreamed of visiting
Jerusalem and the Holy Land and so
have millions of others as well.

This cradle of three religions had always seemed,
somehow, to be a mystic, almost unreal land far off—
scarcely part of this same earth. Now we were to be
privileged to visit this land we had heard so much about
and read about ever since we were old enough to read
the Bible.

And we were to learn that it is, indeed, a real land
right here on this same earth on which we live. The land
there is composed of the same kind of earth we have
always lived on.

Our visit made the Bible *come alive!* The Bible—
the records of Abraham, Moses and ancient Israel,
David, Nehemiah, Jesus Christ, the apostles— suddenly
became *REAL!*

362

Here, now, is the third part of Mrs. Armstrong's diary.

PART III
by Loma D. Armstrong

WE ARRIVED back in Amman, Jordan, May 7, 1956, in the evening, tired and dusty. We then picked up our bags we had left at the hotel and, after looking in vain for mail from home, continued toward Jerusalem.

From Amman to Jerusalem

This trip was so very interesting. The country is more beautiful and every bit of the way filled with the history of the Israelites—with their wars, not only with the pagan nations around them, but among themselves.

We saw the place where Absalom was killed. It is no longer a wooded area, but today a bleak land denuded of trees. There are no oak trees. Remember how Absalom tried to escape the armies of David by riding on a mule through the area called the wood of Ephraim? How his long hair was caught in the thick boughs of a great oak before he was slain by Joab?

We went through Jericho where God caused the walls to fall as the Israelites marched around the city.

We saw the mountain from which Moses viewed the Promised Land before he died.

Every mile of the way was breathtaking. We were seeing in our imaginations, again, the tribes of Israel before and after they reached the Holy Land, then a land of rich vegetation, a land flowing with milk and honey; but now, because of their sins and their idolatry it is a land under a curse. The only trees are those recently set out. Most of the land in Arab hands is uncared for.

363

Nearing Jerusalem

We went through Bethphage and Bethany. Bethany is where Mary, Martha and Lazarus lived and where Jesus raised Lazarus from the dead. When Jesus went into the city of Jerusalem, He often went to Bethany or out to the Mount of Olives to spend the night.

We passed the Garden of Gethsemane on our way to the hotel in Jerusalem which was situated outside the walls of the city. We looked forward to a good bath and a good bed after the long day's ride from Petra. We were quite disappointed however. After viewing the bathroom in connection with our rooms, we felt it would be cleaner to go to bed without a bath. So, after washing ourselves in sponge baths we tried to rest in very uncomfortable beds.

We arose early, anxious to see all there is to see in ancient Jerusalem. The old Jerusalem of Jesus' time is *not* there now, except a few places where excavations have been made some thirty feet below the present surface. Many shrines exist over deep holes or caves. To get to them one has to go down a steep stairway through dank, dark passageways; then there is a cave or hole where candles are burning and where people are kneeling, kissing rocks or cave walls. They believe these shrines to be the places where this or that happened in the life of Christ.

One such place, called the Church of the Holy Sepulchre, was crowded with people all overawed by a stone. Some were rubbing their hands over it and then over their bodies. Another had an airplane bag (the Pan-American bag that is given with purchase of ticket) that he was rubbing over the stone. Another man lifted himself up and scooted around on the rock, rubbing his hip over it. Perhaps he expected healing from this

364

procedure. Everyone backed out of the place crossing himself or herself.

The Site of the Crucifixion

The original level of the ancient city in the time of Jesus was twenty to thirty feet below the present level. Two walls have been built in different places since the original wall around Jerusalem and only a small part of the old wall has been excavated. The base of the old Damascus Gate has recently been excavated under twenty feet of debris.

From this place can be seen The Place of a Skull. No one can fail to see the resemblance. There is a low eroded forehead, two deep hollows that make the eyes, a nose, and near the ground level, twisted lips.

We viewed this skull from a spot near the tomb in the garden; then walked past an ancient winepress to enter the nearby tomb.

It was impossible fully to realize where we were— what we were seeing! To actually visit, to really *see,* and to walk into the sepulchre from which Jesus rose immortal from the dead—the actual spot where the angels sat, at the right of the entrance—was an experience we couldn't fully comprehend until later.

It is an unfinished sepulchre; only one tomb was completed. Two others were partially finished. We saw the stone where the angel sat and also where the linen cloths lay that Peter and John saw as they stooped down and looked into the tomb.

We walked in the garden where Mary met the resurrected Christ. We saw the place where the stone had been moved in the groove to cover the opening of the sepulchre. Near all this are evidences of rocks split by earthquakes. All of this, at the foot of Golgotha, was excavated in the year 1893. This is the place where

Joseph of Arimathaea hurried to bury the body of Jesus as the High Day Sabbath drew on.

The Sepulchre

This tomb is at the foot of The Place of a Skull. There is a garden surrounding the tomb. It all is as the Bible describes, while the place in the city called the Holy Sepulchre is under a church, down a steep stairway, to a hole in the ground where there is a rock.

We visited many places in the old city where churches and shrines were built over spots purported to be where Christ did this or that. They probably are fakes. All have their boxes out for money.

The ancient city of Jerusalem was destroyed. The Arab city now in existence on the site is crowded. Their Mosque or "Dome of the Rock" now is at the site of the temple Solomon built.

Inside this Dome of the Rock, which is built on Mt. Moriah, is a huge boulder surrounded by the dome. This boulder is covered and protected by glass on the circular hall around it. There is an entrance to a cave below this rock to an ancient threshing floor. There we found Muslim women bowing, kneeling, and touching their heads to the floor in their worship. On top of the rock, they claim, is the place Abraham led Isaac to sacrifice and near the place where the ram was caught in the bushes. Near the Dome of the Rock is the "gate called Beautiful" where the lame beggar was healed by Peter and John.

We were driven out to see the Valley of Hinnom (Gehenna), or *hell* as the *Authorized Version* reads.

We drove to Bethlehem to the church built over the place claimed to be the stable where Christ was born. This also is a deep hole under the church, down steep stairs, through dank, dark rat-runs to a cave—*not* a stable or anything resembling a stable or manger where Christ was born as given by Scripture. Here was an idol in a cradle. There were also numerous candles and odd lamps burning; and people were also kissing walls and floors and crossing themselves.

Adjoining this is a Greek Orthodox church over another hole *they* claim is the birthplace of Christ. Here there was another statue in another cradle and other candles and other people kissing stones, floors, and walls. Our guide told us that the two churches, or the priests of the two, get into real fights sometimes. Each church has out its money boxes and each watches the other in jealousy.

We drove by Rachel's tomb on the way to and from Bethlehem and stopped there for a few moments. She died here at the birth of Benjamin.

When Not to Eat "Lamb"!

When we returned to our hotel, we were tired and hungry. I tried to eat. Muslims do not eat unclean meats but the "lamb" they served had been a lamb many years ago. Although I lost a lot of weight, I don't believe I'll be able to eat "lamb" again for months or maybe years. From Egypt on, everything has been "lamb." Strong, smelly, tough lamb! Everyone and every place smells of sheep, goats, and camels. I wonder if I will ever be able to get the sheepy, goaty, camel-ly smell out of my memory!

The next day we went to the top of the Mount of Olives. This was a real inspiration. This is the place where Christ spent much of His time, and the mountain from which He ascended into heaven and on which His feet will again stand when He returns to this earth a glorified Christ and King of kings. We who overcome and are faithful unto the end, will be there with Him.

367

I may never again see the Mount of Olives in my mortal life but I expect to see it again then with Him.

We walked down into the beautiful Garden of Gethsemane among the ancient olive trees—some over two thousand years old. We walked in the place where Christ prayed and sweated great drops of blood in His agony before He was betrayed by Judas. It is impossible to express the thoughts, the sensations, and the inspirations that one experiences here. It is so cold on paper, but to be there and experience it makes it all very real. To me the Bible is a new book now—so *alive* and *real!*

Our time in the old city of Jerusalem, under Arab control, was up. We were driven to the Mandelbaum Gate where we were to pass out of Jordan into Israel— the Jewish section. Yasser took us to the gate and through it to a small shed which is the Arab border customs house. Just outside are cement tank traps, tangled barbed wires, and many bombed-out buildings.

From here on for 100 yards was "no man's land."

Entering Israel

No Arab was allowed to help us across to the Israeli side; so Yasser stood on a cement tank trap waving to us as we started out on foot across this precarious ground. Mr. Armstrong and Dick were loaded down with bags. I had the two cameras, Dick's blue airplane bag, my hatbox, and the handbag. Watched behind by the Arabs and in front by the Jews, we caught the feeling of animosity that exists between the two enemies. Soon we were faced by a sand-bagged shack on the Jewish side. We were watched through a small window used as a place to shoot any intruder.

An Israeli met us when we had finally made it across "no man's land" and helped us into Israeli customs. We had to call American Express from here and found out that our Israeli guide had gone to Tel Aviv. We then called a taxi and went to our hotel—the King David.

What a change! It was like suddenly entering a new world.

All was different here. The streets are clean and wide. The children playing on the lawns are clean and healthy looking. The hotel is beautiful and clean. The luxury of baths in clean bathrooms and eating in a clean dining room was such a wonderful feeling. I spent one day sick abed.

Our tour over all Israel was so different from the Arab countries. There were no more Arab robes, nor diseased, crippled, and deformed people. These were more like the people of our country, yet they are not from America but from the countries of Europe, Asia and Africa.

We spent a couple of days seeing the Israeli side of Jerusalem. It is a comparatively new city, and very modern. It probably was open field in Jesus' day. None of old historic Jerusalem is in Israeli hands [in 1965].

After a visit to the tombs of the Sanhedrin and to the town where John the Baptist was born, we drove to Tel Aviv, over the ancient territories of Judah, Benjamin and Dan. Tel Aviv, of course, is on the Mediterranean seacoast. From here, stopping only to check for mail, we proceeded north along the coast through the ancient lands of Dan, Ephraim, and into Manasseh, then northeast over into the Valley of Jezreel and to Megiddo. This place is the "Armageddon" of Bible prophecy, where armies assemble for the future battle of the "Great Day of God Almighty".

In this valley more battles have been fought than any other place in the world. Once again blood will flow "unto the horse bridles" at this place. In the distance, across the valley, we could see Mt. Tabor.

Approaching Nazareth

We continued along the highway northeast to the town of Nazareth, where Jesus lived as a boy. Nazareth is located on a rather steep hill. The ancient city of Jesus' boyhood is gone—buried underneath today's city. The present city is now and has been for hundreds of years occupied by Arabs. The Arabs have built their city with adobe and stone.

Again we were taken to a dirty cave over which is a church. They claim it to be the boyhood home of Jesus. There was another they called the home of Mary's girlhood. But Jesus was a carpenter; and they did not live in dirt caves. Here again were fakes for money-getting.

We were taken to a synagogue that had been excavated. This was the site of an earlier synagogue where Jesus did attend and where he "stood up for to read" (Luke 4:16).

After another Arab lunch in Nazareth, we drove past Cana of Galilee where Jesus performed His first miracle.

As we neared the Sea of Galilee, we stopped and viewed it first, from a high hill. The sea is approximately 700 feet below sea level.

As we drove over all this country between Nazareth, Cana, Capernaum, and the Sea of Galilee, it brought again to life the New Testament. Jesus walked over these hills along this way. He too viewed the blue Sea of Galilee from this high point, for it is on the way to Capernaum.

We drove along the seashore where even today the fishermen launch their boats and mend their nets. This is where Jesus called Peter and Andrew, and where they left their nets and followed Him.

We went over the hills where He fed the five thousand, and we could view the place, across the lake, where He cast the demons out of the two demoniacs, and the swine ran down the steep embankment into the sea.

We passed through Magdala, the home of Mary the Magdalene, and then on to Capernaum. The town is gone but the synagogue has been excavated. It is in ruins now. It is a much larger place than the one in Nazareth. Here again, though, they have a high iron fence around the place and expect money to be given for looking at it.

Jesus devoted a large part of His ministry to this region around the lake of Galilee, especially around the northwest portion of the lake where we were, and it was a very impressive experience to be there on the very spot.

It was growing late in the afternoon, so we drove on across the valley of Jezreel again, forking northward, arriving in Haifa in the early evening. Haifa is a very busy seaport city, located on a bay overlooked by the north tip of Mt. Carmel. We registered at our hotel and went for a walk around the city. A United States cruiser was in port, and we saw a number of American sailors.

A Jewish Wedding

When we returned to the modern hotel for dinner, we found that hotel guests were not being admitted to the main dining room, located on the lower level below the street-level lobby. A Jewish wedding feast was in progress and the wedding guests completely filled the large main dining room. Hotel guests were being served in a smaller room on the same floor. It was filled, and we had to wait in this lower-level lobby some thirty minutes for a table. This gave us opportunity to observe a

371

little of the Jewish wedding feast. This was most interesting, after having passed by Cana of Galilee that day,
where Jesus attended a Jewish wedding more than 1,900
years ago, and turned the water into wine. We learned
that Jewish weddings are elaborate affairs. The bride
and groom came out in the lobby to have their pictures
taken while we were there.

We spent the night in Haifa. Next morning we were
driven all over the city, and stopped to go through a
Jewish industrial fair being held there at the time. Here
we saw displayed exhibits of the various products now
being manufactured in the new nation of Israel. It was
an eye-opening revelation. It seemed to us that the Jews
who have returned to Palestine are now manufacturing
there almost every commodity and gadget that they
need to be self-supporting. We saw literally thousands
of different items of modern Jewish manufacture, for
home, farm, office or factory.

Then we were driven up on Mt. Carmel, which
overlooks the city.

We ate lunch on Mt. Carmel where Elijah lived. We
drove past the place where Jezebel and King Ahab lived
when she was thrown out of the window and the dogs
ate her. We also saw the place of their summer palace,
and the place where Elijah dared the prophets of Baal
to call down fire to burn up the sacrifice, and where
God, at Elijah's prayer, sent down the fire that not only
burned the sacrifice but the altar, the stones, and the
dust. We were over the hills and dales where the
prophets of Baal were slain.

From there we proceeded south and visited one of
the Hadassah farms where Jewish children, from all
countries, many of them orphans, are entered at the age
of ten and schooled and trained until they are eighteen.
It was a fruitful and beautiful place.

372

The children do all the work—care for the buildings, the chickens, the stock, and the farm. The super-
visors train them to do each job well. They are so happy
there that even though they sometimes leave for a visit
to their homes they are always in a hurry to return.

We took pictures of this place. The overseer turned
on a beautiful fountain for us and showed us the
flowers. We took pictures of them in color.

Some of the boys took Mr. Armstrong and Dick to
show them the stock. They are all very proud of their
place and their work.

As we drove through the fertile fields, I stopped
and picked some of the lovely lavender hollyhocks that
grow wild everywhere along the roads.

Much of our journey from Haifa to Tel Aviv was
along the Mediterranean Sea. It was such a beautiful
trip.

We visited a communal farm between Haifa and
Tel Aviv where families live and have everything in
common. These are very productive farms, and because
the land of Palestine has had its rest, it is very fertile.

These people live in large buildings and have a
common dining hall, kitchen, and living room. The
barns and dairy are nearby, while the fields go for miles
in all directions.

They drive out in the morning to cultivate the land.
Each group has its certain work to do.

That American Tourist Again!

When we reached Tel Aviv we found a modern city. It
was Friday afternoon when we arrived. Our hotel was
a beautiful modern building on the seashore. When we
entered the dining room here again was the woman
whom we had seen and heard at Baalbek, Amman, and
again at the King David in Jerusalem. It seemed

wherever we went she was there. We did not want to start a conversation with her or rather have her try to start one with us, so we veered off to another corner of the dining room.

Our rooms here were very nice. On leaving us after taking up our bags, the boy said, "Shalom." Each time anyone greeted us this was the word they used.

We had a new experience the next day. Everything all over the city was closed. It was the Sabbath—no buses, no streetcars, not even any mail delivery to the hotel. Yet the Sabbath is *not* observed as a sacred day. The only synagogue we saw was a small one. All streets within two or three blocks of it each way were closed to traffic. However, the other streets were full of people out walking or on the beach swimming, surfboard riding, and playing games. It is a day used by many for their pleasure.

The land now called Israel is being rebuilt by Jews who are leaving God entirely out of their plans.

I sat on the beach at the rear of the hotel and a Jewess from New York was there with a Hadassah group. She talked to me of the wonderful things they were doing for the children and of the general upbuilding of the land of Israel. But, when I tried to talk of the part their religion had in the building of the country there was no answer. She just was not interested. God is not in the picture at all.

We had driven out to the ruins of Ashdod, a totally ruined and deserted Arab town since 1948. Thence we went to desolate Ashkelon where some of the ruins of the ancient city have been excavated and where part of the ancient wall still stands. God said that this city would be completely destroyed and it was.

We drove to Ekron where we took pictures of a group of Yemenite Jewish children. They are very dark.

374

■ *With His Majesty Leopold III of Belgium. In 1970 His Majesty presented the last of four watches cast from a World War I cannonball to Herbert W. Armstrong for his contribution toward world peace.*

■ *Prime Minister Golda Meir of Israel invited Herbert W. Armstrong to visit at her Knesset office in Jerusalem in 1971. India's Prime Minister Indira Gandhi reviews copy of* The Plain Truth *during 1970 visit of Herbert Armstrong. Left, below, with President V.V. Giri during same trip to India.*

■ *Climbing aboard the Grumman Gulfstream II on one of numerous trips in the 1970s to visit world leaders. At the garden tomb, Jerusalem.*

■ *The building of Ambassador Auditorium, Pasadena, 1972 to 1974. Above, Herbert Armstrong in his personalized hard hat at the groundbreaking ceremonies in January 1972. Left, addressing the audience at the ceremonies, flanked by personnel of the construction company. In foreground before podium is model of the Auditorium.*

■ *Reviewing blueprints during construction. The completed Auditorium, above, surrounded by mirror pools and egret fountain designed by David Wynn. With pianist Artur Rubinstein.*

■ *Pausing with longtime friend Nagendra Singh, left, and President Manfred Lachs, of the World Court, top left. Greeting Emperor Haile Selassie of Ethiopia in June 1973 and President Suharto of Indonesia 1972, center, opposite page. Bottom left, with South Vietnam's President Nguyen Van Thieu, October 4, 1973. Above, with President Jomo Kenyatta of Kenya, 1975; left, King Sobhuza II of Swaziland, 1976. Below, with King Hussein of Jordan.*

■ *Portrait of Herbert W. Armstrong taken in Japan. Order of the Sacred Treasure, Second Class, conferred on Herbert Armstrong by His Majesty the Emperor of Japan.*

D. WALKER/LIAISON

■ Over a period of more than a decade Herbert W. Armstrong had the privilege to know and to discuss world problems with Japan's Prime Ministers. Pictured here from left to right, beginning at top are Prime Ministers Sato, Tanaka, Miki, Fukuda, Ohira and Suzuki.

■ *With President Anwar Sadat of Egypt, whom Mr. Armstrong regarded as a leader who came to understand the importance of peace among nations. Embracing Prime Minister Menachem Begin of Israel, 1978. With President Suleiman Franjieh of Lebanon, in 1973.*

■ *The redwood Library and social hall on the expansive campus of Ambassador College, Big Sandy, Texas. Mr. Armstrong, even in his late years, attended commencement exercises at the Pasadena campus whenever he was at headquarters.*

■ *Addressing a luncheon in Bangkok, Thailand, after being presented the royal Thai decoration of "Commander of Our Most Noble Order of the Crown of Thailand." Thailand's Prime Minister Prem Tinsulanonda personally congratulates Mr. Armstrong for the royal Thai decoration conferred on behalf of His Majesty King Bhumibol Adulyadej.*

■ *Mr. Armstrong addresses an audience of more than 4,500 in Manila, at the Convention Center,* *in his ninetieth year. Speaking before the Rotary Club in Manila. The Presidential Merit Medal* *bestowed in 1983 by the Philippine President.*

■ *Herbert W. Armstrong being received at 10 Downing Street by Prime Minister Margaret Thatcher.*

Charles, Prince of Wales, greets Mr. Armstrong as a benefactor of the Royal Opera House in London.

■ *Symbolic tree planting at the Jomo Kenyatta School of Agriculture and Technology, a school partially funded by the Ambassador International Cultural Foundation and Japanese friends. Kenya has a population explosion and its leaders, since independence, have had to focus on the country's agricultural and forestry needs. President Moi of Kenya receives Herbert Armstrong in November, 1982.*

■ *His Majesty King Juan Carlos of Spain receives Herbert Armstrong on the King's estate outside Madrid.*

King Hussein of Jordan, a longtime friend. Touring the Bunyat Special Education Center in Amman, Jordan.

After another night in Tel Aviv, we flew to Istanbul, Turkey. We had to fly over the Mediterranean Sea, the island of Cyprus—one of the world trouble-spots—Asian Turkey, over the Sea of Marmara and the Bosporus before arriving in Istanbul, which is located in European Turkey.

We stayed at the Hilton Hotel in Istanbul that was built by the American hotel man, Conrad Hilton.

Viewing the Black Sea Near Russia

Our first trip here was a boat ride up the Bosporus to the entrance of the Black Sea—Russian waters. We saw the submarine nets near the entrance to the Black Sea, put there by the Turks to prevent Russian submarines from coming through.

The trip was tiring because the boat was packed and we could hardly find even standing room. This was because we were there during the time of the completion of the Ramadan—a thirty-day Muslim fast, which is ended with three days of feasting and holiday. Although the Turks are Muslims in religion, they do not wear the Arab dress or the fez, the robes, the veils for women, etc. These were all outlawed by Ataturk, a former ruler.

Our guide this time was a woman. She was a very nice looking Turkish woman, who in summer works for American Express and in winter teaches in a girls' school.

At the end of our boat trip up the Bosporus, we landed at a large village and took a car back through the country to Istanbul.

Many of the buildings in Istanbul are modern, but many also are very, very old frame houses so ancient they look as if they are ready to cave in: yet people live even up in the third and fourth stories of these old firetraps.

Our guide took us through the old mosque and also the palace of the king, now a museum where we saw the largest collection of china on earth. There was room after room filled with it from all parts of the world.

Our stay in Istanbul was short. We left there May 17 and flew over the Golden Horn, the Sea of Marmara, and the Aegean Sea to Athens, Greece.

Greece and Its Statues

The German president and his retinue had taken over this hotel where we had reservations; so we had to find another. The beds were just thin pads on wooden slats with no springs and not enough cover. The bathroom was dirty, so we only spent a few hours in our rooms and the rest of the time looking over the city where the Apostle Paul spent so much time.

There is always a silver lining to every cloud. Even though we had to stay in a very uncomfortable place, we were not in the same hotel with the lady whom we first met at Baalbek who did get in the hotel where the Germans were.

We had to avoid her. She caused trouble wherever she went. At the King David while in Jerusalem, she had several waiters trying to soothe her ruffled feathers and finally, before we left, the head waiter had been called to try to calm her. We scurried out of sight of her in this hotel.

Our guide was a woman—a Greek Orthodox, and our driver was a man. We drove to the museums, then past the palace and back to the hotel for lunch.

During our visit in the museums, our guide was disgusted with us and frustrated at our lack of enthusiasm over the icons and religious trappings and pictures. She would exclaim, "Isn't this beautiful?" over some picture and receive no response from us. Finally, Mr.

376

Armstrong told her what he thought of superstition and gave her a good explanation of what life is all about. She heard the gospel for the first time in her life.

We went to the marketplace where Paul disputed with the Athenians. We also saw Mars' Hill where Paul told the Greek "wise" men that they were too superstitious and declared to them the true God. We went up to the famous Acropolis and spent some time there.

Our stay was not long in Athens, but we were able to see all the Bible places connected with Paul's ministry.

On to Rome

As we flew over the Mediterranean, across the boot of Italy, along the coast of Italy, the Bay of Naples and then to Rome, we were contemplating staying no longer than two days; we were now one week ahead of schedule. However, when we arrived May 18, we called the hotel in London by telephone to try to advance our reservations there five days, but found they were crowded and no space was available until Friday, May 25; so we stayed the full week in Rome.

The city is so very interesting. We spent every day in historic places. On Thursday, May 19, we drove to Naples along the Appian Way where Paul entered Rome after landing near or in the Bay of Naples. It was a very beautiful drive to Naples with many interesting places to see.

After seeing Naples, we drove to the ruined city of Pompeii. This was the most startling place we have seen. In the year A.D. 79, Pompeii was completely covered with ashes from Mt. Vesuvius. It was the city of twenty thousand people. While thousands escaped from the city to the sea, hundreds perished in their homes and in the streets.

377

In the year 1860, excavations began. We walked down the narrow cobblestone streets worn by chariot wheels and saw public buildings still standing. Only the walls remained. The roofs were gone—fallen in from the weight of the ashes and cinders.

We entered the doors of many homes and saw, in some, their household gods. These were near the entrance to the homes.

We saw the bodies of the victims that have been found preserved in the ash.These were in the museum. Even the expressions on their faces are preserved. One dog still with the chain around his neck was twisted, with his head under his body, showing the agony it suffered before it died.

There are two loaves of bread preserved and hardened. Here was bread two thousand years old.

There was also the body of a woman with her arm over her face to protect it. An expression of stark fear and agony was on her face. Some of the bones of the hand and leg were showing through the encrusted body.

We walked past their pagan temples and through the city center. One has to visit the place to really understand. It was overwhelming. One feels shocked beyond expression and has a great pity for these people, even though they have been dead over eighteen hundred years. It is impossible to realize that it happened so long ago when you are there and viewing their bodies.

The Image of Mary

We drove back to Rome. On the way we passed a funeral in one of the villages. The hearse was a highly decorated, immense, horse-drawn affair; and the whole funeral procession was more like a parade.

When we entered the suburbs of Rome, we got into a traffic jam that seemed hours before we moved. When

378

finally we began to inch along, we found what had held up traffic. It was a life-sized statue called Mary that was on a brightly lighted truck used in a political campaign. An election was coming up and the Christian Democrats were urging everyone to vote to defeat the Communists.

It seemed that wherever a statue called Mary was seen in Rome many worshipers would stop and stare in worshipful awe. They will even stop city traffic.

Statue of Peter

We went through St. Peter's cathedral again, once more watching people as they pass the seated statue in the cathedral, kissing its big toe. One after another they kissed the big toe, even lifting up little children. Whether diseased, dirty or clean, all were crossing themselves and kissing the toe that was now worn shiny from years of this procedure.

A halo has been placed over the head—or perhaps it's called a crown, and huge keys made and fastened in the hand. It is now called "St. Peter" with the keys to the kingdom of God.

We went through the treasury in the church and saw millions of dollars worth of jeweled religious robes, crowns, and all sorts of things. Among them was the triple crown of the Pope. In some jeweled objects were bones, small bones, or piece of bone from some pope or saint.

We went through the Vatican Museum on two different days. It was our third visit to these places.

Home Again!

We were glad when we were able to leave Rome and once again fly (even though I dislike flying) to England. We flew over the Mediterranean, and then over the

Alps. We flew very near Mt. Blanc and that was awe-inspiring and beautiful. It is the highest mountain in the Alps. All the flight across those snowcapped mountains was so beautiful that I almost relaxed.

It was beginning to become dark as we flew over France and the English Channel.

When we arrived in London, George Meeker, from our London office, was there to meet us. It was almost like arriving home.

Our long, long trip over Egypt, Iraq, Syria, Lebanon, Jordan, Israel, Turkey, Greece, and Italy was over. The English seemed like home folks. London looked so good.

Here we finally had letters from home and at last good clean food and comfortable beds, and, of course, George Meeker.

67

Touring Europe by Car

MRS. ARMSTRONG, our son Richard David and I returned by air to London from our Middle East tour Friday, May 25, 1956.

Before leaving London on this tour of the Bible lands, arrangements had been completed for holding a two-weeks' speaking engagement at Dennison House, a hall in London's downtown West End near Victoria Station. The office had been left in charge of George Meeker while we were gone. He and the office staff in London had sent out notices of the meetings to those in and near London on our mailing list.

Speaking Campaign in London

Almost two years before, I had engaged a hall and spoken three successive nights in London. So this was the second time for speaking before our radio listeners in London.

Customarily, in earlier years, I had held evangelistic meetings six nights a week for six weeks. But these were not "evangelistic" meetings—but rather speaking engagements for the purpose of meeting those who had become regular radio listeners.

Commencement exercises at Pasadena that year were held on Friday, June 1. Our son Garner Ted graduated on that day—the first commencement at Pasadena I had missed.

Immediately after his graduation in 1956, Ted and his wife, Shirley, flew on over to meet us in London.

Actually, before leaving London on the Middle East tour I had written a letter, to be printed later and mailed to our mailing list for the area, inviting them to these special services. At the time of writing, we did not yet know just where the meetings would be held. I had arranged for our London advertising agency to work out the booking of a suitable hall with Mr. Meeker. Mr. Meeker was to add this information to my letter.

Although I had written this letter in April, before our tour of the Bible lands, it was finally dated May 22, when Mr. Meeker posted it. It was sent only to those radio listeners already on our mailing list. It said: "I hope to meet you personally here in London very soon—and for some of our friends, it will be for the second time." Then the meetings were announced, beginning June 4, for Monday, Tuesday, Thursday, and Friday nights of that week, and Monday through Friday the following week. On the second week, my son Dick spoke one night, and Garner Ted the following night. I did the speaking on all other nights.

Touring Europe

Early Sunday morning, June 17, the five of us—Dick, Ted and Shirley, Mrs. Armstrong and I—left in my car, which we had brought over with us on the *Queen Mary,* for a brief tour of the Continent.

I do not remember all the events of that tour, but we crossed the Channel from Dover to Calais on a ferry, drove on to Paris. Tuesday we drove on to Luxembourg. On the way we examined many scenes of both world wars. Seeing the actual battlefields made the wars seem much more real.

At Luxembourg we visited the radio station, then on to Frankfurt. Mrs. Armstrong, Dick, and I had driven through Germany, and visited Frankfurt am Main in 1954, and Dick had been there in 1952. We were tremendously impressed with the amazing progress in restoration of bombed-out areas, which had devastated most of the city—and other German cities as well.

When Dick had visited Frankfurt in 1952, people were living in quickly erected temporary little cabins or shacks. They were then rapidly rebuilding their industrial sections, with apparently inspired zeal. Retail stores were operating out of temporarily roofed-over, mostly destroyed business district buildings. Their temporary little wooden cabins were being made neat, with patches of lawn and carefully planted flowers.

When we had visited Frankfurt with Dick in 1954, almost unbelievable progress had been made. The giant factories were then restored and steaming full-blast— many twenty-four hours a day. The retail business districts were well toward complete restoration, and almost endless blocks of flats and apartment dwellings being rapidly erected. But there still were many whole blocks of stark devastation, as yet uncleared.

But now, in 1956, few vacant blocks remained from war's destruction. Work was rapidly nearing completion in expanding the retail district and residential areas.

German cities had made far greater progress at restoration than had London.

Even ten years before, people of other countries were saying Germany would *never* rise again—or, as some cautiously admitted, it would take fifty to a hundred years to restore devastated Germany.

We spent a day driving over various parts of Frankfurt. Then on Friday, June 22, we drove on to Munich on the famous German autobahn. Some one of us became careless. The car ran out of fuel. We were out in a wide expanse of country, miles from any town. One of the party remembered passing a petrol station a couple miles back. So, with the car pulled over to the side of the highway, Mrs. Armstrong, Shirley and I waited while Dick and Ted started afoot back along the autobahn.

About an hour later—actually much sooner than we expected them, they returned in a car which had taken them in, with a can of gasoline.

At Munich we saw the same miraculous restoration—streets lined with gleaming modern new buildings. On Saturday night we visited the historic beer hall where Hitler's Beer-Hall Putsch started, November 8 and 9, 1923. Actually, this beer hall might be called the site of the beginning of World War II. On November 12, 1923, Hitler was arrested for leading the putsch, and imprisoned at Landsberg. There he wrote *Mein Kampf.*

We didn't remain long in this beer hall. Hundreds of robust Bavarians were drinking their beer, shouting with deafening, throaty voices, holding their giant beer steins aloft. Mrs. Armstrong wanted to leave immediately. Nevertheless, it was quite an experience.

En Route to Switzerland

Sunday, June 24, we drove on southwest toward Zurich.

En route we passed through a corner of Austria—had lunch at a restaurant in an Austrian town, probably Bregenz. The Bavarian countryside between Munich and the Austrian border was very scenic. We were impressed with the large farm dwellings, where the barns for livestock were part of the same building as the family dwelling. Their system of gathering hay also was something we had not seen before.

Then came a unique experience. We entered and crossed one of the tiniest little countries in the world, Liechtenstein. There was a certain amount of mountainous scenery, and a castle atop a small mountain.

But very soon we entered scenic Switzerland, and, between Liechtenstein and Zurich, one of its most scenic highways. Much of it was along two elongated lakes, the Walensee and the Zurich. There was just enough mountain scenery, combined with the beauty of the lakes, to make it breathtaking and exciting. The higher mountains, of course, are a little farther south. Switzerland undoubtedly offers the most stupendous, breathtaking scenery of any part of the world I have visited—and I have traveled completely around the world.

We merely spent the night in Zurich. A grand-scale festival was in progress, and we were only able to get our car within about two blocks of our hotel. We had to carry suitcases afoot through the throngs of happy festival participants—many in native costumes. The gaiety lasted well past midnight. We viewed the excitement from our hotel windows, but finally were able to get some sleep after the noise and din began to subside.

Monday morning we walked up and down the Bahnhofstrasse—Zurich's main business street, and did some shopping for wristwatches. There I purchased the watch I wore for many years, a Rolex Chronograph. It

385

gave the day of the week, day of the month and was also a stopwatch.

When I purchased this watch, Dick solemnly shook his head in mock disapproval, saying, "It's no good, Dad. It doesn't tell what year it is."

By noon on that Monday we arrived at Lucerne in time for lunch.

Then we proceeded along the way of exciting scenery and beautiful lakes to Interlaken, arriving a little late for evening dinner. However, the kitchen staff hurriedly prepared a special meal just for us. Switzerland is just about as famous for its good cooking as it is for its fantastic mountain and lake scenery, its watches, and its trains which *always* run *on time*—you can set your watch by the arrival or departure of a train.

The Spectacular Alps

Next morning, early, we boarded one of the mountain trains which daily transport awestruck crowds up to the top of the spectacular Jungfrau, one of the highest peaks in the Alps. We changed trains twice, as the climbing became steeper, proceeding on a cog railway.

The steep journey winding upward is simply one breathtaking and exciting view after another. Cameras click constantly. Arriving to the top, we found it necessary to purchase specially dark sunglasses. The brilliant sun, reflecting on the glistening white of the snow and glacier is almost blinding to the natural eye on a cloudless day.

We had lunch in the large restaurant at the top— took the few tunneled side tours, and then started the slow descent on the cog railway. The afternoon was well spent on returning to Interlaken.

Wednesday morning we were back in our car resuming our journey. Retracing our way some little distance, we then proceeded east and south toward Lugano, which Mrs. Armstrong and I had visited in 1947. We passed through some of the most spectacular mountain scenery in the world. Arriving at the famous St. Gotthard Pass, we decided to load our automobile on one of the flatcars which the railroad makes available for that purpose, and ride through the railroad tunnel, rather than drive the car on the winding figure-eight roadway over the mountain.

At Lugano we again contacted and visited Madame Helene Bieber, whom we had gone to Lugano to see in 1947. At that time we had visited Madame Bieber's villa, Heleneum, with a view to its possible purchase for the European branch of Ambassador College. We had envisioned this branch college in Europe even before the opening of the college in Pasadena. We then drove on to Milan, northern metropolis of Italy, for the night.

The next morning, Thursday, after visiting the great cathedral in Milan, we drove on to Genoa, on the beautiful Mediterranean Sea. I had read about Genoa even as a boy. It was exciting to visit it for the first time. We drove around the city a bit, had lunch there, and then proceeded west along the Italian Riviera. I had always heard a great deal about the Riviera. But when one speaks of the Riviera, he is speaking of the *French* Riviera, farther on west—especially that bit of coastline from Monte Carlo on past Nice and Cannes.

Bustling Italian Riviera

But we found the Italian Riviera one continuous winding coastline of jam-packed beaches, with a continuous congestion of town after town, and perhaps hundreds of Mediterranean-front hotels. Only these hotels were not the large, elegant, luxury-class hotels of Cannes and Nice, frequented by the rich of the world. The Italian

387

Riviera, we found, was far more densely populated with pleasure-seeking vacationists than that of the French coast. But that was true because it is a much lower-cost type of resort area.

We found going quite slow along this Italian Riviera because of traffic congestion. We reached Monte Carlo by evening, where we had reservations for the night at a hotel.

Next morning, Friday, now the 29th of June, we drove, first, up to the palace of Monaco, which is ruled by Prince Rainier III. He had married the American motion picture actress, Grace Kelly, April 18, just a couple of months before our visit. As we approached the palace, atop a hill, we began to wonder why all visiting sightseers seemed to be staring at us. We learned that, although we were not driving an expensive limousine, such as one would expect royalty to ride in, but just an ordinary car in the Chrysler line, Prince Rainier and Princess Grace drove the same model car we were driving!

Monaco is another of these very tiny nations. Its entire area is only one-half square mile! Its population is around 20,000, and that includes the city of Monte Carlo, a small city of only 9,500 resident citizens. But of course the hotel population of visitors swells that considerably. This little nation is entirely surrounded by France, except for the Mediterranean coast. Yet it has existed as an independent principality for 300 years! This miniature nation has no income tax. But it is one of the world's famed tourist resorts. It derives its government income from gambling at the casino, the sale of postage stamps, the indirect taxation on money spent by tourists, and a tobacco monopoly. This made two of these very little countries we had visited this trip.

As we proceeded west toward Spain, we made brief

stops at both Nice and Cannes, which we had never visited before. But we had no inclination to join the playboy vacationers lolling around on the beaches in front of the luxury hotels. We continued on to Marseilles, France, where we had hotel reservations.

One interesting thing I remember about Marseilles. The Harlem Globetrotters professional basketball team was there. We did not attend any performance, although we assumed they probably were giving one. But we had seen them at performances back home. They stage a hilarious performance. The things they can do with a basketball must be seen to be believed.

On Sunday morning, now July 1, we continued our trek along the Mediterranean, entering Spain, and arriving by evening at Barcelona. This was our first visit to Spain. It was necessary to visit Spain because Garner Ted speaks the language fluently. We noticed at once something we had not seen previously, in other countries. Dictator Franco had his armed gendarmes stationed at frequent intervals along the highways.

At Barcelona we were put in one of the finest hotel suites I had ever seen. This was not of our choosing. American Express, London, had arranged all bookings. The bathroom off the room Mrs. Armstrong and I occupied had one of these elaborate sunken Roman baths. But when we checked out on Tuesday morning, the hotel office overcharged us rather outrageously— completely above the price quoted the travel agency. Protest did no good. This is somewhat of a European custom. But we had the consolation that we had enjoyed exceptional accommodations, at least. Barcelona is a city of about one and one-half million people. We found it interesting, but I do not remember anything worth recording here.

Tuesday was another day of driving. Tuesday night

we checked in at the Castelana Hilton Hotel in Madrid. It was a comparatively new hotel. Certain parts of the building were still unfinished. But we learned that certain parts of virtually all buildings in Spain are left unfinished. It seems that once buildings are almost completed—sufficiently to be occupied—they simply never do get around to completing them.

Inside Spain

We found Madrid to be an exceptionally beautiful city of two million population. It has broad avenues and boulevards, with beautiful parking alongside, and the streets lined with imposing and beautiful buildings.

Dick had been there before. He had made the acquaintance of a young man of a family of the former nobility—prior to the Franco regime. This young man had visited Ambassador College in Pasadena, so we had all met him. We spent one enjoyable evening at the home of his widowed mother and two sisters. The mother was an accomplished pianist. They had a grand piano, and she played for us.

The next day, July 4, our American Independence Day, this young man—I believe his name was Francisco—arranged for a friend, Juan, to drive us out past the outskirts of the city—I believe the direction was north or slightly northwest—to one of the most unusual structural operations I have ever seen. General Franco was secretly building a *tremendous* cathedral, to become a surprise gift to the Catholic Church. I'm sure there is nothing like it. It begins on the side of a small mountain. Actually this church or cathedral is a gigantic tunnel under the mountain, coming out on the far side of the mountain. As I remember it, it had a ceiling higher than any other room in the world—and it was unbelievably long. Also, it was being done in magnificent and ornate cathedral style. We drove around the mountain to the rear entrance.

There, on level ground just beyond the far side of the mountain, was a most beautiful building. It was beautiful in its very plain simplicity. It had been built as a monastery, which the Generalissimo had wanted to present as a gift to the monks. But the monks had refused to accept it. It was "too fine." The monks have taken a vow of poverty. They seem to feel they must live in surroundings so plain that they are gloomy, depressing, utterly lacking in anything fine and beautiful.

Incidentally, this very experience impressed on me an outstanding *difference* between Ambassador College and other universities. Between the 6th and 12th centuries, the only colleges in Europe were the cathedral schools and the monastic schools. The monastic schools were colleges for training the monks, usually if not always located in the monasteries. After the founding of the first modern-type university in the 12th century— the University of Paris—the monastic tradition seemed to cling to all educational institutions as an inviolable policy. That is the reason classrooms, libraries, study rooms, lecture rooms, halls, in so many colleges and universities have always been so excessively plain, foreboding, gloomy, depressing.

At Ambassador College we strive to create even a physical atmosphere of equality, character and beauty. We find quality and cultural surroundings *much* more conducive to inspiring education than a bare, colorless, depressing atmosphere.

While shopping in Madrid we strolled into the lobby of one of the luxury European-type hotels. At a cigar-news-souvenir counter, we found a beautiful gaily-dressed Spanish doll of perhaps fourteen or eighteen

391

inches in height. Mrs. Armstrong liked it, and I purchased it for her.

That started a hobby. Mrs. Armstrong continued collecting dressed-up dolls in various countries we have traveled through, usually in the native dress or costume of that country. Her doll collection has been used in elementary schools to help children understand the people of other countries, and how they dress.

The night of July 4 we were unable to sleep until long after midnight. In a hotel court below our window a group of Americans were celebrating Independence Day. The alcohol was flowing, and the voices were not only merry—they were loud! So even though we were far from America, there was a 4th of July celebration going on!

On Thursday, July 5, we started driving back north. We reached San Sebastian, in northern Spain on the Atlantic and near the French border, for lunch, and spent the night at the French town of Poitiers. We stopped off at Versailles on the way in to Paris.

The next day we were spending a quiet day in our hotel suite.

68

Purchasing Ambassador Hall

O UR OVERSEAS TOUR of 1956 had been a long and eventful one. From Paris, we drove our car back to London—crossing the Channel, Calais to Dover, by ferry.

At the time, we had left George Meeker in charge of the London office. After checking in at the office in London, within a few days we again boarded the *Queen Mary* for the return voyage to the United States.

The 1956 Return Voyage

All four of the larger British and American trans-Atlantic ships conduct table-tennis tournaments during the crossing. On most voyages I have noticed there are no real expert table-tennis players on board. But on this particular crossing there were four or five who were fairly good—among them the former Maureen Connolly, nicknamed "Little Mo," three times women's world champion lawn tennis player—usually ranked with Helen Wills as one of the best women tennis players of all time. Maureen was rather good at table tennis, although not of the topflight championship class she had been at lawn tennis.

As I remember, our younger son played her during the tournament, but neither he nor I remember now who won. Garner Ted had been, nine or ten years earlier, a rather good table tennis player.

Before sailing from Southampton, Dick had sold his Hillman-Minx car, receiving almost as much for it as he had paid new two years before.

Arriving in New York, Dick purchased a new Mercedes—one of the smaller models—and drove it back to California. Garner Ted and his wife Shirley, anxious to get back to their children, flew home from New York. And Mrs. Armstrong and I drove our car—which we had taken with us to Europe—across the country. That left Mrs. Armstrong and me alone for the drive from New York to Pasadena.

I had wanted to drive through the city of my birth, Des Moines, Iowa, especially to see my uncle, Frank Armstrong, who had virtually steered my earlier life, beginning at age eighteen.

Death of My Uncle

Those who have read the *Autobiography* from the beginning will remember that, at age eighteen, I had put myself through a vocational-guidance analysis, and decided I belonged in the advertising profession. My Uncle Frank was the leading advertising man of the state of Iowa, and naturally I went to him for counsel and guidance. After moving to Oregon, in 1924, I had seen very little of my uncle—especially after my conversion and my being drawn into the ministry—except on rare occasions when I happened to be in Des Moines.

I felt that, since he was now past eighty, this might be my last opportunity to see him.

But, arriving in Des Moines, I telephoned his office and learned that he had died while Mrs. Armstrong and I had been in the Middle East on this same trip. So it already was too late.

However, I felt I should at least telephone my aunt, now widowed. But she did not care to see me. She had been very cordial to me during the advertising days—whenever I was in Des Moines. But her cordiality cooled noticeably after I had entered the ministry. Now, I was disappointed to learn, it had chilled completely. I hung up the receiver, deeply disappointed.

Thousands who will be reading these words have learned this same thing by experience. When God really gets hold of one's life—when that life becomes *changed* by the indwelling of God's Holy Spirit—one's contacts, friends, and especially relatives will often chill decisively. A certain underlying hostility will be sensed, if not openly displayed. Actually it is not the converted human they resent. It is the living Jesus Christ—now living *His* life within the converted one, who is the real object of the hostility. However, the carnal mind does not realize or understand this phase of its own working.

I felt intense sorrow and disappointment over my aunt's cold and blunt statement that she did not care to see me. She said, icily, she had never approved of my "religion." I had always been very deeply grateful to my uncle for his advice and counsel. It had become a long-standing feeling of affection. Some day, in a resurrection, her eyes will open. I think she will be quite astounded when they are opened to the TRUTH.

A Fabulous Property Offered

While we were in London on this 1956 tour, before

leaving for the Middle East, I received a trans-Atlantic telephone call from Mr. Meredith at Pasadena headquarters. It was near midnight in London—but shortly before 5 p.m. in Pasadena.

He asked me whether I felt the college would like to acquire the estate of multimillionaire Hulett C. Merritt. One other 200-foot-wide property stood between this estate and the Ambassador College campus—as it then was. This Merritt property was considered the most fabulous in Pasadena. The mansion on it, built in 1905-1908, had cost $1,100,000 at that time. Several years ago an architect told me that the place could not have been built for six million then—*IF* the rare woods and materials could be obtained—which they couldn't.

The question came like a bolt out of the blue. I had always considered this fabulous property as utterly inaccessible for us. Extending the campus in that direction had not been considered in our future planning.

Mr. Merritt had died before I had left Pasadena on this tour. His wife had died previously. Mr. Meredith explained that the executor of the estate was going to put it on the market, but first, privately, it was being offered to us through an insurance and real estate broker and his associates.

This broker had an offer to purchase the estate for less money than the ornamental iron fence around the Orange Grove Boulevard front of it would cost today. His proposition was that he and associates would purchase the estate at this low figure, and then donate the property to the college.

It appeared they had privately checked with some Internal Revenue people as to whether they could deduct this donation on their income taxes for something like a half million dollars. Apparently they felt assured they could. They could purchase it for less than half of that.

396

How Would We Use It?

My mind was doing some fast thinking. One doesn't turn down such a gift without consideration. But how would we use it?

"Could you gain access to the place yet tonight?" I asked.

Mr. Meredith said they could.

"All right," I replied. "I want you and Dr. Hoeh to go over there immediately. Go completely through the building. List how many rooms could be used as classrooms—and send me a telegram stating how many rooms could seat sixty-five or more students, how many fifty or more, how many thirty-five or more. Your telegram should be here by the time I wake up in the morning. Then I'll give my decision. I wouldn't want to accept this property unless we need it for actual college purposes—otherwise we'd have to pay taxes we can't afford for something we couldn't use."

The telegram was waiting for me on arising next morning. The ornate and fabulous building would be ideally suited to become our chief classroom building of the college.

I telegraphed the decision: "Accept it."

Plain Truth *Grows*

While we were on this Middle East tour, the April issue of *The Plain Truth* came out an enlarged magazine, and with a new front cover. This had been planned before leaving Pasadena.

Only once before, a special issue announcing the new Ambassador College, January, 1947, had *The Plain Truth* appeared with a front cover. It merely had a masthead, with the lead article beginning on the front cover. This April, 1956, number also went up to twenty-four pages. At the time this seemed a big leap forward. It had contained only sixteen pages previously. But the twenty-four pages was small compared to today's thirty-two pages, including cover. It was still black and white—no color printing. But it was advancing, improving, growing!

From Cairo we had a long-distance telephone talk with the Pasadena office about the Merritt property, the purchase of which had hit a snag. The heirs—all grandchildren—had rejected the price tentatively agreed to between the executor and our prospective donors. They insisted the place be sold at auction, thinking it would bring a higher price.

Returning to Pasadena, I found the broker and his associates had bought the property at the auction. They had made the high bid, which was only slightly more than their original purchase offer. However, it seemed their funds were not immediately available, and our office had loaned them $5,000 to bind their bid.

Saving Ambassador Hall

The auction purchase terms had been one half down, with the balance spread over some seven or eight years. The due date for the balance of the one-half down payment had come due, but our prospective donors still had not had the funds available. They had obtained a thirty-day extension.

I contacted these people. They assured me the money would be available by the final extended due date. A week before that date I contacted the broker again by telephone. He was positively reassuring. Two days before the deadline date I was becoming quite concerned.

"My associates and I will be in Pasadena with the money day after tomorrow," he said, positively, over the telephone. "Everything has worked out all right. Don't worry about it."

I had told him that, having gone this far, I did not want to lose this valuable property. It had totally changed our general master-planning for the campus. I told him that, if his people were going to come up short, I wanted time to raise the money myself, rather than lose it.

The crucial day arrived. Our would-be donors were on hand, but the necessary funds were not. They had flunked out completely.

I went to the executor, who had been Mr. Merritt's business manager. I asked another thirty-day extension to allow time for me to raise the money.

Ten-Day Margin

"But this matter is in probate court," he said, "and another thirty-day delay in meeting the obligation would undoubtedly cancel out this purchase, and open the property up to another auction. Some of the people building these multiple-family garden apartments along the boulevard now regret they didn't bid higher. In another auction they would bid up as high as necessary to acquire this property. They realize now that it went for too low a bid."

Nevertheless, he called his attorney. The attorney agreed with his opinion, but felt they might give me a ten-day extension.

I was under pressure, but we managed it. I had an offer of a $20,000 loan from a loyal co-worker, and I had borrowed $30,000 at the bank, neither of which, on the tenth day, I needed. I did accept the $30,000 bank loan, however, and then left it on deposit at the bank to improve our credit standing. It was worth paying the interest.

And so the fabulous Merritt property, which had been named "Villa Merritt Olivier," became ours, and was renamed "Ambassador Hall."

New Adademic Center

To leap far ahead of this chronicle of events for a moment, two exceedingly beautiful ultramodern new classroom buildings were later built flanking Ambassador Hall and the formal Italian sunken garden, with a magnificent plaza in the center, joining the three buildings and the Italian garden into an outstanding academic center. One of the new buildings is our Science Hall, the other the Fine Arts Building. The entire grouping was named in memory of my wife of fifty years, the Loma D. Armstrong Academic Center. An oil portrait of her now hangs in the grand hall of Ambassador Hall.

Escrow at the bank on the purchase of the Ambassador Hall property finally closed October 29, 1956. The 4-acre estate was then ours.

Manor Del Mar Acquired

Meanwhile, we had ourselves negotiated another important purchase of former Merritt property through the executor of the estate. This fine property, a block to the south of the campus as it then existed, had been the three-story mansion of Lewis J. Merritt, father of Hulett C. Merritt. This property, too, was obtained at a very low price and on very favorable terms. An extensive remodeling job was undertaken at once, and two large rooms were added. This property was named Manor Del Mar, since it was located on Del Mar Boulevard, which forms the south boundary of the campus as it is today. Manor Del Mar became our number one men's student residence.

400

After returning from the European trip, my elder son, Richard David, joined Roderick C. Meredith in a long-planned evangelistic series of meetings at Fresno, California, with splendid success.

Dick Needed a Wife

Dick had spent many months—including most of two dreary, lonesome winters—alone in London. Those of us in the family, as well as students and faculty, had somehow neglected writing him most of the time. Dick had come to feel the desperate need of a wife. He was now twenty-eight. It just seemed that the right girl had never come along.

Meanwhile there was a young married man from Iowa here attending college classes. His wife was very pretty. Mrs. Armstrong had become fond of her. This woman had a younger sister, attending university in Omaha. Mrs. Armstrong had heard glowing reports on the younger sister, Lois Lemon, and had shown a picture of her to Dick.

Sensing his mother's interest in the girl from Omaha, Dick immediately set up a prejudice against her in his mind. Much as he felt the need of a wife, Dick was not going to let his mother select her for him. But meanwhile Mrs. Armstrong and Miss Lemon's sister were doing their best by letters to interest Lois in the advantages of Ambassador College.

Would GOD Select a Wife?

During the two years previous to this time I had had a number of talks with Dick about the matter of marriage. I had counselled him to simply put this problem in God's hands, and rely on God to bring him and the right girl together. I had urged him not to rush blindly into any romance.

Even before I had been converted—had come to really know God, His truth and His ways—in my carnal-minded days I had somehow realized that God had given me my wife. I did not "pick her out." Even before conversion I did pray occasionally. Everything about those prayers, however, was selfish—except one thing: I always thanked God for giving me my wife!

Dick always agreed with me that he should "leave it in God's hands." He asked me to pray that God would work it out in the right way. I knew that he had asked others to pray for this same solution. But, even though Dick was willing to have God provide his wife, he was not willing to have his mother pick her out. This, of course, was only human nature at work. Most any other young man would react the same way.

While Dick was on his field assignment, in southern Texas that winter, Lois arrived on campus, and registered to attend classes beginning the second semester. Mrs. Armstrong just could not resist calling Dick long distance.

"Now wait a moment, Loma," I said to her. "If you want to talk to Dick a while, go ahead and call him. I'd like to talk to him, too. But whatever you do, DON'T say one word about Lois being here. You'll only drive him the other way if you do."

Prejudice Aroused

Mrs. Armstrong *partially* heeded my advice. But not altogether! She just would not resist mentioning, in a tone supposed to be very nonchalant, casual, disinterested, and incidental, "By the way, Lois Lemon is here, and has registered for classes."

That *did it!*

She didn't sound one whit casual or incidental to Dick.

When Dick returned to campus a few weeks later, he avoided Lois as though she were poison.

It seemed that everyone on campus sensed "romance in the air" between Dick and Lois, as soon as Lois arrived. It seemed just like a "natural" to everyone. Naturally, Lois had sensed this from talking to the girls. This set Lois against Dick just as positively as he had set his mind against her.

My Advice

So they went around, each determined to avoid the other.

After about two weeks, I called Dick to my office.

"Dick," I said, "years ago when I had been reduced to the depths of financial depression, just after my conversion, I had prayed earnestly for God to provide me with a new overcoat—among other things. We then lived in Portland, Oregon. It was in January, and cold. I needed an overcoat seriously, so I asked God for it. The next day I stopped at my brother's office a moment. He noticed the big hole in the side of my overcoat.

" 'Herb,' he said, 'you need a new overcoat. Today is the 20th of January, and Meier & Frank have a sale on overcoats. Anything I charge on my charge account beginning today will not be billed until March 1. I'll have until March 10 to pay and keep my credit good. Go over and select an overcoat, and during noon-hour I'll come over and have it charged on my account.'

"But I resisted immediately. It would be rather humiliating to have my younger brother buy me an overcoat.

" 'Oh NO, Russ,' I said, 'I couldn't let you do that!'

"And just at that instant it flashed to my mind, almost as if God Himself were speaking and saying,

403

'Didn't you ask me for a new overcoat? And now you don't want to take it THE WAY I am giving it to you!'

"So instantly," I continued, to Dick, "I changed my mind and told Russell I would do as he said. And now, Dick, didn't you pray and ask God to send you the right wife of HIS choice? And didn't you ask me to pray for it, too—and even several others? And here you are, when everyone on campus seems to just *know* that Lois is the answer to that prayer, you are avoiding her like the plague!"

Just Two Dates Only?

"Now I don't want to intervene in your most *personal* problems, Dick, or try to pick out your wife for you. But I *do* say that after you asked God about this, and have prayed about it so long, you are acting rather foolishly to completely and coldly *avoid* Lois altogether. Now all that I'm going to ask you, Dick, is this: I ask you to get a date with Lois—just once. IF this is God's doing, give it a CHANCE! Then don't date her again for a week—but a week later, have just one more date with her. Then if you're satisfied she is *not* God's answer to your prayers, DON'T EVER DATE HER AGAIN! Now how about it?"

Dick grinned.

"O.K., Dad," he said rather sheepishly. "I'll do as you say."

That same evening Dick had a date with Lois. But he did NOT do as I said, fully. He did *not* wait a whole week for the next date. Their next date was the very next night! And for the next few weeks they were seen together quite frequently.

One day in March, Dick and Lois came to Mrs. Armstrong and me, hand-in-hand.

"Dad and Mom," said Dick, "we've got something to tell you!"

404

Of course, we knew what it was!

"We're going to be married," Dick announced.

Later he told me what had happened.

That afternoon they had gone for a talk in Dick's car. Suddenly Dick pulled over to the side of the road, and stopped the car.

"Lois," he said, "I can't stand this any longer. I've been fighting this, trying to steel my mind against liking you, and trying to resist it—but I can't resist it any longer. I know I'm in love with you!"

And he said that Lois then said she had been fighting against him in the same way—and she couldn't resist it any longer, either.

So then they drove straight to tell Dick's mother and me they were going to be married.

The Happy Wedding

I performed the ceremony, as I had for our other three children, on June 11, 1957, in the outdoor garden theater on the Ambassador College campus, with a reception at our home afterward.

Dick and Lois took a honeymoon trip up to Oregon, the scene of his early boyhood. Meanwhile I had given them a little help in purchasing a small but very nice new home, which was ready for them on their return. Their marriage lasted just a little more than a year—when it was suddenly and unexpectedly cut off by Dick's untimely death resulting from an automobile crash while Dick was out on a baptizing tour.

But they *lived* a rather full lifetime in that one year. And Dick left behind a little three-month-old son, Richard David II.

69

Ambassador College Expands

ISN'T IT strange?—when one tries to remember past events, one's memory
seems so much sharper in recalling
events of childhood and early adulthood, than in re-
membering events of ten years ago.

I have not yet come to the year, in this *Autobiography,* of my mother's death. She lived to the ripe and
happy old age of ninety-five and a half. But in her last
years she was becoming noticeably more forgetful. She
would ask a question, hear and plainly understand the
answer—and then a little later ask the same question.
Her mind simply did not *retain* the knowledge as well
as formerly. She had a good mind. That is just the way
of all flesh!

Consequently, I am having to question many people—younger people of sharper memory—to help me
remember events of sufficient interest to record, from
1957 to the present.

Actually, as I write, I am now trying to remember the happenings that were taking place while I was writing the earlier chapters of this serial. The first installment of the *Autobiography* appeared in September, 1957!

Perhaps I should have been writing about what was then happening *while* it was happening. That, of course, never occurred to me. I had no idea, when I started this story of my life, I would still be writing it many years later. Actually, I think I vaguely envisioned it lasting for perhaps ten or twelve installments. But the response showed readership interest, and I began filling in more details.

The Campus Expands

Through 1956 and 1957 the Ambassador College campus in Pasadena began expanding with increasing momentum.

During the lifetime of multimillionaire Hulett C. Merritt, we had envisioned our campus as occupying the area beginning on the north with Mayfair, and the half-block dead-end street of Mentoria Court, and south to Del Mar Boulevard. As I mentioned earlier, the idea of Mr. Merritt's fabulous mansion ever becoming a part of the college simply had never occurred to me.

But with the acquisition of his property in 1956, our whole concept of the future campus was altered. Immediately on acquiring this superb property, we conferred with city officials for a use permit for a change of occupancy. Changing the mansion from a private dwelling into a college classroom building brought it under a different code.

We were required to install a fire sprinkler system throughout. Mr. Merritt had built a penthouse on the flat-roofed central portion of the building, with an elevator running from the basement to the penthouse. We were required to remove the penthouse, or come under a different code applying to three-story buildings that would have necessitated excessively expensive alterations. We were required also to seal off the elevator so it could not be used.

A Real Scare

Next, the city inspectors threw us a real scare. There is a code which requires all public buildings to be reinforced against earthquakes. Pasadena is almost directly over the famous San Andreas Fault. It is "earthquake country." Since Mr. Merritt had built his mansion long before this code was introduced it was naturally assumed the building had not been constructed to conform to this strict code. It was going to cost a fortune to add this reinforcing—if indeed it could be done. We faced the possibility of having to demolish the building and build another, or give up using the property altogether.

City inspectors made a series of tests. They bored through the outside walls at certain points, and looked into the interior walls. We had good news. They found the building had been constructed far beyond code requirements.

Our relief was only temporary. Next, inspectors said the mortar used fifty years ago would not conform to present standards. Once again we had good news. Tests showed the mortar equal to or superior to present standards. Next, they insisted on testing the bricks— but they, too, met all required standards.

Finally, in December, 1956, city engineers approved *classroom usage* of the building. But that did not mean we could start holding classes then. The sprinkler system had to be installed—a major plumbing operation

408

requiring several months. There was serious question about the ornate dual winding staircases. They did not conform to code for our new use. On this point we argued strenuously. To remove those staircases would destroy the beauty of the building. Finally, city officials agreed to let them remain, provided we build a new outside stairway on the west portico. The pillars on that half-circle portico had to come down—more earthquake regulations. A rear staircase had to be taken out.

For several months work was proceeding to put the newly named Ambassador Hall into condition for classroom usage. My elder son Dick set up his office in one of the future second-floor classrooms. One or two other men set up temporary offices in other rooms. This usage, of course, was permissible while the work on the building was in progress.

Certain other remodeling had to be done—like providing adequate restrooms, refinishing much of the fabulous wood paneling, certain painting, a complete remodeling of the rear first floor wing into home economics labs. It was finally more than two years after acquiring the property that it became our finest classroom building. It was first opened to classes with the opening of the 1958-59 school year, early September, 1958.

It had been a lot of work, accompanied by anxiety and suspense—but it was worth it. Few institutions have a building so elegant, and with such magnificent grounds. Actually we had a multimillion-dollar property acquired for less money than the ornate iron fence around the South Orange Grove Boulevard front would cost today. It had come to us for a very small fraction of its actual value.

Our entire concept of the future campus was now greatly altered. We knew the campus eventually would have to include the four-block area from Green Street on the north to Del Mar Boulevard on the south—and from "millionaire row" South Orange Grove Boulevard on the west down to the Union Pacific railroad tracks on the east—a twelve-square-block area.

Earlier we made mention of the acquirement of Manor Del Mar, our finest men's student residence. This had been the mansion of Lewis J. Merritt, father of Hulett C. Merritt. It also was built with rare and beautiful wood paneling. It also had spacious grounds and a sunken garden. Here also we were required to install a fire sprinkler system throughout. This fine property, also, had come to us at an exceedingly low price—actually a fraction of its present value.

New Office Building

From this time, we were in the process of gradual acquisition of additional properties within our ultimate campus area.

Next, by donation, the college acquired a two-story building on the northwest corner of Vernon and Camden Streets, one block east of Ambassador Hall. This building had housed the Jensen's Furniture Store.

Meanwhile we had completely outgrown our circulation and mailing department quarters, and our little printing shop. These departments had occupied the ground floor of our administration building. I have explained before that this building, part of the original initial property purchase, had been built as horse stables, with servants' living quarters on the second floor. Later the large center room on the ground floor had been converted into a four-car garage, with servants' living rooms on each side of it. We converted the larger center room into our main work room, for mailing list files, and mailing room; and the rear rooms into one room for our printing department.

We then operated two small Davidson duplicating machines as presses. We printed all of our booklets on these. Type was set by an outside firm. We had the small hand-lever paper cutter, and the small folding machine we had brought from Eugene, Oregon, also in this small printing shop.

After remodeling the Jensen's Furniture building to our needs, we moved the printing shop into the rear part of it, and the circulation and mailing department into the front portion of the ground floor. This more than doubled our floor space for these operations. But the work was growing—at the average rate of thirty percent increase each year. It wasn't long until we had to partition off the second floor into rooms and offices, and expand these departments into that.

In January, 1958, when we moved into this building, we installed two small-size Miehle presses. But to us, then, after some years with the little Davidson duplicating machines, these seemed like great giant presses! Yes, they made us realize THE WORK WAS GROWING!

1957, 1958 and 1959 were years of gradual expansion and growth on the Pasadena campus.

Neighbor Heckling

As the campus little by little expanded, with occasional additional property purchases, we found ourselves in a situation of trying to operate a liberal arts college with neighbors living next door, across the street, and sprinkled here and there in between us.

Ambassador students always have been exceedingly well-behaved. We were making every effort to keep noises down, and to avoid disturbing neighbors. I'm sure we did a more than creditable job at this. Nevertheless, our student body was growing every year.

411

Careful and courteous and considerate as our students tried to be, a few neighbors became irritated at times.

Once the students were putting on a short play in the Tempietto, which forms the "stage" or "platform" for our "garden theater," in what we have called the Lower Gardens. Two elderly ladies living across the street called the police. Soon a police car drove up. The officers only grinned when they saw what was going on, asked us to do our best to keep noises at a minimum, and asked if they could stay for a while and see part of the show. They explained that even though they disliked to interfere, when a complaint came in they had to investigate.

A short time after that we were having an afternoon wedding in the garden theater. There have been many of these, since. I looked across the street, and sure enough the two elderly ladies were sitting on their front porches. Ah-ha! Were we going to have the police called out to stop the wedding?

Just before time for the wedding ceremony, while guests were beginning to arrive, I walked across the street, smiling, and asked the two ladies if they would honor the young couple by attending the wedding. I have always noticed that women never outgrow their interest in romances of young people and weddings. The ladies graciously accepted, and I escorted them across the street, and ushered them into seats. They could not have seen any of it, otherwise, because our garden theater is secluded by high trees and thick shrubbery along the street side.

These ladies became very friendly and never again raised any objection to any student activities.

412

70

Tragedy Strikes Richard D. Armstrong

B Y January, 1958, the *World Tomorrow* program was being broadcast over every inhabited continent on earth. We were using more than four million watts of radio power every week. We were broadcasting from Okinawa, from Mozambique into the Republic of South Africa, and into India, over into Burma and the East Indies, and into Eastern Africa by the three superpower beams of Radio Ceylon, besides Radio Luxembourg, world's most powerful station in Europe—and beamed over the British Isles.

These were very powerful stations—reaching out as far as 2,000 miles, covering vast areas. With our coverage in South America, we were reaching out over areas containing approximately half of the entire world's population.

Of course I do not mean that that many people actually tuned in and listened to the broadcast—but that

413

many *could, if* they all owned radio sets and tuned in to hear it. Actually, our estimate was that some four or five million actually did hear the program during an average week of broadcasting. But that's a vast audience!

But we knew well that we were only barely *started!*

The BIG growth was yet before us!

By September of that year—1958—another million watts of radio power per week had been added.

Most significant among the *new* doors of radio being opened to *The World Tomorrow* was the powerful KGO, San Francisco. This is one of the few AA-class 50-thousand-watt radio stations on the West Coast that was heard clearly up and down the Pacific coast from Alaska to Mexico. We were given a good time, seven nights a week. Also newly added by that September were such valuable stations as WPIT, Pittsburgh; KGBX, Springfield, Missouri; and KWJJ, Portland, Oregon.

Also, by October, that year, *The Plain Truth* had been increased to thirty-two pages. It had been printed in two colors since February, 1957. With the November, 1958, number we began publishing, serially, the *Bible Story* book written and illustrated by Basil Wolverton. By that time, the circulation of *The Plain Truth* had gone up to 175,000 copies.

During the early part of summer, 1958, Mrs. Armstrong and I had driven once more back up to Oregon, for a period of fasting and rest on one of the Oregon beaches. Dick was left in command at headquarters. In more ways than one he showed excellent executive ability and good judgment.

We returned to Pasadena after two or three weeks.

It was along about this time that two significant events—occurrences that would seem incredible to many—directly involved Dick.

414

One, the birth of a baby. It was a most serious breech birth. The situation was becoming desperate, and since Dick was the ranking minister then at headquarters, he was called in on the emergency. He drove immediately to the home where the baby was being delivered. The doctor and the nurse were near exhaustion—perhaps more of hope than physical—and the mother near physical exhaustion. Of course all Dick could do was pray but pray he did, and in faith. He kept reassuring the others but the situation was fast becoming hopeless.

Finally the doctor gave up hope, said there was nothing he could do, unless to take the baby by cesarean section, which the family refused to allow. The doctor went home. The husband and the wife were counseled by Dick not to become frantic or to lose hope but to rely on God. Dick refused to lose faith. He continued to pray. And finally his faith was rewarded. The fetus turned over in the womb. The doctor was called back, and the baby was born in a normal manner.

The other incident, more amazing, involved a war veteran. He was paralyzed in his back, in his legs and both arms—helpless. He had to be moved in a wheelchair. The military hospitals had done everything for him that medical science could do. It was an incurable case. He was confined to helplessness for life, and put on a life pension for special financial support.

This man called for Dick to pray for him and ask God to perform a miracle, that he might be restored to a life of usefulness.

This was one of Dick's last acts. He did go to this man, and following the New Testament instruction in James 5:14-15, anointed him with oil, and laid hands on him as he prayed, asking the Eternal Creator to do what

415

man was unable to do, and had pronounced impossible to be done.

This man, a former Yale football player, was healed, and quickly restored to the full use of arms and legs and his whole body. He entered Ambassador College, and soon was climbing up and down ladders painting buildings.

The Last Baptizing Tour

It was shortly after this incident that Dick was off, with an assistant, on a baptizing tour up the Pacific coast. A number of people had sent in written requests for counsel with a minister, and for baptism.

At the time I was using, for an office, a very small room in what we called "the penthouse" atop the library building. The room was so small that I was having to use a small woman's boudoir table for a desk—an ordinary business desk was too large for the room.

I shall never forget, of course, how Dick came briskly running up the stairs to say good-bye.

"Well Dad," he said with cheerful enthusiasm, "I'm off on this trip."

A few days later his companion, Mr. Alton Billingsley, called me on the telephone.

Tragedy Strikes

"Mr. Armstrong," he said in a voice that signaled even before his words that something was very wrong, "We've had a terrible accident, and Dick is in very critical condition."

Quickly I asked for all of the facts. The accident had occurred a short distance north of San Luis Obispo, which is about halfway between Los Angeles and San Francisco, on the Coast Highway. It had been a head-on collision. Both our men had been thrown completely out

416

of the car. The right third of our car had been virtually sliced clear off. Dick had been sitting in the right front seat—often called "the death seat"—and had he not quickly moved to the left he would have been killed instantly.

As I learned later, they were driving north on the Coast Highway 101, after having baptized a man that morning. As Mr. Billingsley was driving, Dick had opened his briefcase and was checking his list of people to visit planning their next few stops. They had been on a dual highway—one way traffic only on each side of a divided highway, with a short space in between. The divided highway had ended but somehow neither of them had noticed it. A half block or so to their left was another paved road running parallel to theirs, which Mr. Billingsley noticed, supposing it to be the other two lanes of the divided highway.

Assuming that they were still on the divided highway with only one-way traffic on their two lanes, they were driving on the left lane to pass another car. Suddenly, from over a slight hilltop, came another car in their lane heading directly toward them. At this precise second they were almost past the car on their right— but not far enough to turn right in front of it in order to miss the oncoming car in their lane. There was no time for that, anyway.

Dick shouted, "Turn left! Turn left!"

Mr. Billingsley had only a fraction of a second to turn partly to the left. There was not enough time to turn out of the way of the oncoming car. Two cars, for example, speeding toward one another at fifty miles an hour or more, seeing each other about 150 feet away, will crash into each other in *less than one second!*

The oncoming car hit them head-on, its right side striking our men's car slightly to the right of center, and

417

Dick's car crashed the oncoming car into the third car that our men were then passing. It was a three-car crash!

But I didn't wait for all these details then. I got the essential details, and I was off in a flash for San Luis Obispo. Dick had been unconscious, and taken in an ambulance to a hospital in San Luis Obispo.

I had our switchboard telephone operator call our college physician, Dr. Ralph E. Merrill, asking him to be ready as I would be driving past his office in Glendale, on the way to San Luis Obispo. I asked Mr. Norman Smith, our radio studio manager, to go with me. Dr. Merrill was ready as we drove past. I drove as fast as I dared, consistent with safety.

Right then I was terribly aware of the DANGER of highway driving, and although I wanted to make the fastest time possible, caution and care in driving came first. It was a strenuous drive of approximately 200 miles.

Arriving at the hospital, we found that Dick had been transferred to another hospital—there were two hospitals in this little city.

We found him now conscious, but in very critical condition. His right arm was broken at the elbow; his pelvis had been broken badly, and they had him in traction. His jaw had been broken in three or four places; X-rays showed that his heart had been knocked over to the right—to the middle or slightly right of the middle of his chest; his left lung had been collapsed. Mr. Billingsley had been examined, and released—not sufficiently injured to remain in the hospital.

Dick wanted to rely on God for healing, without medical aid. The doctors asked for a conference with me and Dr. Merrill. They explained that Dick was already in their care and to protect their reputation and that of the hospital, they had to administer medical aid or else have him moved, in which case he probably would die before we could get him home.

Dr. Merrill, who himself had been healed by direct prayer, and understood both sides of this problem, advised us against moving him in his very critical condition. The hospital doctors agreed to give him the very minimum of medical aid consistent with their own and the hospital's protection. I learned later, however, that in practice that meant giving him everything "medicine" knew how to give. It was a very difficult decision to make—but with so many bones broken it certainly seemed that we would be directly *causing* his death to move him out of the traction and other trappings and contraptions that they had him in.

Then followed one of the most tense, strenuous week's vigil of my life. I telephoned my wife, and she with Lois, Dick's wife, and their two and one half month old son came to San Luis Obispo on the train. Of course Mr. Smith and I had anointed and prayed for Dick immediately. It was a week of almost constant prayer.

Registered nurses were required to be in constant attendance around the clock. We had one "R.N." as they are called in hospitals, at the college and another had applied for entrance to Ambassador College that autumn. By telephone, I arranged for these two to come immediately to the hospital, and the hospital supplied the third nurse. We preferred to have our own nurses at his side so far as possible.

It was too agonizing a week to go into in detail. Dr. Merrill had to return to Glendale, but the rest of us remained in the hotel in San Luis Obispo, to be in as constant attendance as possible.

The accident occurred on July 23, 1958. By evening of July 29, a very serious decision had to be made.

419

Dick's kidneys were not functioning enough to keep him alive much longer. The doctors at San Luis Obispo had called specialists from UCLA Medical Center to come up for consultation. They told me that it would be necessary to attempt to remove Dick to the medical center in Westwood (Los Angeles) where they could use an artificial kidney to stimulate normal action by his own kidneys. By carrying him suspended in traction on the special kind of pallet "bed" that he was strapped on, driving slowly in an ambulance through the night, they felt that they could successfully move him to the Los Angeles medical center. Our two nurses and one or more of their doctors went along in the ambulance. Also, Mr. Norman Smith, who had remained the week with me, went along with them.

We tried to get a little sleep through part of that night, rising and leaving about 5 a.m. for Los Angeles. We felt we should arrive not too much later than the ambulance, since it was to drive very slowly.

During the week, Dick had had various ones of us read the Bible to him. In spite of the pain, and the terrible condition, he kept in good spirits. Once, in prayer, he began thanking God for the many, many blessings that had been lavished on him. The nurse in attendance said that this continued a long time—he had so very MANY things to be thankful for.

I had typed out a number of biblical PROMISES that God had made for us, from various parts of the Bible, for our nurses to read to Dick in the ambulance when he was awake.

As we approached the Los Angeles area on the morning of June 30, strange premonitions seemed to come into my mind. I didn't tell the others. I didn't want to cause them any concern, worry, or lack of faith. This I had to fight out within my own mind, by prayer

420

and mental concentration. Finally, it seemed that I had won a victory over these premonitions and I had gotten my mind again into a state of FAITH.

We drove into the UCLA Medical Center parking lot. We left the others in the car while Lois and I went to see Dick or to get a report on his condition. As we approached the entrance, Mr. Smith and our two nurses approached us, with the news that just before they could get the artificial kidney connected, Dick had died.

There were present some of the most famous surgeons and specialists in the nation. They cut Dick open near the heart and tried to massage his heart back into action—they tried frantically everything that such specialists know, but to no avail.

Dick's body was then sent to a mortuary in Pasadena.

It hit Lois as if she had been shot. I grabbed her, steadied her.

"Steady, Lois," I said as calmly as I could. "Remember you have another very precious little life to nurse and keep alive, now. You must keep calm so that your milk will not be disturbed."

Lois responded bravely, like a "trouper." Then we discussed how to break the news to Mrs. Armstrong. We tried to break it gently so it wouldn't come as too much of a shock. We tried to keep normal composure.

"They've taken Dick back to Pasadena," I said, trying to be casual as if everything was OK. But no one ever could mislead my wife. She almost fainted—for she *knew* that we were only trying to ease the blow. But, she always was a real "trouper" too, and she quickly recovered without going to pieces—though naturally wounded to the very depths.

71

25th Anniversary

IT was an agonizing week for Lois, his
mother and me.

No one, of course, *but* a mother, can
describe or fully appreciate a mother's love for her son.
But fathers love their sons, too. And my affection for
Richard David had been greatly deepened by the special
circumstances under which he had been born.

My Time of Trial

It is, of course, natural for every father to want a son.
When our first child was a girl I was not disappointed.
Few fathers would be. Nor was I disappointed when our
second child was another daughter. But when the ranking most famous obstetrical specialist in the world, in
a Chicago hospital pulling my wife through a near-fatal
mid-pregnancy toxemia eclampsia, with 30 percent
albumin in the urine, warned us gravely that she could
never undergo another pregnancy without fatal results

422

to her and the child, I *was* disappointed beyond words to describe. I had to resign myself to a sonless life.

And this medical pronouncement was confirmed by two other doctors.

We didn't know, then. And I'm not sure these doctors knew, the real REASON. Apparently not too much was understood, at that time, by the medical profession about this negative-positive RH blood-factor condition. But my wife and I were opposites in that regard.

I had been forced to resign myself to a future without possibility of ever having a son.

Then, eight years later, in Portland, Oregon, Mrs. Armstrong had been—as recounted earlier—suddenly, completely healed of several serious complications by a positive miracle resulting from believing prayer. We knew then, by faith, that whatever had been the disturbing factor to render another pregnancy fatal, had been removed by this healing.

I knew then that God would give me a son.

And ever since I felt that the day Richard David was born was the happiest day of my life.

I was perfectly satisfied, then. God had blessed me with a son. He had been conceived less than a year after my conversion.

But the great God had plans I did not know. I was perfectly satisfied with the one son. We did not plan to have another. A year and four months later, Garner Ted was born—and I then felt doubly blessed—with TWO sons.

But when God took from me—or allowed to be taken—my firstborn son, on July 30, 1958—less than three months before his thirtieth birthday—well, it seemed that I could have some little understanding of how Abraham must have felt when he expected to have to give up his son Isaac—or even God the Father of all, in giving His Son Jesus Christ for ME as well as for the world.

The Ordeal

Dick's death occurred early Wednesday morning, July 30, 1958. The accident had occurred the preceding Wednesday morning. The funeral was set for Friday, August 1. The day in between, Thursday July 31, Mrs. Armstrong and I shared a very sorrowful 41st wedding anniversary.

On Wednesday we conferred with Messrs. Roderick Meredith, Herman Hoeh and Norman Smith regarding funeral arrangements. They felt unanimously that it was my duty to officiate at the funeral, which we planned for a simple graveside service only. Through the day I drove in my car to inspect cemeteries—which I had not had occasion to do before in Pasadena. I do not now remember whether Mrs. Armstrong and Lois went along. Necessary arrangements were completed. Lois accompanied us to the mortuary to select the casket—selecting one in the type of wood Lois said was Dick's favorite.

To say that my comparatively brief graveside sermon was an ordeal would be a gross understatement. I had learned, many years before, in conducting many funerals, to steel my nerves and remain calm, with controlled emotions. But speaking at Dick's funeral was altogether different. I found myself speaking in a louder, more concentrated voice than usual in a supreme effort to prevent emotional loss of control.

I remember quoting a portion of Lincoln's Gettysburg Address, regarding the duty of those of us remaining to carry on the great work to which God had called us.

424

My first impulse was to remain away from the Saturday afternoon college church service. I didn't want to see anybody. Nor did Mrs. Armstrong. But then I realized it was my duty to attend.

I thought of entering at the last moment, and sitting in the front row before any could speak to me or offer condolences. But then I realized that some of the students had erroneously assumed that ministers were under such divine protection that no such tragedy could occur to one of them. Dick's accident and death might shatter this faith. I knew I had to bring a message that would bolster and strengthen, not destroy, faith.

These experiences were perhaps the most severe test I had ever been called on to experience. But of course I knew where to go for strength, wisdom, and help.

We Travel to Springfield

Lois' parents had come for the funeral. She and they planned for them to stay on a while with her, in the home she and Dick had purchased new just over a year before. Lois felt that perhaps, with her parents in the house, she might adjust to remaining there without Dick.

I had assisted Dick and Lois with the down payment for the purchase of the property, and it probably was still less than half paid off. But Dick had been thoughtful in providing insurance which paid off the property in full. He also had provided insurance for Lois. And there was an additional $15,000 due Lois from group insurance carried by the College.

However, the few days of attempts at adjusting to living in the house without Dick had convinced Lois, by that weekend, that she could not live there alone.

Mrs. Armstrong, Lois and I planned a trip to get away from the trauma-shock we had undergone. I had

425

learned that nothing is so quieting and relaxing to distraught nerves as a long trip on a train. So we planned a trip to Springfield, Missouri, to meet Ted and be with him for the final service of his evangelistic campaign. The death of Dick had caught Ted in a campaign he could not leave at the time.

We left almost immediately, taking either the Chief, or the Super-Chief of the Santa Fe Railroad as far as Kansas City, changing there for a train to Springfield. Little Dicky—Richard David II—was carried in a sort of crib basket.

It did Ted and his wife a great deal of good to have us with them in Springfield. He, too, had undergone a most severe ordeal.

After a few days there, we journeyed on down to the location in Texas that later became the third campus of Ambassador College. We were then building there, of comparatively inexpensive all-steel construction, what we believed to be the largest "church auditorium" in Texas, as a tabernacle for an annual 8-day festival or convention—seating 8,000.

After a day or two there, we journeyed on back to Pasadena. Soon we were engrossed in the many responsibilities of carrying on the work to which the living Christ had called us.

We had, shortly before this, acquired the mansion of Mediterranean architectural design located between Mayfair (girls' student residence), and Ambassador Hall. We had done a certain amount of remodelling to convert this property into another girls' residence on campus—renamed Terrace Villa.

Since Lois felt she could not endure living alone in the home she had shared for a year with Dick, we converted one wing of the ground floor of Terrace Villa into an apartment for her and little Dicky.

426

This proved to be the best solution possible for Lois. She was on campus, where there was much activity. Many other girls were under the same roof, though she had the privacy of her own apartment. Also, she was abundantly supplied with "baby-sitters" whenever needed.

Frequently, from that time, during the next few years, we all dreamed occasionally about Dick. It often seemed, in my dreams, as if he had come back from the dead and was living again—as indeed he shall—and in the not too distant future.

Surprise Banquet

On Sunday, January 4, 1959, Ted and Shirley called at our home for Mrs. Armstrong and me. They had arranged a few days before that we four should go to a restaurant for dinner that evening—since it was the 25th anniversary of *The World Tomorrow*.

It was midwinter and they were wearing coats. We didn't notice that they were in evening dress. After driving a couple of blocks Ted suddenly said:

"Oh, by the way, Dad and Mom, I wonder if you'd mind stopping off at Ambassador Hall first. We've plenty of time, and Shirl hasn't seen the big new chandelier we just installed in the Grand Hall. I'd like to show it to her. Would you mind?"

Of course we didn't mind.

Entering fabulous Ambassador Hall, we found it all dark which was natural on a Sunday evening. I switched on the lights in the Grand Hall. Shirley was thrilled. For a few moments we four stood admiring the ornate chandelier of Czechoslovakian crystal. Then Ted suggested we have a look at the new crystal ceiling light fixtures installed, at the same time, in the Rosewood Room. When the doors to the Rosewood Room were

427

opened, a mystified Mr. and Mrs. Armstrong were bewildered. For there seemed to be many obscure and shadowy figures in the very dim, partially candlelit room.

The lights suddenly flashed on, to the shouts of "SURPRISE!" coming from seventy voices.

All—except Mrs. Armstrong and me—were in evening dress, sitting around beautifully decorated banquet tables forming one large "U" shape filling the large room. Huge floral arrangements of red and white carnations decorated the immaculate linen-covered tables gleaming with sparkling crystal, china, and silverware.

Accompanied by enthusiastic applause, Ted and Shirley escorted Mrs. Armstrong and me to the head table. There, for all guests to see, a red and silver banner at the base of the large floral arrangement read: "25TH ANNIVERSARY."

Student waiters appeared in full dress, and began serving a banquet of superb cuisine, probably prepared by girls in the Home Economics class. Then I glanced over the room to recognize the guests. There were all the ministers so far at the time ordained and their wives (except two who were in England); all faculty members of Ambassador College and wives of male members; intimate personal friends of Mrs. Armstrong and myself who had been associated with the work since the early days; and those business and professional men, who were closely associated in a business or professional way with the work, and their wives.

Perhaps the keynote of the banquet was the playing of a recorded "Memory Tape," prepared by Mr. Norman Smith, director of our radio studio. It recounted, through loudspeakers, by means of re-recording old recordings, even back in the "electrical transcription" days, many memories of the early days of the

428

broadcast back in Eugene, Oregon. There was a running commentary, tracing the history of *The World Tomorrow,* outlining the beginning and progress of the *Plain Truth* magazine. We were vividly reminded of the days in 1934 and 1935, in the stuffy little windowless office, devoid of ventilation. In that little room many mimeographed editions of *The Plain Truth* were edited and printed.

Mrs. Helen Starkey, who had been our first employee in that unventilated "office," was present with her husband, and at my request she rose to relate a few personal experiences of those days.

At Ted's request, I rose to give our guests (or was not *I*—with Mrs. Armstrong—the guest?) a glimpse of the happenings of those days.

Highlight of the Banquet

Perhaps the highlight of the "Memory Tape" was the reproduction of a portion of a *World Tomorrow* broadcast, in which the listening audience had been taken to Paris, where Dick cut in with our first "on-the-spot" broadcast, along the Champs Elysées, reporting the military display of the Bastille Day parade.

But the highlight of the entire evening was a presentation to Mrs. Armstrong and me of a most unusual and superb gift, commemorating a quarter century of broadcasting. Garner Ted read the presentation. He said:

"No anniversary would be complete without a gift. But a gift presents a serious problem. Mr. Armstrong has repeatedly said Mrs. Armstrong was fully 50 percent of his ministry. She has been with him through much of the actual programming during the last twenty-five years. No run-of-the-mill gift would do. And so, in selecting an APPROPRIATE gift for the occasion, I found

429

the article I wanted could not possibly be purchased on such short notice, not even at the finest jewelry stores, silversmiths, or trophy makers on the Pacific coast.

"I found it would have to be MADE, by silversmiths in San Francisco. And so I had to decide whether to have a gift to present to Mr. and Mrs. Armstrong TONIGHT, or to sacrifice presenting it tonight in order to have a wonderful memento specially created by master craftsmen as a permanent, lasting memorial of this first Sunday of 1959, the twenty-fifth anniversary of the *World Tomorrow* broadcast.

"I decided in favor of the QUALITY, instead of the time.

"And so, it gives me great pleasure to make this special presentation to Mr. and Mrs. Herbert W. Armstrong.

"As a lasting memorial of this twenty-fifth anniversary celebration, we are having made, by silversmiths in San Francisco, a beautiful desk set. The thick, long base is to be one solid piece of specially rolled and carved sterling silver! Beautifully matching pens will be specially made by the Sheaffer Company, and they'll also be of sterling silver! They'll repose in sterling pen holders, on each end of the base. In the center, a specially cast, hand-engraved miniature microphone, also of solid sterling, will stand beside a hand-finished miniature solid sterling silver world!

"In the center, immediately in front of the mike and the world, a gold inscription plate will read: 'To Mr. and Mrs. Herbert W. Armstrong. In deep and lasting gratitude for unselfish service as instruments in the hands of God through twenty-five years of radio broadcasting.'"

72

Providential Acquisition of English Campus

N OW WE come to the year 1959. The
office my son Dick had opened in
London had expanded as far as it
could expand. It then occupied the entire floor of an
office building in downtown London.

However, the office building occupied but small
ground area, and each floor consisted of only three
office rooms, beside corridor and lift (elevator to Americans).

When Garner Ted and I boarded an SAS (Scandinavian Airlines System) polar-flight DC-7 plane at Los
Angeles International Airport, in early June, 1959, we
had no idea whatsoever of establishing another liberal
arts college campus in England. Our purpose was to find
larger office quarters.

We did have in mind combining new and enlarged
office space with an altogether different kind of college.
We felt it might be advisable to open a small college for

men only, of various races and nationalities. The idea of such a college was to make it primarily a college for training men either as ministers or for religious service among various races and countries, as the broadcast and *The Plain Truth* developed need.

We arrived in Copenhagen about 3 o'clock in the morning. It was already becoming daylight—because Copenhagen is far north where the days are *very* long in summer and *very short* in winter.

There was some mix-up in our hotel reservations. I think we were to go to one hotel, and learn there what hotel our travel agent had booked for us. Anyway, I remember that after an hour or two waiting in the lobby of the hotel to which our taxi first took us, we transferred to another hotel several blocks away.

First Ship Radio Station

This was our first visit to one of the Scandinavian countries. We took this flight, stopping first at Copenhagen, because we wanted to contact the first radio station that we had heard of operating offshore from a ship. The offices of this station were in Copenhagen. Also, we wanted the thrill of a polar flight, and, as I remember, only this SAS flight from Los Angeles to Copenhagen was then operative as a polar flight. Flying on the pre-jet prop plane, it was much slower than today's jets.

I was not able to contact the manager of the station, who was out of town. However, I did contact him later by telephone. Nothing definite came of it at the time, but it did open to our investigation the idea of broadcasting from offshore ship stations, to countries where no radio time can be purchased or used by *The World Tomorrow*.

We enjoyed a day in Copenhagen, and then flew on

432

to Cologne, Germany. We carried with us a portable Ampex tape recorder. In fact it was the first of the Ampex 600 models—I believe ours was the first set from the factory. This was the first portable tape recorder that was of professional broadcast quality, so that programs recorded on it would be acceptable for broadcast by the largest, most discriminating radio stations.

At Cologne, in our hotel room, I recorded a program, which I wanted to do from inside Germany.

German Enthusiasm for Work

We were much impressed by the phenomenal progress the Germans had made since our last visit, in recovering from the war. Now factories and downtown business blocks and stores and offices not only had been rebuilt, and residence apartments constructed, but we noticed a much finer, more expensive quality of merchandise displayed in store windows.

Cologne suffered one of the worst beatings by Allied bombing of any city—80 percent to 90 percent destroyed. In all their cities, the Germans rebuilt first their factories and industrial and production facilities. People lived in temporary shacks or small temporary houses. They kept them neat, planted roses, flowers, shrubs for beauty outside working hours. Stores operated, at first, from bombed-out wreckage or any temporary kind of quarters.

Production came first, not fine living. In 1956 and 1958 I was awakened frequently in hotel rooms by Germans walking briskly to work about 5 or 5:30 a.m., yodelling or singing lustily. While the English, supposedly the victors of the Second World War, lolled around, came to tea and took an occasional work-break, the Germans worked with enthusiasm, vigor and PURPOSE.

433

Today the whole world sees the RESULT. I talk a good deal about CAUSE and EFFECT. Every condition is the RESULT of a CAUSE. If Britain has gone down economically, no longer a world power, virtually bankrupt today, there has been a CAUSE. The English, in their proud and stubborn attitude, have refused to acknowledge the CAUSE they were producing. Now they are down, and, as an important nation in the world, OUT! They have toppled the bars of moral restraint. They have gone in for laziness, indolence, gambling, and haughty, stubborn indifference. They are beginning now to *really* reap what they have been sowing!

The British have *written* a lesson they still refuse to learn or admit.

But, every visit we made to Germany, we noticed the CAUSE of a dynamic economic upsurge—hard work, industry, vigor, PURPOSE. They have purposed to *come back*. They are once again beginning to shout: "Deutschland über alles!"

Office Hunting in London

From Cologne Garner Ted and I flew on over to London. There, Raymond McNair, in charge of the work in Britain and Europe, and our business manager of the London office had been searching for a larger, more suitable office space prior to our arrival, hoping to have a few desirable selections for our decision. This time we wanted office space in a building where additional office rooms could be leased as our needs expanded.

But up to that point their efforts had not been very rewarding. Most of those they had inspected were not suitable, or worth showing to us. They did have three or four, one of which they termed "the least of the evils." After looking them over, we agreed with their appraisal.

434

One we inspected was a three-story, old, badly maintained apartment building. We supposed it could be used for the kind of college we had in mind—for a small number—perhaps not over thirty-five—men of different races. They could live in the apartment rooms, mostly very small, and the one or two lounge rooms might be enlarged by tearing out a few partitions and doing a remodeling job. These might be used as offices and classrooms. But the place was of third-rate quality, old, ill-kept—*and,* the PRICE was too high.

It was very discouraging.

Lastly, they showed us "the least of the evils." It had once been a mansion, or home of very good quality, three stories, and a block and a half north of Regent's Park. It was fairly close to the downtown business section. The location was good. It occupied a lot of about seventy-five or eighty-five feet width. But it, too, had been neglected, poorly maintained. Of course we knew we could give it a going-over. It could provide sufficient office space, and perhaps we *could* use it for our small, limited-size college of the type we then had in mind.

And Then—Out of the Blue!

We had spent two or three days looking. Mr. McNair had spent several days looking prior to our arrival. It began to seem like we were going to have to settle for this "least of the evils." It could be bought, and on terms we could handle. But we were not a bit happy over the idea.

Mr. McNair had entered Ambassador College in October, 1948, in the second year of its existence. He had always been a steady, balanced, persistent plugger—never quitting—never giving up. He didn't give up, now. He continued to telephone estate agents.

435

Then, suddenly one of these agents suggested something he didn't suppose we would be interested in—but he ventured to suggest it; a place just outside Greater London, north by northwest, in the Green Belt. It was a fairly large house, larger than the "least of the evils." It had a few acres of grounds.

"Could you handle the office work from a location that far out?" I asked.

"Yes," said Mr. McNair, "I think we could if the place were otherwise satisfactory."

"Why don't we go out and have a look at it yet this evening?" I suggested.

It was arranged.

Finally, after we had gotten completely out of London, we had to drive down a lane, and then a still narrower, winding, twisting lane. It didn't raise our anticipations. But then, we were getting used to disappointments.

Finally we turned in to the place. There was a sign, "Hanstead House." I don't know why, but that name sounded very unattractive to me.

Then suddenly we came to the iron gates in front of the mansion. It was like turning suddenly from the back-alleys of discouragement and dilapidated disappointments into a millionaire's beautiful mansion and grounds!

This place, too, had been neglected for two years. Weeds were hip-high. But the house looked proud and majestic. We could not see in very well—it was almost dark—but what we could see appeared to be in reasonably good condition inside. The building was of stone and stucco. It had a very attractive and fairly impressive entrance. There was, on the south side, what appeared to have been an expanse of lawn—now high in weeds. But on either side of that weed-grown lawn were rows of the most beautiful and stately cedars of Lebanon we had ever seen.

We were a little excited. *This* began to look promising!

"I want to see the inside of this mansion," I said. "Can you arrange for us to come back tomorrow morning, with the agent, to let us inside?"

"We'll stop by his home on the way back to the hotel and try to arrange it," Mr. McNair responded. It was arranged for complete inspection at 10 next morning.

This time two others of our staff went along. And we planned to arrive at 9:30, to go carefully over the grounds and talk it over privately among ourselves before the agent arrived.

When we arrived, in full daylight, all four of us were tremendously impressed. We began walking around. I noticed three large urns in what appeared to have been a garden in front of the front entrance—one a very large and costly urn. Then we discovered that there was an aviary. We discovered a little brook running down what appeared to have been a very fine and costly garden. At least I noticed, among the weeds, several plants I knew to be very fine and expensive shrubs.

We also had noticed that there was an informal English sunken garden on the east side of the mansion, and there were four large greenhouses.

We *didn't* know, then, that there was such a beautiful formal garden on the west front, the most magnificent rose garden we had ever seen, and a very exotic Japanese garden through which the little brook ran—these were so thickly covered with weeds we did not discover them.

The young men began to shout.

Almost in unison, we all exclaimed, "This is PROV-

437

IDENTIAL! This means God wants another full LIBERAL ARTS coed college in England, just like the one in Pasadena!" It was like a sudden realization—a KNOW-ING—a recognizing of the divine guidance and intervening to show us HIS will!

The other fellows were shouting for joy.

"Hey, pipe *down!*" I said. "Not so loud! If that estate agent arrives and hears you fellows, the price will double! Besides, we haven't bought it yet, and we don't know whether we can!"

There was not really any doubt in our minds, though. It was like recognizing a revelation straight from God. We KNEW this meant we were to establish a college in England. NOT the kind of college *we* had in mind. The kind we now recognized GOD had in mind.

This may seem preposterous to some readers, I know. But we are engaged in God's work. We have learned how God works. It was like God had flashed a message straight from heaven like a sudden bolt of lightning.

Here was a college campus, already there! We knew that, for this purpose, we would need additional buildings, for administration offices, for dormitories, perhaps for additional class and lecture rooms. We knew, too, that in the Green Belt it would be almost impossible to obtain a building permit to erect additional new buildings.

But on this place we noticed there were quite a number of very superb horse stables, cow barns, and even a building for an electric generating plant. We felt sure we could obtain a permit to REMODEL those *existing* buildings suitable for our usage.

Of course we knew there were many problems to hurdle. We had, first, to see whether the county authorities would grant us a change of occupancy permit to

operate a college at that location. And there was the
rather BIG matter of negotiating for the purchase—and
whether we would be able.

When we inspected the inside we saw that this
Hanstead House, as it was then named, was a very
ornate building of fine quality—comparable in quality
and size to Ambassador Hall on our Pasadena Campus.
Ambassador Hall is the former Hulett C. Merritt mansion and estate, the most fabulous place in Pasadena.
Ambassador Hall had come to us virtually as a gift.
When we saw the ornate interior of Hanstead House,
we began to have misgivings. Perhaps we would find the
price completely beyond our reach.

Beside, the estate agent's office had intimated that
TWA was considering the purchase of the property to
be used as a school for stewardesses.

Yet, this mansion, with these outstanding gardens,
the aviary, greenhouses, cedars of Lebanon, all finally
came to us for £8,000 ($22,800)—the not uncommon
price of a five- or six-room cottage on a forty- or
fifty-foot lot in America,—and *that* on terms that gave
us several years to pay.

[*Editor's note: The events of the year 1959 in the life of Herbert W. Armstrong were written for* The Plain Truth *in the year 1968, some nine months after the death of Loma D. Armstrong. Mr. Armstrong chose not to continue his autobiography serially in the magazine. However, during the years that followed he continued to write up his remarkable experiences and to expound new truths as they came to him. The publishers have therefore gathered together and edited his public letters, together with certain editorials in* The Plain Truth. *So here, in Herbert W. Armstrong's own words, are the highlights of the nearly twenty-seven remaining years of his life that concluded on the morning of January 16, 1986—when he fell asleep in death in his wife's favorite chair.*]

73

June 29, 1959— May 22, 1963

Dear Co-Workers with Christ:

We spent a very busy ten days in London. We planned for having the British and overseas edition of *The Plain Truth* printed hereafter in London. Until now we have shipped the printed copies by air freight....

Also plans were made for establishing a second Ambassador College in Britain, beginning September next year, 1960. God opened to us one of England's fine, spacious country estates. Until the owner died a year ago, this was the home of one of England's wealthiest titled ladies—Lady Yule. It is one of the most recently built of such estates—built in 1924, and in superb condition. Originally this estate comprised over 800 acres. When wealthy titled people die in Britain today, the inheritance taxes take almost everything, and their heirs (Lady Yule left no children) are forced to sell the property in order to pay the taxes. In this case, the estate has been subdivided into many smaller farms, and most of it sold, except for the fine big mansion, with its eight acres of beautifully landscaped lawns, rose gardens, etc., and a two-acre plot containing brick housing units for the former employed staff, the fine brick stables, garages, etc. These will make student housing, as also will servants' quarters in one large wing of the mansion. They had no difficulty selling off small farm plots, and even near-by guest cottages. But in England today nobody could buy such a mansion to live in, and it could only be sold for a college, hospital, or some such institution. The result was, having been unable to sell it in a whole year, the price was reduced to a small fraction of what it cost to build. We obtained it for less than we paid for any of our college buildings in Pasadena, though this is larger than any of them, and even finer than any except Ambassador Hall. It came to us with a small payment now, a large part of which was paid by our British Co-Workers, and except for small payments which I think British Co-Workers can fully pay, no more to be paid for a year, when we establish the college. This also provides adequate office space for our fast-expanding London office. Our London office manager told me the saving in office rent will more than pay for this fine property.

Thus God has providentially opened to us a superb, magnificently landscaped ten-acre college campus, only five miles from the edge of London, walking distance from suburban train, with a fine, stately, thirty-three-room college building, with ample class rooms, and offices and mailing rooms—and without putting any financial burden on our United States and worldwide work from Pasadena headquarters!

Co-Workers, the way God continues to bless His Work and to lead the way just fills me with awe, with gratitude, and almost chokes me with emotion! Constantly Christ shows us that He is in this great Work— guiding it—blessing it! What a privilege for us to have a part in it—to be co-workers with Christ Himself!

I hope it fills your heart with joy and thanksgiving, too, as it does mine—and inspires you to pray harder for this great work—to sacrifice more so you can give more if you have not already done that, as I know many of you have—but far from all!

I am typing this letter in Monte Carlo, and will airmail it to Pasadena, where it will be reprinted and mailed on to you! I hope to be back home before you receive this, or a day or so after.

New York, November 4, 1960

Dear Friend:

I have just completed my first trip around the world! I have thrilling and important news for you. I have come up to the offices of our New York advertising agency to type this letter to you, during a stopover of a few hours between planes. I must fly on across the Atlantic Ocean again tonight, arriving at London airport tomorrow morning at 7 a.m. Mrs. Armstrong is there, and I expect her to meet me at the airport.

Our New York advertising agency is responsible for opening up time for *The World Tomorrow* on overseas radio stations outside the United States, around the world. Constantly more and more powerful stations are opening their doors for broadcasting the *World Tomorrow* message on five continents around the world.

I have had to be in England most of the time since June, preparing for the opening of the second Ambas-

443

sador College. The founding and starting of a new
college is a gigantic task. It seems a thousand and one
things have to be thought of, planned provided, put into
operation. The new college did open on schedule October 14.

Developments on the other side of the world, in
Australia, made necessary a hurriedly planned flight to
Sydney, Australia. The president of our New York
advertising agency flew to London, where I joined him,
and together we flew on to Sydney, and then on around
the world—all in something like two and a half days'
actual flying time!...

I was very much surprised, recently, to learn that
only a very small percentage of all people have ever
flown in an airplane. I used to say that I would never
fly unless I absolutely had to, in God's Work—and then
I would trust God to protect me. The time finally came
when, nineteen years ago, I had to fly from Seattle to
Portland. I had broadcast the program on Sunday
morning from the studios of a Seattle station, and had
to be in the studios of the Portland station for the
broadcast a very few hours later. The only way I could
get there on time was to fly.

Half-way along that first flight of mine, the captain
came through the cabin, speaking very quietly in the ear
of each passenger the tremendous news he had just
heard over the plane's radio that the Japanese were
bombing Pearl Harbor—the United States was at war!
That, of course, was Sunday, December 7, 1941. You
can understand why I shall never forget my first flight
in the air!...

I have had to do a great deal of flying these past
nineteen years. These big 707 jets have been in service
only about two years, and already I have lost track of
the number of times I have flown on them. But this was

my first trip around the world—and the first time I have ever taken time or space to tell you about it.

I did not look forward to this trip with any eagerness. Mrs. Armstrong does not like to fly, and of course could not come along on a trip of this great length and short time, anyway. My entire trip around the world, with six days in Australia, three in Pasadena, and one in Texas, is less than two weeks. I put off this trip as long as I could. . . .

We flew straight through from London to Sydney—almost half way around the world—on the same plane. There were forty-five-minute fuel stops made at Rome, at Cairo, Egypt—flying over the very path of the great Exodus under Moses, and close to Mount Sinai—then Karachi in West Pakistan on the west border of India. We stopped again at Calcutta after crossing India, then southeast to Bangkok, on down to Singapore, then clear down to Darwin, Australia, then across that continent and landing at Sydney about 7 a.m. in rain and a gust of wind. Our office staff there now numbers ten, seven of whom have been sent over from Ambassador College. . . .

During the six days in Sydney, arrangements were made to gradually add thirty-nine additional stations, with daily broadcasting. This will mean we shall cover thoroughly the areas in which about 98 percent of all the people of that continent live.

It seemed very strange on Sunday night as we left Australia to realize we were starting to cross the vast Pacific Ocean. From London we had travelled east and southeast—always, so it seemed—travelling farther and farther away from the Pacific. I had left the Pacific Ocean when I last had left Pasadena, and had steadily travelled farther away from it all the way to London. And from there I was still going on east—and now, all of a sudden, I realized I was way west of Pasadena, instead of east. It really seemed very strange. I had been going constantly farther east of Pasadena, and now here I was west of it! ...

During my brief three days at headquarters in Pasadena, I approved going on our second station in Canada. ...

Now I must hasten back out to the international airport, and board one more big 707 jet, on the last leg of this 'round the world journey, to be with my wife and continue supervision, for a while, of the new Ambassador College in England. ...

February 16, 1961

Dear Co-Workers with Christ:

We now have to realize it! These are the most trying and crucial days for this great closing Work of God since it began! ...

Now I want to tell you how the living Christ has moved swiftly this past week, in a most thrilling manner, to speed His Work ahead! ...

Kansas City is a very important center where we have had no station at all. There is just one 50,000-watt station there, with coverage reaching over much of Missouri and Kansas and adjoining states—KCMO. The management there has been consistently adamant against what radio men term "commercial religion."

Perhaps most of our Co-Workers do not realize how very difficult it is to induce any of the larger, more powerful, top-prestige stations to open time for *The World Tomorrow*. In radio circles there is a feeling that all religious programs are "commercial religion," broadcasting only for the money they get by begging the public over the air. They object to ordinary religious

446

programming, which is sentimental, emotional, interesting only to a very small segment of religiously inclined people. And 95 percent to 99 percent of the entire listening audience tunes out immediately when such programs come on. The stations cannot sell time to commercial sponsors following the average religious broadcast, because the rating agencies have shown that they have no audience left except a few religious people who will turn immediately to some other religious program.

It's difficult to convince radio station managers that *The World Tomorrow* is utterly different—that we speak to, and grip the interest of non-religious people—the whole public—that most of our audience is made up of people who seldom, if ever, go to church. Many of the largest and highest-ranking stations have learned that *The World Tomorrow* attracts a large listening audience of the entire public—and that we are not commercial and never ask for money on the air, or in any of our free literature. You have no idea how difficult it is to induce radio men to realize the true facts about God's own program!

But on Monday of last week, the manager of KCMO was in Los Angeles, in the offices of the Katz Agency, one of the two or three largest firms of radio and TV station representatives in the country, and who represent KCMO. It was hard for them to believe any religious program could hold a listening audience, and turn over a big audience to the sponsor who follows. They demanded proof.

So they got out the rating reports. First they looked at the KLZ ratings in Denver. They were astonished to find that the rating agency surveys in Colorado showed that *The World Tomorrow* is rated number one in Denver. We had the largest listening audience of any

447

station. We held our audience the second fifteen minutes. They called up the management of WLAC in Nashville. They found we were the highest rated program. The management there recommended that they accept *The World Tomorrow.* They found we are the number one rated program on WWVA, according to an extensive Hooper survey.

The manager of KCMO immediately cleared the time of 9:05 to 9:35 p.m., following five minutes' news at 9 p.m. He then called his friend who is manager of KRMG, Tulsa, told him what he had found about our program, urged him to accept the program. KRMG did—9:00 p.m. every night.

Getting on KCMO automatically opened up to us our first station in Arizona—KPHO in Phoenix—every night of the week at a good time.

That all happened between 10 and 11:30 a.m. Monday morning. Then our advertising agent and the top man in radio sales for the Katz Agency telephoned for a luncheon engagement with me. At 1 p.m. they arrived at the college. They were really excited. Things were happening like miracles! There was some kind of tie-up between these stations and the Storer chain.

This Storer company owns several important 50,000-watt stations. These include KGBS, Los Angeles; WGBS, Miami; and WIBG, Philadelphia. We have succeeded in getting on these three 50,000-watt stations on Sunday only, but so far we had been unable to convince them of the true facts about *The World Tomorrow* and they had refused to open up time weeknights, which we need seriously in these important areas.

These men explained that the "home base" original "mother" station of the Storer group is WSPD, the NBC station at Toledo, Ohio. Although this station is

448

only 5,000 watts, its ratings show it has more than half of the total radio audience in its district. Six or seven other stations in the area divide the rest of the audience.

"This station is the key," said its West Coast representative from the Katz Agency. "to getting complete every-night time on those three other Storer stations. We called them on the telephone. We can't convince them. We think that if you go over there and talk to them personally, Mr. Armstrong, you may be able to present the facts in a way so they will come to see how different *The World Tomorrow* is from the kind of religious programs they object to."

He said the management of the Storer stations at Toledo had agreed to listen with an open mind if I came to them—although they advised against my coming, saying they didn't think there could be any facts that would change them.

But the manager of the West Coast offices of the Katz Agency was now so interested and enthusiastic over the *World Tomorrow* program that he had agreed to fly back himself with me, and also to have his top radio-sales man go with us. It was arranged for those two men, who are the West Coast representatives of this Toledo station, our advertising agent, and me to fly to Toledo. Tuesday morning we boarded a non-stop jet plane for Chicago, with reservations to fly on to Toledo, Ohio, early the next morning.

At 7:50 next morning we were out at Midway air terminal in Chicago for an 8:30 plane. At 8:10 they marked the plane up as thirty-five minutes late. Then thirty-five minutes later, they posted on the bulletin board an additional hour delay. Meanwhile our advertising manager telephoned the manager of WJJD, a 50,000-watt Chicago station. He is a former partner of our advertising agent, and has been manager at WJJD only about a month. He was very favorable to giving us a good time seven days a week. I was introduced to him on the telephone, and suggested I stay over in Chicago and see him on Thursday (it was now Wednesday morning).

Finally they cancelled out our flight to Toledo altogether, and announced they were sending us by taxi clear across Chicago to O'Hare Field to catch a 12:10 plane on another line. Meanwhile the Katz manager called Toledo, found the station manager was at the airport in Toledo to meet us. So it was arranged for him to meet our later plane.

Well, it seemed everything was going wrong! Arriving at O'Hare Field, our 12:10 plane was marked up thirty minutes late! It was now going to get us to Toledo just one hour and fifteen minutes before we had to board the plane on our return flight—and it is one hour's drive from the airport to downtown Toledo!

When we stopped off the plane at Toledo, the three top executives of the station were there to meet us. Because of our short time, they arranged for a conference room in a motel across the street.

I had much to tell them, and not much time. We finished our conversation walking through the airport. It was not until we reached the gate to the plane, with its propellers already warming up waiting for us to hurry on board, that final decision came. They accepted *The World Tomorrow*—9 p.m. every night, seven nights a week!

Arriving in Chicago, we dropped off our luggage at our hotel, then had our cab take us on to the large suite of offices of the Katz Agency on Michigan Boulevard. I was introduced to the Chicago manager of the agency.

450

While there the West Coast manager of the Katz Agency called the leading radio station at Spokane, KHQ, long distance. Their manager was in Phoenix, attending a meeting with the manager of KPHO, which had just opened time for us. The KHQ office in Spokane called their manager on another telephone at Phoenix. The KPHO manager recommended that he accept *The World Tomorrow.* The KHQ manager instructed his office that if his West Coast representative, who was making the call from Chicago, also recommended it, to clear the time 9 to 9:30 p.m., seven nights a week.

Thursday morning the manager of WJJD came to breakfast with us, and then we walked over to the WJJD offices. Two station officials were there waiting for the conference. They seemed friendly. Then the president of the company which owns this station along with a few others walked in. There was no smile on his face. He was decidedly antagonistic. Nothing could budge him. His mind was not open to any facts, other than that the answer was a frigid "no!"

About noon we met the manager of a 1,000-watt station, while waiting to see the manager of 50,000-watt WCFL (the CFL stands for Chicago Federation of Labor). This station manager shot sharp questions at me about our program. When I mentioned that we tell people how to live to be happy, and that we proclaim the truth of the Bible, he asked: "What is Truth? Nobody knows! This whole world is all mixed up. There is nothing but confusion—especially in religion." He said he himself was confused.

"I can straighten you out," I said, "if your mind is open, and I can have enough time with you." He was intrigued. Later he called our advertising agent at our hotel, offering to open an early morning time seven days

451

a week. "What shall I tell him?" asked our advertising agent.

"Tell him," I said, "that if he will make it a condition of the contract to come out to Pasadena and see our college campus, and spend a little time with me getting straightened out, we will go on his station." He accepted. . . .

Later we met the manager of WCFL—only he had just recently resigned. However, he is some kind of a top man in Chicago union circles and very influential. He felt that the station would do whatever he recommended. He spent some little time with me personally. God seemed to give me favor in his sight. He became real friendly—seemed to really want to help us get on a 50,000-watt Chicago station. Of course we could not get the final answer at the time, for we had to leave for the airport to catch the evening non-stop jet plane for home.

Co-Workers, does this give you a little clearer idea why I need to ask you continually to pray for this work? Without divine intervention we would not be able to get on any of the really major superpower stations. I know that hundreds—maybe thousands—of you Co-Workers were praying earnestly for this work the past two weeks. That is why all these miracles happened so suddenly all at once!! Never has anything like this happened before!!

This letter is getting long. But there is still more to tell you! . . .

The time has come when we have to open a branch office in Canada. Scores of our Canadian Co-Workers have been unable to deduct on their income taxes the tithes and offerings they send for God's Work, because we have had no office nor recognition in Canada. . . .

Now, finally—I have found that when Christ opens vital and necessary radio doors for us, He expects us to

452

walk through those doors! Soon after this work started on the air, in the late fall of 1934, He opened the door of station KXL, then 100 watts, in Portland. The work could have spread within its first year to Portland. But I hesitated. I was afraid to go ahead. Instead, I sent a letter to Co-Workers asking if they would pledge the small amount of money it would cost. Not enough pledges came! We lost our chance. The doors of KXL did not open for us again until some two years later.

When stations important and necessary to this work have opened up to us in later years, and I walked right through the doors Christ opened, in faith, God has always supplied the means. When I hesitated, the money never came!

Co-Workers, God has performed miracles for His Work this past week! I know he expects me to follow where He leads! In faith, I am going ahead! I know you will back me up, and will not let me down! . . .

Thank you again, and God will bless you—because I ask Him to, and He does bless all of us loyally in His Work!

Written from Ambassador College
St. Albans, near London
May 22, 1963

Dear Co-Workers with Christ:

Again I am writing you from Ambassador College in England. Mrs. Armstrong and I expect to be here for the remainder of the present school year . . . .

I have written you about our austere year, on which I found it necessary to embark some two months ago. Some of you misunderstood! Let me make it clear! God's Work is not going backward!—never! The actual gospel work is going forward faster than ever before! We are not making any cuts that would actually slow the Work.

But this is what we are doing! We are cutting every waste effort or unnecessary expenditure we can. We are continuing to add more radio stations—but, (for this one year) not as rapidly as we had been doing. We are cancelling out some radio stations that have not proved productive and apparently were not being listened to by as many as others.

I did write you two months ago that we had postponed the opening of the third Ambassador [campus], in Texas, for one year. That was because of this austerity year. But we feel that will not slow down the actual proclaiming of the gospel—as long as it is for only one year. And another reason is that we are simply forced to continue a building program at both Pasadena, and at the college in England—or else take in no additional students next school year!

Here in England we are now trying to feed one hundred ten students in one ordinary-size family dining room—designed for only one small family! So we are proceeding right along to complete the new dining hall, which was started last year. We have no place for additional incoming new students to sleep the next school year. So we are continuing the work of remodeling the "Clock Horse Stables," converting them into a new dormitory to house one hundred fifty men.

We are having to enlarge our office space, and space for our printing department here, to take care of the constantly increasing mail from listeners requesting literature.

The Work cannot grow unless the colleges continue to turn out an increasing number of graduates every year. This great Work now encompasses the whole world. It now requires the full time work of hundreds of trained men and women. It now reaches millions of people every week—our estimate is at least twenty-two million!

We are spending no money for just "beautifying" our college properties that is not absolutely necessary for the functioning of the colleges. Our colleges are outstandingly beautiful because multimillionaires built these fabulous estates that way at their expense. Then these magnificently landscaped properties came to us at a tiny fraction of their original cost.

For example, you could not, today, even buy the fine and imposing iron fence and gates around Ambassador Hall on the Pasadena campus for the price we paid for the whole fabulous estate! . . .

But we are certainly not letting these fine properties go to weeds and ruin. God commanded Adam to dress and keep the Garden of Eden, not let it run down and go to weeds. We do work hard to properly maintain what God has seen fit to entrust into our hands. He will hold us accountable for how well we take care of what He gives us!

The building program must go on, or the work cannot grow! Our building program has been costing only a small portion of the total expenditures for God's Work—between two percent and three percent. It would be penny-wise and pound foolish to cut this off. Rather, we are making big cuts in the two biggest items of expense. This enables us to continue right on with the necessary building program, and still reduce expenses, while at the same time increasing and expanding the work itself! God's Work must continue to grow its normal 30% even during this austere year! This does take careful planning, and sound management! . . .

74

April 25, 1966— December 10, 1968

April 25, 1966

Dear Co-Workers with Christ:

Greetings from Australia: Mrs. Armstrong and I are visiting our offices here in Sydney, Australia— "down under," on the other side of the world where the sun circles around the north on its way to setting in the west.

God's Work is booming here in Australia. It is my wife's first visit here and my first since October, 1960. . . .

It has been a tremendous inspiration to Mrs. Armstrong and me to see God's Work booming in rapid growth down here in Australia. While here, I have had conferences with radio station officials in Adelaide, Melbourne and Sydney, and we leave in ten minutes for the airport, flying today to Brisbane. These and other business conferences are resulting in stepping up our program for reaching the people of Australia and New Zealand with Christ's own gospel. Additional radio coverage is opening up. Also arrangements are under way for the purchasing of full-page advertising space in national magazines and metropolitan newspapers. These will carry Christ's dynamic message to hundreds of thousands, and millions, in print.

Many hundreds have been really converted—their lives turned around and changed—since I was here last. God is doing a big work here in Australia. What an inspiration it is to realize that the *World Tomorrow* is heard all over the world.

Let me tell you a rather exciting experience. When I was here in October, 1960, our local manager, a radio station official and I were walking on a wharf to board a ferry when suddenly I heard a sharp, deep bass voice from behind say: "Are you Herbert W. Armstrong?" Turning, I saw a tall policeman. How did he know my name, way down here in Sydney, Australia? Had I done something wrong?

"Well, I want to shake your hand," he said, reaching out his hand. "I hear you on the radio, and I recognized your voice as you were talking to this gentleman."

It was really a startling experience. Well, here is the astonishing sequel. I met this man again the other day, with his wife. He has been converted since I was here, baptized by one of our local ministers. And, more! His wife was also baptized just the other day—since we arrived here—also by one of our ministers. Mrs. Armstrong and I were overjoyed to meet them both.

I am now finishing this letter from Brisbane, where I am to speak tonight to an audience of a few hundred listeners to *The World Tomorrow*. I have spoken before good-sized audiences in Melbourne, and several times in

457

Sydney, since we arrived in Australia. Tomorrow I have a luncheon appointment scheduled with the manager of a Brisbane radio station. . . .

Next Monday we fly on the Hong Kong for two days, to try to make arrangements to put the *World Tomorrow* program on a station there. Then we must take a very long flight all the way across Asia, to Tel Aviv, Israel. We will spend a few days revisiting historic places in the land of ancient Israel. I am especially anxious to visit again the little synagogue in Nazareth, where Jesus spoke from the book of Isaiah (Luke 4:16-30), and other places. Then from there straight to London, and Ambassador College in England.

This 'round the world' trip is an arduous one. I was afraid it would be very hard on Mrs. Armstrong, but thousands are praying for our safety and pleasant flights for her; and so far, all prayers have been answered. We are very grateful. . . .

I must hurry now to the auditorium where I am to speak tonight. Remember, the living Christ blesses you for your generous part in His Work.

February 27, 1967

Dear Co-Heir with Christ:
This letter must be brief, and to the point.

I had hoped that I would be able to announce, in this letter, the biggest, most important, most sensational leap forward in this Work of God, since it started in 1934!

That's why this letter is two or three days late. But I can't delay longer. And now I must make it short so it may be typed and mailed yet today if possible! I feel sure this very sensational announcement will be ready before the next letter. . . .

458

Meantime, dear Co-Workers, I have been under the heaviest cloud for years. My dear wife has been stricken with a serious intestinal condition. For three weeks she has been confined to bed. Everything possible was done, including, of course, anointing her and asking God to heal her. At first we thought it was an attack of appendicitis—and, under fasting, such an attack will resolve itself naturally within about seven to ten days. But that time passed, and the pain was not in the appendix. In such a condition there are, of course, certain things we humans can and ought to do—even though we rely on God for the healing. I assure you, that under the best professional advice, everything we could or ought to do was done.

I would like to explain, for your own understanding, that God does for us what we cannot, and ought not, try to do for ourselves. Healing of sickness or disease is something no doctor nor medicine can do. That is why God has promised to heal us. In my ministerial experience over forty years, literally thousands have been healed—of almost every disease or sickness, including cancer and leukemia—by my prayers, and those of God's ministers in this Work associated with me. Some things we cannot do, and ought leave solely to God. Some He does through us, with certain things we can and should do. Other things we do by ourselves.

But we came to the place where, under "medical" advice of a doctor who is one of our converts (no longer in active medical practice, but in God's service), the time had come to stand still, and commit it into God's hands. The first two weeks, approximately, she was in great abdominal pain, with cramps, unable to hold anything on her stomach. She did sip water, and take crushed ice into her mouth—but always her stomach rejected it, and it was thrown up. Then, a week ago, I'm sure God performed one miracle—I awoke at 6:30 a.m. and was told she had taken about a half glass of homemade grape juice at 4:30, and her stomach had retained it. She has been taking prescribed amounts about every two hours since. For about three days she was able to take small amounts—two or three teaspoons at a time—of a beef juice, then her stomach refused it further. We have been able, however, to alternate some fresh carrot juice, and even some gelatin.

This nourishment, during the past week, has given her some added strength, and she has been getting in better rest and sleep, and is much improved in mind and spirits. . . .

Dear Co-Worker with Christ, this great Work of God is on the very threshold of the greatest leap forward in power and scope in its history. The really big work is yet to be done. God started His Work for this time through my wife. He used her to bring me to Him. God said it is not good for a man to be alone—and He gave her to me to be my help. She has been my partner—the other half of this team God called, and has used in building His great Work. As we now face a greatly stepped-up, bigger Work, I need her desperately at my side. God, of course, knows this.

During this ordeal I fasted ten days. I did not fast for her—because we do not bring God "to our terms" by suffering and "doing penance." I fasted to bring myself closer to God. When that was accomplished I broke the fast. I had been concerned over a heart condition and high blood pressure. I was slowed down in my work. That is now all gone. This heart condition I have felt for some four years is no longer noticeable. I have renewed verve, bounce, energy. God has, in this fasting and prayer, opened my eyes to many things—

changed my entire daily routine, brought me far closer to Him. I am ready, now, for this big leap ahead in this Work. . . .

April 17, 1967

Dear Co-Worker with Christ:

At last I can give you the one greatest most exciting news announcement in the history of our broadcasting Christ's gospel to the world.

But I am deeply sorry to have to announce, at the same time, that my wife's critical illness has ended in the manner least expected—in her death just after midnight Saturday morning, April 15. In the next second of her consciousness she will awake in the Resurrection, completely healed—and, far more than we beseeched God in our earnest prayers, not in the corruptible body of this mortal flesh and blood, but in an immortal spirit body, in glory in God's eternal Kingdom!

Thirty-four years ago, at this same time of year, when my father died having reached his seventieth year, I had to learn that God's promises are absolutely secure—but not always in the way we expect. For His ways are not our ways. In the "Faith Chapter" of the Bible, Hebrews 11, speaking of the example of faith set by Abraham, Isaac and Jacob—"the Fathers"—and of Sarah, we read: "These all died in faith, not having received the promises, but having seen them afar off, and were persuaded of them, and embraced them . . . that they, without us, should not be made perfect." (Heb. 11:13 and 40.)

Had they received the promises by their faith at that time, then you and I would have been left out. But God's promises to them are irrevocably secure! They

461

shall receive them in the resurrection—and many thousands or millions of us also with them.

God has promised to heal the sick, upon real repentance and faith. But God has not promised how, or when! That, we must leave to Him in faith.

We did fully expect that God would heal her now. True, she was seventy-five and a half years of age. Even King David, who has been rescued from death, and healed from near-death more than once, "died in a good old age, full of days," at age seventy. (I Chron. 29:28). In I Kings 1:1, it is stated that "King David was old, and stricken with years," just before his death.

God already had given my wife five and a half years more of this life than He gave David. She was just a few months older than I, though part of each year we were "the same age," as they are counted. Yet neither of us have felt or acted in any manner like "old folks," or "elderly" people. We never thought of her as being anywhere near seventy!

God had called her, and then me through her. He had chosen us for His Work. He had built His great Work through us, bearing great and rich spiritual "fruit." . . .

If you'll read John 15, you'll realize that God corrects, "prunes," or "purges" every branch in Christ which is producing fruit—that they may bring forth more fruit. It is only those bearing none that He cuts off.

This great Work of God not only has produced fruit—but right now God is opening gigantic new doors for His Work to multiply in power!

In our human thinking, it seemed God would heal her now, that she could continue the remaining few years as my help in the closing years of God's Work preparing the way for Christ's coming, and the Kingdom of God, ushering in the wonderful *World Tomorrow!* But, we know now, God had intended otherwise . . . .

To all you who have come to a reawakening through her recent illness, let me plead: Carry on, in this spiritually rejuvenated new life! Never slacken! Never lose courage! Now I need your help more than ever! . . .

June 29, 1967

Dear Co-Worker with Christ:

Since I wrote you, a week ago, things have happened fast. Indeed, world events are racing on now at an ever-accelerating clip.

I want to give you a little advance news, which you will read in more detail in my *Personal* column. Page one, in the July *Plain Truth.* With this coming number, due off the press in a few days, the circulation has reached, at last, the fabulous plateau of one million copies!

It requires about three full freight carloads (large American size freight cars) of paper! Comparatively few magazines on earth publish a million or more copies! That surely is a new milestone of progress! Read more about it in your next *Plain Truth!*

Of that one million copies subscribed for—to be read by probably two and a half million people—about 2,450,000 of them are noncontributors to God's Work. No one pays for his own subscription, as you know. In addition to receiving *The Plain Truth* free, these 2,450,000 people who read it have never contributed— and have never been asked to contribute anything!

In other words, beside helping pay for the *World Tomorrow* broadcast on radio and television, reaching some forty million people every week, your tithes and

463

freewill offerings are helping me to put *The Plain Truth* into the hands of nearly two and a half million readers who are not even asked for financial support!

Actually, it is monumental, phenomenal, and virtually incredible, how much every dollar you and I put into God's glorious Work actually accomplishes! I know of no place else where every dollar accomplishes so much good! That is because the living Christ actually heads, directs, and blesses this Work of God! What a privilege He allows you and me to have a part in it—to be used as His instruments, through whom He works, carrying on God's Work!

One other exciting bit of advance news, which you will read in more detail, in my next *Personal* editorial.

When I wrote you on May 29, I was en route to London, ticketed for a jet flight from London to Beirut and Jerusalem on June 5. I wrote in that letter, ". . . it looks right now as if I will not be able to go to Jerusalem at this time." As I wrote you in the general semiannual letter to all *Plain Truth* subscribers, June 21, I was not able to go. The Israelis took over the old city of Jerusalem, including Jerusalem Radio, belonging to the government of Jordan. . . .

July 31, 1967

Dear Co-Worker with Christ:

This letter should have been written yesterday. Things are happening so fast these days, and I have so many things on my mind, that I completely overlooked the fact this letter was due.

And here it is, the 31st of July. For me it is a very important day—a day of mixed emotions. May I be real personal in this letter? . . .

Today is a day I had been looking forward to. It

464

was to be the fiftieth wedding anniversary of Mrs. Armstrong and me. But she is no longer here to share it with me.

I could not help, this morning, thinking back fifty years ago today. I was living in Chicago. I had been engaged to marry a girl from Iowa. That very morning I disappointed her. I arrived late at the railroad depot to meet her. And there she was, a girl who had never before seen such a big city, alone in the metropolis of Chicago! . . .

Many young ladies would have ended the engagement then and there. They would have become angry, resentful, unforgiving. Because most young brides are in love, most assuredly—but with their own selves! Not with the man they are marrying. And most young bridegrooms also are in love—with their own precious selves!

As soon as the other becomes inconsiderate, or does something, or says something, that "steps on the other's toes," the "injured" one flies into a rage, or becomes sullen and resentful. One thing leads to another, and ultimately to an unhappy marriage—or divorce!

But this young lady forgave me, and later that same day she became Mrs. Herbert W. Armstrong.

This is not to say that in the virtual fifty years of happy marriage there were never any rough spots, misunderstandings, or hurt feelings. There always are, in every marriage. And unless each one is mindful of that fact—mindful that each is human and imperfect—and has enough love for the other to forgive and forget, it would be better to call the whole thing off before the wedding.

Why do most marriages fail? Two reasons. They are not really in love, though of course they think they are. They do not, each, have as much love and concern for the other, as for self. They want the other for what they feel the other means to them. They are on the getting side, not the giving! And when everything ceases to come their way, and the time comes to give, they don't give. And the second reason is part of the first—carnality!! And carnality is vanity, lust, envy and greed. . . .

But since I am a day late with this letter, I must make it brief. . . .

Thank you—I do remember you constantly in my prayers!

December 10, 1968

Dear Co-Worker with Christ:

Today I can announce this big news at last! Now it's official! I have said before I expected to announce it soon.

Jesus Christ is not dead—He rose from the dead—He is alive right now, actively directing this Work of God—and this is the season more than any other, when He needs these gifts for His Work! He has blest us by drafting us as His Co-Workers. We have our part to do!

And speaking of Christ being alive! That is what this big announcement is all about! And even though I need to get this urgent letter off to you immediately, I feel I must take time to tell you what He has just done for His Work!

Let me give you the background facts first. God originally chose Jerusalem as His city, to become eventually the capital of the whole world. But when He removed Judah (the Jews) from their land, He said: "I will remove Judah also out of my sight, as I have removed Israel, and I will cast off this city which I have

466

chosen, Jerusalem." (II Kings 23:27.) God turned His back on Jerusalem. . . .

And today it is heap upon heap of . . . rubble and filth. All this is going to have to be cleaned away before it can be made, after Christ's coming, the capital city of the world. Then for a thousand years it will be the most beautiful, clean city of splendor on earth.

Briefly, let me tell you how it started. The first seven and a half years of King David's reign, Hebron was the capital city. This is a few miles southwest of Jerusalem. But God had chosen Jerusalem to become the capital. It is recorded in II Samuel 5: "And the king and his men went to Jerusalem against the Jebusites, the inhabitants of the land. . . . David took the stronghold of Zion, that is, the city of David. . . . And David dwelt in the stronghold, and called it the city of David. . . . And David became greater and greater, for the Lord, the God of hosts, was with him. And Hiram king of Tyre sent messengers to David, and cedar trees; also carpenters and masons who built David a house" (a palace).

That city of David was the original Jerusalem. Later, Solomon rebuilt, or greatly enlarged, the palace. Solomon also built the Temple. The Temple was probably the most glorious, costly building ever constructed on earth. It was built on a rectangular plateau. Mount Moriah, high above, and directly adjoining the city of David on the north. As the city of Jerusalem grew, it spread to the west and north of this Temple Mount—or Mount Moriah. Near the center of this Temple Mount is a large rock. It was on this rock that Abraham built an altar, when God tested him to see if he would obey even to sacrificing his own son (type of God sacrificing His Son Jesus). This also was the rock used as a threshing floor by Ornan the Jebusite. At God's com-

467

mand, King David purchased this from Ornan. This same rock was the site of Solomon's Temple. Also of Zerubbabel's temple in the days of Ezra and Nehemiah. That Temple was remodeled, renewed and greatly enlarged by Herod—the Temple in Jerusalem during Jesus' lifetime. It was destroyed in A.D. 70.

That same rock is in the very center of the present Moslem mosque, called the Dome of the Rock.

On the south side of this Temple Mount a great massive stone wall was built from the ground below at, or just north of the City of David. This wall was perhaps fifty feet or more high. The original inhabited part of Jerusalem was far below at that point. Long after Solomon's palace and the Temple had been destroyed, Gentiles built other buildings on the rubble. Succeeding generations built on that rubble. As a result, the surface at this site of the original Jerusalem and City of David is perhaps forty to seventy feet higher than it was when David first built his palace there.

Now I can explain to you this important announcement. Ambassador College has just been given the great honor and responsibility of entering joint participation with Hebrew University of Jerusalem in the most important archaeological excavation of our time—uncovering 3,000 years of history! We are now actively engaged—Ambassador College and Hebrew University—in excavating down, layer by layer, removing the accumulated rubble and filth of century after century of Gentile occupation!

Hebrew University is recognized as the top center of scholarship in the Middle East. It is a large university of 12,000 students. Like Ambassador College, its students are serious, studying with purpose. Like Ambassador, there are no hippies, and no student rebellion, or student riots. The fact that they are Jewish and we are not makes no difference (we do have a few Jewish students at Ambassador). This great archaeological project is under the direct supervision of Dr. Benjamin Mazar, one of the world's recognized outstanding experts on archaeology, former President of Hebrew University.

Now I wonder if you can realize how important this is!

First, it is one of the most important scientific projects under way anywhere on earth today. It will mean great prestige and recognition of Ambassador College. If some wonder why we need recognition by the world, remember that we are commissioned to go into the world to preach the gospel. We have to deal with the world. We have to obtain the use of the world's facilities—radio broadcast time on their radio facilities, television facilities, and publishing facilities when we buy large advertising space in the great mass-circulation magazines. This is increasing the readership of *The Plain Truth* by hundreds of thousands. Without favorable recognition and status in our "public image" we simply could not carry out Christ's commission!

Secondly, we are contributing to the known fund of knowledge!

Thirdly, we are preparing the way for Christ's coming as King of kings and Lord of lords—as world ruler, to set up the government of God to rule all nations—and to save the whole world!

How are we preparing the way for Christ's Messianic coming? In three ways. 1) by proclaiming and publishing worldwide the gospel of the kingdom of God (Matt. 24:14; Mark 13:10). This we have been doing for thirty-five years, with constantly increasing and multiplying power! 2) by making ready a people for His coming! These are "the elect" (Matt. 24:21-22) for

469

whose sake God will save humanity alive! Otherwise "no flesh would be saved alive" in the great tribulation now almost upon us! Thousands are being converted—their lives changed—receiving Christ as Saviour, and receiving God's Holy Spirit—every year.

And 3) something that even I did not realize until recently we were also commissioned to do—clean up the filth and rubble in that area that was the original Jerusalem and City of David (actually several acres of ground—this is a major operation of excavation).

Why is that important? Because Christ has said He will yet choose Jerusalem, and make it the capital city of the whole world tomorrow! Jesus is coming in all the supernatural power and glory to rule the world. His throne will be there. Do you not suppose it will be in the very spot He chose for David's throne? Jesus is to sit on David's throne! Where was David's throne? It was on this very spot where we are now cleaning up and hauling off the rubble of century after century of accumulation! And even David is to be resurrected! That is the spot we are cleaning up! So there is a physical preparing, as well as spiritual, in preparing the way for Messiah's coming! Further, God says we are to shout, with amplified power, to the cities of Judah the glad message that the Messiah is soon coming. This is leading to the opportunity to do this (Isaiah 40:1-11).

That is all I have time to say now. I must rush this letter into the mails.

75

September 28, 1970— April 12, 1971

September 28, 1970

Dear Fellow Co-Workers:

I'm writing you from 38,000 feet, over a desolate portion of Australia, en route from Sydney to Singapore. With two other officials in this great Work, we are on a very important round-the-world trip.

I have said for some time that the big world news from now on will be centered on and around Jerusalem. We haven't been getting full details of the present Middle East crisis in Australia. And because I'm so far away it is necessary to write this letter about a week before you will receive it. . . .

Events of the last few days could be leading into a chain reaction of events that would threaten immediate world war. Such a war could—except for supernatural intervention by the "unseen Hand from someplace" probably would—blast all human life off the earth. . . .

A day or two ago, the United States fleet in the Mediterranean moved quickly to the eastern Mediterranean, ready to fly large numbers of Marines, probably parachute troops, into Jordan. The guerillas threaten to kill all Americans, and destroy all American property in Jordan if the U.S. intervenes. Of course the principal reason the U.S. forces have moved up close to Jordan is to block the U.S.S.R. from moving in, as well as to be poised for any emergency. Meanwhile the Israeli forces are on instant alert as of September 23.

This is a serious world crisis. It could explode into a world war at any moment.

Meanwhile, we must put on the pressure, and speed up the great Work the living God is doing through us, for it is yet far from finished. Since we cannot know how much time we have left, we are laying long-range plans for ten years ahead—in case we may be allowed that much time—but also we are planning to speed up the Work as fast as funds allow, in case we may have no more than fifteen months or so remaining.

Now about the present trip. . . .

From England we flew on to New Delhi, capital of India. A conference had been arranged with the Prime Minister, Mrs. Indira Gandhi (daughter of former Prime Minister Nehru). However, she was at the time in Nairobi, in Africa, attending the Congress of Unattached Nations. So Dr. Singh, secretary to the President of India, V.V. Giri, arranged for me to visit the President. Even he was away at the time, in Bangalore, in the far south of India. We were entertained at a luncheon at Dr. Singh's official residence. Arrangements were made for us to fly to Bangalore, en route to Singapore. The President's personal car, with the presidential flag flying at mast in front, met us at the Bangalore airport. . . . There we had a nice visit with

472

President Giri. I presented him with a small gift, and a copy of the college students' yearbook, *The Envoy.* He, in turn, presented me with a large photograph of himself, in a handsome silver frame with his special presidential monogram at the top. President Giri promised to come to Pasadena to speak before an assembly of our students. I have devoted my next *Personal* page in *The Plain Truth* to our visit in India. You may read the rest of it there.

Mrs. Gandhi had expected to see us, and I was told that if we could remain or return on the 18th, we could have a meeting with her. However my own commitments did not allow, and so we were invited to return in December.

At Singapore, we visited a number of top officials. The Prime Minister was in Europe, but while he was away the second in command was the Minister of Education. He already had a copy of our booklet *This Is Ambassador College,* and I presented him with a copy of *The Envoy....*

At Singapore I was invited to be the speaker at a Rotary Club luncheon. I was followed by a very brief speech by a prominent local member, head of one of the colleges. I was surprised to hear him say he was a subscriber to *The Plain Truth,* praising it highly, telling the local Rotarians they should all become subscribers. I am also writing an article for *The Plain Truth* about Singapore.

We have just visited our offices in Sydney and our printing plant there, and we also flew over to New Zealand to see our office, and staff, there....

While in Sydney ... we were able to host a reception in a private room in our hotel last evening. Present were about thirty executives of radio and TV stations, newspapers and magazines. One local newspaper had

473

given us a rather bad image in Australia, and at this reception I was able to speak to all these executives for about twenty-five minutes, completely correcting all the misconceptions that had been given out by an uninformed hostile newspaper. Handling things in this manner is very vital to this great worldwide Work. Last evening's reception was of untold value of the Work.

Just now we are flying back to Singapore. I was to have had a conference with the President of Indonesia, but he was in Europe when we were in Singapore. So arrangements were made to see him tomorrow, at Djakarta, the capital of Indonesia. We preferred to go back to the same hotel in Singapore where we were a week ago, and just hop on over to Djakarta and back tomorrow—it's a short distance by our jet aircraft from Singapore.

Today is Wednesday. Friday I have a conference set up with the President of the Philippines, at Manila. Then Saturday night we plan to fly across to Hong Kong, where a meeting is arranged with the Governor-General. From there on to Tokyo. I have been informed that at Tokyo Prince Makasa, brother of Emperor Hirohito, has invited ... me, with his wife and my daughter who are with us, to be dinner guests of the Prince and the Princess, his wife. I am to address a group of some 300 college and university professors, which the Prince is arranging, while in Tokyo. Plans are now developing for the opening of our Work to reach the Japanese people. . . .

I am especially grateful that we have been provided with our own jet aircraft, for I could not make these important commitments otherwise. I have before my seat on the plane a built-in bookcase with an electric typewriter that lets down. I can write as we fly. It is my office in the skies. I arrive fresh and alert, but on smoke-laden commercial planes I have always been very fatigued at destination after long flights. . . .

It is certainly providential that I have been invited to meet so many world leaders, and heads of state in so many nations that are of prime importance right now, with world conditions moving as they are. I have sought none of these meetings, yet the invitations come. They are aware that through our media of *The Plain Truth,* our broadcasts, telecasts, etc., we reach and influence into the hundred millions of people worldwide, and it is significant that I have been given favor in their sight. Naturally they want to favorably impress me, for they know I am going to write about our meetings.

Co-Workers, I think this gives you an idea of the tremendous progress of the Work. As world conditions worsen rapidly, heading on into the grand smash climax that will end this age and this society, this Work is speeding up, as never before, to get the job done, before it is too late. . . .

We cannot know, now, just how much more time we have. But this we do know—we must get back of this great Work to our utmost, as never before! Our great reward is not far ahead, now. And in the meantime getting the job done is all that matters!

Thank you for your prayers—fervent, earnest prayers—and your interest and sacrifice.

October 28, 1970

Dear Fellow Co-Workers:

. . . When I wrote you a month ago, I was in our jet aircraft, returning from Sydney, Australia to Djakarta for my conference with President Suharto, of Indonesia. An appointment had been set, but he was unable to see me until the following day. On that following day I had

475

an appointment with President Marcos of the Philippines at his palace in Manila. I felt it incumbent on me to keep that appointment, and so was unable to wait over in Djakarta.

I had an important meeting with President Marcos. And while in Manila, President Suharto tried personally to reach me by telephone to arrange a meeting the next day. Prior commitments did not allow time to fly back down to Djakarta. Result, I am now scheduled to meet General Suharto the middle of December.

In Tokyo we met Dr. Binyamin Mazar, Director of our big archaeological exploration in Jerusalem, and also Professor Werblowsky, of Hebrew University of Jerusalem, who is professor of Comparative Religions. They were invited with us to the dinner hosted by Prince Mikasa (brother of Emperor Hirohito), and his wife and daughter. Next day, at 2 p.m., we met the Prince at the palace grounds. He took us first to the palace office building, where a number of candid camera shots were taken. Then to the beautiful new palace, completed since I was there two years ago.

Then at 4 p.m. I addressed a group of the very top professors of several Japanese universities, arranged by Prince Mikasa. The professors invited were those whose principal area of interest is the Middle East. All were greatly interested in archaeology. After I spoke, Dr. Mazar showed them many slides of our archaeological project.

In my talk before them ... I mentioned the following:

About 150 years ago, leaders of science decided the human mind was so near perfect that society could safely discard its swaddling clothes, throw away the "crutch" of religion, and reliance on God. Science had come to the place it could deliver the world from all evils. Given sufficient knowledge, science could solve all problems, they believed. So gradually moral and spiritual values were dropped. Colleges and universities began putting emphasis solely on the intellect, and instruction in the professions, technologies, and sciences. World Wars I and II shot moral and spiritual values to the cesspool.

As scientists and educators added to the world's fund of knowledge, the world's troubles and evils increased. During the past ten years knowledge doubled—and likewise, troubles and evils have doubled in the same decade! Today world-famous scientists are frankly frightened. It is now possible to erase all human life from this planet. Human survival is the number one world problem. Scientists and heads of state say publicly the only hope is a super world government, and at the same time admit its utter impossibility. . . .

I told them how, if we are to place credence in the Hebrew Bible, the entire fault in the production of knowledge took place in the Garden of Eden, in the account of the "forbidden fruit," or the "tree of the knowledge of good and evil." The Creator had set in motion an invisible but inexorable law to cause every good result. That invisible spiritual law is the cause of all good. Its transgression is the cause of all evils. When Adam took of the fruit of the tree of the knowledge of good and evil, he took to himself the divine God prerogative of producing the knowledge of what is good and what is evil. Rejecting the revealed knowledge of God, and disobeying that Law revealed by God, man became an adversary of God, and always has tried to decide for himself what is right and what is wrong. All his knowledge production has been of the way of life that transgresses that cause of all good. Consequently his knowl-

477

edge production has brought only evils. As knowledge increases, so do the problems and evils.

I told those scholarly professors that they are betting their very lives on the existence of the Creator God, and His soon supernatural intervention in world affairs, to save humanity alive. No one sneered or jeered. Those high-ranking professors were sobered. They know world conditions. They knew what I said made sense—it was the truth.

Afterward, Prince Mikasa talked to them for some fifteen or twenty minutes, saying some very nice things about my address.

Co-Workers, this new turn of events throwing me personally into direct contact with heads of state of many great nations is highly significant. It is a door through which God is, I feel, using me to get His warning message to the leaders of nations. It is an additional signal of the fast-approaching end, and the soon coming of the living Christ as King of kings, setting up the government of God to rule all nations.

World conditions are worsening as never before. You know that! This great Work of God must now leap forward as never before! . . .

Tokyo, Japan
February 27, 1971

Dear Co-Worker with Christ:

I have just returned to my hotel from a forty-five-minute audience with His Imperial Highness the Crown Prince of Japan. Last Tuesday and Wednesday I was in Okinawa. I had gone there at the suggestion of Prime Minister Sato of Japan. It may well be called one of the trouble spots of the world.

When I was here in December an anti-United States riot occurred there on the day of my arrival.

478

Okinawa is the principal U.S. military base between the U.S. and the Vietnam war. Entire island is under U.S. military government. Some 800,000 Okinawan citizens are Japanese people. The whole government is scheduled to revert back to Japan next year.

I interviewed the Japanese Chief Executive there, Lt. General Lampert, who is High Commissioner and President of the University. I also spoke at a banquet there to some thirty-five leading citizens and their wives. I will say to you what I said to them:

I am now completing my third round-the-world trip in six months. Everywhere I find troubles, high tensions, frightening evils, problems that governments cannot solve!

In Jerusalem I had a long talk with Mrs. Golda Meir, the Prime Minister. She explained the high tensions between Israel and the Arab nations—they are merely in an armistice. Actually the '67 war has not yet been settled. Jerusalem, as I have told you before, will become the number one news issue in the world.

At New Delhi last December, Mrs. Indira Gandhi, the Prime Minister, explained to me in a half-hour interview the overwhelming problems of starvation and death, poverty, illiteracy, filth and squalor. And besides, thousands of refugees were pouring daily into India from both East and West Pakistan—poverty stricken and needing to be taken care of. It is a pitiful and hopeless situation.

In Nepal I had interviews with both the King and the Crown Prince. They told me of their insolvable problems of getting education and other help to the isolated mountain people.

At Bangkok I had a fantastic audience with the King of Thailand—formerly Siam—in which for an hour and a half he poured out his heart to me of the

479

problems in his country. It was a heartrending, emotional experience, difficult to keep the tears back. He said nobody could help him with these overwhelming problems and burdens unless I, perhaps, personally could. He said, with some emotion, he would welcome any ideas, suggestions, or help I might be able to give and asked me to come again.

At Manila, in September, President Ferdinand Marcos told me of the serious problems they have in the Philippines and what he is doing to help. But, of course, it is only a start. Everywhere I find on personal contacts with heads of nations, the world's troubles, problems and evils are completely beyond the human ability of kings, presidents, prime ministers or their governments to solve. . . .

You and I are shouldered with that gigantic commission to prepare the way for the intervention of that strong hand that will usher in at last the happy, joyous and peaceful World Tomorrow. You and I are having a part in changing the world and in saving the whole world before all human life is blasted from this earth!

Isn't that honor and responsibility worth sacrificing for? Nothing else is important anymore.

I am doing my utmost to carry out my part. Giant doors are being opened before me and I am walking through them. But I can only do my part as you make sacrifice and generously do your part. It is urgently needed in the most important work on earth!

I Visit the War Zone
Saigon, South Vietnam: March 16, 1971

At the suggestion of Ambassador to South Vietnam Ellsworth Bunker, I decided to visit Saigon, war capital of South Vietnam. You will ask the same question I first asked him: "Is it safe to fly into Saigon?"

"You are more safe than you would be on the streets of Washington, D.C.," responded the Ambassador. Actually, many government officials in Washington, and many senators and congressmen, have visited Saigon.

This is Tuesday afternoon, March 16. We flew over here from Manila this morning, arriving shortly before noon. En route from the airport to our hotel, I was surprised to see so little evidence of the war. I was mostly impressed by the congested traffic. Automobile congestion was heavy. But for every car there were two to four "Hondas"—Japan-made motor bikes.

"Before the war, everybody rode bicycles," said an American now resident in Saigon, who met us at the airport. "Now everybody rides motor-bikes and automobiles. They have to pay cash for them, too. No time payments."

"They must be sold at a low price," I suggested.

"No, they cost about three times as much as they would in the U.S., due to the heavy tax."

Since the partitioning of North and South Vietnam, the same thing has happened here that happened in East and West Berlin, East and West Germany, North and South Korea. Noncommunist South Vietnam has prospered economically—Communist North Vietnam has not.

"How much of this new South Vietnam prosperity has come from United States dollars?" I asked.

"About 99.98 percent," grinned my Saigon friend. It has come from American "aid," and from G.I. spending. Traffic moves slowly, through mid-day, and almost not at all during morning and evening rush hours. Saigon is a city listed in our aircraft atlas as having

481

about 1,750,000 population. But locally they claim four million now. But the unbelievable thousands of motorbikes and automobiles are a spectacle to behold.

At 2:15 this afternoon we left, in company of our two American local-resident friends, for an interview with the Minister of Social Welfare in the Government of the Republic of Vietnam, Dr. Tran Nguon Phieu.

I asked Dr. Phieu—he's a medical doctor—what was the main social welfare problem in Vietnam, and what effect the war was having on it.

"Refugees," he responded quickly. "More than a million have been rendered homeless by the war. And then, orphans—that is, fatherless children, whose fathers have been killed in the war. They still have mothers, but most mothers, who formerly remained at home, are now forced to work, while the men fight—or, widows whose husbands have been killed. And this is destroying the Vietnamese family structure."

"And," I added, "when a nation's family structure breaks down, that is the beginning of the destruction of the nation." The doctor nodded assent.

Refugees—women leaving the home and working—family life breaking down—juvenile delinquency! I have found this, it seems, EVERYWHERE in the world recently. . . .

The drug problem is acute here in Vietnam, too. But although it is illegal to sell marijuana (or hashish) here, the bigger problem in Vietnam is opium. This is spreading among our American G.I.s even more than among South Vietnamese soldiers. There is a serious problem of education here, too.

There has not been, up to now, a system of compulsory education in the elementary grades, but compulsory education will soon begin. As it has been, many children will run away from home to *avoid* school. Then it becomes a problem after two or three drop-out years. They cannot start in again with others their own age. And often it is impossible for them to go back and start over.

Why is it? The most wonderful thing we can know in the material creation is the human mind. Why are so many mentally lazy? Why do so many resist educating their minds? Why do so many "blow their minds" with dope or drugs—ruining their minds beyond reclaim? Why?

Here, as elsewhere, there is a tragic shortage of teachers. . . .

And now I have to come back to my interview right here in Saigon with Dr. Tran Nguon Phieu, Minister of Social Welfare of the Republic of Vietnam.

"If the war should be over—or, looking toward mid-year 1972, when President Nixon says the American troops will be pulled out of here—what do you envision as the social welfare problems then?" I asked.

"They will worsen," was his grave answer . . .

Jerusalem, Israel
April 12, 1971

Dear Co-Worker in the
Greatest Mission on Earth:

Once again, I am in this remarkable "new" country, Israel. From now on, Jerusalem will be the pivotal center of world news. While here, I want to bring you up-to-date on the almost unbelievable, exciting, and momentous things now happening in this great Work.

Giant doors have been opening before me, one after another, with invitations for personal conferences with heads of state—presidents, kings, prime ministers—and many others in high offices of power, in many countries

483

around the world. The remarkable thing is that I did not seek or initiate these meetings—not once! I was invited.

Do you realize how impossible it is for anyone, except those in official capacity, to initiate and obtain a personal private conference with a chief of state? These people occupy offices of great power in the world. They are all surrounded by the most effective and well-organized security systems. No one except their own closest secretaries or ministers is ever allowed to contact them direct, either in person or by telephone. Nobody, except those in official office with official business, ever gets to see them, unless personally invited by the head of state, or unless most carefully screened, checked on, approved by secretaries, and then, finally, approved by the chief of state. If I, by my own initiative, had tried to arrange all these many personal meetings and conferences, it would have been utterly impossible! . . .

Even though the time has come, in this great Commission, when it is necessary for me to have these personal meetings, there is absolutely no way I could have taken it into my own hands and accomplished it. It had to come like a continuous chain of miraculous occurrences. And it is having tremendous significance to the finishing of the most important Commission on earth in 1,900 years!

Of course you've been reading, in *The Plain Truth,* of some of these meetings with the world's rulers. And many more such articles and reports are coming in future issues. Then later, I will take you into my confidence and give you the exciting facts of the incredible circumstances, and the surprising providential manner in which these giant doors have opened before me, one after the other in time order.

These very important meetings have suddenly catapulted the entire Work up onto a new and higher plateau! The Work has moved suddenly into a totally new phase! These providential new developments signal the warning to you and to me that we do not have much time left to get done the most important job on earth in 1,900 years! We have now been moved into the last and final phase of the Work for this age!

Before I tell you more of that, however, I want to inform you of the tremendously important happenings to the Work right here in Israel.

I am here this time to make final arrangements for the arrival in June of seventy-five of our Ambassador College students. They are coming to work for the summer on our huge archaeological project in Jerusalem. As you know, we are in joint participation with Hebrew University of Jerusalem and the Israel Archaeological Society in the largest, most important such project of our time—probably of all time.

We are not only uncovering 3,000 years of buried history. We are clearing off the accumulated rubble, decay and debris—some fifty to sixty feet high—over the very throne of David—in the original Jerusalem of 3,000 years ago, also known, then, as the City of David. The biblical prophecies of Isaiah 9:7-8, of Luke 1:30-33, and of Amos 9:11, say that the Messiah—the returning Christ in supreme and total supernatural power and glory—is soon, now, to rule the entire earth—all nations—from that very spot! What a providential thing it is, that we are clearing it off—preparing the way for His coming, in this, as well as in other ways!

And here's another exciting and important development: I am here also to confer with officials of the Hebrew University Institute of Urban and Regional Studies. Ambassador College now is in a joint-participa-

485

tion with this institute in a city-planning project, designing and planning the Jerusalem of the future! The probability is that for the remainder of this age, the government will adopt the planning we recommend.

Still another very important development here: I am here also to consult further with Mayor Kollek of Jerusalem. He was our guest at Ambassador College in Pasadena only eleven days ago. . . .

It's hard to realize how this Work—in which you and I are privileged to be Co-Workers—has grown to such worldwide power and scope! It is exerting tremendous impact on more than 150 million people around the world. That is about every twentieth person on earth! . . .

Until recently we had reached, in this Great Commission, primarily the grass roots—the masses of the common people—the ruled. But in this greatest mission in 1,900 years, it now has become necessary that we get directly to those in top positions of power—at the top—the rulers! The Work had, of necessity, to begin where it did. The time now has come when those who wield the power must also be reached! Of myself—or with the human ability of our entire organization—it would, indeed have been impossible! . . .

In the June number of *The Plain Truth*—and I hope we'll be able to print and send out such a vast number of copies—I'll give you my report on my conference with Mrs. Golda Meir, Prime Minister of Israel, and also of Mrs. Indira Gandhi, Prime Minister of India. I will give you my own close-up personal portrait evaluation of those two outstanding women— sitting in seats of tremendous power in a very sick, war-inflamed world! . . .

486

76

May 28, 1971—
July 1971

Dear Inner Family of Co-Workers:

I am able, now, to disclose to you privately and confidentially the almost unbelievable manner in which giant doors have been opening before me. As you know, one after another, the doors have opened for personal meetings with presidents, kings, prime ministers—and many other high government officials, in many countries around the world.

As I wrote you a month ago, all of a sudden this great Work has been catapulted onto a new and high plateau! It has been moved into a totally new phase.

So many high-level personal conferences could not have opened to one in private life, in so short a time, by mere happenstance. I could not have planned them and brought them about if I had tried! As I now disclose these astonishing circumstances, I think you will see the providential guiding Hand maneuvering them!

As I mentioned in my previous letter a month ago, the Work of necessity had to begin by reaching the grassroots—the masses of the common people—the ruled. We now are reaching more than 150 million of them. Think of it!—that is one in every twenty-three of all the people on earth, or one in every sixteen persons above age fourteen.

But we have reached the point where it has now become necessary that we reach also the rulers—those in the very top echelons of power in the world. Because, whether we have realized it or not, this Work is the greatest, most effective activity on earth for world peace!

Actually this new phase in the Work began about three years ago.

Here is "Coincidence" #1: The wife of our office manager at Bonn, West Germany, happened to show a copy of the 1966 Ambassador College year book—*The Envoy*—to an industrialist friend in Brussels. He was much impressed by the book, and the high character of Ambassador students, reflected in their photographs and action shots. This industrialist happened to be a personal friend of King Leopold of Belgium. He asked if he might show *The Envoy* to the King. The King was quite impressed, and said he would like to meet the founder and Chancellor of this unique high-character educational institution.

His request was passed on to me through the manager of our Duesseldorf office. That was the first I knew of this. Through the Brussels industrialist a meeting was arranged.

That is how the first such meeting came about. On my first visit, the King asked me to come again. During

488

the past three years a cordial and warm affection has developed. And also a fifty-fifty collaboration in scientific expeditions between King Leopold's Belgian Foundation and Ambassador College.

Now, "Coincidence" #2: In September, 1968, our Dean of Faculties wanted Ambassador College to conduct an archaeological project at a location in Israel. I was personally not interested in such a project. But I consented to visiting Jerusalem to see whether permission could be granted from the government authorities.

He found Dr. Mazar at the time in charge of the most important "dig" so far undertaken, starting from the south wall of the Temple Mount. Three major United States universities had sought participation in this outstanding project. All had been rejected. But Professor Mazar offered a fifty-fifty joint participation to Ambassador College! . . . About mid-October (1968) I did fly to Jerusalem to look over this project. The "dig" had been begun a few months before. I met Professor Mazar and inspected the project.

It was much more impressive than I had expected.

I began to realize the scientific and educational value to Ambassador College. A luncheon was held in a private dining room in the Knesset—the government's capitol building. Present at the luncheon were five high-ranking officials of both the university and the government.

It was a most memorable luncheon. The favor we were given in their eyes—the warmth of their attitude toward us—was inspiring, astonishing, and most unusual. The Israeli Minister of Tourism and Development, Mr. Moshe Kol, proposed that we build an iron bridge that could never be broken between Ambassador College and Hebrew University. After two and a half years that "iron bridge" has been greatly strengthened.

I did not make final decision, however, at that time. We agreed to meet again in Jerusalem on December 1, for final decision. Meanwhile, Dr. Mazar, with Dr. Aviram, Dean of the College of Humanities at the university, came to Pasadena, and visited also the Texas campus, to look us over. They liked what they saw. And on December 1, at the official residence of Israel's President, Zalman Shazar, we made the joint participation official.

I did not learn until later that we were actually clearing away the decay, rubble and debris—some fifty to sixty feet high—over the very spot where prophecy says the returning Messiah—Jesus Christ—is to rule the whole world. Tremendous things have happened in this relationship since.

So that is the manner in which this vitally important leap forward in the Work was started. We have been given very great favor in the eyes of both government and university chiefs in Jerusalem!

Now, "Coincidence" #3: After our midOctober meeting in Jerusalem in 1968, . . . I caught a Pan Am round-the-world plane for Hong Kong and Tokyo, for conferences with advertising officials of *Reader's Digest.* We had begun purchasing double-page advertising space in many editions of their magazine around the world. Arriving Tokyo airport, we were met by our . . . Chairman of the Department of Asian studies at Ambassador. . . . He was acquainted with Prince Mikasa, brother of Emperor Hirohito. Unkown to me he had shown the 1966 *Envoy* to the Prince, and the Prince had expressed a desire to meet me. . . . The Prince had asked me to be his guest at luncheon the following day. . . . We also were introduced at that time by the Prince to his very charming and lovely wife.

This first meeting with Prince Mikasa has led to

other important meetings. I did not visit Tokyo again until last September. But when Prince Mikasa learned I was coming, he, his wife and daughter planned a dinner in my honor. Also he arranged for a meeting with some sixty leading professors from various Japanese universities, which he invited me to address.

The meeting with Prince Mikasa has led to a number of things vitally important to the Work. It is paving the way for opening the Work in Japan on a big scale. And unlike all other nations so far, we are starting in Japan from the top down—and reaching the 100 million Japanese people as a whole will come later, hopefully by midyear.

It led to further contacts with the most important educators in Japanese universities. Perhaps the highest ranking educator in Japan is Dr. Nobumoto Ohama, former president of Useda University. His reputation is worldwide in educational circles. He is to speak at Ambassador College in Pasadena this coming September.

Incidentally, these meetings are beginning to result in bringing many world leaders to Ambassador College to speak before our students.

Also my acquaintance with Prince Mikasa led to my forty-five-minute private conference with Prime Minister Sato in December. Privately and confidentially, Mr. Sato requested me to go to Okinawa in February (the tension was too hot to go on the December trip). And I did go. This has already been reported in *The Plain Truth*.

I think it pertinent to say to you, here, that private meetings with heads of state on this high level are something vastly different than a handshake with a crowd of tourists—or, for that matter, even magazine or newspaper correspondents. A magazine correspondent or editor may, on occasion, have a private conference with a head of state. But he does not meet the ruling official on an equal level.

An interesting example of this, was an incident that occurred during a reception at the residence of the United States Ambassador of Nepal this past February.... I had just returned from a visit with King Mahendra at the palace. We were hosting a dinner for important local men and their wives at the hotel that evening, but stopped off at the reception to which we had been invited.

The Ambassador in Kathmandu happens to be a lady, and her husband is Ambassador Ellsworth Bunker at Saigon—U.S. Ambassador to South Vietnam. He and his four or five chief assistants were in Kathmandu for the weekend.

On learning that we had just come from meetings with the King, and with the Crown Prince the evening before—following meetings with President Giri of India, and Prime Minister Golda Meir of Israel—and on the previous trip with Prime Minister Indira Gandhi of India—at which time King Leopold was traveling with us—and that two days later we were to have a private meeting with the King of Thailand (Siam)—this government official looked puzzled, and asked, "Well how in the world do you do it? We've been trying for six months to arrange meetings with some of these people, and yet we haven't been able." And they had the power and prestige of the U.S. government!

I couldn't tell him how I arranged these meetings—because I didn't! Could you believe a Higher Power than the United States government opened these doors?

I had been invited to visit Kathmandu, the capital of Nepal, and visit King Mahendra, because my good friend Dr. Singh, official Secretary to President Giri of

492

India, had wanted me to do so, and unrequested by me, had arranged it.

And that was "Coincidence" #4. And at that "chance" meeting with Ambassador Bunker he urged me to see him at his embassy in Saigon. And that was "Coincidence" #5. That has been reported in the May *Plain Truth.* . . .

And when you realize the doors have opened before me for eight such meetings in six months, you can believe it has been a series of providential or miraculous circumstances!

"Coincidence" #6: I will take space to tell you of just one more. On our December trip, King Leopold accompanied us from Brussels to Athens, New Delhi, India, Singapore, and Djakarta. At Djakarta, my planned visit with President Suharto had to be postponed because the King of Thailand (Siam) was there on an official state visit. This required President Suharto's entire time. He had scheduled a meeting with King Leopold (who was on a private, nonstate visit, with us), for the following Monday, and wanted to see me then. But I had meetings scheduled in Manila and Tokyo, and was unable to remain over that long.

But a special dinner was held on Tuesday night in Djakarta, attended by six or eight of the chief officials under President Suharto, and their wives. That night I was simply too exhausted to attend—the only such appointment on any of these trips I was unable to attend. My elder daughter has been accompanying me, since there have been many such occasions, and she takes her mother's place as my hostess.

At this banquet, my daughter became acquainted with Mrs. Sunirat Telan of Bangkok, who had accompanied the King of Thailand on his state visit. Mrs. Telan owns the Rama Hotel in Bangkok, besides at least two more skyscraper hotels, and some large Thai industries. When she learned from my daughter that we had never visited Bangkok, she insisted that we simply must see Bangkok on our next tour, in February. She wanted to host a dinner in my honor, and wanted me to meet the King.

And that chance meeting with my daughter is the manner in which the one and a half-hour visit with the King of Thailand, this past February, came about. I did not seek it—I was invited! . . .

One thing more I will tell you, then I must not make this letter longer.

Last November King Leopold, his wife, Princess Liliane and daughters—the Princesses Daphne and Esmeralda—visited us in California. They were dinner guests in my home. After dinner that evening the King and Princess Liliane asked for a private talk. We excused ourselves from the other guests and retired to a private room.

Then in subdued, solemn and hushed tone they told me that, after World War I had ended, the King's father, King Albert, had visited one of the battlefields. He was appalled, and emotionally sick at heart at the realization of the human slaughter that had occurred there. It moved him deeply. He had one of the iron cannonballs remaining on the field melted and cast into four watch cases—pocket watch size—to encase four fine watches. It was his intention to present these to the four men whom he felt had made the most significant contribution toward world peace.

World War I was the war supposed to "make the world safe for democracy"—the war to end all wars! King Albert therefore felt the chief generals and French Premier contributed most, and gave one watch to Field Marshal Foch, Supreme Commander in Chief over all allied armies. The second watch was given to General Pershing, Commander in Chief of all United States forces. The third went to Georges Clemenceau, Premier of France during World War I. King Albert apparently found no one he felt qualified for the fourth watch. It was passed on to his son, King Leopold to give.

In solemn and subdued voice the King said he felt the fourth watch, in a red leather case now showing age, should go to me. Both the leather case and the watch are embellished with a gold design with a royal crown in the center.

I feel it was the very highest honor the King could have paid anyone. Whatever contribution to world peace I may have made you have shared with me, and it has not been through war, but through education, teaching millions worldwide the way to peace! And I believe King Leopold feels, and that he saw here, that we have set an example by the real peace that we do have on our three campuses! He has visited both the Pasadena and English campuses.

Co-Workers, something very great is being accomplished through this great Work, in which you and I are both privileged to be Co-Workers. It is a greater power working through us that is producing peace, and happiness, and abundant well-being in ever-increasing thousands all over the earth! And truly, this Work is leading the way into world peace!

This greater power is opening more and more important doors for finishing the Work for this age. I am walking through them in faith and confidence. My life is dedicated to this Work, and doing my part diligently. But it takes your part, too—and the whole Work can go only as far and as fast as you do yours.

The financial condition, the past year, has been very serious. I feel we are slowly on the upswing once

495

again. We have weathered a very serious financial storm—our rate of gain the past two years has been slowed—but the Work has survived, even grown slowly, and now it needs seriously the biggest push we can give it. Let's make every sacrifice to give it the big push! God bless you for your part—I am very grateful—and I must remind you the need is now very great.

Visit with Prime Minister Golda Meir
June 1971

Is it significant of this time, that growing girls and young women are reflecting increasing qualities of leadership, while young men are evidencing less and less?

Every college president, I am sure, has become painfully aware of this modern trend. The young people born since World War II are, indeed, a new breed.

Today three nations, one of them modern Judah, are ruled by woman Prime Ministers. They are Mrs. Golda Meir, Prime Minister of Israel; Mrs. Indira Gandhi, Prime Minister of India—second largest population in the world—and Mrs. Sirimavo Bandaranaike, Prime Minister of Ceylon.

In the past few months I have had personal meetings with two of these ruling women—Mrs. Meir and Mrs. Gandhi. Each told me of the overwhelming problems that beset her. It seemed to me that these problems are too stupendous to have to come crashing down on the shoulders of a woman.

Never before has the whole world been embroiled in such weighty, apparently unsolvable problems. It is indeed a frightening world in which we live today. The fact that these are women of exceptional abilities does not lessen the burden.

I have said before, and I say again, Jerusalem is

destined to be the focal point—the nerve center—of world news from here on out. And on the human level, the destiny of the Israeli people is presently in the hands of a woman.

What are the crushing problems that confront her?

What kind of woman is Mrs. Meir?

I am able to answer both questions much more intelligently since spending forty-five minutes with the Prime Minister in her executive office last February 7. She told me her problems, and how she views them. And after this personal contact, seeing and hearing her at close range, I understand much better than before what kind of woman she is.

Of course I was previously aware generally of Israel's problems. But I had not previously seen them through her eyes, as she views them. Also I had observed Mrs. Meir in extended television interviews, as have millions of others. But seeing her in person, chatting with her, listening to her in real life, gave me a much clearer perception of her as she really is.

In one sense Mrs. Meir is most certainly no ordinary woman. Yet, paradoxically, that is because she *is,* after all, such an ordinary woman. She is small of physical stature. From having seen her many times on television, I had expected to see a taller woman. But in character and ability she is of unusually great stature.

Without apology to anyone, I have to attribute to this so common, yet so uncommon a woman, humanly, the quality of greatness, such as is possessed by so very few—if any—men in public life today.

Emphatically, that is not flattery. I never flatter.

Why do I attribute the almost non-existent quality of greatness to Mrs. Meir!

Because she is humble. Because she is just an ordinary, plain, down-to-earth, unpretentious homespun woman and mother. She puts on no airs. She makes no effort to impress anyone. No pretenses. But to lead His people Judah, the Eternal God of Abraham, Isaac and Jacob has bestowed on this daughter and mother in Israel an exceptionally intelligent, capable, balanced and understanding mind.

She has that rare quality of seeing things precisely as they are. Her vision is in sharp focus. Her mind pierces through the extraneous and confusing details to the central important point. She remains unconfused by the labyrinth of branches and twigs, and has the trunk of the tree in clear view.

One man, well experienced in worldwide political affairs, said "the subject of world peace is a very complicated one." I was very happy to observe, in our conversation, that it is not at all a complicated subject to Mrs. Meir. To her, peace is a very simple matter—if leaders and their peoples were *willing* to have it. For forty years I have been presenting the subject to the world as a very simple one. There is a *cause* for every effect. The way of life that will cause peace is what I term very simply as the "give" way; and the world insists on living the "get" way.

I was quite impressed by the fact that when speaking of soldiers risking their lives for her country, this woman sees them through a *mother's* eyes. Yes, Mrs. Meir is common clay—a mother, a former Milwaukee, U.S.A. school teacher who loved and taught children. Yet at the same time she is a capable executive of firm purpose and uncompromising, unbending will against what she sees is wrong. For with all her common, down-to-earth qualities is joined the quality of firmness and determination . . .

But now, what did she say? What happened in our meeting?

498

It has been custom for thousands of years to present a gift when visiting a king or ruler. I presented Mrs. Meir with an original crystal sculpture, made exclusively for her by Steuben. She seemed very pleased with it, commenting that she did not deserve something so beautiful. She had received other pieces of Steuben— one from Governor Nelson Rockefeller of New York. . . .

Mrs. Meir was already well informed about Ambassador College, and our joint participation in the great archeological project, and also in Mr. Kol's international youth movement.

I asked Mrs. Meir what Ambassador College could do to promote peace and understanding in the Middle East.

The Prime Minister then spoke at some length in answer to my question.

"What Israel wants," she said, "is really quite simple. It's as simple as two plus two equals four. Yet other nations and other peoples seem to be able to understand Einstein's theory of relativity more easily. What Israel wants is peace, and this seems to others to be so very complicated."

Mrs. Meir said that Israel must remain free and independent within secure borders in order to continue to provide a haven for all Jewish people.

"We must be free," she continued, "to provide a place for people who have been persecuted throughout the world for so many centuries. Only Israel has been willing to receive with open arms so many people from so many places. In the last fifteen years Israel has received more than 800,000 people from the poorest areas of Africa and Asia. They were people who were ill-fed, ill-clothed, illiterate, in poor health. Some actually came from dwelling in caves in Libya.

"And yet," she explained, "with such human mate-

499

rial, Israel has been able to create useful citizens. They have now learned a new language. They have learned to live in a modern society. They are now well fed, reasonably well clothed, gaining education. Their children will be even better educated, more useful to themselves and their new homeland country, and will live fruitful and fulfilled lives."

When these people—destitute refugees—arrive in Israel, they are immediately housed and cared for. I learned a good deal about this program on my second visit to this remarkable new country in 1966. These poverty-stricken newcomers are given jobs. Often they have to live in tents at first. But they are paid, and given instruction on saving a portion of their wages. In a reasonably short time they are able to move into a house or flat. As I now remember it, they can buy their own flat on the installment plan, and it is to a considerable extent subsidized by the government. Some are taken into a kibbutz.

Mrs. Meir made a special point of another astonishing achievement.

"An extraordinarily high infant mortality rate plagued these immigrants before their arrival in Israel. There was a correspondingly high death rate of mothers in childbirth. But now one may contrast those figures with what is one of the lowest infant mortality rates and mother childbirth death rates in the world."

Then she told us of the Israelis' ability and willingness to help their Arab neighbors. This small but remarkable nation now sends its experts and its technology throughout the deepest parts of Africa and to even more remote places in the world to help under-developed nations.

"How easy it would be," she said earnestly, "to send the same teams across the border into Jordan, or

500

across the canal into Egypt, and how much prosperity and happiness would be brought to this entire area of the world by peace. . . ."

"We don't want to have to go on winning more and more victories," she added. "We only want peace. . . ."

I would like to mention, at this point, that I feel King Hussein would gladly welcome such peace, cooperation and help in improving his people. Three times I have had appointments set up for a personal meeting with King Hussein. Each time a war incident prevented. Once he had unexpectedly been called away from Amman in an emergency. Another time, war conditions made it unsafe for me to go there.

I have read King Hussein's autobiography. He was educated in England, and also in Cairo, as well as in Jordan. There is much to admire in him. He yearns to help upgrade his people and improve their status in life. Above all things, he is an Arab at heart, and that is the principal reason he went along with President Nasser in fighting against Israel. I personally feel Hussein would have been glad to make peace with his Israeli neighbors, and have entered a cooperative arrangement for the benefit of his people. But his dedication as an Arab, and the political pressures from Cairo and other Arab capitals, prevented. Hussein also is under constant pressure from within his own country. . . .

What a deplorable tragedy that the whole world cannot *now* have the kind of peace, with prosperity and happiness that Prime Minister Golda Meir expressed a desire for—each nation cooperating with its neighbor.

But the reason is summed up in the biblical statement: "The way of peace they know not." There has, of necessity, to be a cause for every effect. There will have to be a cause to produce peace. That cause is a way of life.

501

It is the way Mrs. Meir said she would like to see in practice with Israel's neighbor, Jordan—the way of cooperation! It is the way of outgoing concern for neighbor equal to self-concern.

For the past forty years I have taught that way. Thousands of lives have turned to it—been changed— and now set the living example of peace!

Today in this great Work of which you and I are a part, we proclaim that way to 150 million people—one in every twenty-three people on earth. Today on three college campuses we practice that way, and we are setting the living example of peace—three campuses where there is radiating happiness, beauty, harmony, and no protest, riots or violence.

Many are beginning to recognize that this is the most effective contribution toward world peace in active operation on earth today.

Mrs. Gandhi Tells Me of
Her Frightening Responsibilities
July 1971

One of the most horrifying calamities ever to visit masses of humans—as one of numerous problems to solve—has just fallen on the shoulders of a woman.

The whole world was shocked as news headlines told of the mounting mass deaths caused by the cholera epidemic hitting victims from East Pakistan fleeing into India.

Last December in my personal meeting with the Prime Minister of India, Mrs. Indira Gandhi told me of the crushing burden of the problems that are her responsibility. One of her most serious problems was that of the Pakistan refugees, then at the rate of about 1,500 per day, streaming across the border into India—desti-

502

■ *Linked by satellite and microwave network to dozens of halls and auditoriums worldwide, Mr. Armstrong addresses more than 100,000 during annual Church conclave.*

Senior students in conversation with the Chancellor.

■ *A lighter moment in conversation with Egyptian President, Hosni Mubarak, top. Above left, President of Israel Yitzhak* Navon receives a personal protocol gift from Mr. Armstrong. With children in Liberty Bell Park, Jerusalem.

■ *His Majesty King Bhumibol Adulyadej of Thailand and Her Majesty Queen Sirikit receive Herbert W. Armstrong in 1984. Mr. Armstrong became acquainted in 1971 with the many agricultural, engineering and cultural projects of Their Majesties on behalf of the Hilltribes and rural and needy Thais. As a result of the royal projects, opium growing has been reduced 95 percent. Medal bestowed on Herbert W. Armstrong by Her Majesty on occasion of the royal visit.*

■ *Enjoying a light moment, Prince Mikasa of Japan and officials of the Mideast Cultural Center in Tokyo examine artifacts the Ambassador Foundation helped the Center to acquire. In the office of Prime Minister Nakasone of Japan. Children in Summer Education Program in Australia.*

■ *At the typewriter on the Grumman Gulfstream III working on* Mystery of the Ages, *the last book written by Herbert W. Armstrong.* The Plain Truth *appears in Norwegian, Spanish, Dutch, French, German, Italian. All seven languages are printed compatible each issue—a quantitative challenge no other magazine has undertaken to date.*

■ *Holding up the*
50th anniversary
issue of The Plain
Truth *at the R.R.*
Donnelley and Sons
Printers in Kentucky.

■ *Mr. Armstrong did* World Tomorrow *television programs into the beginning of his ninety-fourth year.*

■ *Teleprompters
were long in use
when Mr.
Armstrong's eyesight
failed. Here are
first pages of scripts
written by his hand
in his ninetieth to
ninety-third years.*

■ *The Honorable Deng Xiaoping, leader of China and Honorary Chairman of the Soong Ching-ling Memorial Foundation, greets Mr. Armstrong as Chairman of AICF. King Birendra of Nepal received Mr. Armstrong in November 1984. In conversation with President Jayewardene of Sri Lanka.*

■ *Her Majesty Queen Sirikit of Thailand explains to Mr. Armstrong and staff the goals of the royal cultural projects among the Hilltribes in Northern Thailand.*

■ *Her Majesty Queen Sirikit toured the United States in March, 1985. The Queen visited Ambassador College in Pasadena March 19 to 26 and honored Mr. Armstrong with a most special royal gift.*

■ *The Ambassador International Cultural Foundation sponsored a tour of the United States for China's Little* *Ambassadors of Shanghai. Top, a visit with "Grandpa" Armstrong on the Pasadena campus* *of Ambassador College. A highlight of the tour at the White House with First Lady Nancy Reagan.*

■ *The formal presentation of* Mystery of the Ages *to students at Pasadena. Cutting the ribbon, left, on walkway by the Library; enjoying piano playing in his home.*

THE WONDERFUL WORLD
TOMORROW
WHAT IT
WILL BE LIKE

The
Incredible
Human
Potential

This is the eye-opening story of the real gospel message
of Jesus Christ—of how this missing dimension was
withheld, and the whole world deceived.

THE
MISSING
DIMENSION
IN SEX

HERBERT W.
ARMSTRONG

THE
UNITED STATES
AND
BRITAIN
IN PROPHECY

Herbert W. Armstrong

MYSTERY
OF
THE
AGES

Did you ever ask yourself: "Who am I?
What am I? Why am I?" You are a mystery.
The world about you is a mystery.
Now, you can understand!

HERBERT W. ARMSTRONG

■ *Though most of his writing was in the form of advertisements,* *magazine articles, booklets and broadcast scripts, Mr. Armstrong summarized his literary work in* *these five volumes— and, of course, the* Autobiography.

■ *In the last summer of his life Herbert W. Armstrong traveled to Des Moines, Iowa, his hometown. Joseph W. Tkach, Mr. Armstrong's designated successor, visits with him at airport. The official portrait of Joseph W. Tkach.*

tute, helpless, for her overburdened government to feed, clothe and house.

Then, since my visit with her, the Pakistani problem erupted as if "all hell had broken loose." East Pakistan exploded into civil war. The refugee problem was increased to an overwhelming extent. Then, late May, the cholera epidemic started, spreading to a gigantic calamity in early June. On top of this, the monsoon rains broke over eastern India June 5. By that time Indian estimates were that the spread of cholera had already killed 5,000 refugees in India who had fled from East Pakistan.

Mrs. Gandhi had flown promptly to Calcutta to obtain first-hand information on the raging epidemic. She had appealed to other nations for help. Medical aid was being air-lifted to Calcutta and Eastern India from Britain, the United States and other countries. On June 5th three Indian States, Meghalaya, Tripura, and Assam, sealed their borders against further refugees. Inside East Pakistan, with no medical aid, conditions were reported worse. Huge refugee camps were quickly organized to prevent spreading the cholera epidemic into Calcutta and other cities and towns.

I happen to be writing this month's personal in Israel, where seventy-eight Ambassador College students have just arrived to spend the summer working on our huge archaeological project west and south of the Temple Mount in Jerusalem. And this is as far east as I will go at this time. I have no desire to investigate personally the cholera area. Last night the International Cultural Center for Youth staged a special program to welcome the Ambassador students. Ambassador is a joint participant in this cultural center for youth as well as in the archaeological project. The center was founded by Minister of Tourism Moshe Kol and Eleanor Roo-

503

sevelt. Tomorrow night is a special dinner in my honor being given at the King David Hotel in Jerusalem....

Last December, when I had the meeting with Mrs. Gandhi, rumors were rife about Mrs. Gandhi's "supposed" turn toward the left, and her "supposed" autocratic tendencies. I had been told I would find her cold, haughty and overbearing. The prediction was made of an impending clash between her and leaders of the conservative opposition.

Quite the contrary.... We found Mrs. Gandhi very warm and cordial, with a charming personality and welcoming smile.

And within a very few days after our visit she, in fact, dissolved parliament and announced that elections would be held forthwith. When we were passing through New Delhi again in February, she was away from the capital, campaigning shortly prior to the election, which she won with a landslide victory. Her power has been consolidated to a degree totally unexpected from her opposition.

When she received us in her office at the Parliament in New Delhi, I presented her with a piece of Steuben crystal. Before I could open the distinctive Steuben red leather gift box, her face lit up with a happy smile, and she exclaimed: "Ah, a piece of beautiful Steuben." She said she had always admired Steuben crystal. Her father, the late Prime Minister Nehru, had received several gifts of this type of art. It is often given to heads of state....

I then explained to the Prime Minister of the second most populous nation on earth that Ambassador College would like to send its television crew to do a television documentary on India. Mrs. Gandhi responded that she would welcome an Ambassador College television production on India. I had promised her that it would present India's problems fairly and honestly and in an educational manner.

Mrs. Gandhi then expressed great interest in the Ambassador College agricultural research program at our Texas and English campuses. In answer to questions I explained at some length these activities and the gratifying results being achieved.

I then asked the Prime Minister to tell us about India's problems and also her problems as Chief of State—and of progress being made. She then spoke, uninterrupted (except by notes being handed to her by a secretary of the arrival of cabinet members for appointments with her). But she rejected interruption and spoke for the next twenty minutes in answer to my question.

She explained first that India does have immense problems of every description. There are no problems confronting mankind that cannot be readily found without effort in India. But she was deeply concerned that journalists, television producers and commentators, and other writers and observers, fail to note carefully the way India is attempting to cope with, and improve, each of the problems. Also, they too often fail to report the progress that India has made during her brief history as an independent nation since 1947.

Mrs. Gandhi explained that most of India's problems stem from immense population, its enormous birthrate and its agricultural resources—or its lack of the same. For the sake of comparison, she noted India gives birth each year to a population equal to the entire population of Australia. India is making every effort to lower the birthrate, but education and time will be needed.

There have been agricultural reforms. Much progress in agricultural production has taken place but there have been significant setbacks because of the natural elements. As irrigation becomes more widespread, many of the agricultural needs will be alleviated. In the meantime, India is grateful for the aid received from the U.S. and elsewhere.

The Prime Minister was very much interested in Ambassador College's worldwide educational extension program, and she noted that the educational needs of India should be significantly helped by such a program. But that, again, much time would be needed to correct India's educational system. Efforts had been made to make education compulsory, but the means of enforcing the compulsory education were not readily at hand. . . .

I mentioned, or possibly she noted independently, our association with Hebrew University in Jerusalem, and a brief discussion ensued about the kibbutz system. She seemed to suggest some interest in the adaptability of such cooperative efforts in India.

Mrs. Gandhi said that India has been confronted with an ever-increasing problem of refugees from East Pakistan. These refugees were then coming into India at the rate of some 1,500 persons per day. Most of them find their way to Calcutta and make conditions there, already bad, increasingly worse. She called our attention to the increasing political and civil strife in East Pakistan and also Calcutta as a result of this refugee problem.

Democracy, Mrs. Gandhi insisted, will prevail in India despite the rumors to the contrary. She said that she believed very strongly in democratic institutions herself and was confident that they had been successfully adopted by her people.

I then alluded to the Palestinian refugee problem in the Middle East. I advised Mrs. Gandhi of Ambassador College's efforts to promote world peace and understanding everywhere and explained how Ambassador College had given assistance to the Jordanian Government refugee problem through the purchase of radio time. Also I advised the Prime Minister of our support of the International Cultural Center for Youth in Jerusalem where young Arabs and young Israelis are brought together and taught to respect the customs and traditions and individual differences of the other.

I then explained that I had recently visited with Deputy Prime Minister Allon in Israel and that Mr. Allon had sent his very warmest regards to Mrs. Gandhi and expressed great admiration for her and her father, Mr. Nehru. Deputy Prime Minister Allon had asked me to convey to the Indian Prime Minister that he was deeply concerned that India did not have diplomatic relations with Israel and was, therefore, unable to learn firsthand about Middle East problems as viewed from Israel's vantage point. Mrs. Gandhi shrugged and explained why the government of India was unable to establish diplomatic relations with Israel. She expressed admiration for Israel as well as sympathy for Israel's difficulties, but she said her problems were very much complicated in relation to Israel because of Pakistan, which is a Muslim state.

Mrs. Gandhi said that she had heard very nice things about Ambassador College and myself from President Giri and from her minister of information. She said that she would look forward with great interest to our articles about India, and to a *World Tomorrow* television production dealing with India's problems today. She then extended a warm invitation for us to return.

77

March 26, 1972— June 1973

Dear Inner Family of Co-Workers:

I am writing while our plane is being refueled at Teheran, Iran (which is Persia). We are en route from Colombo, Ceylon, to Israel. Now our engines are starting up. I will have to fold my typewriter back up into its place until we are airborne.

In Ceylon I had a . . . meeting with the Prime Minister, in the living room of her official residence, Friday afternoon. Last night (Saturday night) my daughter and I . . . were guests at dinner at "Queen's House," residence of the Governor General. It is really a palace—quite huge for a private residence. It was built over 400 years ago by the Dutch, when they were in control of Ceylon, before it came into British hands. Ceylon is now independent, but a member of the British Commonwealth. The Governor General is appointed by Queen Elizabeth of England.

508

We had been invited to Ceylon by the Prime Minister, Mrs. Sirimavo Bandaranaike, through the Ceylon High Commissioner (same level as Ambassador) to India, at New Delhi. The High Commissioner accompanied us on our plane to Colombo. I will give you a report of the meeting with the Prime Minister in the *Personal* article in the May *Plain Truth.* I just thought in this more personal and confidential letter to our inner family of Co-Workers you might enjoy some of the more personal highlights.

At the dinner at "Queen's House" last night besides our party, were the Governor General and his wife, his Chief Aide and wife, and the High Commissioner of Ceylon from New Delhi.

This morning, we brought the High Commissioner with us as far as Bombay, where he caught a commercial flight back to New Delhi. We have had to make the one fuel stop between Bombay and Israel, at Teheran. While we were on the ground at Bombay, one of our Indian Co-Workers who is a mechanic with Indian Airlines, recognized our plane, and came aboard for a few minutes' visit. I have met him two or three times before. His daughter graduated from Ambassador College, English campus, and until her marriage was also a faculty member.

Earlier, at New Delhi, I had another visit with President V.V. Giri, and also a meeting with our U.S. Ambassador Keating. He is the former Senator from New York. I am sorry that there have recently been more or less strained relations between the Governments of India and the United States. For that reason protocol made it inadvisable for me to see Mrs. Gandhi, the Indian Prime Minister, when I had had a talk with our American Ambassador on the same visit.

However, at New Delhi we were entertained twice

at the home of the Executive Secretary to the President, Dr. Singh—and there we met two or three maharajahs, and the Ambassadors from Chile, Argentina, and Sudan, and we received invitations to visit their countries in South America and Africa. . . .

On this present trip, we left Pasadena Monday, March 6, flew out to Honolulu, stopped overnight, then Tuesday morning flew (one stop for fuel at Wake Island) to Tokyo. We did not disembark, but Dr. and Mrs. Ohama came aboard our aircraft and flew with us to Seoul, Korea. Dr. Ohama is the leading educator of Japan, and perhaps the leading nonofficial adviser to the Government. He has visited both our Pasadena and Texas campuses, and addressed the student bodies.

I had never been to Korea before. Dr. Ohama and I had expected to have a meeting with the President of Korea, but, as frequently happens with heads of state, emergency matters came up that prevented. However, I did have a very fine meeting with the Minister of Education and his two chief aides. . . .

We flew back to Tokyo on Friday. Had dinner Saturday night with the new Ambassador, from Israel, and his wife. Had tea with them at their Embassy Sunday afternoon. Had tea with the Emperor's brother, Prince Mikasa, on Monday afternoon at his palace. On Monday night we were guests of two of the most influential Members of the Diet (the Japanese governing body—Congress-Parliament), both of whom had accompanied Prime Minister Sato on his trip to San Clemente (the Western White House in California) for the meeting with President Nixon. . . .

The big day was Wednesday. About eleven in the morning, we were driven to the House of Representatives office building, where Mr. Bunsei Sato (no relation to the Prime Minister, but a leader in the

Diet), together with Mr. Keiwas Okuda, the other Diet Member who had visited our Texas campus, joined us and took us to the Japanese national capitol building.

There, Minister of Commerce and Industry Tanaka, considered to be the probable next Prime Minister, excused himself for about fifteen minutes from a very important conference, to meet me. He invited me to have a longer meeting with him on my next visit to Tokyo. I also met the Minister of Pollution (the official title uses a different word), the Secretary of the leading political party, and another top ranking Diet Member—a Mr. Ishii, a graduate of Stanford University, besides one or two other Diet Members. We had lunch in the Diet building restaurant.

Then, a fourth Diet Member, Mr. Shionoya, whose son is in his second year at Ambassador College, Pasadena, joined us. And these four leading men of the Japanese Government accompanied us to the Prime Minister's official residence for my meeting with him.

Prime Minister Sato reminded me at the outset, that this was a very historic occasion. When I first had a meeting with him, in December, 1970, the newspaper headlines were blaring forth the news of the great riot against American forces on Okinawa. The Prime Minister had asked me to visit Okinawa, on my February, 1971, trip—which I did, and wrote an article on my survey there in *The Plain Truth*. The Prime Minister thanked me for the help I had given, and reminded me that immediately following our meeting, which was in his private office, he was to step into an adjoining conference room where the U.S. Ambassador and staff were to exchange the ratification instruments with the Japanese Foreign Minister and staff, legally affirming the reversion of Okinawa back to Japan. This

511

was the big moment in Prime Minister Sato's administration. We visited with him for some forty minutes, leaving at ten minutes to 3. As we left, the United States delegation were driving up. Their meeting was scheduled for three o'clock. It was the big news on front pages next morning. . . .

Meeting with President Suharto of Indonesia
November 1972

At last, the long-awaited, twice-postponed meeting with President Suharto took place, yesterday morning, in Djakarta.

We flew on here today, en route to Jerusalem, where eighty of our Ambassador College students have been working this summer on the giant archaeological project adjoining the Temple Mount. Then a stopover at our campus in England, a luncheon visit with King Leopold, and then back to Pasadena.

At this point we are approximately halfway around the world on the present trip. We really had a most interesting and profitable meeting with General Suharto. . . . I wanted to know what President Suharto's plans were for keeping the Communist forces out of Indonesia. Any Communist takeover there would imperil the entire free world. That is a major reason why President Suharto is of vital concern to the United States, Canada, Britain and Western Europe.

The first time I had a meeting set up with the General he had been called to Europe. The second time a meeting was planned, the King of Thailand was in Djakarta on a state visit, and of course that required the full time of the President. He had been desirous of seeing me all along, and this was made doubly evident

512

by the warmth of the reception at this meeting yesterday morning.

If you could be with me in meetings with heads of governments in different parts of the world, you would have an altogether new concept of the insurmountable problems facing this whole, very sick world today. These heads of governments tell me of problems beyond their human power to solve . . .

Before I tell you of the things President Suharto and I discussed, I think you might be interested in a brief description of our arrival at the Presidential office building in Djakarta.

Yesterday morning, at 8:45, we arrived at the Presidential office building in Djakarta. Immediately it was evident that the President was expecting us. At the entrance of the building we walked into a battery of official and press photographers, and a number of Presidential staff members. The Chief of Protocol stepped forward to greet us. The signing of the official guest book was carefully documented by a staccato of flashbulbs.

First we walked into a reception room and talked briefly with the Chief of Protocol and the Presidential interpreter, while awaiting General Suharto's arrival.

Remember that President Suharto is the leader of the fifth largest nation in population [1972 figure]—with a population in Indonesia of approximately 125 million. Indonesia is one of the richest countries in the world in natural resources, but, as yet, one of the least developed. Incidentally, you might understand better where and what Indonesia is when I tell you we used to call it the East Indies. It composes many islands, the largest of which are Java, Borneo, Sumatra, and the western part of New Guinea. If you have an atlas, I suggest you look at the maps to locate this important nation of Indonesia. Djakarta is a short distance south of the equator, and not too far northwest of Australia. It is in the far Southeast Asian district, south of Burma, Thailand, Malaysia and Singapore. I know how most people are unfamiliar with geography and the location of continents and nations on this earth on which we live.

Shortly, we were ushered into the President's rather large and well-appointed office. The smiling President met us at the doorway with a very warm greeting.

I thanked him for giving official approval for our forthcoming scientific expedition into the Irian, that is, the western portion of New Guinea, and for the cooperation given by the Indonesian government to King Leopold of Belgium, when he was there planning the expedition. I've mentioned previously the joint participation of Ambassador College with the Belgian Foundation, headed by King Leopold, for the exploration of land inhabited by Aboriginal peoples, the study of these peoples, and other activities in the field of anthropology.

We then moved over to a seating area, where I was seated next to the President. I then presented him, as is customary in visiting a head of state, with a small gift—a fine piece of American Steuben crystal. This presentation brought on a flurry of activity by the official photographers—as there had been when I first shook hands with the President. . . .

President Suharto explained his country's policy of National Resilience. This is a program of united mobilized people's efforts to improve the country's economic, social and military position, in order to

514

withstand successfully the continuous effort by subversive forces, supported, if not directed, in large part from outside the country.

Indonesia is largely one of the undeveloped and very poor countries. Mr. Suharto emphasized the efforts being made to relieve the conditions of poverty and misery and discontent—and the continuing effort by the government to show the people the proof—the evidence—of the benefits of the national policies. He urged that other nations in Southeast Asia adopt the same policy of National Resilience to insure their social, economic and military growth in the face of subversive elements, and to improve the standard of living of their peoples, and promote peace everywhere.

As this man, responsible for the welfare and the future of some 125 million people, continued to tell me his problems, and his efforts for peace and for the betterment of the vast number of his people, I had to think, in my own mind, of the magnitude of these problems—and the complexity of the thousands of factors with which he is trying to cope.

General Suharto is having to work to try to improve, or change, the conditions of poverty, illiteracy, and misery of the vast majority of 125 million people within the framework of this world's pattern and ways of society—its ways, traditions and customs of living—the ways and traditional methods of dealing with other nations. . . .

President Suharto faces the evils of poverty, illiteracy, degeneracy of mind and body, people living, or rather eking out an existence, in misery and the lowest of living standards. President Suharto didn't cause these evils. They were there before he was born. He inherited them. So he set in order this policy of National Resilience in an effort to improve

515

the country's economic, social and military position....

June 1973

On this present trip around the world, now almost ended, I have been discussing important domestic and world problems once again with a number of heads of state. But just what is the connection between the conditions and problems of the governments around the world and the gospel of Jesus Christ?

The connection is very vital! If people knew just what the gospel of Jesus Christ is, they would understand that very important and urgent connection....

...Christ's gospel was the good news of the Kingdom of God. It has to do with the evils confronting the world's peoples, which the governments in the world have tried to cope with, but have been unable. It has to do with the way people live—with the cause of all the world's evils—and it has to do with the solution that will be made—and the government that will bring peace and universal, right education and prosperity and abundant, joyful well-being to the peoples of the world! It has to do with the problems faced by heads of state today and how those problems are going to be solved!

Therefore, as the minister of the living Christ, and of his gospel, it is very much a vital part of my commission to discuss these very problems and conditions with those closest to them, the heads of governments. My commission is not a local one, but a worldwide ministry.

This present trip, almost ended, has been of very special significance and concern in this regard. Also, it has sparkled with interest! There were some personal

516

and human-interest incidents as well as the more serious and vital.

First, we stopped off in New York to break the time-lag of eight hours between California and England. I took a short flight to Washington, D.C., where I spoke to a combined Worldwide Church of God assembly of between 2,000 and 3,000 people. Then I went on to the campus of our Ambassador College in England on March 4. March 5 and 6 I was busy writing and doing a Sunday radio broadcast in our recording studio on campus. Tuesday night, March 6, I attended our college's annual spring concert at the Watford Town Hall. These concerts are given annually by our college, as a contribution to community cultural interest. This year, the concert was provided by the London Symphony Orchestra, with guest conductor Van Remortel and the world-renowned Huddersfield Choral Society, combining with our own Ambassador Chorale.

We left Luton Airport (where we garage our plane when in England) early Wednesday morning March 7. We flew all the way to New Delhi, India that day.

For more than three years we had been planning a series of scientific expeditions, a joint participation between Ambassador College and the King Leopold III Foundation in Belgium. This morning, at last, was the "kickoff" of the expedition. It was to be made in the wilds of New Guinea. We first landed at Brussel's airport where King Leopold and Monsieur André Capart, Director of the Royal Museum of Natural Science in Brussels, also a member of the foundation, boarded our plane. Mr. Capart is one of five scientists participating in this present expedition. The others were to meet them in New Guinea, traveling by commercial airlines.

At New Delhi airport that night, we were met at the plane by the Chief of Protocol of India and the

517

Belgian Ambassador and members of his staff. Because of King Leopold's presence, we were put through immigration and customs with diplomatic speed, and cars were waiting to whisk us to our hotel.

One of the most helpful people in our worldwide work has been Dr. Negendra Singh of New Delhi. He is a recent appointee as judge of the World Court at The Hague—a position of great worldwide power and importance, due to the fact that the nations have feared to defy a decision made by this World Court. The court's sole power is its moral power—but that has proved very great. Prior to his high appointment, Dr. Singh was Executive Secretary to President V.V. Giri of India. He has been a guest speaker before Ambassador College students and faculty at all three campuses.

On Thursday night, March 8, Dr. and Mrs. Singh were our dinner guests at our hotel. On Friday, March 9, was a luncheon in my honor at Dr. Singh's residence. Two distinguished guests present were His Excellency Abdul Hakim Tabibi, the Ambassador from Afghanistan, and the Ambassador from Ethiopia, Getachew Mekasha. Mr. Tabibi was educated in the United States at Georgetown University and George Washington University, and was formerly Ambassador to the United Nations. He invited us to visit his country and his king, Muhammed Zahir Shah, who has ruled forty years. At his invitation, a meeting with the king of Afghanistan was set for a later date.

The Ethiopian Ambassador extended an invitation from Emperor Haile Selassie, one of the best-known rulers in the world, for a personal meeting in Addis Ababa in the near future. Emperor Haile Selassie, known as "the Lion of the Tribe of Judah," has been regarded as a descendant of King Solomon of Judah, through the Queen of Sheba.

He was crowned the 225th ruler in 1930. It was in 1935 that Mussolini's Italian forces overran Ethiopia, in fulfillment of the prophecy in the latter part of Daniel 11:40. The Italians ruled Ethiopia until 1941. Emperor Haile Selassie's appeals to the League of Nations made world news. They were often cited as the warnings unheeded that led to World War II. Ethiopia is rich in biblical history, and I am looking forward with great interest to this meeting with Emperor Haile Selassie.

Also present at this luncheon were several other distinguished guests, including V.B. Giri, eldest son of President V.V. Giri, whom I had met previously.

I have had a personal meeting with President Giri each time I have visited India, once at the governor's mansion in Bangalore, once at the governor's mansion in Madras and all other times at his palace in New Delhi. This visit was no exception.... I, with Dr. Singh, paid another visit to the President at the impressive palace. The President's face lit up, and he stretched forth his hand in a very warm greeting. I had not presented a gift since our first meeting, some two and a half years ago (it is not custom on subsequent visits), but this time I presented him with a beautiful, sparkling piece of Steuben crystal for his desk. We posed together for official photographs. Then we discussed the cooler relations between the United States and Indian governments and his official state visit to Malaysia. In fact, he had just returned the night before and had made special arrangements for our visit without prior notification.

When I visit President Giri, he talks about the serious and tragic need for one hundred fifty million jobs—and of the poverty and other serious problems in the second most populous nation in the world. All nations have problems and troubles. India is no excep-

519

tion. Millions walk around aimlessly, with nothing to do—no jobs. Such problems weigh heavily on officials at the head of national governments.

I am learning more and more about these problems and man's efforts to solve them, in such meetings. And, I am having an opportunity to get more and more of this good news over to those struggling with this present world's problems, through its governments.

I have, in my lifetime, met hundreds of the great and the near great—multimillionaire heads of great industrial corporations, heads of great educational institutions, heads of great banks and governments, and no matter how lofty the position or status, if one is allowed to look deeply into their personal lives, he discovers that they have their personal troubles, disappointments, unhappiness—because they don't know the way! Christ's gospel reveals the WAY—both for the individual and for the nation. But the gospel has not been gotten across to the comprehension of the world! . . .

But my commission is merely to proclaim or teach it—not to force any to accept it. God's own Kingdom and solution to world problems and individual, personal problems is going to come, on schedule—and your believing it or not believing it will neither prevent it nor hasten it. . . .

But back to the trip. . . .

At Dr. Singh's residence I met the younger son of Prime Minister Indira Gandhi. This young man was trained as an engineer in India and trained on the job in the Rolls-Royce factory in England. He is presently embarking on a private enterprise to produce an all-India automobile of the Volkswagen type. His name is Sanjay Gandhi. He extended an invitation to our party to dine at the Prime Minister's home on our trip in May.

520

Dr. Singh also invited us to visit the World Court at The Hague on our May trip.

At 10 a.m. March 11, we were again airborne for Jakarta, on the island of Java, in Indonesia. It was a six-hour forty-minute flight nonstop—lasting virtually all day.

That morning I had come down with the flu and a severe head cold. It was the start of a three-day fast for me. On the plane, I occasionally sipped lemon juice and honey—but took no food. The next day at Jakarta, I ran a temperature of over 102. At Jakarta I remained confined to my room. Jakarta is just south of the equator, and it's steamy hot there. The air-conditioning in my room at the hotel was one of these window contraptions, and it was almost a choice of sweltering or being in an ice-cold draft.

At the Jakarta airport, we were met at our plane by the official Indonesian protocol people, the Belgian ambassador Mr. Georges Elliott, the Belgian economic advisor, and Dr. Sarwono, head of the Indonesian Educational and Scientific Institute, which had helped make many of the arrangements for King Leopold's expedition in New Guinea.

March 12: Due to my flue attack, several appointments were canceled for me. But my assistant Mr. Stanley Rader called upon our friend Mr. Adam Malik, the Indonesian Foreign Minister—second man in the government, next to President Suharto, and until this year, President of the General Assembly of the United Nations at New York. President Suharto was addressing and being reelected by the National Assembly that day. But he sent greetings and his personal best wishes for the success of the expedition and an invitation to visit him on our next return to Indonesia.

That evening, a banquet was held for King Leopold....

March 13: We flew to Biak, in West Irian (New Guinea). It was a five-hour flight, at nearly 600 miles per hour. We must have flown over hundreds of islands, all part of Indonesia, many of the islands as yet uncharted.

At Biak, we were met by a contingent of military personnel, including the general who is administrator for the area. Some of the other military officers had been detailed there to escort and protect King Leopold and the scientists on the expedition. They were going into some of the wildest jungle on earth, among totally uncivilized natives—perhaps headhunters—who may not have seen civilized people before.

We spent about an hour at Biak, had photographs taken and bid good-bye to the King. [The king's party was] to spend the night there, then rendezvous the following day at a place called Djajapura (formerly Hollandia) with the other scientists who had flown there by commercial airlines. From there, the expedition was to get under way.

We again boarded our plane for an approximately five-hour flight to Hong Kong. I was still running a fever, and it had been a rather trying day for me. It seemed very nice to be in a properly air-conditioned hotel room with an even temperature and no drafts. I said that I was going to remain right there until I recovered from the flu.

March 14 and 15: Resting and recuperating in Hong Kong.

March 16: We boarded our plane at 8 a.m., arriving in Bangkok, Thailand (formerly Siam) about 9:30. We were met at the airport by Madam Sunirat Telan, owner of hotels and other enterprises, and also a close friend of the King and Queen and Princess Dusdi Sukhuma. These two ladies have accompanied us in all visits with King Bhumibol Adulyadej. On this morning, we had a meeting with the King at 11 a.m. We were driven to the palace. Having some extra time, we were driven around the city so that we arrived at the palace just before 11.

We were greeted by the admiral who is the King's number one aide. We were first escorted, as usual, into a reception room. Then shortly after, we were shown into the room where the King was waiting for us.

On entering, we were met, as usual, by a barrage of brilliant lights, TV cameras and still photographers. The King greeted us warmly. He expressed great appreciation for our interest and cooperation in the education of the hill-tribe people. He was most happy to report that very pleasing results are being achieved in the area of Ambassador College's participation in the King's program (as part of the Ambassador College Extension Program of Education for all peoples at all levels, getting the missing dimension in education to people worldwide). Not only are the people being taught the true values and purpose of life, but they are also being shown how to do new things with their hands.

They are now replacing the former poppy crops (for making opium) with vegetables, now being canned for the market in newly established canneries. And the people are much happier and better off economically. The Ambassador College motto is "Recapture True Values," and some of these mountain tribes are beginning to do just that.

After the meeting with the King, we were driven directly to the personal residence of Prime Minister Kittikachorn for my second meeting with him within six weeks. He arrived ten minutes late, apologizing unnecessarily, but greeting us warmly and enthusiastically.

He had been detained in an important meeting with his highest officials, dealing on that day with a Communist intrusion at the northeastern border of Thailand (North Vietnam is only a short distance from that point). The Prime Minister was still dressed in his military uniform. On our previous meeting with him, he was dressed in civilian clothes. The Prime Minister's son-in-law, whom we met on the previous visit, was there, talking with us until Mr. Kittikachorn's arrival.... The Prime Minister's son-in-law has a Ph.D. in Education and was trained at Boston University in the United States.

Again the Prime Minister and I discussed the Vietnam cease-fire situation and the future prospects of the new bastion in Thailand against the communist threat in Southeast Asia. Once again he stressed the threat of communism and said he fully expects increased communist efforts against Thailand when the cease-fire becomes more effective in Laos and Vietnam. But he said his people are prepared and vigilant, as well as experienced in dealing with the communist menace.

Prime Minister Kittikachorn then presented me with two beautiful full-color portraits, one of himself alone and the other of himself and his wife. They had just celebrated their forty-second wedding anniversary. I congratulated him, mentioning that my wife had died just 3½ months before our fiftieth or golden anniversary. I had presented him with a beautiful piece of Steuben crystal, which he seemed to like very much.

We returned to the airport, taking with us as guest, as previously planned, Princess Sukhuma, who accompanied us to Pasadena. We returned that same afternoon to Hong Kong. My temperature was gone and the flu had nearly disappeared, but we remained in Hong Kong for the weekend, because our next scheduled meeting was for Monday night in Tokyo.

Monday, March 19: We flew into Tokyo to attend a banquet with Prince Mikasa, brother of Emperor Hirohito, Ambassador Ron of Israel, Dr. Ohata, archaeologist from the university, and six other young Japanese archaeologists and Middle East scholars. They are to participate in the archaeological project at Tel Zeror—an ancient biblical site between the modern cities of Tel Aviv and Haifa. The project is cosponsored by the Japanese government and Ambassador College. Perhaps some of our Ambassador students may be working on this project this summer, as well as on the large archaeological project at the base of the Temple Mount, digging down to the palace, location of the throne of David, in the ancient city of David. This project is sponsored jointly by Hebrew University, the Israel Archaeological Society and Ambassador College.

Tuesday, March 20: We had dinner with the Ambassador from Thailand and his wife, invited by Princess Sukhuma, who was accompanying us, and, of course, who had attended the banquet with us on Monday night. The Thai Ambassador had formerly been stationed at the United Nations in New York and also had been stationed in Bonn, West Germany. One of the children of the Ambassador and his wife had been born in the United States and was educated in a girls' school in Virginia.

March 21: At the suggestion of former Prime Minister Eisaku Sato, we had been invited to make a second visit to Okinawa, where I was guest of honor at a small and intimate banquet sponsored by the governor of Okinawa and the President of the university there.

We were met at the airport by Mr. Matsumura,

525

Director of General Affairs of the University of the Ryukyus, and Mr. Ichimura, President of the university's alumni association and Rector of the university's law institute....

At five that evening, I was visited in my hotel suite by the parents of a girl student at our Pasadena campus, a transfer from the university at Okinawa, on our new exchange program with that university, and also by the father and one of the brothers of a young male student at Pasadena, also a transfer from the Okinawan university.

At six, President Takara of the university came to my suite for an informal chat and renewal of acquaintance prior to the banquet.

At 6:30 p.m., we entered the private banquet room in our hotel, the newly opened Okinawa Hilton. Present were Governor and Mrs. Yara, university President Takara and wife, Mr. and Mrs. Matsumura, Mr. and Mrs. Ichimura, a Mr. Sho, grandson of the last king of the Ryukyus, now a businessman and member of the Board of Trustees of the university. These Japanese women appeared in their bright and beautiful Japanese kimonos....

Both the university president and the governor spoke at some length.... The governor's speech, especially, was full of feeling, sincerity and emotion. He wanted me to convey to former Prime Minister Sato his deep appreciation for his tireless efforts in bringing about the reversion of Okinawa (from the United States) to Japan.

A portion of his deeply felt speech was this: "Please convey to Prime Minister Sato that nothing is lost in Okinawa. We have many problems facing us. But we hope to create a new Okinawa. Please convey this additional message: We believe and desire, because of the friendship of America and mainland Japan, for a better Okinawa—a better tomorrow. The new Okinawa is like a woman expecting a child—it will be painful, but a priceless and precious new life will be born. It will take a long period of patience to create this new Okinawa. The reversion is precious—not because of yesterday—not because of today, but because of tomorrow!"

The Governor said he was expressing his personal opinions and feelings. He had wanted, originally, to be a teacher, so at this important meeting, he was speaking as an educator among educators. He also said that before the reversion, the big goal was to achieve the reversion.

But now that that was accomplished, he had discovered his problems were far greater than they were before. He was then chief executive of the Japanese people under American government and authority. Now that he is Governor, and in authority, he finds that the problems confronting him and his administration are greater than when under the authority of the United States. Problems previously submerged now confront him.

The university President expressed his appreciation over the exchange program of the univeristy with Ambassador College.

I spoke on the problems confronting both Japan and the United States, and the causes of the trade and monetary imbalance, asking for understanding and patience, and asking them to look forward to the world of peace we are proclaiming worldwide. But this was neither the time nor place for a sermon on how that happy result actually will be brought about in the world tomorrow.

However, such meetings and conferences as I have had on this most recent round-the-world trip definitely

527

are paving the way for getting that happy and wonderful good news in great power before the peoples and
nations of this unpeaceful and unhappy world today.

78

September 24, 1973— December 1973

September 24, 1973

Dear Co-Workers in Giving God's
Last Message to a Dying World:

I am writing from Tokyo where I look forward on the night of day after tomorrow, to a very great opportunity. It may be the first time in all history such a thing has happened. I am invited by Prince Mikasa, brother of the Emperor, to explain the Bible—proclaim Christ's gospel of the Kingdom of God—to a most impressive audience. It is the most impressive audience before which I have ever been given opportunity to give Christ's message.

I am informed that what I originally thought was to be a private Bible study with the Prince alone, will now include some fifty or more of the very top people of this nation—members of the government, scholars and heads of universities, and their wives.

I want you to realize how very important this is to the Work of the living God. The Work is moving forward at greatly accelerated pace now, taking on an entirely new dimension in giving God's last message to a dying world in these last days! . . .

In the Bible, a king, or chief of government, often represents and stands for the nation. In one sense when Christ's message is delivered to the heads of government, it has been delivered to the nation.

Jeremiah was sent to kings. Daniel was sent to kings. God called the apostle Paul to "bear my name before the Gentiles, and kings, and the children of Israel" (Acts 9:15).

And now, kings, presidents, prime ministers and leaders of many nations are inviting me.

Last Wednesday night, in Bangkok, capital of Thailand, I was given just such an opportunity. I did not know of it in advance. But a banquet was held in a special banquet room of my hotel in my honor. Present were Ambassadors representing the governments of Japan, Korea, Cambodia, Ethiopia and Israel, the President of the University, and Her Royal Highness the wife of the recent Prince Regent of Thailand, and other important guests.

I was given a very warm—even emotional— introduction, and asked to speak. I had no idea how long I was expected to speak, so I confined it to exactly 12 minutes. But I spoke earnestly and God gave me power.

I will give you a quick summary of what I said:

"One who travels over the world, as I have, is forced to see the pitiful condition in which a majority of all people on earth live—in utter ignorance, deep poverty, semi or total starvation, wracked with disease, living in filth and squalor. I have to ask, why? You

530

people should be concerned about it! We have mind power to fly to the moon and back—yet we find the majority living in such conditions—we can't solve our own problems here on earth—we don't know how to have peace! Why? Even where people are educated and prosperous, they are not happy! Why?

"For every effect," I said, "there had to be a cause. Years ago, I made surveys. I learned people are not happy. Why? I finally found the answer—in the Bible! It's a book people have refused to understand—which people have interpreted all out of natural and intended meaning—but taken for what it plainly says I found it makes sense—and answers the big questions! It contains the missing dimension in knowledge. The world doesn't know: What we are—why we are—the purpose for which humanity was put on earth—how to fulfill that purpose. What are the true values in life? What is the way to peace, universal abundance and happiness? Those are the basic things we need to know! Those are the necessary things to know which man, science, technology cannot discover! Those are the things the Bible reveals."

Then I covered the incident of the "forbidden fruit"—how our first parents rejected God's revealed knowledge, which He had started teaching them—how mankind cut himself off from his maker, and has turned to imaginary and false gods, how man ever since has tried to reason out what is good and what is evil—what to do and how to do it—and has brought on humanity this colossal tragic mountain of human woes and anguish! Then I explained God's way of life—the way of "give"—of love which is outgoing concern for the good of others—of cooperation, instead of competition, strife and violence—because mankind has cut itself off from God.

"As Adam and Eve disbelieved God, rebelled, and disobeyed His inexorable spiritual law—sinned—so now man, by repentance of that disobedience, and faith which is to believe God and His Word, can be reconciled to God and receive eternal life." Then I explained how "Christ is coming again as the divine Messiah in supernatural power to rule all nations, and lead nations in God's way, which will bring world peace, abundance, happiness, and eternal life as God's gift."

Twelve minutes is not very long, but they did get the message! And there was a very enthusiastic response! It did make important people think—and want to know more!

On this present trip, I spent one week in Lebanon. I had important personal meetings with President Franjieh (several hours with lunch), the Prime Minister (we talked for an hour and ten minutes), the Foreign Minister, and the Minister of Education. . . .

We were welcomed at Beirut airport in VIP manner. Our meeting with the President and First Lady was on Friday at the summer presidential palace, high in the mountains, and a two-hour automobile drive from Beirut. Our entire party was invited.

No other visitors were there. The President had reserved this entire day for our visit. We spent about an hour, before luncheon, in explaining about our Work, the truth we teach, and going through an Ambassador College annual publication, *The Envoy,* which the President carefully went through page by page. . . .

The Prime Minister had to be seen on Saturday morning. He had just returned the night before from the Conference of Nonaligned Nations at Algiers. But, my visit with him was really to go into phases of the gospel, and for an hour and ten minutes, we were remarkably in accord in regard to principles and philosophies. He, too, surprised us with a remark, "Your appearance and physical presence denote your character and the nature of your activities. Great men accomplishing important things bear their age well."

On our last Saturday night a special reception and dinner was held in my honor at a very large building on the outskirts of Beirut, facing the sea. Among other things, it contains a large casino. . . .

The reception and dinner was held on a very spacious veranda on the second story, overlooking the sea and the lights of the city. It was a warm evening, and delightful in the open air. Many important people were present, to whom I was introduced. At dinner, I sat with a Dr. and Mrs. Charles Malik. Dr. Malik is a former President of the General Assembly of the United Nations, New York, and today he is a member of the cabinet and legislative body. He asked many questions about Ambassador College and our worldwide Work, and seemed pleased.

As a coincidence, I also know Mr. Adam Malik, also a former President of the General Assembly of the United Nations, and Foreign Minister of Indonesia. He is President Suharto's right hand man, and second in authority in the government of Indonesia. I have visited him in his home in Djakarta. Also, I happen to know another very important Mr. Malik, of New Delhi, a good friend of King Leopold. . . .

Hong Kong
November 26, 1973

Dear Co-Workers in Giving God's
   Last Message to a Dying World:
   . . . While in New Delhi I had another very nice meeting with President V.V. Giri.

On last Friday I flew to Dacca, capital of the new

country Bangladesh (formerly called East Pakistan). I wish I had time and space to tell you the tragic, almost unbelievable story of that country and its recent war. It must be told. I will write an article on it for *The Plain Truth,* which you may read later.

Bangladesh is the eighth largest nation on earth, in population—with seventy-five million people. It appeared, from what little I saw of it, to be the most impoverished country I have seen.

In early 1971, when I was visiting New Delhi, India, Prime Minister Indira Gandhi took some twenty minutes of our meeting to tell me of the many thousands of East Pakistanis daily fleeing as refugees across the border into India—no earthly possessions except what they carried on their backs—no food, no money, no employment. India, already impoverished with millions of poor—needing to provide an additional hundred and fifty million jobs—had no way to take care of these refugees. Many were half-starved and starving, many diseased, their clothes in tatters.

After the war, freed from the yoke of a government that was machine-gunning people by thousands because of political differences, the refugees have been returning. The number of refugees fleeing into India had reached nearly ten million!

The present Prime Minister, Sheikh Mujibur Rahman, had been a political prisoner, jailed in West Pakistan. In January, 1972 (last year), he was released in London and immediately returned to his people in the new Bangladesh.

Thirty minutes after my plane landed at Bangladesh airport, I was ushered into his temporary office in a frame house that had been a private residence. At a glance it was apparent he was a leader of his people. He is big, strong, alert, active, aggressive,

534

emotionally and compassionately aware of the dire needs of his people. His conviction and sincerity impressed me.

He told me how his country had suffered—three million were killed—six million homes were destroyed—more than one and a half million farm families were left without tools or animals to work their farms. The transportation and communication systems were totally destroyed. Roads badly damaged, bridges knocked out, inland waterways blocked. He described the basic need of food—education—every basic need. The educated had been systemically killed by thousands. Now education is a dire need. He lamented the fact that the major nations are spending so much of their resources for military purposes of killing, and giving only lip service to the improvement of the lives of the overwhelming majority of all mankind.

We discussed the possibility of possible cooperation in some way with Ambassador College.

After lunch . . . I had a private meeting with the Head-of-State, President Aby Sabeed Choudhury. He is a former Justice of the Supreme Court.

The President asked me frankly for my appraisal of what I had seen of his country. When I hesitated, he smiled, and said he wanted my frank and honest appraisal. I told him that it appeared to me to be the most impoverished country I had seen. I added that I had involuntarily uttered the prayer, on seeing it, "Thy Kingdom come"—as the real answer to the plight of the country. He said he knew quite a little of Ambassador College, of our worldwide Work, and of me personally, and then:

"Mr. Armstrong, I want to appeal to you for your candid counsel and advice. I know of your contacts with so many leaders of government and their problems, your wide experience, your age and wisdom. You can see

535

the colossal problems we have here, struggling with the reconstruction of this nation of seventy-five million impoverished people."

This was not the first time a head of a government over many millions of people has asked me for counsel and advice in trying to solve their virtually unsolvable problems. And I think our Great God will show me a way to help—at least to uplift the morale, the spirits and the hope of those millions of poor, downtrodden people. In spite of their tragic recent war, their spirits right now seem good—they, with India's help, won the war, and their freedom from a most cruel rule. A very large portion of their people understand English. If the President, the Prime Minister, and present government will allow, I think it might help the spirits and morale of the people greatly if I took to the air over their government radio, admonishing them, as in James 5:1-11. The great hope of all the world, now, is the coming of the Lord Jesus Christ, to bring the world not only peace, but universal prosperity. Perhaps this President may see that the gospel will give his people more hope and encouragement than anything. . . .

I Visit Emperor Haile Selassie
December, 1973

What if the League of Nations had heeded Haile Selassie's plea and warning in 1935? Might it not have prevented World War II? And would that not have changed the whole course of world history? . . .

Think how that might have changed the whole course of *your* life!

The Fascist Mussolini invaded Ethiopia in 1935. He was saying, "The time has come to make the Fascist voice heard!" . . .

Emperor Haile Selassie went before the League of Nations in Geneva in person. He pleaded with them to stop this fast-mounting Fascist threat to world peace at Ethiopia, before it invaded France and Britain, and started the greatest conflagration of world war in history.

Did not this man, who claims to be a direct descendant of the ancient King Solomon of Judah and the Queen of Sheba, prophesy that if they did not stop the Fascist armies before they invaded Ethiopia, that all Western Europe would be invaded?—that the British Empire would cease to be an Empire—that nothing but trouble would come upon the democracies of Western Europe and the United States?—war troubles, economic troubles—political troubles?

But the League of Nations had no power ! And the democracies didn't think any such big war would come. So they left helpless Ethiopia to her fate. And Mussolini took Ethiopia. He added it to Libya and Italian Somaliland and Eritrea. After having previously made a concordat with the Vatican he now proclaimed another resurrection of the Fascist Roman Empire! . . .

The Ethiopian Emperor Haile Selassie was forced into exile. He went to England, and did not return to his capital. Addis Ababa, until May 5, 1941, at the head of his resistance forces, and with British troops. They had fought their way into Ethiopia from Sudan.

From the time of his personal appearance before the League of Nations, in 1935, Emperor Haile Selassie became one of the best-known heads of state in the world. He ascended his throne in 1930, and has had the longest reign, or tenure in office as head of state or head of government, of any man in the world.

Of all the heads of nations or of great corporations,

537

I think none could have triggered greater anticipation prior to meeting than this longest-ruling of all rulers.

All my life, from age nineteen, I have had more or less close contact with many of "the great and the near-great" of the world—heads of large corporations, presidents and chairmen of major banks, publishers, educators—and in these recent years government heads and world leaders. But none had seemed a more outstanding personality than Emperor Haile Selassie.

So when, last March, the invitation came unexpectedly to visit him, it was an intriguing anticipation.

It was in New Delhi, capital of India. Once again I was luncheon guest at the residence of Dr. Nagendra Singh, one of the world's leading exponents for world peace through international law. He had been Executive Secretary to the President of India, V.V. Giri, and recently appointed judge on the World Court at The Hague.

Among other guests was his Excellency Ato Getachew Mekasha, the Ambassador from Ethiopia, and wife. Also the Ambassador from Afghanistan and wife, and the elder son of President Giri. . . .

During the course of the luncheon both Ambassadors extended invitations to visit their respective countries and their kings. Tentative arrangements were made for the Ethiopian visit in May. I was unable to meet that schedule, but did manage to make it in June. . . .

Meanwhile a second invitation had come by telex to visit the Emperor in Addis Ababa.

At a luncheon in Jerusalem, attended by several high-ranking university and government officials, it was mentioned that Emperor Selassie had spent over two years in Palestine during his exile, and our Israeli friends at the luncheon knew him well.

It so happened that in our archaeological project, a very ancient seal, used by kings of Judah more than 2,500 years ago, had been discovered. A lion was engraved on the seal, representing "The Lion of the Tribe of Judah." This title is applied to Christ in the Bible, but Emperor Selassie claims to be the direct descendant of King Solomon and the Queen of Sheba, and is often called "The Lion of the Tribe of Judah."

Our Israeli friends thought it would be nice to make a blown-up photograph of the seal, frame it, and let me present it to the Emperor, which was done. Also our friends at the luncheon told me that the Emperor understands and speaks English very well, although as all heads of state do, he would speak through an interpreter at our meeting.

While in Jerusalem I was received for a personal visit by Israel's new President Katzir.

We had a really spectacular flight from Tel Aviv directly to Addis Ababa (capital city of Ethiopia), over the straits of Tiran, the Gulf of Aqaba, and the Red Sea, with Saudi Arabia on our left, and Egypt on our right.

Ethiopia is a mountainous country, in east-central Africa, south of Egypt, and north of Kenya. It covers an area about the size of Texas, Oklahoma and New Mexico combined. Much of its area is a high central plateau, ranging from 6,000 to 9,000 feet elevation. Addis Ababa is over 8,000 feet, and I did have some little difficulty breathing, especially early mornings, because of the thin air at that altitude.

We arrived Sunday, June 17, about 1:30 p.m. at Addis Ababa airport. Our party was met at our plane by the Ambassador to India and his wife, who had flown from New Delhi to welcome us, as well as the President of the Haile Selassie University, and others.

His Imperial Majesty the Emperor had sent to the airport one of his Mercedes limousines and driver, which was put at my personal service for the duration of our stay. Other cars were waiting for the others of our party. . . .

The capital city of Addis Ababa was an eye-opener for me. In the main it is a very modern city—a generous sprinkling of new, modern high-rise buildings, and a goodly number of imposing and impressive public buildings. These included the headquarters building of the Organization for African Unity (OAU). This is an organization of African nations, brought about primarily through the initiative and leadership of Emperor Haile Selassie.

Other impressive buildings were government buildings, hotels, the university, hospitals. Addis Ababa is a city of over 800,000 population, approaching a million.

We were driven to the comparatively new Addis Ababa Hilton Hotel, one of the better Hiltons, and I was given the Presidential suite.

That evening our party was hosted at an informal dinner by His Excellency the Ambassador to India, and the Minister of Information, at the home of the latter.

On Monday morning, due to shortness of breath I remained in the hotel. . . .

Monday evening the Minister of Education and Chairman of the University Board of Governors, His Excellency Ato Seifu Mahteme Selassie, hosted a reception for us. Of course the President of the University was there, as well as most Vice Presidents.

But now came the highlight—the meeting with the Emperor. Our entire party had been invited to come along with me. . . .

The meeting had been set for 4:30 Tuesday afternoon. At that time we arrived at the Jubilee Palace of the Emperor. There were, of course, at the gates, and at the entrance of the palace, the usual battery of armed and colorfully uniformed guards. We were met at the entrance by aides in military attire, with the President of the University and the Minister of Education.

We were escorted up a long grand stairway with heavy red carpet. One of the aides, taking my arm, cautioned me to "take it easy," because of the high altitude and length of the stairs.

Arriving on the upper level, we turned into an ornate and very long room. There was a wide strip of red carpet down the center, the length of the room, and at the far end, seated behind a table with flowers, was the lone figure of His Imperial Majesty, the world-famous Emperor Haile Selassie. I led the way down the length of the room, and was warmly greeted, as was the entire party on being introduced one at a time.

I then presented the Emperor with a gift of Steuben crystal, and also with the framed picture of the 2500-year-old seal, with the engraving of the lion, "The Lion of the Tribe of Judah." This seemed to please him very much, as I explained about our archaeological project, and our mutual Israeli friends.

The university President acted as interpreter. I then began to mention some of the things the Emperor and I have in common. We are virtually the same age—he is just eight days older than I. But I mentioned that his hearing seemed better than mine. We both enjoyed long marriages, and both are now widowers. The Empress died in 1962, my wife in 1967, after almost fifty years of marriage.

Then I mentioned that I have the genealogy of my ancestry, and that I too, [on one side of the family] am a direct descendant of King Solomon of ancient Israel.

"Well why not?" blurted out the Emperor sponta-

541

neously, without waiting for the interpreter to tell him what I had said.

At that responsive quip we all burst out in laughter. From that point the interpreter had very little to do.

Early in our talk, His Majesty mentioned that he was well aware, as were the others in the Ethiopian government, that I was the spiritual leader of a large worldwide following. During the first fifteen or twenty minutes of our meeting, he tended to answer whatever I said with a philosophical observation, apparently inspired by Solomon's Proverbs, which I rather deduced he has studied continuously and religiously.

The general sum and substance of our conversation revolved around the basic fundamental principles of world conditions, evils and problems, and how in our work we are putting solutions and true values to actual practice, setting a living example of the way to peace and happiness, both in our college campuses, and in the Church throughout the world. He took keen interest in my explanation of the two divergent philosophies or ways-of-life. which I call the way of "get" practiced in this world, and the way of "give" which leads to peace, happiness and success.

"Philosophy, and moral philosophy," he commented, "is commendable, but it is far more commendable to put into actual practice the principles upon which the philosophy is based." He said he recognized fully our achievements of both our institutions putting into practice *the way* that we preach worldwide. . . .

The Emperor gave no indication or move toward terminating our visit, but after some forty-five minutes, I felt it proper to do so, and rose to my feet, expressing what an honor and delight the meeting had been. Then Haile Selassie presented me with an already autographed full color photograph of himself, with a sterling

542

silver frame, bearing his Imperial insignia centered over the top of the frame. Also, he gave me another duplicate photograph (not autographed) for publication.

Then I received a real surprise. Out of a beautiful leather case, handed him by an aide, the Emperor took an extremely beautiful gold bracelet which he presented to me as his personal gift to my daughter, whom he had expected to be with me. In the center of the bracelet was a solid gold coin (twenty-four karat), made forty-three years ago in celebration of his coronation. The coin had the Emperor's face engraved on it. The rest of the bracelet, except for the clasp at the underside, was twenty-two karat gold, with beautiful garlands engraved with exquisite craftsmanship. Jewelers have since evaluated it as the finest gold bracelet they had ever seen.

Naturally, I thanked His Majesty very sincerely, and on returning to the hotel, I rushed immediately to my suite and put in a telephone call to my daughter in California. On describing it to her, she said she would send His Majesty a telegram of thanks immediately. It is naturally quite a conversation piece, and so far as value is concerned, priceless. The very exquisite work was all done in Ethiopia, where they mine gold in limited quantities, and produce some of the world's finest jewelry.

That evening, I hosted a reception and dinner in a private room off the lobby of our hotel in honor of the Minister of Education, the President of the University, the Dean of Faculties, the Head of the Institute of Ethiopian Studies, the Vice President for Academic Affairs, the Vice President for Planning, and other distinguished guests, and their wives.

On Wednesday, June 20, I paid a morning visit for two or three hours to the University. There my host and guide was the President of the University. We also paid

543

a most interesting visit to the embryonic Museum of Natural Science. Later this proved to be of special significance at a subsequent meeting with Prince Bernhardt of The Netherlands, husband of the Queen. He has a very active interest in the conservation and preservation of wild life throughout the world.

That same day, June 20, I was guest of honor at a *very* important luncheon hosted by His Excellency the Ambassador to India. He had invited other Ambassadors. In attendance were the Ambassadors from 19 different nations, and their wives. Included, and seated on my left, was the very impressive-appearing Ambassador from the People's Republic of China, who, during the luncheon, extended an invitation . . . to visit China. . . . Also present were the Chargé d'Affaires and acting Ambassador from West Germany, and the Ambassadors from Argentina, Ghana, Indonesia, Iran, Kenya, Mexico, Nigeria, Spain, Thailand, Colombia, Tanzania, and the Chargé d'Affaires from the United Kingdom and from Yugoslavia. The Ambassador from China, His Excellency Yu Pei-wen, has held some very important posts for his government, including that of Chief of Protocol in Peking. . . .

I was called upon to make a brief address before this distinguished gathering. The entire room was buzzing with laughter and conversation—all in an exceedingly happy mood. After making a toast to His Imperial Majesty, the Emperor of Ethiopia, I stated that we were gathered in a World Peace-Conference, proving that so many people from so many nations could gather together in jolly and happy friendship. I spoke briefly, some seven or eight minutes, on the way to world peace—*the way* of God's law, briefly proclaiming the coming world of peace—the World Tomorrow—the Kingdom of God.

The following day, Thursday, was the day of our departure, and we were planning to be at the airport in the early afternoon. But that morning we were the very special guests of His Imperial Majesty at the graduation ceremonies of the University, held in the Grand Palace (not the Palace which is the Emperor's residence and from which he rules the government). We were seated on the large front platform, immediately to the left of the dais on which was the ornate gold throne where the Emperor was to sit, personally handing the diplomas to each graduate.

A large band was playing at the rear. Finally the graduates marched in, completely filling the large auditorium. There were close to 3,000 graduates.

It was a very colorful ceremony. But, with so many graduates, the Emperor handing each individually his diploma, it was a very long ceremony. On the front platform, but to our left and farther from the throne, was the entire Board of Regents, and on the other side Faculty and other dignitaries. Members of the royal family were seated immediately in front of us. As the spectacular ceremony dragged on, an official whispered to us that it would be quite all right if we wished to leave, as the ceremony would carry on for more than another hour.

We were driven directly from the palace to the airport, where our crew had our plane ready for boarding. And there, to personally bid us good-bye were the Ambassador to India and his wife.

It was, we felt, a most profitable, as well as enjoyable, four days.

79

March 28, 1974—
May 21, 1974

Dear Inner Family of Co-Workers with Christ:

When I surrendered completely to the Living Jesus Christ, giving my life literally to Him to use as He might see fit, I counted the cost! It meant giving up my business, and career in the business world. I was well aware that Jesus had said to His disciples—and this included all who would follow Him fully—"If they have persecuted me, they will also persecute you." I had to be willing to accept that.

When God inducted me into His ministry more than forty years later I knew what He had commissioned me to do, to "go into all the world and preach the gospel"—"go ye therefore, and teach all nations."

Teach what? Christ's gospel, which is the good news of the Kingdom of God.

And for our time, now, Christ said, "This gospel of

the kingdom shall be preached in all the world for a witness unto all nations, and then shall the end [of this present world] come."

Not to proselyte—not aggressively to seek Church members—but to announce the good news of the soon-coming Kingdom of God—which will bring us world peace, universal happiness and prosperity, and eternal salvation. To prepare the way for the coming of Christ again to earth in all the divine splendor, power and glory of the Eternal God, as the King of kings and Lord of lords to rule, and to save the world.

This is not the time when God is trying to save the world, spiritually. We are preparing the way for the time when He will do that. If God had been trying to get the world spiritually "saved," He would have saved it! Nevertheless, though we have made no direct active effort to make converts—and absolutely none to compete or take members from churches, there have been thousands of conversions of those who heard the proclamation of Christ's gospel.

And, of course, since God did add to His flock, it became our responsibility to "feed the flock." For this an educated ministry was provided through Ambassador College. There are, at the present time, some 600 ordained ministers, worldwide, in the Worldwide Church of God. The number one purpose and function of these hundreds of ministers and churches is their part in helping us in getting the great commission accomplished! And that job has been getting done—in a very powerful manner!

But in regard to Christ's Church, even in the first century, there were false brethren and even false ministers. The Apostle Paul had called to him at Miletus the elders (ministers, pastors) of the chruch at Ephesus, where there was a good-sized church.

Paul said to them: "And now, behold, I know that ye all, among whom I have gone preaching the kingdom of God, shall see my face no more, . . . take heed therefore, . . . for I know this, that after my departing shall grievous wolves enter in among you, not sparing the flock. Also of your own selves shall men arise, speaking perverse things, to draw away disciples after them. Therefore watch, and remember, that by the space of three years I ceased not to warn one night and day with tears" (Acts 20:25-31).

There are many more New Testament statements of ministers turning false, and leaving God's Church, trying to draw away members after them, and trying to destroy the Work of God. We would not be doing the true Work of the Living God if the same things did not oppose us today—persecution, false accusations! . . .

Yes, there was a conspiracy. But the back of that conspiracy has been broken by our God! On what do we rely in such an emergency? We rely on the throne of grace in heaven! We go to our knees before the living Christ! He heads this great Work. He guides it, blesses it, produces abundant fruits for His Kingdom through it. And we leave the dealing with adversaries in His hands, only praying for them, that God will cause them to see the serious error of what they have yielded themselves to do and restore them to Him and His Work.

This angry attack has, of course, given us a temporary setback. Undoubtedly it will hurt the income for God's great Work. But it has at the same time actually strengthened us—for it has welded the great loyal majority closer together than ever before.

It came at the very time when I had just arrived in Manila, the Philippines, for the very first public Personal Appearance Campaign. . . .

548

Now I cannot go back to Manila and pick up where I had to leave off to rush back to Pasadena headquarters.

What a tragic shame!

But we shall immediately carry right on with these campaigns! The next one is scheduled for Ethiopia in May. Many others will follow.

I wrote you previously, I think, about the eight high-ranking Japanese Diet Members (Japan's Congress or Parliament) who traveled two weeks with me into the Arab oil-producing countries. As we said "goodbye" at the end of the trip, they called themselves my "eight Japanese sons." The following telegram from them, when they heard of this attack causing me to fly immediately back to Pasadena, brought tears to my eyes when I read it. They are loyal! Here is what they telegraphed:

"Dear Mr. Herbert Armstrong. Our sincere prayer for you that you may have precious direction and protection upon your present task which we learned that you had to go back to the States. May the Almighty give you wise wisdoms, peaceful mind and splendid health so you'll be able to carry through your mission.

Yours respectfully,

Your eight Japanese sons

Bunsei Sato and other Members of Japanese Diet"

I also received telegrams of assurance of loyalty from important officials in other world capitals, and from a judge of the World Court at The Hague, Holland.

Dear Co-Worker in the most important Work on earth, from the bottom of my heart, I thank you beyond words to express for your loyalty, your confidence, and for standing behind me, when such crises threaten! We have had to weather many storms, but God has always

549

been with us, as we are with Him, and Jesus Christ has never left us nor forsaken us, and He never will!

Thank you for your prayers for me. . . .

I pray for you, and am very grateful for your prayers!

May 21, 1974

Dear Inner Family of Co-Workers with Christ:

. . . Co-Workers, Satan exists! And Satan hates this work of the living God, and seeks by every subtle deception and maneuver to destroy this Work! He did it in the first century. He tried it now. But God is more powerful than Satan. And this is the activity of God. And Christ has promised He will never leave nor forsake His Church nor His Work. The living Christ broke the back of that conspiracy! The handful of dissident and disloyal ministers took a certain number of deceived brethren with them. But already, I am informed, more than that number of new brethren have been baptized, replacing those who went with the self-seeking disloyal ministers. They were deceived. They may not have realized Satan was using them. I pray their eyes may yet be opened—that they will be brought to a real repentance and will return to God's Work.

Yes, Satan did strike a blow at this new dimension in God's Work. Satan did not want the very first of the public campaigns to succeed, getting Christ's gospel message into the nations where it had never gone before. He did prevent the originally scheduled date for the Manila campaign. For awhile we wondered if the campaign could ever be picked up again, once it had to be called off. But remember this is the Work of the living Christ! And it finally was carried on much bigger than planned the first time!

But now, more than two months later, all three nights' meetings were held in the Coliseum! All things do work for good, to those who love and obey God!

So let me tell you about the past eventful week.

On arrival at the airport I was met by Dr. Angeles, the Executive Vice President of Angeles University, and other important people, as well as the press—newspaper, radio, television. A government Highway Patrol car, with flashing red light and siren, escorted us to our hotel. This same patrol car, with siren going full blast, escorted me everywhere I went for the nine days we were there. It plowed our way through snarled traffic. and saved much time.

On the first Saturday I spoke to some six hundred people. On Sunday, for a noon luncheon, I was guest speaker before a group of more than two hundred—a combined luncheon of the Knights of Columbus and Daughters of Isabella, where for some twenty-five minutes I opened the gospel of the Kingdom of God to them. . . .

Monday, at 10 a.m., a visit with the Mayor, and a ceremony in which the Mayor presented me with the Key to the City—a very ornate work of art, by the way. At 12 noon, a luncheon press conference, in a private room at the Manila Hilton Hotel. We received a most favorable press, by the way—more often on the front page of newspapers—every day we were there. Also on television and radio. One evening Channel 2 put on a twenty-minute documentary supplied by our own television people. . . . The Channel 2 crew came to my hotel room for a ten-minute televised interview which—following the twenty-minute documentary—filled the entire thirty minutes. I later heard from many people who had seen it. This was put on as a public service, without cost to us. . . .

Continuing, on Monday evening our dinner guest, in a small private dining room in the Hyatt Regency Hotel, was the mother of the President, Mrs. Josefa E. Marcos. She is a delightful person to know, virtually my age. . . .

Tuesday was another busy, event-packed day. Our four-car caravan (including the pilot siren car), left our hotel Tuesday morning at 8:30 a.m., for Angeles City, a two-hour drive. We passed through three or four other towns on the way. It was almost 10:30 a.m. when we arrived at the Angeles University, a school younger than Ambassador College, yet a full university with some 5,000 students. I was hurried into a changing room where my coat was removed, and the commencement ceremony robes—bright and colorful—put on. At Ambassador College we never use such robes, nor the four-square cap and gown. But so far as I know all other colleges and universities do.

Anyway, once I was robed, as well as many faculty members, we started on a procession, led by the band, to the gymnasium, which already was filled with faculty and students. There, in dignified ceremony, the university conferred on me the honorary degree of Doctor of Humanities. After the ceremony, back in my own clothes, in another auditorium, there was an entertainment program by students, and then a luncheon, hosted by university officials. Then, the long ride back to Manila.

That evening, Tuesday, another private-room dinner with Mrs. Oliveras, President and General Manager of the *Times Journal,* which has a circulation of 30,000 copies daily. Her newspaper carried many stories about us and the coming campaign.

Wednesday, I was guest of honor at the Kiwanis Club luncheon, at which I spoke some twenty minutes.

At 5 p.m. we arrived at the University of the East, largest in the Philippines, with 68,000 students. The President of the University, Dr. S.F. de la Cruz, had just returned about three weeks before from visiting the Ambassador College campus in Pasadena, with Mrs. de la Cruz. Dr. de la Cruz was one of the three university presidents from this part of the world who attended the grand opening concert at the new Ambassador Auditorium. At the U. of E. I met the Chairman of the Board and Founder of the University again (I had met him on a previous trip), and several administration officials and faculty heads. We soon went to their auditorium, where students gave an entertainment program, which was followed with speeches introducing me, and I addressed the filled auditorium of students and faculty.

From the university we were driven to the studios of Channel 13, where I was interviewed... in a half-hour telecast.

Thursday, there were more press interviews, and a dinner with officials of the Greater Manila Junior Chamber of Commerce....

But now we had come to the big event! Friday night was the first night of the Manila campaign—there were to be three meetings in all (lectures they were called in the newspapers). They were for Friday night, Saturday night, and Sunday night—the meetings started each night at 7 o'clock.

We should have arrived very late, had it not been for the police siren pilot car, for traffic was extremely heavy. We were a little tense on arriving, wondering whether there would be a big crowd.

"What if only two or three thousand come?" I wondered. They would look like a tiny handful of people in that huge 24,000-seat Coliseum. They would look as if they were lost! We entered at the rear, behind the stage.... The Coliseum seemed well filled—a few scattered empty seats here and there—what a relief to see such a great crowd present!...

A most complimentary short speech by the Vice President of Angeles University was followed by a very vigorous speech by Dr. de la Cruz, mentioning enthusiastically his visit to the Ambassador College campus. It was 7:30 p.m. when I stepped up to the podium. I spoke one hour. Following is a brief summary of my first sermon of the campaign:

First, I asked the audience how much they knew about the conditions in the world they live in. Then I outlined the evil conditions I see in all parts of the world, asking why such evils exist in a world where men have learned how to fly to the moon and back, but not how to solve their own problems on earth. This world, I said, is headed toward the supreme crisis at the end of this age—this present evil world. Human survival is now our number one problem. For thousands of years, heads of governments have striven for world peace—but, no peace! There will have to be a cause to bring about world peace. I mentioned my early surveys, learning of this world's unhappy conditions. Finally, beginning 1926, I received the shock of my life, discovering the true answers in the Bible—answers never revealed by science, nor taught by religion or education. Then I went into some detail in the incident of the forbidden fruit in the second and third chapters of Genesis. I explained God's way of life revealed to but rejected in that incident by Adam and Eve—and how humanity has rejected or overlooked the revealed knowledge of God's way of life (based on the Ten Commandments) ever since. Of course the third chapter of Genesis introduced Satan the Devil, symbolized by the serpent. After thoroughly explaining God's way of life, I asked the

554

questions, Where did this Satan come from? What is "human nature"? What is the difference between human mind and animal brain? Why was humanity put here on earth—what is the real purpose in our being here? How is God's purpose being worked out?—and saying that on Saturday night I would answer those questions, and explain how and when world peace is coming, in a message of hope and assurance.

These questions are something most of the audience had never heard answered before!

These questions were gone into on Saturday night—explaining the gospel message, which God sent to mankind by Jesus Christ—and how that gospel— that vital message from God to humanity, has not been proclaimed to this world for eighteen and a half centuries. I reminded the audience that most of them were now hearing that gospel message for the first time! ... I read from Malachi's prophecy about the coming of Christ (Mal. 3:1), and of the beginning of the gospel of Jesus Christ, Mark 1:1, and verses 14-15.

But to understand that gospel, it was necessary to go all the way back into prehistory. I then explained the presence of pre-Adamic angels on earth, ruled by the government of God. And as long as that government of God ruled the earth, there was peace, happiness, joy! It might have been millions of years. Then, Lucifer and his angels rebelled (did precisely what some ministers were recently doing) and became the devil and his demons. That involved many Scriptures which I read from the Bible. Then the renewing of the face of the earth (Ps. 104:30) described in the first chapter of Genesis. Then I went into an explanation of the human mind compared to animal brain, reading the Scriptures about it; how God put what He wanted into the mind of King Cyrus of Persia (Ezra 1:1); and how Satan has swayed all humanity, injecting what we call human nature—vanity, lust and greed, envy, jealousy, competition, antagonism, rebellion and violence—and how man, swayed by this spirit contrary to the government of God, has caused all the problems and evils that have plagued suffering mankind.

I ended Saturday night with Acts 3:19-21, showing how Jesus Christ is now in heaven until the time when the government of God shall be restored on earth, and once again bring peace to this earth.

On Sunday night, the Coliseum appeared to be packed. It is a huge auditorium, with many tiers or balconies—like a vast bowl with a roof over it....

Again the President's mother came—all three nights. There were more preliminary ceremonies, with Mrs. Marcos presenting certain honors to me on the platform, and enthusiastic speeches from others, before the sermon. I spoke exactly one hour Friday night, 70 minutes Saturday night, and an hour and 15 minutes Sunday night. Not a soul was seen leaving until the end.

The final Sunday night I quickly reviewed the state of the world, and the number one problem, survival of humanity on earth. Never before was it possible to erase all human life from the earth fifty times over! One H-bomb could destroy all of Manila (four million people). Again, there had to be a cause for this alarming condition—and if we are to have peace, something must cause it. I explained in retrospect how Friday night I showed how the first humans, Adam and Eve, had rejected knowledge revealed from God, and turned to the way that has caused all the world's evils. I explained the two ways of life—God's way of love—the giving, sharing way of outgoing concern, and the getting way of self-centeredness, and rejection of God and His way. Then a quick summary of how God's government, based

556

on His spiritual law of love had once caused happiness on earth, and the rebellion that turned the archangel Lucifer into Satan, and his angels into demons. Then the creation of man, and his rejection of knowledge of God, and rebellion against God's way. And how the all-important dimension in knowledge has been missing since. Then, the fact man is created of matter, dust of the ground, but God is composed of Spirit. God's purpose for man, shown in Genesis 1—the reproduction of Himself! This was startling new knowledge to nearly all there. His purpose also, through man, to restore the government of God to earth, bringing world peace. The seven days of Genesis 1 and 2, a type of God's plan for working out His purpose. Adam rejected God's way. Then how the second Adam, Jesus Christ, qualified to restore the government of God (the Kingdom of God) to this earth. I read the Old Testament prophecies of Christ coming to rule, setting up the Kingdom of God on earth, then in Luke 1:30-33, how Christ was born to rule as King. Then the beginning of Christ's gospel (Mark 1:1, 14-15), and teaching we may be born of God (John 3:1-8 which I read and explained). This was new to nearly all. How we may be converted, receiving the impregnation of God-life (eternal life) by the Holy Spirit from the very person of God. I read Romans 8:9, 11, 14, 16. I explained how we may receive the Holy Spirit, being begotten as a son of God (Acts 2:1-4, 37-38 which I read). I explained how God created all things by and through Christ (John 1:1-5, Eph. 3:9)—He is our Maker—therefore when He gave His life on the cross, by His shed blood He paid the death penalty for all humanity—for His life was greater than all He created! Christ rose from the dead, making eternal life possible for us. Christ ascended to the Father's throne in heaven. I went through the parable of the pounds, Luke

19:11-20, 24, showing we who grow in grace and knowledge in the Christian life will rule in God's Kingdom. Then I quoted Christ's promise, that we shall reign over the nations with Him, (Rev. 2:26-27; 3:21), and we shall reign with Him on the earth (Rev. 5:10). I read of the Second Coming of Christ to rule all nations, restoring peace—Revelation 19:6, 11-16. Then I read of putting Satan away for a thousand years, and the Kingdom of God ruling a thousand years, Revelation 20:1-6, and how converted Christians, then resurrected and changed to spirit composition, will reign with Him.

I explained how that will complete the 7,000 years. But, then what? What is our ultimate destiny? I read of man's ultimate transcendent glory, once real God-like character is developed in him in this life. I had explained how God is a family, into which we may be born, and now in Hebrews 1-2, how Christ is now very God, sustaining the whole universe (explaining that "all things" means the entire universe) with His power. Then, in Hebrews 2, beginning with verse 6, how God has put the entire universe under man—but (verse 8) we see not yet the whole universe under man, but we do see Jesus, having gone on before as our Leader—the firstborn of many brethren (Rom. 8:29). I ended by stating how much more wonderful is the knowledge God reveals in the Bible than that taught by science, religion or education! They had heard the good news (gospel) of the Kingdom of God! The people were astonished, as in Jesus' day (Matt. 7:28).

After this last sermon, we were dinner guests at the lovely home of Minister (Mrs.) Lim.

I have taken the time and space to give you a full synopsis of all three sermons before those many thousands in the first of these new public appearance campaigns in the world capitals around the world. For I want you to see and realize that Christ's great commission is being effectively fulfilled—that what He has commissioned you and me to do is getting done—and done effectively—for the first time in 1,850 years and more! I want the living Christ to be able to say to you and me, "Well done, good and faithful servants."

I wanted you to realize it fully, because this is the most important of the things God's tithes which you send in are going for! God has opened the doors. God has been in it—it has gone out in His power! . . .

It is now full steam ahead! A glorious new start, on a new plane! We are moving on in rejuvenated power!

Thank you, dear Brethren and Co-Workers, for your loyalty, for standing by us faithfully. We forge ahead unitedly, now, as never before. God's blessing will continue to be with you, and His Work!

80

June 18, 1975— December 24, 1976

June 18, 1975

Dear Co-Worker with Christ:

Suppose God had called you, yourself, individually, to start His Work for this time—to think out the plans and ways to go about it, to preach and publish Christ's gospel message for the soon-coming Kingdom of God in all the world for a witness to all nations! Would you be overwhelmed? Would you know how to go about it? Ever think about that?

Forty-two years ago God laid that awesome responsibility upon me. I had no money then—not even a car. I had to hitchhike to preach in a country schoolhouse. There was only a very small handful of brethren to help me....

Gradually others began joining and standing behind me as Co-Workers with Christ in His Work. The Work grew slowly but steadily. In three of four years we

560

were reaching the Pacific Northwest. In due time I was reaching the entire United States and Canada, coast to coast. . . .

It took us forty years to get Christ's message with fairly good coverage over the United States and Canada, and to a far lesser extent, Australia, New Zealand, South Africa, Britain, and the countries of western Europe—the nations descended from the so-called "lost sheep of the House of Israel." Meanwhile, of course, more and more Co-Workers got back of this most important operation on earth. . . .

Since 1968 God began opening doors through seemingly unusual circumstances for personal meetings with kings, presidents, and leaders in education, commerce, and industry. It was absolutely providential. Many came to have a warm, and even affectionate feeling toward me.

At first I didn't understand why this was happening. But I did know it was God's doing. For doors were opening miraculously and the warmth of their feeling toward me was far beyond normal. In most cases I soon became acquainted with high-ranking officials under these heads of state—such as members of the cabinet, members of their law-making bodies (Diet, Parliament, etc.). Dinners were hosted in my honor. Opportunity began opening for "testimonial dinners" where one or more high officials acted as host, sent out invitations to the most influential leaders, and I could have thirty-five to forty-five minutes to present a message of the soon coming Kingdom of God.

About two years ago, God began showing us how to develop these open doors into large-scale Public Appearance Campaigns, reaching hundreds and thousands of leading people in these countries.

I have come to see that the commission to take the

gospel of the Kingdom of God to all the world for a witness to all nations could only be accomplished through the very heads of government!

I have explained this time and time again in letters, editorials, and articles. I am now actively holding campaigns in world capitals, speaking before professional groups, even with heads of state worldwide! I am explaining why there is no peace—what is the way to peace—why humanity cannot solve its problems—why Christ's coming world government is the world's only hope!—and what is our very purpose for being! And I am being given grace and favor in their eyes!

These are miraculous events—God's doing! But we all share a human responsibility. I appreciate, more than words can express, your faithful support—your financial contributions, your encouragement and prayers. I think you appreciate my efforts as well. . . .

Some weeks ago I authorized the formation of a new foundation—the Ambassador International Cultural Foundation (AICF). It is nonprofit, dedicated to serving humanity worldwide. It has become a necessary adjunct to this new world-wide dimension of getting Christ's true gospel to the nations through heads of government.

Within the scope of AICF, we are participating in humanitarian projects in several areas of the world. Some of the more publicized activities you are undoubtedly already familiar with—the archaeological excavations at Jerusalem, the International Cultural Center for Youth, explorations with King Leopold III of Belgium, etc. All provide important opportunities for demonstrating our concern for all nations. And the Foundation—with its message of universal understanding and hope—is receiving greater prestige and favor than we had hoped. It is truly becoming a wonderful tool for getting the Work done. . . .

562

August 21, 1975

Dear Brethren and Co-Workers with Christ:

It keeps on happening—at accelerating pace! Another head of state—President Mujibur Rahman of Bangladesh—whom I have recently visited, was slain last Friday morning at predawn, in a military coup.

Bangladesh is, politically, a new country. It emerged from the very recent Pakistani war as probably the most poverty stricken and illiterate nation on earth. I learned while there that during the last three or four days of the war, the enemy sought out all the leaders and people of education they could corral together, and executed them before firing squads—so as to leave the country almost destitute of educated people for leadership.

President Rahman had been confined in the enemy jail as a political prisoner. On release, he was acclaimed as a great hero, and took over the lead of the nation. He was a "rough-and-ready" type of man, yet I was much impressed with his abilities, and told him so.

Governments are being overthrown at the rate of one a month around the world now. In many cases these overthrows have involved either men I knew, or circumstances in which I had some indirect contact. When men I have known personally, like this, are being mowed down in government violence, it strikes home. It makes me realize the times we are living in—how close we are now, to the end of this world (or age).

Such government overthrows have prevented my planned campaigns in South Vietnam, Ethiopia, Afghanistan and Chile. I have said before, we must move from now on as swiftly as possible, for nations are

563

being continually overthrown where we have made progress in planning campaigns.

The world picture right now is in a sort of paradox. On the one hand, conditions of violence are worse than ever. But on the other, the general economic worldwide recession seems to have turned the corner. Economic conditions in the United States are looking up for a gradual upswing, which I hope and pray will help you Co-Workers.

In this Work of the living God, the new Foundation (the Ambassador International Cultural Foundation—AICF) is making a sensational start. Several prominent Members of the Japanese Diet (their Congress) are coming to Pasadena for an important meeting here next Wednesday night. I shall be leaving the next morning for Tokyo, for a meeting there, to be followed by meetings in Bangkok and Munich, West Germany.

Wednesday, August 27, 1975: Morning news on radio and television—too late for morning papers—Haile Selassie of Ethiopia is dead. Nothing more than that announced so far. No one knows where he has been held, except a few top officials of the new military government which overthrew his government about a year ago, taking the Emperor captive. He was just eight days older than I. One of his last acts before being taken captive was to send me a telegram of congratulation on my 83rd birthday.

Tonight is a big night here on campus. There will be a concert in the new Ambassador Auditorium, and dinner welcoming the Honorable Bunsei Sato and the Honorable Toshio Yamaguchi of Japan, (two of my "Japanese sons"), Members of the Japanese Diet, and the Honorable Keiichi Tachibana, Consul General of Japan (Los Angeles).

Then, early tomorrow I leave for Tokyo. . . .

Johannesburg
May 28, 1976

Dear Brethren and Co-Workers in Christ:

I have just come from a press conference attended by reporters who are representatives of all newspapers, television and radio stations. After the main conference, which lasted over two hours, I did a television interview and then, by tape, a radio interview. This is Friday, and we hope we catch all Sunday papers. The television interview was also taped and will be on the one and only television station here in this city of one and one-half million people at 8 o'clock tonight.

This is my first visit to South Africa. . . .

We made stops at Oman and Kuwait, two of the oil-rich Arab countries of the Middle East. Conferences were set up at Oman for a stopover on our return from South Africa. At Kuwait I had a very fine meeting with the Head of State, Sheikh Saba Al Salem Al-Sabah. He is an absolute ruler, since the form of government is an absolute monarchy. Kuwait City has grown to be a city of about a half million people and, since the virtual destruction of Beirut by civil war, Kuwait is probably due now to be the financial capital of the entire Arab Middle East. Our conference there was very successful and will bear much fruit. . . .

This is the time when we must all put our shoulders to the wheel—make any and every financial sacrifice possible to move ahead with ever-increasing momentum.

Here in South Africa I have a very heavy schedule. I will be speaking constantly before such business men's groups as Rotary, Kiwanis, Lions, etc.—before our local churches and with public campaigns in Capetown, Durban and here in Johannesburg.

Hopefully we shall now be going back into *Reader's Digest* with double-page ads in the South African edition. . . .

June 28, 1976

Dear Brethren and Co-Workers with Christ:

I have just returned from one of the most—possibly the most— successful trips ever in God's Work.

First I flew to two Arab oil states—Oman, and Kuwait. I met important leaders at Oman, but Sultan Qaboos bin Said was out of the country, so I plan to return. At Kuwait I had a very fine meeting with Sheikh Sabah Al-Salem Al-Sabah, who is both Chief of State and executive leader in an absolute monarchy.

Since Beirut—capital of Lebanon—has been almost destroyed by civil war, it probably will no longer be the financial capital of the Arab world, and Kuwait may now assume that position. It is a very new and modern city, exceedingly oil-rich. . . .

We went directly from the Sheikh's palace to the airport and flew on to Johannesburg, South Africa, arriving after dark. . . .

Mr. Robert Fahey, our Regional Director for South Africa, and one or two of his assistants, met us at the airport.

This was my first visit to South Africa. I was several years overdue there. We had many students from South Africa all through the years of Ambassador College at Bricket Wood, England. It was a joy to renew aquaintances with some of them; now married couples with children.

. . . It was one of the busiest periods of my life. Most days I had to appear at planned meetings virtually morning, noon and night. I must have spoken before some twenty-nine or thirty groups—from a few small groups of thirty to fifty up to public meetings of *Plain Truth* subscribers of over 1,000. I spoke before the Rotary Clubs of Johannesburg, Durban and Cape Town; Lions Clubs; Zionist groups in two cities; at press conferences in all three major cities, and was interviewed on radio and television. I had a half-hour meeting with Mr. John Vorster—the Prime Minister—and more than an hour with the former President of South Africa, Mr. J.J. Fouche. . . .

There was a special noon-day meeting of community leaders in the neighboring town of Edenvale, where I was personally invited by the mayor, an avid *Plain Truth* reader. There was another luncheon in the very elaborate office in Cape Town of the Chairman of the South Africa Foundation. He also is the Chairman or President of the largest bank in the country. He, too, is an enthusiastic reader of *The Plain Truth*.

I was actually astonished when nearly every official, or person of importance (including the President), mentioned being a *Plain Truth* reader, most of them for years. The *Plain Truth* circulation in South Africa is currently 100,000.

We received a special telephone invitation from a former mayor and civic leader at Port Elizabeth, fourth largest city (250,000), to speak and be his guest at dinner that evening. Present at the meeting he had arranged were the mayor, sitting next to me at the speaker's table, and the head of just about every phase of government, university, what-have-you—all leading citizens and wives—660 altogether.

We also took the time to fly to the capital city of South-West Africa, Windhoek, where the South Africa Foundation had arranged a noon luncheon with the nine leaders of that state—including two blacks and two Colored. . . .

The semipublic personal appearances came last. I say semi-public because there had been virtually no effort to get the general public out to these larger-scale meetings—little or no advertising—just invitations sent to *Plain Truth* subscribers. The first was at Durban, on our second visit there. They had engaged a hotel ballroom seating 800. About 950 came. People were standing all along the side walls and back wall, and even an overflow in an adjoining room.

At Cape Town the same thing happened. More than a thousand came—with standing room only.

The final two nights were for the Johannesburg meetings. But the riots had started two nights before. And a sudden cold snap with winds (it was winter in the southern hemisphere) caused perhaps more than half those who planned to come to stay home. We had perhaps about 800 the first night and 750 the second. But they were very attentive and interested audiences. A local motion picture theatre manager said his attendances had been cut to one-fourth those evenings.

Those audiences heard the true gospel of the Kingdom of God which the world has not heard for 1,900 years. . . .

July 20, 1976

Dear Co-Workers with Christ:

This morning at 5.12 a.m. (Pacific daylight time), I sat in our Ambassador Auditorium here in Pasadena, looking in on Mission Control headquarters, located only walking distance away, as scientists manipulated at JPL (Jet Propulsion Laboratory) the safe landing of Viking I on Mars.

The JPL scientists had cooperated with Ambassador College so that everything at Mission Control—as the scientists maneuvered the Mars landing—was shown on a large screen in our auditorium. We had opened the auditorium to the public. A thousand or more were there.

I had risen at 3.30 a.m. Many had been watching in the auditorium from 11 p.m. last night. I arrived in the auditorium just before 5 a.m.

The Viking I spacecraft is a marvel of mechanical precision. It landed safely right on schedule at 5:12 a.m. (It actually landed at 4:53 a.m. Pacific daylight time, but due to the vast distance, the signal did not reach Mission Control at Pasadena until 5:12 a.m.).

Enthusiastic applause—filling the auditorium—greeted the landing.

Very soon, just before 6 a.m., the first strip of two spectacular pictures arrived. We at the Ambassador Auditorium were looking in, just as if we were in Mission Control ourselves. Dr. Thomas Munch, geology professor and leader of the team of scientists in the Mission Control room, gave a cry of delight as the first strip of the first picture came through. As strip after strip of the pictures came through, he was unable to conceal his excitement. As the strips were pieced together, the scientists were absolutely amazed at the quality and clarity of the pictures of the Mars surface—pictures taken perhaps only four or five feet above the surface. It was just as if a man were standing there, pointing his camera straight down, taking close-up pictures of the Mars surface.

Later, the second picture looked out over the landscape to the horizon. The pictures showed a Martian surface as a sandy desert littered with rocks—from very minute size up to perhaps a foot or more in diameter.

569

But I had to think—it showed precisely what I had expected from what is revealed from the God of Creation in the Bible. It was a dry, barren surface of decay and futility—total unproductiveness.

So you can realize the thrill I experienced, seeing in our own House of God Auditorium, the first real close-up photographs from the very surface of Mars, confirming the state the Bible reveals such planets are in today....

August 19, 1976

Dear Brethren and Co-Workers with Christ,

...I have just spent another four days and five nights in Jerusalem.

Jerusalem!—the city God chose over all places on earth. The city from which for a span of time God has hidden His face (Jer. 33:5)—yet the city God shall yet choose as His city (Zech. 1:17). The city soon to become the capital of the whole world—when, finally, we shall have world peace!

Jerusalem is a city important to God—it ought to be important to us! So I want to tell you about my most recent visit there. It is a city I have visited many, many times.

My first visit to Jerusalem was a mere short stop at Jerusalem airport (not now in regular use) in 1956— twenty years ago—en route from Cairo to Baghdad. Just setting foot on the ground of its airport for the first time was a thrill. It gave me sort of a sense of awe. With my wife and elder son, Dick, we stopped again at Jerusalem on the return—first visiting the "old city" then in Arab hands—then walking, luggage in hand, through the "Mandelbaum Gate" (no man's land) into the newer Israeli Jerusalem.

Back in 1969 and 1970, when our joint participation with the Hebrew University in the huge archaeological excavation at the east wall of the Temple Mount was getting well under way, General Yigal Yadin, organizer of the Israeli army and Chief of Staff from 1948, referred to my arrivals there as "monthly visits." In many ways I have had a deep personal interest in Jerusalem since December 1, 1968. On that date, in a formal ceremony at the palace of the late President Shazar, Ambassador College entered into this joint participation formally with Hebrew University and the Israel Archaeological Society.

"Do you want a formal, legal contract?" I was asked. "My word is good," I replied. "And I believe yours is, too, without any legal entanglements." That was good enough for them, and our friendship and mutual participation has grown ever since.

Our very important friends in Israel—from the President and Prime Minister of the country on down in the government—and from President Harmon and Vice President on down in the University, have been not only most friendly and cordial, but more—affectionate! And so I thought that in this letter, you might like to hear a report on this latest Jerusalem visit.

We arrived Thursday—late afternoon. Friday morning, Mayor Teddy Kollek met us at the Jerusalem Hilton Hotel at ten. He took us on a two and a half hour tour of portions of the "old city" where the Mayor has been supervising rejuvenation and rebuilding. After all the years of being "trodden down by the Gentiles" the old walled city has become dirty, decayed—anything but beautiful. But Mayor Kollek is restoring much of its original beauty.

Israel is a very poor country—economically. The government does not have billions upon billions of dollars for such purposes. Much of this restoration is being done by volunteer labor. It made me think of the early days in building Ambassador College.

In those days, as we purchased gradually more and more property, we used old, dilapidated frame houses for many purposes—we used volunteer student labor—we improvised as was necessary to keep building and growing. That is the way the Israelis are doing in building up their country.

First the Mayor took us through the citadel—or the "Tower of David." This is an agglomeration of old buildings, inside the northwest corner of the walled city. Some of these old brick and stone buildings date back to the second century B.C. The northern tower of the citadel has been known as the Tower of David since Byzantine times—but neither the citadel nor Tower of David have any connection with the ancient King David.

There are many walls and many rooms, and it is being restored into beautiful and modern condition.

From the citadel we were taken over to the old Jewish quarter of the old walled city. Here are a cluster of low, domed houses. Very old. Very unimpressive from the outside. But entering, we were struck by the beauty, the majesty of the rooms—the high ceilings which had looked like very low buildings from the dingy old outside. But Mayor Kollek had done a remarkable job of restoring this area. There were about four synagogues—each in a different room in the same building—now very modern, very bright and beautiful on the interiors.

I was really impressed with all the plans Mayor Kollek told us he has in mind for renewing and re-beautifying the city of Jerusalem.

I could especially appreciate it, personally, since I have—the past thirty years—gone through the job of building Ambassador College in Pasadena (not to speak of similar jobs at the other two campuses). It was built out of what—at the lower down-hill level—had been the nearest thing to a slum section Pasadena had. We were then buying up the property—a forty-foot lot at a time—usually with two old shacks—one behind the other—on each narrow forty-foot lot. With the fine help I have had, we have built this area of Pasadena into a campus that twice in the past two years has won the national award of being the most beautiful, the best landscaped and best maintained campus in the United States! . . .

Mayor Kollek then took the group of us to a special restaurant for lunch. There, several other friends joined us. After that, we drove to the site of the new Liberty Bell Park.

I was scheduled to be there on July 2 for the official ground-breaking ceremony for building the new park in the heart of the new city. I had undertaken to build the children's playground area of the new city park. The last day of June, I had boarded the G-II jet aircraft, bound for Jerusalem. We were forced down at Bangor, Maine after crossing the United States from southwest to northeast, as I think I wrote you before. We had a cracked window in the cockpit. We were forced to return to Pasadena—flying at low altitude. So the Mayor conducted that ceremony alone.

When we reached the park area, I saw a large sign posted, in both Hebrew and English, saying:

"Under Construction Here:
A Children's Playground
A Gift Of
The Ambassador International Cultural Foundation
H.W. Armstrong, President"

573

Sabbath afternoon we had a Bible study in my hotel suite at the Jerusalem Hilton. About thirty came. . . .

December 24, 1976

Dear Brethren and Co-Workers in Christ,

Very few men in this world know personally as many heads of governments as I. Yet I am absolutely amazed at how short a period of time most of them last. Many have a tenure in office—if they stay healthy—of only four to six years. Many die in office. Some are assassinated—others shot down in a military coup or violent overthrow of government. Some are forced to resign.

I think over, in my mind, about many I have known, some closely and intimately—now gone! One was Prime Minister Eisaku Sato of Japan. . . . Before he died last year, he received the Nobel Peace Prize.

There was Emperor Haile Selassie of Ethiopia, taken prisoner in a military coup which overthrew his long-established government. He died in military custody.

There was President Allende of Chile, machine-gunned in the very room where I had the private conference.

There was President Rahman of Bangladesh, as-sassinated in an overthrow of his poverty-stricken, illit-eracy-cursed country.

There was the king of Afghanistan, whom I was invited to visit, but who was overthrown and driven to European exile before my visit could be arranged.

There have been others, affectionate friends of mine, whose terms of office have expired, such as V.V. Giri, ex-President of India.

Prime Minister Thanin Kraivichien of Thailand

574

has been driven from office in a military coup, again overthrowing the Thai government. He is being held in "protective custody." Three weeks before this military coup, I had a private meeting with him in his office in Bangkok, and that night he sat next to me at a banquet.

I see these heads of state personally. I see them in trouble. And, very often I soon get news that they are dead! Men I know! Men with whom I have had private talks!

Perhaps it is not quite as real to you. You have not known those men in a close, personal way, as I have. It has struck close to me! Yet I try to share my experiences with all of you to help you also feel the reality of what is going on.

For what it portends as absolutely certain soon to strike is going to affect you, personally, just as much as me—and perhaps a lot more terrifyingly unless you are as ready as I.

It means the end of this world, as currently organized, is upon us!

God Almighty sent Jonah to warn the Gentile city Nineveh! They heeded his warning. And the destruction did not come, because God saw their deep repentance— their turning from their evil ways—He heard their desperate prayers asking for mercy!

But God said that if He sends a prophet to modern Israel as He now uses us to warn the people of America, Canada, Britain, Western Europe, Australia, New Zealand and South Africa, they by nature will not heed! So, if they don't, then I tell you what is certain to happen.

Let me give you a picture of it from God's own Word, as God Himself had it pictured!

"Howl ye, for the day of the Lord is at hand; it shall come as a destruction from the Almighty. There-

575

fore shall all hands be faint and every man's heart shall melt: and they shall be afraid: ... pangs and sorrows shall take hold of them; they shall be in pain as a woman that travaileth: they shall be amazed one at another; ... Behold, the day of the Lord cometh, cruel both with wrath and fierce anger, to lay the land desolate: and he shall destroy the sinners thereof out of it" (Isa. 13:6-9).

These world happenings now are not just routine world news! They signal the great world crisis that will usher in the government of God to finally and effectively bring peace at last. They are God's loving warning to us, of the fast-coming supreme crisis at the end of this world's society, civilization, governments—man's whole evil system.

Then, afterward, shall come the happy, peaceful World Tomorrow, ruled by the government of the living God!

Dear Co-Workers, I hope you realize ours is not an easy job. The living Christ has called us to labor together to warn this world. In Jesus Christ is the only hope and safety! Some are going to heed our message and receive God's protection through the tribulation (Luke 21:36).

Together we have been given the job to prepare the way for Christ's return (Matt. 24:14). It is a privilege and responsibility no other generation has shared. It will also mean a better reward! God rewards us individually according to our works—our zeal and wholeheartedness in supporting and carrying out the greatest task in this world.

81

February 25, 1977—
June 22, 1978

February 25, 1977

Dear Co-Workers With Christ:

I am writing from Bucharest, Romania. I am spending two or three weeks at the Otopeni Clinic, famous over all of Europe, recharging tired batteries.

I have kidded about being thirty-seven going on thirty-six. It is acknowledged by all, so far as I know, that I appear to be at least some twenty years younger than I actually am....

But there may have been a slight misunderstanding in some of this, and I wish to be utterly frank, and not to pretend. It is true, the dynamic power, energy and drive has been there. It is true that probably not one in a hundred half my age could do the work that I have been doing.

But what I feel most of you have not realized is that much if not most of all that energy, vitality, drive

577

and power has come from two sources—God, of course (Isa. 40:29-31), and sheer determination and self-drive, even when I did not feel up to it.

But it's like one lady wrote to me years ago: "You may stand in that pulpit and preach with the energy and power of a forty year old, but you must remember you are standing on eighty-year-old legs."

Under the strenuous travel, with the continuous speeches before Rotary Clubs, Lions Clubs, Kiwanis, Knights of Columbus, etc., etc., besides numerous other meetings with leaders around the world, I have had to keep up constant writing, besides the oversight of the entire vast worldwide Work. . . .

I feel that God will continue renewing my youth and physical vigor and mental powers as long as necessary to get His job done. I have had to come to realize that this excessively arduous job of this new dimension, getting into nations where doors were closed to the gospel before, traveling the whole wide earth—is one few could endure. While I was driving myself on, even in fatigue, my physical body was taking a beating.

There was a time when Jesus needed to take off a little time and go aside to a quiet place and get some rest. So I have decided I must also.

I am not here because of faith in man's modern methods, but by faith in Christ, for all healing is in Christ—and being here in a position of enforced rest from strenuous routine and travel keeps me in regular hours of health-meals—and I cannot have this opportunity to recoup vitality while still traveling and constantly speaking. . . . In a couple of weeks I'll be back on the job as vigorously as ever.

My left ankle received a serious sprain three months ago, after speaking to a packed auditorium in Port Elizabeth, South Africa. A sprain, as I have learned, is worse than a break. It seems to me mostly healed by now but is still far from being back to normal. I have had to learn to walk all over again, and still am a bit unsteady. But God is with me, and I need your prayers!

I have at least ten more years of vigorous active work needed to finish the Work that God has committed to me—or less, if God cuts time shorter.

Meanwhile, news from Pasadena is that all is well. Our Great God is on His throne!

> In Flight, Republic of Transkei to
> Cape Town, South Africa
> March 22, 1977

Dear Co-Workers with Christ:

An hour ago I had just ended an address before the ministers of the world's newest government, the entire legislative assembly and others of the general public....

It was a rare once-in-several-lifetimes experience. Because a week ago across Africa on the west coast I addressed the eighty or eighty-five delegates who were drafting a new constitution for another soon-to-be new nation, Southwest Africa. I addressed them in their famous Turnhalle in Windhoek, their capital city. They held this special session for the sole purpose of hearing my address. Everyone I talked to in Cape Town, it seemed, was simply amazed that such a special session had been called to hear an address from one of another country.

So far this has been one of the busiest, most productive trips of my life. Mr. Robert Fahey, Manager of our South African office in Johannesburg, surely takes me seriously when I give my age as "thirty-seven going on thirty-six." Not many of that age could keep up the pace he has set for me—and he does the planning for my South African trips before I come. There have been meetings, addresses, speeches, interviews, luncheons, dinners planned for morning, noon, afternoon and night nearly every day. . . .

However, my badly sprained ankle (it happened last November 11 just after I finished a campaign speech before hundreds in Port Elizabeth, South Africa, on my last trip down here before this one) has improved.

I will try to fill you in on what's happened so far on this trip.

I had been in Bucharest, Romania, expecting to stay two more days, when I was suddenly called to London by telephone. This got me out of there just barely the day before that devastating earthquake (7.2 on the Richter scale). In London on Thursday night I had dinner with all the ministers stationed in England we could get together. On that Sabbath I preached once again at Bricket Wood. By telephone they managed to reach about all from the London church and also several from churches to the north in England, so the gymnasium was well filled.

After another day or two in London and stopover in Rome, we left Rome Wednesday, arriving Johannesburg at 1 a.m. Thursday morning. It was 3:30 a.m. by the time I had gotten from the airport into the city, my luggage brought to the room, and I had turned out the bedside light to get some sleep. I had to rise early enough to drive to Pretoria to speak at a luncheon before the Rotary Club of Pretoria. At 2:45 of the same afternoon we met with the new Mayor of Pretoria in his very elegant office at City Hall. We found him to be an ardent reader of *The Plain Truth*. He asked me to autograph two different issues for him and another piece of white paper for his son. Dinner that evening in Johannesburg with Mr. Fahey and his chief assistants.

Friday, March 11: Luncheon engagement with Mr. and Mrs. Owen Williams at Ellis Park (he is the leading tennis promoter in South Africa), together with Arthur Ashe (he is President of the Black Tennis Foundation). A connection is being considered with AICF to assist underprivileged and promising blacks to develop and enjoy tennis. During our talk following lunch we were able to watch Bjorn Borg (Swedish and Wimbledon champion) defeating Fred McMillan. That night we had dinner with several of our South African ministers and their wives. . . .

March 13: . . . I had a day of rest—but I wrote an article or two. . . .

Monday, March 14: In the morning flew to Windhoek, Southwest Africa (Namibia). Arrived 12:30 p.m. . . . At 3 p.m. met Mayor and Mrs. Yssel, Mayor of Windhoek. Mayor Yssel is a *Plain Truth* reader, though he holds to his own Protestant beliefs. Also present were the City Secretary and the City Engineer. The Mayor welcomed us to Windhoek and presented me with the Windhoek Yearbook. We discussed my worldwide work and portions of the book of Revelation. Our visit was forty-six minutes. . . .

6:30 p.m. Came the big event. Representatives of eleven population groups who were framing the constitution for the new nation . . . came in special session to their grand meeting room to hear my address. They had been meeting since September, 1975, in a constitutional convention at Turnhalle to draft a constitution. . . .

I emphasized the difficulties they face in starting a new nation and new government in today's world with governments of nations crumbling at the rate of one a month. I then explained how this whole confused world—chaos in government—as well as in all society worldwide—had started at the incident of the forbidden fruit. How angels had first inhabited the earth—rejected God's government based on God's law of love and turned to the way of life of "get" instead of God's way of "give" or love. How Adam and Eve had disbelieved God, believed Satan's deceptive lies, took to themselves the knowledge of right and wrong, rejected the government of God and cut themselves and their posterity (all mankind) off from God.

Whereupon God adopted the "hands off" policy toward humanity for 6,000 years. Now man had been left to devise his own government, his own religion, educational system, commerce and industry and total society and way of living.

Today's world with its scores of varied man-made governments and all this world's evils was the result. I explained how God knew that, left to himself, man would within 6,000 years destroy himself—and that we have reached the very last generation of this present evil world. For the first time in human history the weapons of mass destruction exist that can erase all human life from this earth—unless Almighty God intervenes to save us from ourselves. How God reserved to Himself the right to intervene if and when necessary for His ultimate purpose—that mankind learns that only God's way of love can bring peace and happiness.

I mentioned how God had intervened in the case of Abraham, Moses and the ancient nation Israel; Christ and the Church. How Christ's gospel was the announcement of the restoration of the government of God to bring the world peace and happiness—but how they put Him to death and suppressed His gospel announcement of the Kingdom of God before the end of the first century. The world went on ignorant of God and His ways.

Today we approach the end of the 6,000 years and of this civilization. We have reached the last generation—the very generation in which the nations would destroy all humanity in nuclear war—unless God intervenes to save humanity alive. He raised me up for the purpose once again in this final generation of getting out the gospel announcement just before it happens.

Then I said: "You gentlemen are faced with the solemn task of trying to hammer out another new government in the kind of world we live in today. In such a world you have to deal with other nations, and you will not be able to form a government based on God's law, for you would be a lamb among wolves. But you can try to form a government that gives equal justice, opportunity, protection and concern for the welfare of your own people in your domestic policies. And the nearer you can come to forming foreign policies and pursuing dealings with other nations as nearly like God's way as possible, the more you will be specially blessed by the God who is Creator and supreme Ruler over all. And you will live into His wonderful World Tomorrow—when the Kingdom of God rules your people and all the world in peace and happiness and well-being and joy. It is the way—and the only way that will lead to God and the welfare of us all."

That in essence was my message to them. God strengthened me to deliver it to them in power and with authority and I can say truthfully that they were really moved and impressed.

I give you this much detail because I wanted you Co-Workers to know just how this urgent and necessary gospel message is now reaching the heads of governments around the earth. I feel that my message this afternoon . . . was even stronger, with greater power and authority, and I know it shook and moved the audience, including the lawmakers and the heads of those who execute the law in that nation.

Much more work lies ahead for me here in South Africa the next several days. Expect to be in Durban for Passover. . . .

April 18, 1977

Dear Brethren of God's Church:

This is a very personal announcement. Forty-three years ago God committed to me His great commission—to carry Christ's gospel—the Kingdom of God—to all the world. It is a staggering responsibility! In many ways He had prepared me for it in advance. Apart from organization, I have had to rely on God for private, personal needs as well.

Even before He thrust me into His Work, God provided the wife of my youth. He used her in bringing about my conversion, and for fifty happily married years giving me the needed closeness and warmth of companionship, love, affection and inspiration only a wife can give.

Since her death, God miraculously has opened to me doors (Rev. 3:8) to kings, emperors, presidents and prime ministers, so that Christ's message may be taken into nations whose doors were closed to this message. At this stage no one but myself can do this. And I could not endure the grueling worldwide travel had not God blessed me with youthful vigor, vitality, and energy (Isa. 40:28-31), enabling me to carry on more vigorously than one in a hundred half my calendar age. This almost constant travel (last year 300 out of 365 days) and loneliness has reawakened me to the serious need God recognized when He said, "It is not good that a man should be alone."

584

Directly or indirectly, you brethren are all my sons and daughters in the Lord. But I am nonetheless human. Like the Apostle Paul said, "We also are men, of like nature with you." God says through James, "Elijah was a man of like nature with ourselves." Paul said, "Am I not an apostle? . . . Do we not have the right to be accompanied by a wife?" (RSV). People do sometimes forget an apostle has personal needs.

Of course no one could take the place of my beloved wife of fifty years. But the Work of God must go on, finishing the great commission God committed to me, in this new and most important phase of the entire Work. And God now has graciously provided the wife to be constantly at my side—a woman truly led by God's Holy Spirit. We have given the matter much time, to be sure it has grown into true love and like-minded rapport, as well as definitely sure it is God's will.

This is to announce my marriage to Ramona Martin, in an informal and simple ceremony, attended only by our respective families on Sunday, April 17.

May 16, 1977

Dear Brethren of God's Church,

This may be the most important letter I have ever written . . . .

I have just returned from the Big Sandy (Texas) campus graduation. I have not been able to go to Big Sandy but rarely—I think a year ago was the last time—and what I saw there was a real eye-opener. Attending graduation exercises were two or three bank presidents, presidents and vice presidents of other colleges in east Texas; important business men, multi-millionaire oil men, Several of these—the most important men in east Texas—congratulated me on the

585

fact that Ambassador College at Big Sandy has given all of east Texas a new cultural awakening—and made a tremendous uplift in the morale and the uplifted life of the whole area.

But it made me sick at heart—my heart literally ached to realize that the financial situation may probably cause the closure of Ambassador College, Big Sandy. This college has earned and now has the enthusiastic goodwill and praise of the whole section—within an area of at least a 100-mile diameter. Pray with me God will send a miracle to prevent it. . . .

But, as I wrote you in the letter read on April 27, God committed to me in July, 1933, Christ's great commission—to take Christ's gospel announcement to the whole world for a witness to all nations.

God did not call me into the college business—as a business. I must keep the priorities straight as He gives them to me, for I shall have to give account to Christ when He comes!

But by 1947 it finally became necessary to found Ambassador College. There were reasons why it had to start in Pasadena. God miraculously opened the doors to start it there, when we had no money to start it with.

I had been used to raise up the parent church at Eugene, Oregon with nineteen members in 1933. It grew. God opened radio to me January, 1934. *The Plain Truth* was born February 1, 1934. I held nightly evangelistic meetings in or near Eugene for some two years. We went on radio in Portland, Seattle, Spokane. I began holding meetings in Seattle and elsewhere—where God had added members to form a small local church. But I could not preach at Eugene, Jefferson, Portland, Seattle, Creswell and other churches all at once on the same Sabbath. There was not enough of me.

Ambassador College became necessary to train ministers for new local churches beginning to rise up rapidly. The college started October 8, 1947, after I had learned what birth pangs were.

The purpose of the college was to provide personnel for the work—and ministers to feed the flock that was growing 30 percent per year.

As I said, I have to consider the priorities.

Let me give them to you.

First, above priorities for the Work itself, priority number one is the necessity of a spiritual revival in the whole Church. Without that, the whole Work is skidding on the way down—and out! It is just that serious!

I have started setting the example by five days fasting and prayer, and I am going back to it with my whole heart—I hope for the next five days! . . .

First priority in the Work is the open door program—in which Christ is opening doors which I am personally walking through, to kings, presidents, emperors, prime ministers, their cabinet members, parliament members, and others of high position—judges, bank presidents, university presidents, etc. Right now this is first on the priority list in God's sight, because the first thing on God's mind is restoring the government of God to this earth, and this new phase of the Work—the open door operation worldwide is the present activity leading to it.

How significant that the very first priority—the most important phase of the Work, is lowest on the budget-cost allocations. Of course tied with it is the AICF which has been producing sensational results.

Today, among other major priorities is *The Plain Truth*, especially the newsstand circulation. Along with this is the *Correspondence Course*. . . .

Another equally important part of the great commission is television and radio. This must be tremendously stepped up.

Exceedingly important to all of us, and to you brethren is our Pastoral Administration Department. . . .

You can't perform miracles. But God can—has done it always before when we put our hearts fully into our beseeching Him—and will now. I know that what you can do by sacrificing other things and sending in money is limited—but what can be done by your urgent prayers is unlimited. We need now a miracle. We will need miracles in the future.

Please go to your knees and ask for it. Ask believingly!

July 21, 1977

Dear Brethren and Co-Workers with Christ:

It is Tuesday morning July 19. We are in flight in our G II from Tokyo to Hong Kong. We have on board one of my "Japanese sons"—a high Member of the Japanese Diet, with his very charming wife and two of their three sons.

Last Sabbath we had a private dinner in the private dining room connecting with the Fontainebleue Restaurant atop the Imperial Hotel with the Ambassador of Israel and his wife, with other members of the Israeli Embassy and their wives, making it a total of twelve at the dinner. There immediately followed a Sabbath afternoon service attended by some 200 *Plain Truth* readers.

Last night was the big night of the visit to Tokyo— a most important banquet with about 150 in attendance, including several high in the Japanese government with thirteen ambassadors from as many countries. Most of my "Japanese sons"—all Members of the Japanese Diet—were present. I was guest of honor and main speaker. I did get over to them the good news announcement of the Kingdom of God.

I mentioned, first, that I had a very happy announcement to make. I then mentioned that some three years ago I had been guest speaker at a luncheon in Addis Ababa, Ethiopia, attended by nineteen ambassadors—official representatives of nineteen nations—and most of their wives. Everyone was so jovial in a bedlam of laughing conversation that I then said this was evidence that all our nations could live happily at peace as we were doing. I said, last night, that "tonight I will go further. I announce to you tonight, that, in our very present living generation, all nations will come to live happily and joyfully together in world peace. We will not bring this about ourselves," I said. "We humans have brought only trouble, pain and suffering—discontent, injustice, and unhappiness on ourselves!

"Governments are now being overthrown at the rate of one a month. This will accelerate. For the first time in all history, since 1950, man has created the weapons of mass destruction that can erase all life from this planet Earth. We humans are going to bring conditions to the very brink of total disaster! Our number one problem now is survival of the human race!

"Many world-famous scientists say our only hope is the emergence of a one world super-government to rule all nations. One of our great weekly news magazines in the United States said in an editorial that it would seem that mankind's only hope now is the sudden intervention of an unseen strong hand from some place.

"The editor meant," I said, "the intervention of God, the Creator of the Japanese people and all the

589

peoples and races of the earth.

"I am here to announce to you tonight that in our present living generation humanity will bring things to the place that, unless there is that supernatural Divine intervention, no human would be left alive. But, just before that happens, God Almighty will intervene, and save humanity alive. And He will then set up over us the Kingdom of God—the same super-government to rule all nations which scientists say is our only hope.

"Mankind then will be governed by God's laws of love—of giving—of helping, sharing, serving. It makes no difference whether you believe that or not. It is sure! It is as certain as the rising and setting of the sun. I have announced it to you. Your ears have heard it! It's your only hope. Thank you, ladies and gentlemen!" . . .

In Hong Kong I will speak at a special dinner of the highest people, and hope to give them the same message.

Remember our serious needs in your heartrending prayers. I am on a very long and strenuous trip. From Hong Kong we go to New Delhi, where I am to speak to a very large audience, then on to Israel, and then to three countries on the West African coast, and then Pasadena.

P.S. From Hong Kong. This is Thursday, July 21. The dinner last night had to be canceled because of a typhoon which hit Hong Kong yesterday.

Excerpts from Address to the
1978 Ministerial Conference.
March 1978

First, I want to say a few words about my illness. Last August I was scripturally dead. The doctor called it heart failure. When I first realized what had happened, that my heart and breath had both stopped, I will say here what has subsequently been told to me, because I don't remember a bit of it. But the nurse who was in charge has told me that she came in and saw that my face was ashen white, and immediately she took my pulse and there wasn't any.

So the blood was not circulating, not to show even one point on the blood-pressure instrument.

So then they started working over me, and I think Ted anointed me. My wife's sister was there. This was because my wife, who feared something like this, had kept her there, because she was experienced in first-aid and things of that kind. She and the nurse used mouth resuscitation and heart massage until they got me breathing.

The nurse's estimate from the time she had noticed this until I began taking the first breath was at least thirty seconds. She said it was a minute and a half, though, that it was touch and go, because I'd lapse back and quit breathing. And after about a minute and a half I was breathing enough on my own, and I've continued all right since, and I hope the rest of the life that God wants for me on earth.

Had not skilled nurses been present to administer instant mouth-to-mouth resuscitation and heart massage, I tell you that as far as I was personally concerned I wouldn't be here today.

Shortly after they'd told me what had happened, I felt that if my work in God's hands were finished and God didn't have any further use for me in His Work, that I would rather have remained dead. Because if they hadn't intervened I would have been buried in two or three days.

But I realize that God had shown me something by

591

two miracles. No. 1, He restored my life when I was already past eighty-five years of age. And this was very shortly, as a matter of fact, about twenty days after my eighty-fifth birthday.

And, second, neither I nor my nurses had ever heard of anyone of like age being restored by that process after almost complete loss of mind, my brain virtually a vegetable. And I was restored with my mind just as intact as it ever was.

Back at conversion over fifty years ago, I gave my life to Jesus Christ. I had come to the place fifty years ago that I figured I was—I called it then—a burned-out hunk of junk that wasn't even fit to throw on the junk pile. And I said to Jesus Christ. "If You can use this worthless life, I'm giving it to You, and my life is not my own from here on."

I have never claimed that I had built any part of this campus or of the Work. I take a walk every morning, as I used to before this attack, and I've been staying down at Tucson since, but I used to take a morning walk around the campus. I would always remark about the beauty and what a wonderful thing that God had given this kind of beauty, not only that I could enjoy but share it with thousands of others.

But I didn't say, "Look what *I* have done," because I hadn't done anything. This is the Work of the living Jesus Christ, and He alone has done the Work, but He has used me as an instrument.

Now, medical opinion was that it would be many months, eight or ten, before I would be fully back in harness. It has been just barely over four months so far. I would like to remind you of that and that I know the medical authorities all say I'm making extraordinary progress. Well, I think you know why.

Now, again, this is the Work of the living God,

through Christ. It is not the work of man. We must never forget this. It could be a tendency to think that this is just something that I started. No, this is what God started, and God through Christ is going to determine what happens in this Church and in this Work.

Jesus Christ heads this Work, and I work as His instrument through and for Him.

May 21, 1978

Dear Co-Workers and Brethren in Christ,

God's great Work—to the whole world—is, truly, going ahead now as never before, with a new start!

Soon you will hear new programs from me, on both radio and television. Just as Moses, the man of God, had not abated in his strength of mind and spirit, in leading the children of Israel out of Egyptian bondage into the Promised Land, after eighty years of age, so the same God has sustained my mind, energy and power for the completion of His Work in this world.

On July 4 there will be a big "4th of July Celebration" in Jerusalem, hosted jointly by the Mayor of Jerusalem, Mr. Teddy Kollek, and myself. The city of Philadelphia had an exact duplicate made of the Liberty Bell—crack and all—and gave it to the city of Jerusalem. In the spring of 1976—Passover time—the Mayor came to me privately, and asked my help in building an important downtown park in Jerusalem, to be named the "Liberty Bell Park." Through the AICF, I was able to agree to supply the children's playground area, at the very opening of the park. The park is now completed, and Mayor Kollek has asked me to be present on July 4 for the opening and dedication of the Liberty Bell Park.

July 8, I am scheduled to co-host an important

premier of a charity motion picture to raise funds for the handicapped children in Britain. Queen Elizabeth II has promised to co-host this premier and banquet—and in the event she is unable to be present, either Prince Charles (the next king) or Prince Philip will be there.

In early August, I am again to go to Japan—and perhaps other points in the Far East. Other campaigns in world capitals are now being planned—as before my heart failure and illness. December 1, the Israeli government is planning a celebration in my honor—on the 10th anniversary of the beginning of our participation in the great archaeological excavation, starting southward from the Temple Mount. This date will mark the beginning of the second decade of this major project—now starting further south, in the area of the ancient City of David, to uncover 2,500 years of accumulated debris (some 50 feet high) over the ancient palace and throne of King David. The AICF is following through on this—preparing the very site of the throne on which Christ will sit at His coming. This is just one of the ways in which we are preparing the way for His coming and establishment of the Kingdom of God, ushering in world peace. . . .

Pasadena
June 22, 1978

Dear Co-Workers and Brethren in Christ:

I just want to have a real heart-to-heart family get-together with you.

I have said many times that, directly or indirectly, all you who have God's Holy Spirit are my children in Christ. Even those of you who have come into the Church more recently.

The aged Apostle John, writing in the 90s A.D.,

addressed his first letter, in the second chapter, to "my little children, these things write I unto you."

From the bottom of my heart, I thank you for the wonderful letters and telephone calls that have been pouring in, since I have been back on the air and also in regard to the recent changes Christ, the Living Head of this Church, has been making to set His Church back on the right track.

Let me first assure you that I have not "moved away from Headquarters." Jesus Christ has chosen and used only one apostle in our time. Let me say to you emphatically that the Living Christ has taken over as the head of God's Church, and established me in firm control, under Him, on the human level. I am back on the job. I am back on the air—both on television and on radio. Every effort is being made to put the programs on more and more radio stations—especially the major 50,000 watt stations—and on television coast to coast. We must realize it is impossible to get back on so many hundreds of stations all at once. But, as fast as we can we are now bending every effort to increase our radio and television coverage. . . .

Brethren, it is wonderful and inspiring to know that you do love me so much and are praying for me. This awareness gives me the incentive and inspiration to press on until Christ's great commission is finished.

But let me tell you that I do love all you—pray for you—and am grateful from the bottom of my heart for your faithfulness, loyalty, and loving support in the Work.

And now, the first letters after hearing the first radio broadcast (that is, the first I personally have done in a few years) are beginning to flood in. . . .

82

July 25, 1978— December 18, 1979

July 25, 1978

Dear Brethren and Co-Workers with Christ:

Now we are beginning to prepare in earnest for the greatest Feast of Tabernacles ever.

Last Friday night, in addition to the weekly Bible Study in the House of God (Ambassador Auditorium), I recorded on television an opening Festival greeting to be shown by 16mm projector on large screens in every Feast site on the opening night.

Then on the Sabbath I did a full sermon, televised, to be put on 16mm tape to be projected at all Feast sites over the earth on the first Holy Day.

Last year, I was in the early stages of recovery from the heart failure of last August. But the four or five years before that I spoke personally at every Feast site in the United States and in Penticton, B.C., Canada.

596

This year I decided to speak at all sites worldwide, by having it projected on motion picture screens.....

I am sure you will experience a new uplift and inspirational surge forward at this great Feast of Tabernacles!

I am now turning over to the printers what I believe to be the most important book since the very first century! The printers are setting up a speedy crash program, to give us first delivery of this book by October 1—in time for the Feast. Never in our time has any book or writing spoken as this new book will! Its title is *The Incredible Human Potential.* It is the message of the entire Bible—put together as never before—from the prehistoric existence of only God and "The Word," through the creation of angels, the creation of the endless physical universe and the creation of this earth—on through the sinning of the angels, the renewing of the face of the earth for man—the creation of man—why man was put here on earth—why God left Satan here up to now—why the Old Testament congregation of Israel—and why the Church and its mission—on through the World Tomorrow for one thousand years—and then—the incredible potential of man throughout eternity—over all the vast material universe.

Much of this has never before appeared in print. Much of it will be new Bible truth to you! It explains the mind of man, and the actual source of human nature.

This book—full book length—will be available in virtually all bookstores in the United States and the English speaking world. It will reach an entirely new audience with God's message, heretofore unreachable!

Also we are updating, and getting before the world, such books as *The United States and Britain in*

Prophecy—back to full length! Also such booklets as *Why Were You Born?*, *What Do you Mean—Born Again?*, *Just What Do You Mean—Salvation?*, *What Do You Mean, The Kingdom Of God?*, and *The Seven Laws of Success,* and many of those vital booklets that built the Work!

God is rapidly increasing my personal strength, and I am now turning out more work than I have in the past twenty years!

I pray earnestly for you, and I also need your prayers! The Work is now fast picking up!

P.S. God willing I plan to speak in person at the Saint Petersburg, Florida, site the first night and Holy Day, and at the Tuscon site on the final Holy Day.

September 1978

Two of my personal acquaintances and friends, both heads-of-state, died—one yesterday, the other this morning.

Yesterday, August 21, President Nicolaas Diederichs of South Africa died in a Cape Town hospital after a second heart attack in eight days. He was seventy-four. President Diederichs was founder of the Afrikaner nationalist movement.

... I spent about two hours with him about a year and a half ago in Cape Town. We spent some little time taking photographs and in friendly conversation.

Then this morning my good friend, Jomo Kenyatta, president of Kenya, died at the State House in Mombasa in his sleep.

I had visited with him ... at his office in the State House in Nairobi and the better part of a whole day at his residence thirty-five miles outside Nairobi. He customarily spent every night in his suburban home, driving the thirty-five miles every morning to his office in Nairobi.

We had luncheon at his home with members of his family. He conducted us on a tour through a suburban self-help hospital, which he had built. He was, as am I, a staunch believer in helping others to help themselves—to help them get on their own feet so they can make their own way, rather than supporting others outright in pure charity while they do nothing to help themselves.

Through the Ambassador International Cultural Foundation, we had undertaken to join with President Kenyatta in founding in Kenya a self-help school to help reduce the illiteracy of the country. He was apparently just my age—eighty-six, though he did not know his exact birth date. He was a very close friend—like two close brothers with Emperor Haile Selassie of Ethiopia.

The emperor was just eight days older than I, and one of his lasts acts before he was taken prisoner by the military coup that overthrew his government was to send me a telegram of congratulations on my eighty-third birthday.

President Kenyatta defeated the British in the fight for Kenyan independence in 1963. He ruled one of the most stable governments in Africa. After spending several hours with him, I rated him publicly with the evaluation of greatness—one of the few such persons I have known in a life of acquaintance with hundreds of the great and near-great.

God rates people according to how well they do according to what they have to do with. Jomo Kenyatta started out with very little—as an African tribesman. He was a self-educated and self-made man whom I felt had reached the status, in this world, of true greatness.

January 18, 1979

Dear Brethren and Co-Workers with Christ:

This may be the most important letter I have ever written. The very life of God's Church and His Work hangs in the balance. This letter may have to be long. I want you to know all the facts about this master-blow of Satan to destroy the Church of God through the civil power of the State, in flagrant violation of the Constitution of the United States!

I thought on January 7, when I wrote you, that God had then given us the victory in this decisive life-and-death assault against Almighty God, Jesus Christ and God's Church. It was reported to me then that the judge in the hearing of that day had said he found no evidence of any wrongdoing. And that was true—and no evidence of any wrongdoing or justification for this monstrous outrage against God's Work has been found against us. Nor will they find any in our records—for few, if any, corporations have kept as accurate and clean-cut records as God's Church. . . .

Let me illustrate to you brethren, just how this great Work of God started. To start the Work, I needed to broadcast over radio. That required physical facilities for which I had to pay (at that time, $2.50 a week). To print and send out *The Plain Truth,* I had to have a typewriter, a secondhand one I bought for $10, and an old secondhand ancestor of the Mimeograph, a hand-cranked Neostyle, which I procured also for $10.

This Work always has required physical facilities to operate. Now the receiver is locking up our executive and other office facilities. This Work started with a little inside office room with no ventilation—no outside window or door—just a transom over the one door leading to a corridor and another transom over a covered window leading into a large room used for labor union meetings. Tobacco smoke rolled in. We could work in the office only one or two hours at a time, then had to stay out two or more hours until the air cleared—and the office rent was $7 per month.

These physical facilities are part of the operation of a Church. God commanded His apostles to go into all the world with His gospel message. Satan suppressed that message from going to the world for 1,900 years. And now he is trying to destroy the Church of God in order to stop that message from going out to all the world. . . .

Brethren, anyone can sue anyone for anything at any time. That's the kind of justice system in Satan's world. This present outrageous civil action by the State of California was brought by false charges and no proof by only five or six malcontent former members. It's a tremendous travesty of justice that such a thing can be done.

The very purpose of the Church, first of all, is to stand back of and support the carrying of Christ's gospel message out to all the world as a witness to all nations. The second purpose is to prepare those God has called into His Church in holy righteous character so that they may enter—at the time of the resurrection—into the Kingdom of God as a king and/or priest under Christ when He comes to rule the world! But the first mentioned purpose, standing behind the proclaiming of the gospel around the world, is the means God has given us of developing all in God's Church into that holy and righteous character of God.

God's Church cannot carry out either prime purpose without facilities!

But, my dear brethren, let us stop and realize that Christ, the Head of our Church, has allowed this unprecedented monstrous attack by state government and state courts of law to come upon us. God will give us the victory in the end.

But meanwhile we as God's called and chosen people need to ask ourselves, why has God allowed it? He tells us all things work together for good to those who love and obey Him. In what way, then, has this very traumatic, monstrous injustice been allowed by our God? Not that He wanted to punish us. Not that he wanted to bring suffering upon us. But because we were drifting into a careless, lukewarm, spiritual condition! God has allowed Satan to bring this upon us. First, to wake us up spiritually and to bring us back closer to God, and second, to draw us closer together and third, to sift out from our midst some of the chaff from the wheat.

Brethren, this terrible ordeal is accomplishing those three things! It is a sifting time. Some "liberals" who wanted to water down God's truth are being sifted out.

It is also the time of Daniel 12:10: "Many shall be purified, and made white, and tried. . . ." It is speaking of this very time shortly before Christ's Second Coming!

God has allowed it exactly as He allowed Satan to take away everything from Job, and then afflicted Job with boils from head to foot—Job was self-righteous. . . .

But just as once Job came to realize his sin of self-righteousness and repent of it, God restored to him twice as much as he had before, even so, my brethren—my own children in the Lord—God will restore to us and His Work double, or much more than double, once His purpose, as I stated above, has been accomplished.

602

My children in the Lord, we need to go to our knees! We need to fast and pray! True, I need you to stand back of me now as never before in special generous offerings to fight this monstrous miscarriage of justice—but even more—you need to draw closer to our wonderful and great God.

Don't ever worry about God or Christ forsaking us or His Work! He won't! We need to be concerned about whether we have begun to veer away to some extent from Him—have we unknowingly begun partly to forsake Him? . . .

I call now a special day of fasting and prayer—not only for the Work and the Church but also for our own selves that we may be brought closer to God—on Sabbath, January 27, worldwide! We under Christ shall prevail!

I thank you with all my heart, and I love you all as never before.

Tucson, Arizona
January 28, 1979

Dear Brethren and Co-Workers with Christ:

Thank you! Thank you for your great response and coming to the aid of God's Work in this most monstrous and outrageous travesty of justice ever heard of by any state government! . . .

We have never objected to any government authority checking our books and records. They contain proof we have done nothing of which we are falsely accused. They started rumors we had secreted away some of the books. On the contrary, we stood guard that no one could destroy or remove our records and books! . . .

Now we need all the brethren to continue to rally behind Christ's Apostle until a higher court releases the

Work from its virtual captivity. If arrested, our brethren would not have resisted. At all times they behaved like God's people, orderly, neat, polite. Many people outside our membership have noticed this and commented on it.

Brethren, remember what I wrote in my last letter. This is drawing all our brethren closer together than ever before—but it must also draw us closer to God! I called a day of fasting and prayer for last Sabbath. If any did not receive that letter in time, then fast and pray on the very next Sabbath—both that we shall all be drawn closer to God, and that God will release this grip of the State over God's Church. . . .

We now begin to notice a little change in attitude in the press. At first news reports were slanted, practically condemning us as guilty without evidence or proof. Now they are more objective. The attorney general's office has changed its language from using the terms "siphoning off," and "pilfering," to "possible mismanagement," at least in the last newspaper notice.

Some of our enemies have tried to construe my work of personally walking through opened doors to carry Christ's gospel message into nations around the world as "mismanagement," and "siphoning off" money so spent for our own personal use! That is simply a lie! Before my marriage nearly two years ago now, I took my elder daughter Beverly Gott with me as hostess—for there were many banquets, receptions, luncheons and dinners at which I was privileged to speak to people high up in various nations, and even royalty. This required additional and better clothes, and some jewelry that was not mere "costume jewelry." But every such item was paid for by my own personal money on which both federal and state income tax had been paid. Later I had to purchase the same sort of things for Ramona my wife—out of my own money—not a cent from corporate funds or expense money. While I think this should have been a legitimate expense, I did not so construe it, and all such purchases, were paid out of my personal funds. . . .

They have tried to treat as "extravagance" such things as the purchase of Steuben crystal—which is about the only type of art object made in this country fitting for presenting to a king, president, or prime minister. Look into your Bible, Matthew 2:11, and see that the wise men presented gifts to Christ as an infant. This was not a birthday present, for it was many days after His birth. But since long before Christ it has been custom to present a gift when visiting a king or head of government. It would indeed look strange if we did not present an acceptable gift when visiting a monarch.

There has been no mismanagement! Just the opposite! I have written you at times through the years how we have made a dollar go further than any other operation of which I know. Read Revelation 10:11. This shows that after we thought we had completed the Work, or were to complete it by January, 1972, how God says, "Thou shalt prophesy [preach] again before many peoples, and nations, and tongues, and kings"! Most of the doors to kings and heads of governments have opened since January, 1972.

Christ has called and chosen His Apostle for this end-time job of the Great Commission! We have been getting that job done! Often there are as many as twelve to fourteen of us travelling—especially on such trips as when I twice took eight top-ranking Japanese Congressmen on trips to the Middle East oil countries, and to South America. On such trips I have introduced them, and arranged receptions for them, in countries where I already know the heads of government. And, in turn, they opened the door to me on an official basis in other countries where I had not been before! Often there were banquets, receptions, and such occasions, Yes, that cost some money.

But, of all the departments of God's Work, that cost the least, and was the most important!

Today, Monday, I believe this case is to go before the California Supreme Court. Then we will take it into the federal courts, and if necessary to the Supreme Court in Washington. As I wrote you before, we are making this fight not only to protect God's Church from State encroachment, but all churches and even the freedom of the press and right of free assembly....

I thank you all for your wonderful response in sending God's tithes and your liberal freewill offerings to me, personally, here at Tucson, Arizona. A Tucson newspaper has reported that the receiver at Pasadena will try to induce the State of Arizona to shut off my personal mail. If so, we will get word to you quickly, through your local ministers, where to send it—even if need be, to your Area Coordinator, and we will find a way to pick it up from there. I have already signed legal papers making me personally custodian for the Church's funds. Remember money sent to Pasadena will go to the receiver.

God is still on His throne, with Jesus fully alive there beside Him interceding for us! Let us realize God has allowed this to draw us closer to Him as well as each other. Keep praying—fasting and praying. God will win!

Tokyo, Japan
May 15, 1979

Dear Brethren and Co-Workers in Christ,

For some twenty months, due to total heart failure in August, 1977, I was prevented from proclaiming

Christ's gospel in person in the far-flung nations around the world.

But God has been with me. There has been no diminishing of the vital faculties, especially of the mind. And while I was having, for the time, to defer the ordeal of physically demanding worldwide travel, I have been able to write almost faster than you brethren can read, and to continue full leadership of God's Work here on earth.... There must have been 250 or 300 or more at the banquet last night. It was held in a large banquet room of the Imperial Hotel. This is a large hotel with several private dining rooms. Many of the eight Congressmen who call themselves my Japanese sons were there. They are Members of the Diet—the Japanese Congress or Parliament. The speakers' table seated at least a dozen. Some of them spoke briefly, and stood, one at a time, to be introduced. All others, including wives, were seated at many round tables—ten or twelve seated at each table. All who spoke were saying complimentary things about me. During the evening a few other Members of the Japanese Diet said they wanted to be counted as one of my "Japanese sons," all of whom are important Diet Members—the number of my "Japanese sons" in the Diet is now twelve ...

I had said earlier that I was not going to plan ahead what to say, or speak from any notes. I knew the living Christ would put into my mind what I should say—and He did!

There were at least a half dozen ambassadors representing other nations present (with their wives). So, I knew that a number of different religions was represented.

Suppose you were to be asked to stand up and speak to some 300 highly distinguished people.... You knew that Jesus Christ wanted you to proclaim to them

607

the good news about the Kingdom of God, and you had to get this gospel message over to these important people. Just how would you go about it? If you had two or three days beforehand to think and plan what to say, what would you say?

I think all of you ought to know a little about how Jesus Christ leads His chosen Apostle to do it.

I knew the living Christ would guide me. Like you, I am only human, but I trusted the living Jesus. He did put in my mind what to say. . . .

I then said I had read an editorial in one of the world's leading news magazines, which said our "world problems and evils are now so great it would seem that the world's only hope lies in the intervention of a great unseen hand from someplace." In this manner, I brought to the attention of these many government officials of different religions the supreme God—and then explained that this great "Unseen Hand" was the unseen Creator, who made of one blood all of the nations represented in this banquet.

I did not know until I stood up before the microphone that I would say that. But you see, Jesus Christ put words in my mouth that showed them I was speaking of the Supreme Creator, regardless of their religion. Jesus gave me the words to show God's power, without offense to any because of his religious belief.

I then said that many consider me an ambassador without portfolio (that is, no official political authority), but in fact, I told them, I was an official ambassador of the Great God who created us all. I brought to them, from Him, good news—news of the world's only hope— that we are now in the very last days of this present man-made civilization, with more problems and evils than mankind can solve—and that soon now—in our generation—God will intervene, and set up the world ruling Kingdom of God and that we shall then have world peace, happiness, joy and economic abundance for all in all nations.

I said, "I don't ask you to believe what I say. We humans won't bring this about—it will be done to us—and in spite of us—whether we believe it or not—whether we want it or not. I have just announced it to you, and it definitely shall happen!"

Thus, in few words, and, even waiting at every sentence for the interpreter to repeat it in the Japanese language, Jesus Christ, through me, delivered the gospel of the Kingdom to some 300 of the leaders of Japan and several other nations!

I might mention, this is what the attorney general's office in California is trying to call "siphoning off millions of dollars every year for my own use." In the past two years, we have not spent one tenth of one million dollars on this important Work of carrying the gospel into nations worldwide. For the past ten years, this part of the Work has cost less than one million dollars a year—whereas our budget calls for several million dollars per year for salaries to ministers and the staff at headquarters plus several million for radio, TV and printing.

I must break off now and hurry into a business suit—for I am to have a meeting in less that two hours with Prime Minister Ohira. I have met and visited with every Japanese Prime Minister in the past ten years—Prime Minister Eisaku Sato, Prime Minister Tanaka, Prime Minister Miki, and now Prime Minister Ohira. I have been highly honored in Japan. There's a saying that a prophet is without honor in his own country. That's where the persecution comes from. But here, I am honored above any unofficial non-Japanese. And though the persecution comes in many forms at home,

609

I am deeply grateful that you Brethren and Co-Workers of God's Church have deep love for me, and you have certainly proved that. I love and pray for you continually.

Later: In flight back home, April 29.

I have now had private personal meetings with the last four Prime Ministers of Japan.

Perhaps the most important news that I can give you of this trip is that definite plans are now under way for me to make an official visit to China—officially the People's Republic of China—in company with two or three of the highest Members of the Japanese Diet. Two of the high-ranking Members of Japan's law-making Diet are definitely working on arrangements. The trip will be made in our own G-II jet, and probably in August. Private meetings are being set up with the Communist Party Chairman and Prime Minister Hua Guofeng, and the Deputy Prime Minister Ding Xiaoping.

As you know, I have been waiting a long time for the Head of our Church, Jesus Christ, to open doors—if He wanted His Apostle to go to the leaders of China and the Soviet Union. Of course, I can't know yet what Christ may have in mind, but He is able to open doors wherever He wants me to go as His ambassador and Apostle.

Plans are now being made for a visit with the government heads and many other leaders in a country I have never yet visited—Tunisia, on the southern shore of the Mediterranean Sea, east of Egypt. (I already had a personal meeting with President Sadat of Egypt.)

Before leaving Japan on this present trip, I had further meetings with a few other Japanese leaders. This has certainly been a very succesful trip. We are now on the descent for a refueling at Cold Bay, Alaska—the furthermost western tip of Alaska, where the Aleutian Islands virtually join up with Alaska at its farthest western tip.

I close asking you to continue your earnest and fervent prayers for me and the Work.

Returning from China
December 18, 1979

Dear Brethren and Co-Workers with Christ:

I am back from probably the most important and successful single trip overseas. I was honored to be. . . invited as a guest speaker and for personal conferences with leaders of the Communist People's Republic of China. There I spoke with leaders who shape the minds and thinking and beliefs of one fourth of all the people on earth! . . .

Government limousines drove up to our aircraft as we landed. A welcoming delegation had come to the airport, including the president and vice-president of the educational system, which includes the national library. . . .

We arrived on Sunday evening, December 2. On Monday evening I spoke for about a half hour at a banquet in my honor, attended by prominent members of the government and their wives. Tuesday evening I spoke again before the Diplomatic Corps, including ambassadors—many with wives—representing seventy-six other nations from all parts of the world, beside a number of high-ranking Chinese.

Both of these speeches were taped, and will be heard in most of the local churches of the Worldwide Church of God around the world. . . .

We were taken on a virtual all-day visit to the

611

Great Wall of China—undoubtedly one of the seven man-built wonders of the world—on Tuesday. Wednesday was a very full day. In the morning we visited the national library, the "Forbidden City"—a walled city within the city of Peking—former palaces and buildings of the emperors. Then a noon luncheon, and at 4 p.m. the real highlight of the visit—the private meeting at the Great Hall of the People (government headquarters) with the Vice-Chairman of the Standing Committee of the National People's Congress—one of the three top men in the government, Mr. Tan Zhen-lin. . . .

Wednesday evening we attended a special program sponsored by the Ambassador International Cultural Foundation at a Peking theater. The theater was crowded and there was vigorous standing applause as our party entered. It was a semiballet program and was excellent. We were guided up on the stage at the end of the show, as audience applause continued, and we shook hands with the whole cast. The AICF will endeavor to arrange for this show to be staged at the Ambassador Auditorium in Pasadena, and also in New York, Philadephia, Chicago, San Francisco and other major cities.

Thursday noon we left for the airport. There, to see us off and bid us good-bye was a delegation, again including the president and vice-president of the government's educational system.

We were royally received and entertained by the government people. They could not have been more friendly. And we were enthusiastically invited to come again.

On Saturday night there was a banquet in Tokyo at which, among many toasts, I was privileged to speak again. Then Sunday the long trip home to Tucson, with one fuel stop at Cold Bay, Alaska.

God was with us. He gave us great favor in the eyes of our Chinese hosts.

I had been invited to visit China some five or six years ago, by the Chinese Ambassador in Addis Ababa, Ethiopia. At that time the government at Peking refused to admit me, saying I had written articles against communism. However, they said, they had noted that it had been many years ago, and I had not written things against communism in recent years, so they said then they might invite me later. And this they did.

It is true that I did write anticommunist articles, because they are atheist and anti-God, rather than because of their political persuasion. However, I hope I have grown in grace and the knowledge of our Lord and Savior Jesus Christ, as Peter instructs in II Peter 3:18. It has been impressed on me in more recent years what I only partly realized some thirty to fifty years ago, how, when our first parents rejected God's teaching, God's government over them, and God's salvation, that God, in driving them out of the Garden of Eden, barring entrance to the "tree of life," said, in effect: "You have rejected my government, my teaching, and me as Savior. Therefore, I sentence you and your children which shall populate and form the world, for 6,000 years, to being cut off from me and my Holy Spirit. Therefore, go, and create your own religions, form your own kinds of governments, devise your own knowledge and educational systems, and your own types of society. Yet I will call a very few who are predestinated to be called for use in preparing for the final Kingdom of God."

It actually was God who cut mankind off—except for those specially called—rather than man having turned from God (except for Adam and Eve, of course).

God simply has not called most of the millions in China and Russia and India. He will, either in the coming millennium, or in the Great White Throne Judgment, when Satan will no longer be here to deceive.

So I no longer write articles condemning Communism, or their governments. Instead I go to them with the message of hope—the Kingdom of God, when God will open all minds, and bring them to salvation.

Jesus did not come on a soul-saving mission! The gospel is good news, which God has called me to proclaim.

On this basis, not judging or condemning them, but bringing to the leaders of the most populous nation on earth Christ's message of hope, I was enthusiastically welcomed. The most universally believed lie and false doctrine with which Satan has deceived the whole world of "Christianity" is that all not now "saved" are lost. That is not true. They are neither saved nor lost—they are not yet judged.

Jesus said plainly, "No man can come to me, except the Father which hath sent me draw him" (John 6:44). Unless the Father draws them, atheists and communists cannot come to Jesus. He said so in plain language! ...

We are closing a great year for God's Work in spite of the massive assault by the attorney-general's office of the State of California. We have gotten through this year without having to borrow from the bank, as in former years. Income has been up—and it is up to you and me to keep it that way. Meanwhile God's Church has been getting back on God's track after a several-years' conspiracy to secularize and liberalize it. We are now really getting closer to Jesus Christ and God our Father through more prayer and Bible study. Keep up the good work.

83

November 26, 1980—
July 24, 1983

Tucson, November 26, 1980

Dear Brethren and Co-Workers with Christ:

I have very recently returned from another Middle East visit. It was very profitable for the Work that God is doing through us.

En route I stopped off in London, and spoke on the Sabbath, October 25, to the brethren in the London area. There were more than 1,000 present, including a number who came over from the Continent.

On Monday evening, the 27th, I addressed a large banquet in Cairo, Egypt, of people prominent in the Egyptian government and universities, and the Egyptian-American League, hosted by Dr. Mohammed Abdel Kader Hatem, chief personal adviser to President Anwar el-Sadat and former prime minister. Then on to Jerusalem.

Our brief flight to Jerusalem was a "first"! We were

given government permission to fly direct from Cairo to Jerusalem airport. Since the hostilities between Egypt and Israel, there were no flights permitted between the nations until the Camp David peace talks, and then flights were permitted only from Cairo to the Ben-Gurion airport at Tel Aviv. But our plane was given government permission to make the first flight direct to Jerusalem airport. . . .

I spoke at a banquet hosted by Mayor Teddy Kollek. We attended a Sunday afternoon entertainment by the Arab section of the ICCY (International Cultural Center for Youth) in the "old city" Arab section of the city. It was a performance by both Arab and Israeli youth, with a very hilarious "belly dance" by a little nine-year-old Arab girl. This youth center is succeeding well in bringing together the youths, of both Arab and Jewish children and young people, in harmonious peace instead of hostility. We've been participating in this foundation for twelve years. A whole square in front of the main headquarters building in the newer area of Jerusalem is named "The Herbert W. Armstrong Square."

Also we visited again the new downtown city park in Jerusalem, where my name is engraved in a stone marker at one of the park entrances, at the children's playground area. . . .

Our meeting with President Sadat in Cairo had to be postponed, because President Yitzhak Navon of Israel was in Cairo on a state visit while we were there, and we were planning a full televised private meeting with him. . . .

We returned Sunday, the 9th, to Cairo. On Tuesday the 11th—the sixty-second anniversary of the end of World War I (and how well I remember the wild and jubilant reveling of that day)—we had our televised

616

meeting with the Egyptian president, Anwar el-Sadat.

Mr. Sadat was speaking at 11 to 12:30 that morning at a teachers' union graduation in a downtown auditorium. We were driven during that time to the auditorium building and taken to a reception room on about the 20th floor of the building. From there we could watch the ending of President Sadat's speech to the nation on television, and the graduation ceremony taking place in the auditorium on the ground floor of the building. . . .

At the palace, the president entered first, and we were met at the entrance portico by the first lady . . . and Dr. Hatem.

Inside, awaiting a brief meeting with Mr. Sadat, was a group of U.S. congressmen. I was told that they stared in amazed disapproval, wondering, "Who are those nonofficial Americans, and what are they doing here?"

The President's wife accompanied us into an elegant reception room where we chatted for some fifteen or twenty minutes. She and I were photographed together.

Then, the American congressmen dismissed, the President entered. The TV lights were flashed on.

It's a coincidence that the last time I met President Sadat, in Alexandria, he also was then about to address the nation on television. It was at a university in Alexandria. At that time . . . I was waiting in a reception room off the entrance lobby when the President entered. He had then come in a motorcade with streets lined with people trying to get a glimpse of their President. At that time, Mr. Sadat entered with his wife, followed by his cabinet and other top government officials. The President waited at the rear of the room, while his cabinet and officials lined up on each side facing the middle. Down the middle was a long red carpet. I walked down the red carpet to be formally introduced by Dr. Hatem to the President and the First Lady.... That had been my first meeting with President Sadat, although we were already well acquainted with his close adviser Dr. Hatem.

But in this present meeting, Mr. Sadat and I sat together in the corner of the room where seats had been arranged for telecasting. Both our own TV cameramen and the government TV cameramen were shooting us, until the meeting was under way, and then they left, and we were able to continue without the blazing TV lights....

There are other things I wanted to say, but this letter is getting overlong, and I will reserve other things until next time or in *The Plain Truth*....

Tucson, Arizona
February 8, 1981

Dear Brethren and Co-Workers with Christ:

We are off to a running start in the new year, 1981. Never before has God given us such a leap forward at the very beginning of a new year! ...

I returned a week ago from the last important meetings in Japan and the Philippines. They were the most successful so far in all these years.

In Tokyo I spoke a vigorous message on the soon-coming Kingdom of God at a banquet of some 400 important and leading people of that energetic and upcoming nation. Then I spoke on the Sabbath afternoon to 100 Japanese subscribers to *The Plain Truth,* mostly college students and professors. Then again about the same number three weeks later on the return from the Philippines.

At Manila, reporters of newspapers and TV news met me at the airport and we had a press conference....

I was guest of honor, and spoke a full message in power at a huge banquet of 750 members of the very important Philippine Constitution Association, a power in the Philippines. I was guest of honor and speaker at a luncheon of combined Rotary Clubs. I spoke to a packed auditorium a full message of the Kingdom of God at the very prestigious Adamson University....

Then there were the two main public meetings in the city's leading auditorium, seating 4,500, on successive Saturday and Sunday nights, virtually packed houses. I believe these were possibly the most effective speeches proclaiming Christ's gospel message of my life. God was with me, and did inspire me....

I returned home Sunday morning just as the very first of our new TV series was coming on. I was really thrilled at the way our TV staff had tailored that program, with exciting film clips illustrating my sermon all the way through. When I spoke of a meeting with Mrs. Golda Meir, the late prime minister of Israel, a picture of me talking with her was flashed on the screen. When I spoke of the oratory at the San Francisco Conference, which I attended in 1945, there appeared a film clip of President Harry Truman speaking at the conference—and so on. The new TV series, I feel, is the most effective of all our TV programs, so far.

I plan to record two more TV programs and two radio half hours next Tuesday and the same amount on Wednesday, when the whole TV crew will be in Tucson. I plan to keep this up until we have six months or more of programs ahead on tape—and possibly we then may start daily TV and radio broadcasting in major cities in the U.S. and Canada.

It is now Sunday as I write. Today's TV program was a half hour devoted to our China visit as guests of the People's Republic government. It showed a certain amount of several of my speeches there. What I am doing now, as televised, is, I feel, vastly improved and more effective than I was doing a year ago. I may be a year older, but I appear younger, smooth-speaking, more vigorous and effective. God is invigorating and inspiring me. I need your prayers that He will surcharge me with His Spirit and power for still greater effectiveness as we plunge on to finish His great Work before Christ's coming.

But of course His coming will be preceded by the Great Tribulation, the Day of the Lord (initiatory phase, with terrifying signs in the skies).

Just a few months ago God gave me a new idea for turning the hearts of the children to their parents and of the parents to their children—the new magazine *Youth 81.* The first two issues are out, and I honestly feel it is far superior to any youths' publications ever published. When I was young there was a prominent magazine called *Youth's Home Companion.* But I feel that *Youth 81* is far superior, and I'm sure our young people will be much profited.

Now God has given me a new idea for our youth! I have set a ceiling of a total of 500 students in Ambassador College. If we go beyond that we would be unable to maintain the high morale of God's college. That means we can accept only 150 new freshmen each year. But we have between 300 and 400 acceptable applications—young people—almost altogether your children—those of our Church members—and at present we can accept only about one in three of them.

We are besieged with letters from high school seniors asking us what can they do if we can't accept them? Can they go to some other college or junior college? Our experience is, candidly, that if they go to some other school they will be indoctrinated in the materialistic evolutionary approach to all knowledge, and in too many cases, ruined so far as God's teaching and way of life are concerned. . . .

God gives me this solution: For some reason God has blocked the sale of our Big Sandy campus. We still have it on our hands. So I now have in mind, as I believe God leads me, that we immediately start a junior college at Big Sandy. We would accept one-hundred new freshmen for Big Sandy for this coming fall. We would transfer seventy-five out of this year's freshman class at Pasadena, who will then be sophomores, to Big Sandy, to implant there the Amabssador character and atmosphere. That means that, in addition to the one-hundred additional new students we can accept for Big Sandy this fall, we can accept an additional seventy-five freshmen at Pasadena. . . .

The new junior college at Big Sandy will thereafter accept up to 150 or more per year. After two years at Big Sandy, some who qualify would transfer to Pasadena for the third and fourth years, and graduate at Pasadena.

I have to consider this budget-wise, of course. But, with tuitions helping, study of the budget situation indicates we can squeeze this new junior college in. Plans are already well under way for providing faculty.

God is blessing His Church and its Work!

We are now all set to plunge forward in the Work as never before! New time availabilities are opening up on both radio and TV. God is generating in me increased power and energy, and better programs are coming. . . .

Pasadena
January 20, 1983

Dear Brethren and Co-Workers with Christ:

I have to tell you now that the outlook for the United States and the entire world is bleak and foreboding indeed! Based on world news, observation and personal contacts with world leaders—based on Bible prophecy and a long life of experience, I have to tell you now that the entire world economy is in a drastic nose dive. Civilization itself is stricken with spiritual, moral and economic sickness unto its death—the end of this world!

But there is also good news! There is good news for the Work of God—the best ever! And the big good news (the word gospel means "good news") is the new civilization—the World Tomorrow—the Kingdom of God—is soon to follow! God's Church—the living and the dead in Christ—will then emerge into a new world of peace, happiness, abundance, with eternal life.

Bible prophecy shows what soon shall occur—why the world is now sick on its deathbed—why the rising unemployment, the sick economy, the immorality, crime, violence and world evils.

I have seen much of this in ninety years of event-packed experience.

In November, 1919, I was a member of the Chicago Association of Commerce. At a regular weekly membership luncheon, the noted Boston statistician and economist, Roger Babson, was guest speaker. He astonished major bank officials and industrial leaders saying that in one year we would experience the most drastic depression our generation had known. Economic executives ridiculed. We were then in an upward trend of prosperity.

A year later Roger Babson again was our guest speaker. He said, "The year has passed, and I am back and depression is here with me." There was no ridicule or laughter. Mr. Babson told us why he knew, and why business and financial executives did not.

"When I want to know what the temperature in this room is going to be an hour or two from now I don't consult the thermometer on the wall. I go to the boiler room and see what is going on down there. I go to the factor that causes the future temperature. You men were looking at bank clearings, retail sales, wholesale indexes, stock car loadings and trends—the thermometers on the wall." But Mr. Babson said he had learned that when fifty-one percent or more of the people were righteous in their dealings with another, prosperity was just ahead. But when fifty-one percent or more of the people were unrighteous in their dealings, economic depression was coming.

Was Roger Babson right?

In January, 1914, I was in the editorial department of a national magazine—the nation's largest trade journal. I was assigned to cover the story of the very beginning of the conveyer-belt assembly-line mass-production system at the Ford Motor Company plant in Detroit. Ford initiated this system of mass machine production. At that time only the U.S. provided a mass market for such mass production.

Soon other auto companies followed suit, and then virtually all American production in other lines. This swelled profits enormously for capital and management. But labor unionism immediately engaged in a crusade of strikes to raise wages. Also labor leaders adopted the false philosophy of "get" instead of cooperation and sharing. Labor union wars ensued, like the Herrin, Illinois, coal mine massacre, in which more than twenty were murdered and many injured. Labor turned to the attitude that the employer was the enemy—slow down your work, give as little as you can get away with, then fight with the weapon of the strike to increase wages and lower hours of work.

Result? The quality of industrial production diminished.

Meanwhile a burgeoning affluent middle class—also motivated by the way of "get"—developed in the United States. Before World War II the United States had mounted to a position of wealth and power such as no nation ever possessed.

God had blessed us with the natural resources. Selfishness and greed on the part of both management and labor temporarily increased our prosperity. But those very evils are now bringing this country down!

As late as 1969, the American wage was three times that of England and four times that of Japan.

Meanwhile, the Common Market (EEC) in Europe gave that continent a mass market for mass machine production—at low-cost labor. Even with machine production, labor had to direct the machines and remained the largest item of cost in production. Development of modern transportation gave Japan a mass market—in fact, a world market. Now Europe and Japan compete with mass production and low-cost labor against the U.S. with its high-cost labor. Not only that, but both in Japan and West Germany, labor is patriotic, regarding conscientious work as a duty to their country. Result, Japan and West Germany export to the U.S., underselling U.S. competition with better quality merchandise.

In 1970 Prime Minister Sato of Japan told me he foresaw and feared a real trade war with the U.S., and hoped it would not happen. It is here! Japan has figuratively bombed and almost destroyed Detroit. I am leaving Monday on a Far East trip, and expect to discuss this situation with Prime Minister Nakasone in Tokyo. He just departed from talks with President Reagan in Washington yesterday—apparently with no good results for the U.S.

Again, was Roger Babson right?

What does your Bible say? What does God say?

Actually applying to our nation, God says, Deuteronomy 28:1, ". . . If thou shalt hearken diligently unto the voice of the Lord thy God, to observe and to do all his commandments . . . the Lord thy God will set thee on high above all nations of the earth." In Deuteronomy 4:40: "Thou shalt keep therefore . . . his commandments . . . that it may go well with thee. . . ."

In many scriptures God tells us he prospers those whose ways please him. But our people as a nation have not obeyed God. The whole world has been founded and built on the philosophies and ways of life of Satan, not of God. This has been Satan's world—not God's. But the Church of God is God's world in embryo—begotten but not yet born. We are called—drafted—to be trained to be teachers and rulers in the world to come.

When this Work pleases Him, He prospers it. He has been getting us back on the track. We have just closed a record-breaking year.

The world has not lived God's way. Now the final result of the selfish way of living is converging on the whole world in its final climax at the end of this world.

But God is blessing His Church. We suffer because of the sins of the world among which we must live. But unemployment is not as high among our members— God does bless the commandment keeper and tithe payer.

1982 was the most successful year by far in the

history of this Work. *The Plain Truth* circulation took a big leap ahead—now well over five million copies a month. There was a big increase in number of TV stations. A big increase in people asking for counsel about baptism.

Pray for continued success in the Work. Remember, whatsoever we ask, we receive from God because we keep His commandments and do those things that are pleasing in His sight. Pray for me, even as I do for you. Pray for the continued economic stability and financial needs for God's Work.

Pasadena
July 24, 1983

Dear Brethren and Co-Workers with Christ:

A staggering turn in world events may occur suddenly at any day from now on. God has been holding back these world-shaking events. But now they may strike suddenly while the world least expects it.

The very first issue of the *Plain Truth* magazine appeared February, 1934—just fifty years ago lacking about 6 months. The article starting on the cover page warned of a coming sudden appearance of a resurrected "Holy Roman Empire" in Europe—a union of ten nations in Europe under one government, with one united military force. For fifty years I have been crying out to the world the Bible prophecies of this coming "United States of Europe"—a new united superpower perhaps more powerful than either the Soviet Union or the United States!

No one believed me then. But since then the European Common Market has appeared, with ten nations cooperating commercially in a tariff-free common market.

Also there have arisen in Europe two outstanding political leaders, both writing and speaking out and writing books, saying "Europe must unite politically." One of those was called the "Strong Man of Europe," Dr. Franz Josef Strauss. Some twelve years ago I entertained him at dinner in my home in Pasadena, and he spoke to the faculty and students of Ambasador College. I have maintained contact with him. He wrote the book *The Grand Design.*

The other arrived two weeks ago from Munich, West Germany, to have a meeting with me. He is Dr. Otto von Habsburg, head of the 700-year-old House of Habsburg, which ruled the Holy Roman Empire in the dynasty prior to Napoleon, and one of the most prestigious royal families in Europe. Dr. Habsburg was born the Archduke of Austria. His family was exiled during World War II, and he rejected Nazism and sided with the Allies during the war. He has since renounced his title. He very probably has a more clear grasp of international affairs than any man today. He is author of the famous book *The Social Order of Tomorrow,* giving a design for reunification of Europe startlingly close to the biblical description of this prophesied resurrected Europe to occur just prior to the Second Coming of Christ.

I had long wanted to meet Otto von Habsburg personally. I missed meeting him in Athens, Greece, last November, returning from my visit to our churches in South Africa and in Nairobi. However, Ellis La Ravia, vice president of the Ambassador Foundation, had arrived in Athens a couple days ahead of me from Pasadena. He attended a meeting there of the European Parliament, of which a leading member is Dr. Habsburg, who expressed regret at missing a meeting with me. He said then he would be so occupied with the then coming West German elections and sessions of the European Parliament, the very first date he could be free would be July 10 of this year. He said that on that day he would fly to Pasadena for a meeting with me. He kept his word and arrived on schedule in Pasadena two weeks ago this afternoon.

Dr. Habsburg addressed students and campus employees on Monday at 11 a.m. Mr. La Ravia and I took him on a brief visit through the Auditorium and then to luncheon in the faculty dining room. That evening he was guest at a formal dinner in my home with other Church officials and their wives. I also had a private meeting with him, as did Mr. Gene H. Hogberg, chief of our world news staff. While here he stayed in a guest apartment on campus. Tuesday night he addressed the Los Angeles World Affairs Council in Beverly Hills.

Wednesday morning he flew with me and some of our staff in our G-II jet to Washington, D.C. There he addressed the John Davis Lodge Center for International Studies at the University club.

In my private meeting with him, Dr. Habsburg expressed disappointment that progress on the European reunification had moved so slowly. I expressed the conviction that some totally unexpected world-shocking event could occur suddenly at any time that would high pressure European nations to go together overnight, adopting the constitution already prepared by the European Parliament. This Parliament, although without substantial power, is composed of leaders who are framing the constitution in advance. He mentioned that there are madmen such as Kadafi and Khomeini who could pull off some startlingly unexpected international act that would press the panic button in Europe.

Incidentally, Drs. Habsburg and Strauss are close friends, and for some reason I do not understand—but

628

may be of God's designing—both are very friendly to me and to Ambassador College.

Now let me tell you why I know God has held back end-time world events—and why He will cause things to snap together suddenly when least expected and bring this world suddenly to its end, and the coming of Christ in supreme power and glory to rule all nations, ushering in the Kingdom of God and the World Tomorrow! . . .

In Matthew 24:32-35 Jesus said that when we see world events now occurring, we are to know that this end is very near—within this generation. Yet of the day and hour (verse 36) we cannot know. Yet when it strikes it will strike suddenly, unexpectedly, like a trap that springs shut on a hapless rat without warning. If one knew at what hour a thief would come in the night to burglarize his house, he would have watched and been ready to resist him.

We have been seeing these end-time world events coming for several years now. God has delayed—held up world events. Yet He will suddenly cut his Work short, and end things, as unexpectedly and suddenly as when the trap springs on a rat before he can move.

When Europe suddenly unites, our work, which Christ is doing with and through us, will quickly be over, and Christ's coming very soon thereafter.

Brethren, thank you for the generous response to my last month's request for special funds for needed construction at the Orr, Minnesota, camp for the Summer Educational Program (SEP), for youths between ages twelve and eighteen. These camps are so very important. These youths will be leaders in the World Tomorrow! We must all pray all the more as we see end events coming to pass. Pray for one another. And, please, also for me. I do need your prayers. The Work needs our support.

84

January 11, 1984—
January 10, 1986

Brisbane, Australia
January 11, 1984

Dear Brethren and Co-Workers with Christ:
   . . . I am writing you from Australia. On this present trip I first visited New Zealand. There I attended the Summer Educational camp for teenagers, held on an island just offshore from Auckland. There were about 150 teen campers there besides a number of Ambassador College students serving as counselors and camp assistants, and ministers to supervise recreational activities and teach summer classes. Then I spoke on the Sabbath to 768 members at the Auckland church, and on Sunday flew to Wellington where I held a two-hour Bible study with 375 members of the Church. Also sixty bicyclists finished a cross-country cycling tour, composed of eleven college students and five college faculty members with forty-four teenagers—YOU members.

630

Last night I held a one-and-a-half-hour Bible study before 1,020 Church members in Brisbane. Tomorrow I will visit the SEP camp here, where some 300 teenagers are finishing the summer camp. These summer camps are doing a magnificent job of showing teenagers a better way to have fun and study at the same time. The camps are doing much to "turn the hearts of the children to the parents."

I will be preaching to brethren at Melbourne and Perth, then on to Malaysia, then a visit to Thailand, Hong Kong, Tokyo and back to Pasadena.

Again, thank you, sincerely and deeply, for your prayers and help with Christ in His work.

April 1, 1984

Dear Brethren in Christ:

This is a special personal letter to you members of God's Church, written in between monthly Co-Worker letters.

I recently visited my brother, Dwight, who composed all of the music in our Church hymnals except for three or four songs we felt worthy of being included. He has devoted the last thirty-five years of his life to composing the music of these hymns for us. For years, even before that, I had felt we needed our own hymn book, with words from the Psalms (the word *psalms* means songs) and other scriptures from the Bible.

I had noticed that in the hymn books sung in Protestant churches, the words are not scriptural, and sing the praises of the congregations of people instead of the praises of God.

Wherever I travel over the whole earth, visiting our churches on all continents, I find you brethren all enjoying the same hymns and the same music with great joy and gladness.

631

Perhaps most of you have not even realized it was my own brother, twelve years younger than I, who produced the beautiful music we have all come to love and joy in. On this recent visit to speak to the churches in the area of Vancouver, Canada, I stopped off to spend a few minutes with my brother. It was probably our last meeting together in this life.

I found him in the last stages of cancer in the bone structure, going through the marrow of the bones. He is a little discouraged, not realizing what a real success his life has been, and with the mortgage on his home still not paid off as he faces the end of this life. He is not expected to live much longer.

He has not had the opportunity to see and hear you brethren in congregations all over the world singing with such joy the music he composed for you, and I'm sure he can have no realization of how greatly he has contributed to God's Church and consequently what a successful life he has lived. He will be eighty, if he survives until September 15. He has continued up to the present to compose more and more new hymns, most of which have not been as yet published. These may come out in a new hymnal book, much enlarged over our present book. . . .

However, if some of you brethren do feel you would like him to know how much his beautiful music has meant to your Christian life, and would care to just write him a few words of appreciation, I know that would brighten the few remaining days he probably has in this life.

Write to his local pastor. . . .

Dacca, Bangladesh
November 18, 1984

Dear Brethren and Co-Workers in Christ:

I, with the small entourage accompanying me, am

632

now in the midst of a five-week tour in the Far East. I am writing from Dacca, capital of Bangladesh. Bangladesh borders India on three sides. It is a country about the size of Wisconsin in area, but with approximately 100 million population—almost half of that of the United States. It is one of the poorest countries on earth. Less than 29 percent can read or write and many of this number can only barely be called literate.

You people in America, Western Europe and Australasia cannot conceive of the condition in which uncounted millions of human masses live in parts of the world such as we are visiting. We came from Nepal, where I had another meeting with King Birendra and Queen Aishwarya in the palace at Kathmandu, Nepal's capital. Nepal is in the Himalaya mountains with Mt. Everest and other peaks almost the same fantastic height. There also, 80 percent of the people are totally illiterate. Most of them have no idea of sanitation. One of our pilots, in a car driven out of the city in a more rural area, saw children on the ground picking lice out of one another's hair.

You people in supposedly civilized countries have no conception of the poverty and ignorance of masses of human beings in this part of the world, or even in some areas in Africa and South America. Yet in our more "advanced" and supposedly civilized countries, we are plagued with crime, violence, illicit sex, drugs, excess alcohol, broken homes, and hospitals filled to overflowing, and jails and prisons likewise. The evils are appalling in a Western world of awesome progress and advancement. We certainly should pray, as Jesus said, "Thy Kingdom come." Only the coming of Christ in supreme power and authority can save humanity.

I visited this country about eleven years ago, soon after the end of the Pakistan war, when Bangladesh became a new country. I thought then that it was the most impoverished nation in the world. But great strides have been made since. This is due to two factors. The United States, Japan and other developed countries have poured many millions of dollars into this country to help get it started on development. This has resulted in many new modern buildings. The other cause we saw this afternoon. A one-hour drive to one of the villages to inspect one of the village elementary schools. I was driven in a government Mercedes, since I am here as a guest of the government. On the road to the village we had a flat tire. On the return we lost the muffler because of knotty tree roots protruding through the rough unpaved road. The schoolhouse was a dilapidated sort of shed built of old corrugated iron or tin, half rusted. One class of about sixty children were being taught in a shady spot outside this makeshift building. I visited a third grade mathematics class in a small room of thirty-five children. At least the country is beginning to teach many of the little children, although the Minister of Education told us many drop out because their parents can't see any need for education.

On this present tour we have visited Tokyo, where I met several Cabinet Members and Congressmen who call themselves my "Japanese sons." One senator in the Diet flew here with us.

In China I and my entourage were guests of the government that rules over nearly one fourth of all humanity. Our visit was on national TV and on front-page newspapers with nationwide circulation of some 200 million. It was even on Hong Kong television news. I was received in both Beijing and also in Shanghai with all the honors of the head of a nation. We were housed in both major cities in government VIP guest houses. In fact, I was told I slept in the same bed in Shanghai as President Reagan.

Deng Xiaoping admitted to me that China has made some serious mistakes which he is trying to correct. It was heartening to hear so powerful a man admit mistakes and work to correct them.

More than ever before I see the need to pray earnestly, "Thy Kingdom come, Thy will be done on earth as it is in heaven."

I have been given opportunity to speak some very straight truths in China and Nepal, and I may have a similar opportunity at the banquet tomorrow night.

Brethren, this world is being destroyed for lack of knowledge of and from God, as we read in Hosea 4:6. Through my personal visits, and the *Plain Truth* magazine, on TV and radio and through other literature, we are proclaiming that knowledge in power and authority. Some listen. It is God's last witness against those who do not. But we must drive right on until Christ comes!

More than ever I need your earnest prayers. God's great Work needs your generous support. And you need the great matchless blessing that comes from having your part in such a wonderful Work.

We go from here to Sri Lanka, then another visit to the King and Queen of Thailand, then Tokyo once again, then home. All my love to you all.

PS: 11/19/84: Word has just come by telex and telephone of the death of my brother, Dwight Leslie Armstrong. He composed the music for all but twelve of the hymns in the hymnal used in all the local churches of the Worldwide Church of God. He died on Saturday morning, November 17, of cancer. A full account of his life and work will appear in *The Worldwide News.*

July 25, 1985

Dear Brethren and Co-Workers in Christ:

Many things have happened since I last wrote to you a month ago. The passing time seems to speed up. These are the summer months in which we cannot afford to bask lazily in the warmth of the sun in idle leisure. Rather, more than ever, we need a sense of urgency. Events in the world are not taking a vacation, but speeding to the climax of this world and civilization as we know it.

Since my last letter I, with several members of the editorial staff and the television crew, attended the fortieth anniversary of the San Francisco Conference of 1945. Ambassadors to the U.N. from many nations were there. I was one of three or so who attended the entire Conference of forty years ago. Most are not still living. I was honored by sitting at lunches and dinners at the speakers' table, and introduced to all delegates each time.

I was glad to renew acquaintance with General Carlos Romulo of the Philippines, with whom I have maintained an acquaintance on my frequent visits to Manila. The Ambassador from the Soviet Union spoke to me twice and said I am too hard on the Soviet Union on the air, although he admitted I was not as hard on them as other TV evangelists, and invited me to visit the Soviet Union.

On June 25 I attended the twentieth anniversary of the church at my home city of Des Moines, Iowa. It was an experience to be photographed at the very spot where I was born, and to see the tremendous change that has come to the city where I grew up. The anniversary service was held in a new hotel located over the very spot where I worked for three years as editorial

representative of the nation's largest trade journal—
The Merchants Trade Journal—during the years of
1912–1915.

Since, I have visited the YOU camp sites at Orr,
Minnesota, and Big Sandy, Texas, and spoken to the
campers at each. All international camp directors were
in session at Orr. What these camps are doing for the
youths of the Church is amazing. There is no other
youth program in the world that remotely equals what
is being accomplished at our YOU camp...

September 12, 1985

Dear Brethren and Co-Workers with Christ:

Since last December I have been working diligently
on the largest and most important book of my life. In
real fact I feel I myself did not write it. Rather, I believe
God used me in writing it. I candidly feel it may be the
most important book since the Bible.

It is named *Mystery of the Ages*. Actually it might
be called a synopsis of the Bible in the most plain and
understandable language.

But first, before I tell you more about it, let me say
I am overjoyed to be able to send you one of the very
first copies off the press, hardbound—the same beautiful copy that will be sold in bookstores all over the
United States—in gratitude for your cooperation and
financial support of this wonderful Work of the great
God.

All baptized members will be given the book, one
copy to a family, at the coming annual Feast of Tabernacles. All nonmember Co-Workers are being mailed
your copies, but allow a few weeks for delivery, for this
kind of mail goes much slower than this letter.

We want to reach the largest audience possible with

this book. I know you will feel the same way when you read it. There is a very large audience which would never request this book if offered free—who would never send their name and address to us—but would gladly buy a copy in the bookstore. By putting it in the bookstores we will reach a very great audience that we can reach in no other way. We will not sell the book ourselves, but it cannot be made available to this large audience of book buyers unless the bookstores do put a price on it.

Now let me tell you something about this new book.

The Holy Bible is the world's best-selling book, but not the most read, and certainly just about the least understood. Why should this be? Several reasons.

First, God did not intend it to be understood until now, in these last days before the return of Christ and the setting up of the Kingdom of God to rule all nations and usher in world peace. For example, in Daniel 12, Daniel wrote that he heard what the angel was telling him to write, but he did not understand. The angel told him to write the words anyway—that their meaning was closed and sealed from understanding until the time of the end of this present world.

Secondly, when the first man, Adam, rejected the tree of life—rejecting God and reliance on God, taking to himself the knowledge of good and evil, relying on himself instead of God—God closed the tree of life until the coming of Christ, the second Adam. And even then the gifts of the Holy Spirit and eternal life were still closed to all except those whom God the Father would draw to Him through Jesus Christ (John 6:44). The natural mind of man cannot understand the Word of God except by and through the Holy Spirit dwelling within. We read in I Corinthians 2:9 that the human eye has not seen, nor the ear heard, nor has it entered into

638

the human mind, the spiritual things of God. But, verse 10, says God does reveal those things to us through, and only through, the Holy Spirit dwelling in us. No matter how great the human mind—no matter how many Ph.D.s or high degrees one may have after his name, he cannot understand what God has put in His Word—the Holy Bible—without the Holy Spirit. Jesus said, "I thank thee, O Father, Lord of heaven and earth, because thou hast hid these things from the wise and prudent, and hast revealed them unto babes [mentally, educationally]" (Matt. 11:25). No others can understand the Bible, which is the Word of God.

Thirdly, the Bible has not been written like the books written by natural-minded humans. It is a coded book, like a jigsaw puzzle divided into thousands of parts, and cannot be understood except these many different parts are properly put together. And they will fit together in only one way. They must be put together "here a little, and there a little" (Isa. 28:10).

I feel like shouting "Glory, hallelujah" and "Praise God" that He has revealed His Word to His one true Church through the Holy Spirit which He has given to us. Daniel 12 continues to say that in these last days the wise would understand but all others would not. The Bible says the fear of the Lord is the beginning of understanding, and a good understanding have they who do His commandments.

We of God's true Church do keep God's commandments. But the churches of this world say the commandments were done away. Therefore their eyes, even though they do not realize it, are blinded to the truth as revealed in the Bible. That is why the churches of "traditional Christianity" do not and cannot understand the Bible.

This new book *Mystery of the Ages* does put

many "pieces of the jigsaw puzzle" properly together. Because the world has been unable to do this, the Bible and the things in the Bible have certainly been a mystery.

The Bible itself is a mystery to nearly all people. God and the nature of God—what God is like—God's purpose—have been a mystery. No religion on earth has ever truly understood just who and what God really is. Many people, and even different religions, have had some vague ideas about the unseen spirit world. Yet it has been a total mystery to them.

Even the appearance of mankind on the earth and any purpose for human existence are a mystery people have never understood. Human civilization as it has developed is a mystery people simply do not understand. They cannot understand why twentieth century progress has made such phenomenal strides and yet its troubles and evils have escalated and multiplied.

Even the existence of the Church is a mystery. Why should there be such an institution as the Church? The very gospel that Jesus Christ brought from God the Father—the good news of the coming world-ruling Kingdom of God—has never been understood. It, too, has been cloaked in mystery.

This new book *Mystery of the Ages* unveils all these mysteries. It puts the many different parts of the "jigsaw puzzle" together. It is, in fact, a synopsis of the entire Bible. It is my prayer that you will read it along with your Bible—that it will make your Bible come alive and understandable. And with God's Holy Spirit dwelling in you, I feel sure that it will. I am now in my 94th year and I feel that this book is the most valuable gift I could possibly give to you. This book is a partial expression of my thanks and gratitude to you for being a co-laborer with me and with Jesus Christ. With all my heart, I do appreciate and thank God for your part with me in the wonderful Work these closing days.

November 25, 1985

Dear Brethren and Co-Workers with Christ:

This has been the most serious year of the Work of God so far. Never before has God given us such a leap forward in television coverage and *Plain Truth* circulation as in these past six months.

God's time has come to speed up His Work with dynamic and tremendous power! Time for completing the great mission of God in this dying world is fast running out on us! . . .

With the writing of the new book *Mystery of the Ages* God has helped me this year to do the best work of my ninety-three years of life! But now, for over three months, I have been suffering a serious illness that started from a flu bug in August. Since then I have been confined to my home, with a doctor, who seldom makes house calls, coming to see me every day—sometimes twice a day. I have been unable to rid myself of a fever that has left me with low blood levels and very little strength. Even so, I am working as energetically as possible from my home . . .

December 9, 1985

Dear Brethren:

At this time I feel I must make a statement regarding my own physical condition and also changes being made in the Work. I have delayed a definite statement about my health hoping that my physical condition would improve and that the statement I now make could be alleviated.

641

Last August 3, I left Pasadena for Orr, Minnesota, having planned to continue to the Summer Education Program camp in Scotland, then to London, and from London across the North Pole to Tokyo. A trip has been planned from Tokyo to Seoul, South Korea, to meet with the President. I was to be accompanied by the Japanese Minister of Labor, Toshio Yamaguchi. I had become ill and was forced to return to Pasadena from Orr, Minnesota, early in the morning, too ill to be fully dressed. I returned immediately to my home. I was able to make a few trips to the office until the first day of the Feast of Tabernacles in late September. I have not been outside of my home since that day. From that date, my regular physician has been making daily, and sometimes twice daily, trips to my home.

I had hoped for a turn to the better—so that I could return for daily work in my office—and a recovery from this illness, but unfortunately, that has not occurred. My blood level is far below normal and has left me in a very weak condition. I have not been able to dress further than bed clothes and robes since the day before the Feast of Tabernacles.

My physician says that with blood transfusions I could go to the office for three to four weeks. But then another blood transfusion would be necessary. It is my judgment that such a transfusion would be risky and of very short duration. And my physician acquiesces in this decision. Frequently I have very serious and painful angina attacks of the heart. I have been able to make certain necessary decisions in a brief telephone contact with those at the office and will continue this as and when my very limited physical strength permits.

Until the present moment I felt that God might provide a way for complete recovery, and He still may. So I have withheld this statement until now, but I feel it is better that you all know the condition. I am now in my ninety-fourth year. God may grant that I may continue in this very limited manner to direct the Work for some time, but the occasional severe heart pains that I have endured have made me feel the necessity of letting the entire membership know of the condition as it is. . . .

Remember, brethren, this is the Work of the living Creator God. We are now very near the end of this present age. I will continue to give my all to the Work of God up to the last breath. I hope you will all realize the seriousness of the time in which we live and that nothing is important any longer than to be close to God and assured of a place in His soon-coming Kingdom.

This world is not God's world, and of that we may all be thankful. It is now in its very last days. This illness has impressed heavily on my mind, more than ever before, the uselessness of this present evil world. Thank God we are all very near to its end. I thank you, beyond words to express, for your loving concern and for the many thousands of cards and well wishes that have been coming in from great numbers of you from all over the world.

P.S. I have had to dictate this letter due to lack of the physical strength to type it.

January 10, 1986

Dear Brethren and Co-Workers,

This is my first letter to you in 1986, and could very well be my last. Now in my ninety-fourth year I am in a very physically weakened state enduring severe pain and with virtually no strength whatsoever. I briefly described my condition in last month's Co-Worker letter to you, and now it has worsened. It may be that the Work God has given me to do is complete, but not the Work of God's Church, which will be faithfully doing God's Work till Christ, the True Head of this Church, returns.

After much counsel and prayer over the past months God has led me in announcing a decision last week to appoint Mr. Joseph W. Tkach, Director of Church Administration, to the office of Deputy Pastor General, to assist me while I am in a weakened state, and should God choose to take my life, to place himself totally in Christ's hands to lead God's Church under Christ, succeeding me as Pastor General, in the difficult times ahead. Christ will lead in the decision about which men will continue the telecast.

Remember, brethren, this is not the work of Herbert W. Armstrong, nor will it be the work of Mr. Tkach, or any man. It is the Work of the Living Creator, God. You are supporting this Work of God, and it is the Great God who will pour out His blessings on you for your generosity. Continue to sacrifice through 1986 to finish the commission God has given His Church. The greatest work lies yet ahead. Christ confirmed that in John 4:35, "Say not ye, There are yet four months, and then cometh the harvest? behold, I say unto you, Lift up your eyes, and look on the fields; for they are white already to harvest." Never before in the history of the Church has it been possible to reap so great a harvest. It has only been made possible through modern technology, beginning with the printing press, radio, television, and rapid mass transit and mass communication. I personally have seen nearly all of these technological advances in my lifetime, starting in the last century through the horse and buggy age to the current space age.

It was prophesied in Daniel 12 that in the last days knowledge would be increased. This has been fulfilled, yet with this awesome progress we are experiencing even more appalling and continuous evils, which will culminate in the Great Tribulation ahead of us now. Then, just before humanity blasts human life off this planet, God will once again send His Son Jesus Christ. This time in power and glory as King of kings and Lord of lords to rule with all the power of the Great God and usher in utopian peace, happiness and prosperity. Thank God, Satan will then be gone.

Are you ready for the return of Jesus Christ? Will you escape the Great Tribulation soon to occur? Christ said to watch and pray always, that you will be accounted worthy to escape (Luke 21:36). Now is the time of the end.

Each of you must commit yourself to support God's Work, to fast and pray. God's Work must push ahead this coming year as never before. God is opening new doors in television and in the *Plain Truth* distribution. Help us walk through them. Praise and thank God, and pray for His Work. Thank you very much from the bottom of my heart for your prayers for me personally.

85

January 16, 1986— May 1986

Death of Herbert W. Armstrong announced by Joseph W. Tkach

January 16, 1986

Dear Brethren and Co-Workers with Christ,

I am deeply saddened to have to inform you that Herbert W. Armstrong's illness has ended in the manner least expected by all of us. Mr. Armstrong died peacefully in his sleep at 5:59 this morning while resting in the favorite chair of his late wife Mrs. Loma Armstrong.

In the next second of his consciousness he will awake in the first resurrection, completely healed, not in the corruptible body of this mortal flesh, but as an immortal spirit-composed body, in *glory* in God's eternal kingdom!

Through the years, we have learned that God's promises are absolutely sure—but not always in the *way* we expect. Because His ways are not our ways. God says to us, " 'For My thoughts are not your thoughts, nor are your ways My ways,' says the Lord. 'For as the heavens are higher than the earth, so are My ways higher than your ways, and My thoughts than your thoughts' " (Isaiah 55:8-9).

God has *promised* to heal the sick, upon real repentance and faith. But God has *not* promised *how,* or *when.* That we must leave to Him in faith.

The Eternal God, in His infinite mercy and wisdom, faithfully answered our prayers in the way *He* chose, rather than the way *we* would have chosen. "Precious in the sight of the Lord is the death of His saints" (Psalm 116:15).

God is *faithful.* He is merciful, compassionate and loving. Herbert W. Armstrong is merely awaiting the day of his *change,* along with the other thousands and thousands of God's saints, into immortal, glorious spirit-life, born into the very Family of God at the soon coming *return* of Jesus Christ.

God granted Mr. Armstrong 93½ dynamic years, the last 53 of which were fully immersed in doing the work of God, proclaiming the gospel of the kingdom of God to a world blinded by the deception of the god of this world, Satan the devil (Revelation 12:9).

Even in the last year of his life, with declining strength, he completed with God's help, his most powerful and effective book *Mystery of the Ages.* This after half a century of articles, letters, booklets, books, sermons and broadcasts, preaching and teaching the truth of God's Word, of His plan for mankind, of the glorious and radiant future that is the ultimate destiny of humanity.

We don't know what trials lie yet ahead of us in completing God's work of proclaiming the gospel to the world. Perhaps God saw fit, as He describes in Isaiah 57:1, to spare Mr. Armstrong, at his advanced age, from the persecutions and trials prophesied to come as we finish the work of God for this age. Indeed, as Mr. Armstrong wrote in his final letter to you, "The greatest work lies yet ahead... Never before in the history of the Church has it been possible to reap so great a harvest."

Now look at Revelation 3:10-11. Jesus tells us, "Because you have kept My command to persevere, I also will keep you from the hour of trial which shall come upon the whole world, to test those who dwell on the earth. Behold, I come quickly! Hold fast what you have, that no one may take your crown."

Let us persevere. Let us *carry on,* redoubling our efforts to draw closer to God in *prayer* and Bible study, fasting often, and striving to *overcome,* as well as putting our hearts into doing the work of God! As Mr. Armstrong so often stated, "When our ways *please* God, He will bless us."

I am reminded of Loma D. Armstrong's admonition to several Headquarters ministers at her bedside just before her death nearly 19 years ago. She said, "Well, go on now, all you men, and do your *work.* I'll be all right."

Herbert W. Armstrong has given us the same admonition so many times. As he would say, "Go! Carry on with *God's work.* Never slacken! Never let down!"

The greatest tribute we can give Mr. Armstrong is to *do the work* we've been called to.

He often pointed us to his mother's favorite verse in the Bible, Psalm 133:1, "Behold, how good and how pleasant it is for brethren to dwell together in unity." We do need that unity now as never before.

Jesus Christ, the Head of His Church, has PROMISED us that He will *never* leave us nor forsake us (Hebrews 13:5)! We must make *sure* we do not leave or forsake *Him,* but remain steadfast in His calling, working together in unity and harmony, led always by His Spirit!

Pray especially fervently for God's Church at this critical time, and for *one another.* And please pray for me and the other men here in Pasadena. We *need* your prayers, and our daily prayers are with you.

Let us *carry on* in FAITH. There is much yet to do!

January 19, 1986

Dear Brethren and Co-Workers,

. . . And now, GOOD NEWS! In his final letter to you, Mr. Armstrong mentioned that decisions would be made about which men would continue the *World Tomorrow* telecast. He had already discussed with me at length several preliminary ideas.

Mr. Armstrong knew, and we know, that no one can "replace" him or *duplicate* his unique style. But as he pointed out to me in our discussions about the telecast, the *work of God's Church* is not done by might, nor by power, but by the *Spirit of God* (Zechariah 4:6)! *Jesus Christ* will give His ministers the POWER to preach HIS TRUE GOSPEL—the gospel of the soon-coming kingdom of God!

The *message* of God's Church has NEVER changed! And it never will! The *World Tomorrow* telecast will continue to boldly announce Christ's own gospel—the gospel He Himself preached.

I believe God has led me in selecting, for now, *three* men who will begin *immediately* recording new programs in our own television studio here in Pasadena. All of these three men are dedicated, *humble* ministers of Jesus Christ, who have shown themselves to be *yielded* to Him as *faithful* servants.

649

I'd like to introduce them to you *now,* so that you can begin *praying* for them, asking God to empower them and lead them WITH HIS SPIRIT, and to *bless these programs* with abundant fruit!

First, Mr. David Hulme, a pastor rank minister, 17 years serving God's Work, and currently Director of Media Purchasing.

Next, Mr. Richard Ames, an evangelist rank minister, who has served God's Work for 23 years, and is currently Director of Admissions and a Professor of Theology at Ambassador College.

Also, Dr. David Albert, of pastor rank, serving for 26 years and now Director of Career Counseling and Professor of Psychology at Ambassador College.

I call upon each of you brethren and co-workers to join me in heartfelt prayer for these three men—and their wives—in their additional responsibilities now with the *World Tomorrow* program. And pray that God will bless His Work *financially* at this critical time of transition.

God *will* supply the POWER and grant *his blessing* for the EXCELLENT SUCCESS of these programs *if we do our part*—on our knees in diligent prayer throughout this coming year.

I hope none of you will miss the January 26 telecast, which will be a *special tribute* to Mr. Armstrong, and will offer to the viewers a softbound copy of Mr. Armstrong's final and most important book, *Mystery of the Ages.*

Thank you for your earnest prayers for me, and for the many letters and cards of support and encouragement. I do *need* your prayers and I *deeply appreciate them.*

And finally, thanks be to the GREAT GOD, by whose Spirit His work will be done!

From *The Good News*
May 1986

"Passing the Baton"

Though God has chosen to take the life of Herbert W. Armstrong, the late human leader of God's Church, both the Church and the work of God continue unabated under the leadership of Joseph W. Tkach.

Jesus said the gates of the grave would never prevail against God's Church (Matthew 16:18). The announcement of God's coming kingdom must still be made to all the world (Matthew 24:14). Disciples must still be made of all nations (Matthew 28:19).

Jesus Christ, the living Head of the Church (Ephesians 1:22-23), is at the right hand of God the Father in heaven. He continues to actively lead and govern the Church through Mr. Armstrong's designated successor, Joseph W. Tkach.

Mr. Armstrong termed his appointment of Mr. Tkach "the passing of the baton." It's interesting how a baton is passed. It is not passed to end a race, but to continue a race, with a temporary readjustment as the baton is handed from one runner to the next. Once the baton is received by the next runner, there is a speeding up. That's what's going to happen in the work today! Readjusted, we're going to go on running, under the human leadership of Joseph W. Tkach, with the baton that was given to Mr. Armstrong before us, with the teachings God revealed through him, using what has already been accomplished, building on the foundation and continuing toward the finish line.

A native of Chicago, Illinois, Mr. Tkach served in the U.S. Navy during World War II. Following his military service, he studied industrial management, industrial safety and human factors in industry. In

651

1946, he was employed by a midwestern manufacturing corporation, where he began his management experience. Before he resigned to assume a full-time role in the ministry, Mr. Tkach was responsible for several hundred employees.

He was once fired for keeping God's Sabbath, which falls on Saturday.

"I was threatened if I didn't come in on that Sabbath for a special meeting that I would be fired," Mr. Tkach recalls. "Upon coming home from church services there was a telegram waiting for me stating that I was fired.

"Monday morning I received a telephone call from the personnel manager saying, 'Management would like you to come in immediately, as fast as you can get here. I didn't know what to expect," says Mr. Tkach. "But after arriving at the plant, out in the parking lot there were over 200 people milling around on a wildcat strike because they heard I was fired.

"You see, we serve a God who fights our battles for us. My job was given back to me."

March 31, 1951, Mr. Tkach married Elaine Apostolos, a native of Chicago. Mr. and Mrs. Tkach have a son and two daughters. Mr. Tkach was baptized on March 1, 1957, in Chicago, Illinois, and began to assist the ministry in the Chicago churches. He was ordained a deacon January 7, 1961, and a local elder June 3, 1963.

Mr. Tkach—now the Pastor General—helped establish churches in South Bend, Fort Wayne and Indianapolis, Indiana; Rockford and Peoria, Illinois; Davenport, Iowa; Grand Rapids, Michigan; Milwaukee, Wisconsin; Cincinnati, Ohio; and St. Louis, Missouri.

In 1966 Mr. Tkach entered Ambassador College, where he attended for three years before being assigned to serve in congregations in Southern California. In 1970 he began working in Ministerial Services. In 1974 he was raised in rank to preaching elder.

Mr. Tkach was named director of Ministerial Services (now Church Administration) in July, 1979. That same year, Mr. Armstrong ordained Mr. Tkach an evangelist and named him associate pastor of the Pasadena Auditorium P.M. church, pastored by Mr. Armstrong. Mr. Tkach was also appointed by him in 1981 to the Advisory Council of Elders, an advisory body to the Pastor General.

"He taught us the importance of why we were called," Mr. Tkach says, referring to Mr. Armstrong. "We are here to be trained. Now is not the time to throw up our hands and to quit. Now is the time to stand up and be counted to do God's work. Remember, this is our life.

"So as the chapters are increased in the living book of Acts, there should be no gaps, but merely a marker of faithfulness to help us start building where Mr. Armstrong left off. This is the legacy that has been left to us, to carry on with the work. We have an awesome responsibility."

From "Good News Personal"
by Joseph W. Tkach,
Pastor General
May 1986

Our Work Is Cut Out for Us

By now you all will have heard of the death of Herbert W. Armstrong on January 16, 1986.

God's ways are higher than ours, and He sees what we are *incapable* of seeing. He knows our needs and He *does* take care of them, though not always in the way we might expect.

I learned long ago, when my own father died in the faith, that although God does give us His faithful and unbreakable promise to *heal*, upon repentance and *faith*, He reserves the decision as to *how* and *when*. If indeed God does choose to allow the faithful to die, that death is not *permanent*, but only a temporary state of peaceful rest from the suffering of this present evil world, awaiting the *redemption* of our bodies into the glorious liberty of the sons of God!

God mercifully granted us what Mr. Armstrong considered several additional years of his leadership. God used him powerfully to get the Church to a dedicated, concerted *unity* carrying out the *purpose* of our calling, the proclaiming of Christ's gospel of the *soon-coming* kingdom of God, and feeding the flock that is the body of Christ.

I am personally, of course, deeply sobered and humbled by the responsibilities God has placed on my shoulders as Pastor General of the Worldwide Church of God. The apostle Paul stated that he was the "least of the apostles" (I Corinthians 15:9). In another passage he said he was "less than the least of all the saints" (Ephesians 3:8). Like Paul, I am also the least of the brethren. Yet I know, as Paul did, that "I can do all things through Christ who strengthens me" (Philippians 4:13). Jesus Himself set us the example. He did not speak on His *own* authority. He spoke the words and did the works of His Father, *who dwelt in Him* (John 14:10). He and His Father were ONE! They were (and are) in perfect *unity*. That same *godly* unity must be the binding of God's Church.

Our work is cut out for us. God has called us to *unitedly* and *wholeheartedly* carry on till Christ returns.

We must make *overcoming* the priority. The time for this world's civilization is *short*. But there is *much*

86

One Year Later

To Mr. Joseph W. Tkach
Update from Mail Processing
January 9, 1987

1986 Records in Review

As 1987 begins, we thought you would like a recap of new records set during 1986. Some of the more outstanding are these:

- Largest number of WATS calls received in one year—1,996,494. A record total of 1,661,226 came in response to the telecast alone.
- Highest number of calls taken by volunteers on the WATS In-Home Program in one year—224,896. Our record weekend was November 8-9 when in-home operators took 8,996 calls.
- Over 96 million publications were mailed in the United States.
- Highest mail income for one year.

yet to do. As we submit to God, carefully and diligently seeking His will in our lives, and FORSAKING THE WAYS OF THIS WORLD, God will continue to bless His work. He will lead us, direct us, guide us. But we must follow his lead *together,* as ONE BODY. Jesus is not fragmented and *never will be.*

After Jesus was crucified and buried, several of the disciples decided to go fishing—back to their old trade. Maybe they thought the work was over. But what they didn't realize was that the greatest work was *yet ahead!*

Pray as *never before*—for God's people, for one another, for the work, and please pray for me. My prayers are with you. I deeply appreciate and love each one of you members and co-workers. Keep reading *The Good News* and *The Plain Truth.* They will continue to be what we believe are the finest magazines on earth. And keep growing spiritually.

Will Christ find us doing His work when He returns? I intend to be. And I'm calling on all of you to stand with me in Christ's service, *holding fast* to the great commissions He has given us, enduring *patiently* and *faithfully* to the end.

- Largest semiannual ever sent out. Your fall letter went to 3,377,316 people on our mailing list.
- Largest direct mail offer. We offered *The Plain Truth* to 3.5 million people on purchased mailing lists as well as to those who had let their subscription lapse in 1985.

To Mr. Joseph W. Tkach
Update from Mail Processing
January 12, 1987

Half of 1986 Telecasts
Surpass Previous Records

For your information, we would like to report that more than half the programs in 1986 (27 out of 52) surpassed the previous year's record of 26,020 telephone responses for one telecast. . . .

To Mr. Joseph W. Tkach
Update from Mail Processing
February 27, 1987

Fifty Percent of TV Responses
from Subscribers

We have witnessed a marked change in the number of *Plain Truth* subscribers who respond to the telecast each week. We felt you would be interested in knowing that about half of our responses, including both phone calls and mail, now come from subscribers to *The Plain Truth*.

The new speakers, new programs and new literature offers have helped generate this increase. More than half of the 37 books, booklets and brochures we offered on the program last year had either never been offered before or were being offered for the first time in at least a year. Just two years ago, only about a third of the response to the telecast came from those on our mailing list.

> To Mr. Joseph W. Tkach
> Update from Mail Processing
> March 6, 1987

Record Number of Names and Calls

Although the work has taken measures to control the expansion of the mailing list, last month a record 175,686 names, the highest number for any February in our history, were added to the *Plain Truth* list.

This increase is 6.5 percent higher than last year's growth for the same period, when we put 164,912 new names on file. The two primary sources for these new adds were the *World Tomorrow* telecast and *Plain Truth* blow-in cards.

Telephone call volume in the WATS area continues to grow at a record pace. By the end of March 1, we had already received more than half a million calls for 1987, which is more than we have ever received in the first two months of a year.

A breakdown of our new records follows:

Calls	Jan/Feb 1986	Jan/Feb 1987	Percentage Increase
TV Calls	276,298	404,915	46.6
Total Calls	337,574	470,519	39.4

International Responses to TV/Radio Programs

The *World Tomorrow* telecast and radio broadcast produced excellent responses in international areas in 1986. Since Mail Processing has statistics available from our offices around the world regarding these responses, we thought a compilation would be useful.

Our international offices received 89,930 responses in 1986 as a result of the telecast and radio program. This number is 75.6 percent higher than the 51,202 responses they received in 1985.

U.S. responses for the same period were up 88.9 percent.

The work of God is certainly continuing to grow!